How to Enable the Employability of University Graduates

PART III   EMPLOYABILITY AND THE CURRICULUM

8   Employer input to curriculum and assessment   79
    Gillian O'Brien and Darren Siggers

9   Real work opportunities in the curriculum: three different
    approaches   89
    Charles Hancock, Tracy Powell, John Day and Alison Lawson

10 Using a professional skills module to develop student confidence   100
    Parminder Johal and Ruth Smith

11 Developing an ecosystem: employability skills and
    authentic assessments   109
    Sarah Montano

PART IV   INNOVATIVE APPROACHES TO CAREER GUIDANCE

12 Using career pathways to tailor and personalise
    employability activities   118
    Rebekah Marangon

13 The Career Studio: peer-to-peer support   127
    Emma Moore and Paul Gratrick

14 Supporting employment outcomes for students from Asia   136
    Louise Nicol

PART V   PRACTICAL EXAMPLES OF EMPLOYABILITY ACTIVITIES

15 Using social action to support skill development   149
    Fiona Walsh

16 The Big Challenge: interdisciplinary development of
    employability skills   159
    Valerie Derbyshire, Laurice Fretwell and Caroline Harvey

17 Modifying the journey to graduate employment through
    changes to work-based learning   168
    Catherine O'Connor

PART VI ENTERPRISE/ENTREPRENEURIAL OPPORTUNITIES

18	'One for all and all for one': the 3Es (employability, enterprise, and entrepreneurship) *Emily Beaumont*	179
19	BSEEN: extra-curricular enterprise and entrepreneurship support *Carolyn Keenan*	188

PART VII WIDENING PARTICIPATION

20	Employability monsters: breaking barriers to employability for widening participation students *Dawn Lees and Kate Foster*	198
21	Supporting 'first in family' students: My Generation Career Coaching Programme *Heather Pasero*	207
22	Unlocking the potential of under-represented students *Iwan Williams and Pamela McGee*	215
23	Social mobility and London's left-behind graduates *Emily Dixon*	224

PART VIII INTERNATIONAL STUDENTS

24	Using the net promoter score to understand international alumni satisfaction *Shane Dillon*	234
25	Meeting the employability expectations of international students in transition to higher education in the UK *Victoria Wilson-Crane and Linda Cowan*	244
26	How partnerships can make a difference to securing jobs for international students *Jacklyn Tubb and Caroline Fox*	253

PART IX INSIGHTS FROM AROUND THE WORLD

27	How England's policy and regulatory levers have shifted accountability for graduate employment *Lizzy Woodfield*	263

Tables

3.1	Participant profiles – final year undergraduate students	27
10.1	Schedule of delivery: professional development for Accounting and Finance graduates	104
17.1	Institutional Change Project summary	171
20.1	Breakdown of participants' WP markers	200
21.1	Activity types	211
33.1	Alignment of the Employability Framework to the third-generation approach to transition pedagogy strategies	328

Reflections

1.	Reflection from a senior director of a major retail organisation	12
2.	Reflection from a graduate recruiter	23
3.	Reflection from a graduate who works for a national law firm	34
4.	Reflection from an employer in manufacturing	46
5.	Reflection from a law graduate	55
6.	Reflection from a senior manager in manufacturing	66
7.	Reflection from an accounting graduate	77
8.	Reflection from an HR director in service banking	88
9.	Reflection from a Biomedical Science student	99
10.	Reflection from an Accounting and Finance student	108
11.	Reflection from a Costume Design graduate	116
12.	Reflection from a Psychology graduate	126
13.	Reflection from a public sector senior manager	135
14.	Reflection from a Geography graduate working in a major retailer	147
15.	Reflection from a graduate	158
16.	Reflection from a manager in an SME	167
17.	Reflection from a student studying to be a teacher	177
18.	Reflection from an Economics and Politics graduate	187
19.	Reflection from a graduate entrepreneur	196
20.	Reflection from a mature student	206
21.	Reflection from a career coach	214

22.	Reflection from an International Business and Economics student	223
23.	Reflection from a languages student	232
24.	Reflection from a director of a property consulting firm in Vietnam	243
25.	Reflection from a senior manager in financial services	252
26.	Reflection from a Media Studies graduate	261
27.	Reflection from a lecturer who has moved into a management role	272
28.	Reflection from an international student	283
29.	Reflection from a New Zealand graduate	294
30.	Reflection from a student working in a large American video game company	303
31.	Reflection from a French graduate	312
32.	Reflection from a Speech and Language Therapist	322
33.	Reflection from a PhD student	333
34.	Reflection from a marketing graduate	342
35.	Reflection from an Education graduate	350

Contributors

Dr Efimia Anastasiou, Assistant Professor, Department of Accounting, Economics and Finance, School of Business and Economics, Deree – The American College of Greece

Ida Andersson-Norrie, International Strategy Officer, Örebro University, Sweden

Dr Emily Beaumont, Associate Professor Enterprise and Entrepreneurship at the University of Gloucestershire, President of Enterprise Educators UK

Professor Dawn Bennett, PhD(Dist), MMus, GradDipEd, PFHEA, Assistant Provost, Bond University, Gold Coast, Queensland, Australia

Brett Berquist, Amokapua | Assistant Vice-Chancellor Engagement, University of Canterbury, New Zealand

Anna Chudy, International Relations Officer, University of Jaén, Spain

Elaine Clarke, College Director of Education and Students, Lincoln International Business School, England, UK

Linda Cowan, Managing Director, Kaplan International Pathways, UK

Professor Kathy Daniels, Associate Pro-Vice Chancellor (Engagement), Aston University, England, UK

John Day, Senior Lecturer in Strategic Management, Derby Business School, University of Derby, England, UK

Dr Valerie Derbyshire, Impact Officer, University of Derby, England, UK

Shane Dillon, PhD student at the Bankwest Curtin Economics Centre at Curtin University (Australia) and the founder of the EdTech companies Cturtle and JOB+

Emily Dixon, London Programmes and Communications Coordinator, London Higher, England, UK

Martin Edmondson, Managing Director, Gradcore Ltd, England, UK

Dr Omolabake Fakunle, Chancellor's Fellow, Moray House School of Education & Sport, University of Edinburgh, Scotland, UK

Associate Professor Sonia Ferns, Adjunct, Curtin University, Australia

Dr James Forde, Global Professional Award Manager, University of Huddersfield, England, UK

Kate Foster Employability and Careers Consultant (Widening Participation), University of Exeter, England, UK

Caroline Fox, CEO, Twin Group, England, UK

Dr Laurice Fretwell, Course Director of Human Sciences, University of Derby, England, UK

Patrick Glauner, Professor of Artificial Intelligence, Deggendorf Institute of Technology, Deggendorf, Germany and Ramon O'Callaghan Professor of Technology Management and Innovation, Woxsen University, Hyderabad, India

Paul Gratrick, Head of Operations, University of Liverpool, England, UK

Dr Charles Hancock, Senior Lecturer in Marketing, Derby Business School, University of Derby, England, UK

Saskia Loer Hansen, Deputy Vice-Chancellor International and Engagement, RMIT University, Australia

Dr Caroline Harvey, Senior Lecturer in Psychology, University of Derby, England, UK

Professor Helen Higson, Professor of Higher Education Learning and Management, Aston Business School, England, UK

Kaye Howells, Senior Lecturer in Law and Director of the Student Legal Advice Centre, University of Derby, England, UK

Emily Huns, Head of Careers and Entrepreneurship, University of Sussex, England, UK

Melpo Iacovidou, Director of the Academic Compliance Office, University of Nicosia, Cyprus

Sue Jennings, Head of Law, Derby Law School, University of Derby, England, UK

Parminder Johal, Head of Discipline for Accounting, Economics and Finance, University of Derby, England, UK

Thea Jones, Data Lead Quality Co-ordinator, University Centre South Devon, England, UK

Madelaine-Marie Judd, Manager, Career Development Learning, The University of Queensland, Australia

Judie Kay, Vice Chair Programs and Partnerships WACE (World Association for Co-operative Education), Australia

Carolyn Keenan, Head of Aston Enterprise, Aston Centre for Growth, Aston University, England, UK

Dr Alison Lawson, Head of Discipline of Marketing and Operations, Derby Business School, University of Derby, England, UK

Dr Dawn Lees, Student Employability and Development Manager, University of Exeter, England, UK

Colombine Madelaine, Vice-Rector for International Affairs, University of Tours, France

Rebekah Marangon, Teaching Fellow, Aston University, England, UK

Pamela McGee, Project Officer, University of Liverpool, England, UK

Fiona McGonigle, Business Engagement and Innovation Lead, Anglia Ruskin University, Peterborough, England, UK

Dr Sarah Montano – Senior Lecturer in Marketing and Deputy Director of Education (Digital) College of Social Sciences; University of Birmingham, England, UK

Emma Moore, Director of Careers and Employability, University of Liverpool, England, UK

Professor Siobhan Neary, Head of the International Centre for Guidance Studies (iCeGS), University of Derby, UK

Louise Nicol, Founder, Asia Careers Group SDN BHD, Malaysia

Gillian O'Brien, Employer Connections Manager, University of Liverpool, England, UK

Professor Catherine O'Connor, Pro-Vice Chancellor for Education and Experience, Leeds Trinity University, England, UK

Heather Pasero, Career Consultant, University of Southampton, England, UK

Bice Della Piana, Associate Professor of Cross-Cultural Management, University of Salerno, Italy

Tracy Powell, Assistant Head of Discipline of Marketing and Operations, Derby Business School, University of Derby, England, UK

Professor Ross Renton, Principal, Anglia Ruskin University, Peterborough, England, UK

Anna Richards, Senior Manager (Learning Partnerships), The University of Queensland, Australia

Darren Siggers, Employability Business Partner, University of Liverpool, England, UK

Ruth Smith, Lecturer, University of Derby, England, UK

Susan Smith, Associate Dean (Education and Students), University of Sussex Business School, England, UK

Renáta Tomášková, Vice-Rector for International Relations, University of Ostrava, Czech Republic

Jacklyn Tubb, Head of Business Operations, Faculty of Engineering and Science, University of Greenwich, England, UK

Dr Matthew Vince, Academic Outcomes Facilitator, University Centre South Devon, England, UK

Fiona Walsh, Partnerships and Development Director, Student Hubs, UK

Iwan Williams, Employability Business Partner, University of Liverpool, England, UK

Dr Dino Willox, Director Student Employability and Member of Senate, The University of Queensland, Australia

Dr Victoria Wilson-Crane, Senior Director of Innovative Student Learning, Kaplan International Pathways, UK

Lizzy Woodfield, Policy Advisor, Aston University, England, UK

Yuchen Xiao, MEd graduate, University of Edinburgh, Scotland, UK

Foreword

Does higher education need another book about employability?

Employability has become a buzzword that pervades everything from policy to learning outcomes, and yet there is scarce agreement on how it should be defined, delivered and measured.

The dominant rhetoric has over the past two decades shifted from job-getting, individual gain and the neglect of inequalities to one of collectivism, social good and addressing the impacts of disadvantage and multiple disadvantages. Over the same period, attention has shifted to temporal, spatial and geopolitical concerns. Informed by both the nature of work and individual choice, employability is now viewed as something which demands consistent work across the career lifespan.

It goes without saying that employability and employment are not the same; however, once something is measured, it is also scrutinised. Scrutiny is fine when the metrics make sense, but many governments expect employ*ability* and measure employ*ment* within months of graduation. Workers can be employable and not employed, and the labour market is such that many workers intersperse employed and self-employed work with periods of learning and both planned and unintended downtime.

This is not new; other than a brief period during which limited professions offered permanent full-time roles, work has always been project-based and at least partly self-employed. At each industrial revolution and at multiple points before and since, workers have proactively or reactively managed their careers by engaging in employability work. What matters most in higher education is graduates' ability and preparedness to manage this curation.

The success of employability work, or career curation, is not underpinned by the functional employability skillset which results in a nicely formatted CV; rather, it demands cognitive employability without which a skillset has neither foundation nor direction. Mirvis and Hall wrote back in 1996 (p. 334) that workers need to '*learn* a living rather than to *earn* a living'. We can perhaps expand on this by asserting that people who want to earn a living need to both *learn* and *think* a living. It is this cognitive aspect of employability that underpins the ability of graduates to create and sustain meaningful work, and cognitive employability which aligns it with the educative and social purpose of higher education.

The ability to curate a career through informed employability work is learned as a student. This volume goes beyond definitional matters, measurement and geopolitical differences to present a shared narrative on how university graduates' employability can be enabled. Despite the multiple volumes and articles, the need for an authoritative, evidence-based voice on employability has never been more vital.

So yes, the world needs another book on employability.

Professor Dawn Bennett PhD(Dist), MMus, GradDipEd, PFHEA
Assistant Provost, Bond University, Gold Coast, Queensland, Australia

Reference

Mirvis, P. H., and Hall, D. T. (1996), 'New organisational forms and the new career', in D. T. Hall (ed.), *The Career Is Dead: Long Live the Career*, San Francisco, CA: Jossey-Bass, pp. 72–100.

Preface

Working in a university, whether in the UK or further afield, we are very aware of the importance of employability. Universities in the UK and worldwide are measured in several ways, and one of those measures is graduate outcomes. A university is expected to provide students with an excellent education, and the opportunity to move into a graduate level job.

Over many years we have seen cohorts of students graduate from university, and successfully enter the world of work. However, we know that some have not managed to get the job they wanted, whereas others have exceeded their expectations. We know that some students have needed lots of help to get their career started, whereas others have seemed to need very little help.

Employability matters, and as we worked with our students we became aware of many exciting and diverse initiatives being tried by different institutions. We also became involved in the debate about employability – who is responsible for it, should it be regulated for, should it be what universities are about, or is the subject content more important ... and many more questions.

The more that we explored the topic, the more convinced we became that it would be useful to bring together the diverse range of ideas and initiatives into a book. This book is intended to give a platform for the debate about employability, and also to provide ideas for all those who are supporting the next generation of students to become employable.

Interspersed between the chapters you will find a number of reflections. These are written by students and employers, and are an opportunity to pause and think. They are an opportunity to gain an insight into what those who are seeking to be employable, and those who are looking for employable graduates, really think.

We are delighted that we have a range of authors from around the world contributing to this book. All authors have written their contribution within their national context.

Introduction and Context

The book is titled 'How to enable the employability of university graduates', but who is responsible for making this happen? Is it the responsibility of the university, or does the student have some responsibility for making themselves employable?

We start the book by exploring the nature of employability, and what it really means for the student and for the institution which is increasingly measured by the outcomes that it achieves for graduates. We then ask what the responsibility of the university really should be, and we also listen to the student voices giving their opinion of employability.

What Employers Want from Graduates

We now turn to look at the issue of employability from the lens of the employer. What is it that employers want, and are they getting this from the graduates that they employ?

To answer these questions, we look at specific examples from the disciplines of law and accounting. We also look at a specific competency, that of creativity, which employers indicate they want. We ask how that can be taught, and how developing creativity in the student can help to improve employability. We also look at the influence employers have had on the creation of a new university in the UK.

Employability and the Curriculum

If one of the main reasons for going to university is to improve the student's employability, then should employability be taught as part of the curriculum? If it is part of the curriculum, should this be through a specific module that relates to the curriculum, or should employability be integrated into the subject content?

In this section we answer those questions, and we also look at some specific examples of work-based activities that have been embedded into the curriculum. We conclude this section by addressing assessment, looking at the way that assessments can be written to link with the work skills that graduates will need.

Innovative Approaches to Career Guidance

Careers services have been providing invaluable guidance to students for many years. In this section we look at the way that one institution has developed specific career pathways, and how these have been used to tailor careers guidance. We also look at an innovative approach to engaging students to assist peers with career guidance.

We then look at the specific challenge of supporting international students, and we explore how careers services can tailor their support to meet this challenge.

Practical Examples of Employability Activities

Many of the chapters in the book contain specific examples of employability activities that have been tried by a range of institutions. In this section we focus on three specific examples – an interdisciplinary challenge for a large group of students, using social action programmes to develop employability skills and adapting a more traditional placement model to fit the varying needs of students.

Enterprise/Entrepreneurial Activities

Not all students want to work for an employer; many students have an interest in, and a desire to, set up their own business. We start this section by thinking about the nature of entrepreneurism and how this fits with enterprise and employability.

We then look at a large-scale offering which gives support to entrepreneurial students across a group of universities in the West Midlands.

Widening Participation

There has been a lot of focus in recent years on universities doing more to enable students from under-represented groups to enter university. Equal focus is needed on supporting these under-represented students once they get into university, both to be successful in their degrees and in their graduate outcomes.

Across a number of chapters we look at some of the specific issues faced by students who are part of this 'widening participation' agenda, looking broadly at ways of unlocking their potential and also looking specifically at challenges faced by the 'first in family to go to university' students, and under-represented students based in London.

International Students

International students have particular needs when it comes to employability support, especially in countries where post-study work opportunities exist. We start this section by looking at research relating to international students from the UK and Australia. We then look specifically at the expectations of international students and how those expectations can be met, and how to use placements effectively to support international students who want to further develop their skills.

Insights from Around the World

Universities across the world are challenged by the need to support the employability of their students. Universities also have to operate within the regulatory framework within their country, which often has an employability focus.

In this section we look at insights from the UK, Australia, New Zealand, Germany and from a consortium of universities from across Europe.

Institutional Response

Employability is not the responsibility of one department within the university. Supporting a student to achieve their long-term career goal is the responsibility of all departments, working together effectively, across the university.

In this section we look at the way that two institutions have integrated employability into the university strategy. We also look at the way that an employability programme spanning the full length of an undergraduate degree has been successfully introduced, and the initiative to make employability part of the pastoral support offered by a university.

A Final Reflection

The debate about employability is not new, indeed it has been a topic that universities have grappled with for many years. Our final reflection is from a researcher who has over 20 years' experience researching into employability, with insights into the way that the agenda and debate have developed over that time.

Over 60 authors have contributed to this book. It has been a privilege to work with them to create a guide to employability which will be useful to all those working in universities and to employers. Ultimately, we hope that this book will give inspiration to help all those involved in higher education to enable the employability of university graduates.

Saskia Loer Hansen
Kathy Daniels

Abbreviations

ACEN	Australian Collaborative Education Network
AGCAS	Association of Graduate Careers Advisory Services
AI	artificial intelligence
AiG	Australian Industry Group
APP	Access and Participation Plan
Augar Review	Review of HE, chaired by Lord Augar, reported in 2019
BAME	Black, Asian and Minority Ethnic
BEIS	Department for Business, Energy and Industrial Strategy, UK
Brexit	The exit of the UK from the European Union (January 2020)
CBI	Confederation of British Industry
CDAA	Career Development Association of Australia
CDL	career development learning
CFE	Centre for Entrepreneurs
CITB	Construction Industry Training Board, UK
CLE	clinical legal education
CMI	Chartered Management Institute, UK
CPD	continuing professional development
CRM	customer relationship management
CSA	Centre for Social Action
CV	curriculum vitae
DELTAs	Distinctive Elements of Talents
DfE	Department for Employment
DLHE	Destinations of Leavers from Higher Education survey, UK
EDI	equality, diversity and inclusion
EDO	employability development opportunities

ERDF	European Regional Development Fund
FE	further education
FiF	first in family (to go to university)
FSB	Federation of Small Businesses, UK
GEM	Global Entrepreneurship Monitor
GO	graduate outcomes
GOS	Graduate Outcomes Survey
HE	higher education
HEA	Higher Education Academy (now known as Advance HE), UK
HECSU	Higher Education Careers Service Unit
HEFCE	Higher Education Funding Council for England (closed April 2018)
HEI	higher education institution
HEP	higher education providers
HEPI	Higher Education Policy Institute
HESA	Higher Education Statistics Agency
IFS	Institute for Fiscal Studies
ILO	International Labour Organization
IMD	Index of Multiple Deprivation
ISE	Institute of Student Employers
KEF	Knowledge Exchange Framework
KIS	Key Information Set
KTN	Knowledge Transfer Network
LEO	longitudinal education outcomes
LLE	lifelong loan entitlement
MOOC	massive open online courses
NSS	National Student Survey
OECD	Organisation for Economic Co-operation and Development
OFFA	Office for Fair Access, UK
OfS	Office for Students (UK's HE regulator)
ONS	Office for National Statistics
PGR	postgraduate research

PGT	postgraduate taught
POLAR	Participation of Local Areas (in Higher Education)
PPI	pre-professional identity
QAA	Quality Assurance Agency for Higher Education
QS	Quacquarelli Symonds
Russell Group	Self-selected association of 24 UK research-led universities
SDG	Sustainable Development Goals
SIG	sector interest groups
SMEs	small and medium-sized enterprises
STEM	science, technology, engineering and mathematics
TEF	Teaching Excellence Framework
T levels	UK post-16 qualification with a vocational focus
TUNDRA	Tracking Under-Representation (in HE) by Area
UCAS	Universities and Colleges Admissions Service
UCENZ	University Careers and Employability New Zealand
UG	undergraduate
UNSDG	United Nations Sustainable Development Goals
UUK	Universities UK (representative body of UK universities)
VLC	virtual law clinic
WEF	World Economic Forum
White Paper	Government policy document setting out proposals for future legislation
WIL	work integrated learning
WP	widening participation
WURI	World's Universities with Real Impact

PART I

Introduction and context

1. Why employability matters
Saskia Loer Hansen and Kathy Daniels

EMPLOYABILITY: WHAT ARE WE CHASING?

As we applaud another cohort of fresh graduates, walking across the stage and going through the formal process of receiving their degree, what are we celebrating? We are certainly celebrating a lot of hard work that has gone into achieving that degree, but we are also celebrating the future. We hope, and believe, that the degrees the graduates have achieved will pave the way to them having a great career. We hope that their time in university has made them more employable.

Students across the world invest significant time, effort and money in coming to university. Some students are from backgrounds where university study is an ingrained expectation, whereas other students may be the first in their family to go to university. Irrespective of background, students come to university to learn and to be better equipped to pursue the career of their dreams.

Alongside learning the content of their degree, students are expecting to become employable; but what does that mean? Are all graduates walking across the stage equally employable, or are some more employable than others? What does employable 'look like', and how do we know if our fresh graduates have done enough to achieve 'employability'? Can a graduate be 'employable', but not employed? What is the difference between the two?

The idea for this book was stimulated by asking these sorts of questions, but before we get into the many fascinating contributions from colleagues across the world, we need to understand what we are chasing. What does 'employability' mean?

EMPLOYABILITY: WHAT DOES IT MEAN?

Several authors in this book refer to Yorke (2004/2006) when describing employability and that is a common thread through the chapters. Yorke describes employability as 'a set of achievements – skills, understandings and personal attributes – that makes graduates more likely to gain employment and be successful in their chosen occupations, which benefits themselves, the workforce, the community and the economy' (2006: 8).

This suggestion that employability benefits the workforce, the community and the economy is strongly aligned with the academic valuing of the learning experience (Knight and Yorke, 2003). Higher education (HE) can make a difference to the viability and quality of people's lives and the societies in which they live. In this regard, contributions to human flourishing can be seen as an intrinsic good as well as preparation for work. HE is not necessarily an unequivocal public good, but educational development that supports human flourishing has a positive impact. The question this raises is less about how we teach and how students learn, but more about the way that HE contributes through such practices of teaching and learning to human flourishing and personal agency. Agency can be seen as one's ability to pursue goals that one values and is important for the life an individual wishes to lead and is inextricably linked to human flourishing (Walker, 2005).

Another perspective of agency is captured by Roulin and Bangerter (2013), who present recent graduates as either 'players' who treat employability as a 'positional game' or as 'purists' who believe that the right degree credentials will open the door to the right job, or as a mix of the two. Players are much more active in leveraging social networks and actively unpack employer requirements to develop a story about why they are the very best candidate for the job. Purists also look at employer requirements, but mainly to ensure that they are qualified to apply for the role and then to present their formal credentials for consideration.

The early academic work on employability identifies the complexities of many different components coming together. Employability, as a concept, has become intertwined with employment outcomes, but importantly, they are two different things. The distinction between the two was made by Pegg et al. (2012) when they defined employment as the graduate outcome which universities measure, and employability as a 'range of knowledge, skills and attributes which support continued learning and career development'.

A common theme of definitions of employability is that they are seen as individually focused. In 1999 the Confederation of British Industry (CBI) used the definition: 'Employability is the possession by an individual of the qualities and competencies required to meet the changing needs of employers and customers and thereby help to realise his or her aspirations and potential in work.'

However, this definition presumes that the individual has responsibility for, and control over, their employability, which is not necessarily correct given the strong connection with gaining meaningful employment. If meaningful employment is not available, does this mean that the individual has not become employable? Surely this does not make sense, because the cohort which graduates into a tight labour market, with low unemployment and many job vacancies, is almost certainly going to find it easier to secure a job than a cohort which graduates some years later into a loose labour market, with high unemployment and few job opportunities. It is not that the cohort is less employable, but that the cohort has less opportunity to be employed.

This distinction is picked up by Cheng et al. (2021), who identified a number of themes of employability, therefore extending the definition beyond the characteristics of an individual. They concluded that:

- Employability depends on the capabilities of individuals, of intrinsic characteristics which relate to the personal attributes and skills of the individual.
- Employability depends on the labour market and depends on the chance of finding and keeping different types of employment.
- Employability is linked to social capital. Those with lower social capital are less likely to have had the opportunity to engage with work experience and to develop employability skills.

This approach to defining employability sees it as a mix of different factors, both from within the individual and from the outside environment.

The definition from Cheng et al. (2021), also leads us to see some potential inequity in employability. Individuals with lower social capital might always be catching up with those who have had more opportunities earlier in life.

An important consideration throughout this book is how to provide strong graduate outcomes and career opportunities for all students, irrespective of background. Some of the very initiatives that are meant to level the playing field can end up making the field more uneven, for example the use of placements. Siebert and Wilson (2013) focus on the creative industries and identified the importance of students having the 'right connections' to find the important placements that often subsequently deliver employment, and having the financial backing to work for free to get 'their foot in the door'. Smith et al. (2015) further explore this issue and suggest that the emphasis should be on finding ways to provide exposure 'to the world of work' within the learning environment, which is managed by universities, and which would avoid the inequalities associated with unpaid work experience.

The practical examples of employability activities in this book, from a range of universities, offer an illustration of how students are supported in developing their skills and credentials, with the aim of becoming employed. However, many of these activities require students to engage, maybe with doing something additional to their studies. To have the motivation to engage, students need to see the benefit of the activities in helping them to become employed. What do students understand by the concept of 'employability'?

THE STUDENT VIEW OF EMPLOYABILITY

Universities and colleges presume that students are studying a course with them to enhance their job opportunities. This is evident from the emphasis on employment prospects in recruitment literature. It is not always clear, however, whether this is a focus on employability or employment outcomes.

Tymon (2011) carried out research with undergraduate students across a range of business programmes at a post-1992 university in the UK. Students typically had a narrow view of employability, particularly first and second year students. She concluded that the students saw employability as a 'means to an end, being about finding a job, any job, or employment'.

In comparison, Tomlinson (2008) worked with final year undergraduate students in a pre-1992 university to explore how they viewed the role of their degree in shaping their future employment prospects. Students perceived that what they studied, where they studied and what grade they got would assist them to get a job. However, they also saw the need for additional credentials such as developing personal and social skills, due to the high level of competition for graduate-level jobs.

O'Connor and Bodicoat (2016) looked at responses from graduates in relation to their take up of graduate internship opportunities and found a clear distinction between the engaged and the disengaged in a specific internship scheme. Misunderstandings, or concerns, about unpaid internships might result in less-privileged students missing out on opportunities that would support positive career outcomes. This makes it even more important that universities clearly articulate the benefits of opportunities, and the links to employability, not least if these opportunities sit outside the core curriculum.

Research by Tholen (2012) suggests that employability might have a cultural element. A study comparing final year students from Dutch and British universities found that British students expressed their employability in terms of competition. They saw employability as standing out from the crowd, and as being adaptable, flexible and having knowledge and skills. In comparison, Dutch students perceived employability as being about finding a niche in the labour market. They saw employability as developing an understanding of themselves, their strengths and weaknesses, and then finding a job that matches their qualities.

Gedye and Beaumont (2018) concluded that students describe employability in a broad range of ways, much like other groups, but are less likely to emphasise the longer-term aspects of employability, such as being able to thrive and move within the job market. They also concluded that the student view of employability develops during their studies. This is supported by the work of Brown et al. (2003), who found that final year undergraduate students link employability to securing future employment, with first- and second-year students linking employability to qualifications and grades.

If employability is about practical intelligence as well as academic intelligence, as Yorke argues, students need to make the most of both the degree content that they study as well as co- and extra-curricular opportunities. Indeed, there is extensive literature on the importance of extra-curricular activities. Clark et al. (2015) looked at a group of alumni and how they compared the qualities and skills developed through their formal degrees and those developed through extracurricular activities. Alumni reported that their interpersonal skills, self-confidence and communication skills were developed more through extra-curricular activities than through their degrees, whereas analytical skills and problem-solving were developed more through their degrees. If employability requires a broad range of skills, then this points to the importance of students engaging not only with the curriculum but also with activities that complement the formal learning experience, including sports clubs and societies. However, to have the motivation to do this, students need to understand the breadth of the definition of employability.

THE EMPLOYER'S VIEW OF EMPLOYABILITY

In this book we see examples of employability initiatives driven by employers wanting to see that students have had practical experience (e.g. the law clinic referenced in Chapter 5, or the use of social action referenced in Chapter 15). The student focus of employability may arguably be about getting a job, but for the employer, the focus on employability is longer term, going through a number of stages of the employee life cycle. There are the employability skills needed to get a job, then the employability skills needed to be adaptable in the workplace (maybe moving to a new job, maybe moving along with changes in the work of the organisation) and then the development of new skills as the employee looks to enhance their career. Having a broad range of practical experience gives employers the confidence that an employee can develop and bring benefit to the organisation.

The development of employability through this life cycle is shown in the ways that employers define employability. Mason et al. (2009) report that employers see employability as the readiness for work, 'the possession of the skills, knowledge, attitudes and commercial understanding that will enable new graduates to make productive contributions to organisational objectives soon after commencing employment'.

This definition suggests that employers see employability as more than subject knowledge, with the reference to attitudes and commercial understanding. This is supported by de Weert (2007) who concluded that employers value employees with the ability to learn, in addition to having generic skills such as teamwork, problem-solving, planning, communication skills and taking responsibility.

Hinchliffe and Jolly (2011) also concluded that subject knowledge was not sufficient, and that interpersonal skills were valued more than any other skills, and that employers expected new employees to have the qualities of honesty, integrity and trust.

Securing a job is very much something that a prospective employer can control, and therefore the qualities wanted on employment can be dictated by the employer. However, the expectations further on in the employee life cycle, once the employee has gained employment, tend to shift. The employer needs the employee to do the work as assigned, but the employee also has demands on the employer – for personal development, new opportunities and values that align with their own. For example, there is evidence that younger employees, in particular, seek authenticity in an organisation's ethical, diversity and sustainability policies and practices (Rzemieniak and Wawer, 2021).

These demands on both sides of the employment relationship were first referred to as the 'psychological contract' by Argyris in 1960. This is not referring to a written contract, but rather to the expectations and beliefs that the employer and employee have of each other. In the context of employability, this could be the employee having the unwritten expectation that hard work will lead to the opportunity to develop further, and therefore to become more employable as the employee pursues their career.

If there is a breach of the psychological contract, the employment relationship breaks down, as explained by Schein (1978). The contract can be breached by both the employer and the employee – the employer by not providing the opportunity for the development of employability skills, and the employee by not being adaptable and developing new skills. Conway et al. (2011) found that such breaches had greater (negative) effects on outcomes than increases in fulfilment, especially in impacts on well-being, job satisfaction, and organisational commitment.

THE UNIVERSITY'S VIEW OF EMPLOYABILITY

If students come to university to enhance their employability, then this means that they are looking to universities to equip with them with whatever it is that they need to be successful in the job market. Graduate outcomes feed into university league tables and are measures that help students determine where to study. Given the importance of performing well in these measures, Frankham (2017) reports that universities are driven to create employability strategies that fit with government policies.

Boden and Nedeva (2010) develop this argument further, observing that the government has control over universities by using employability as a measure of performance. However, again we see this tension between equipping students with employability skills, and students gaining employment. Government targets tend to focus on employment outcomes, which can be measured more easily than 'employability'.

This focus on employment outcomes is common in regulatory systems across the world, as shown in chapters in this book from countries including the UK (Chapter 27), Australia (Chapter 28) and New Zealand (Chapter 29). Chapters 28 and 33 refer to the impact of Australian government policy through the Job Ready Graduates Package, which provides funding for universities to work with industry to produce job-ready graduates. This is an example of a direct financial incentive causing universities to focus on delivering employment outcomes for their students.

In addition to emphasising the difference between employability and employment outcomes, this leads us to question the purpose of universities. Are they there to prepare students for future employment, or are they there to educate students in the subject knowledge that they have chosen to study? In asking why universities exist, Collins (2012) asks whether the underlying purpose of a university education is to create new avenues of interest, questions and research, or to reduce learning to acquiring specific skills, attitudes and behaviours.

It could be argued that focusing on the development of employability skills detracts from the academic rigour of a degree course. Sin and Neave (2016) argue that addressing the short-term needs of an unpredictable labour market, by focusing on teaching of skills to meet those needs, threatens the quality of academic courses.

McCowan (2015: 279) argues that a university has little impact on individual attributes and qualities, as these are established before entering university, and that the role of the university should be to focus on 'developing critical thinking, the development of values associated with research and scholarship, and the experience of living and working with diverse others'.

This debate about the purpose of universities presumes that there is one overall purpose, but Stoten (2018) disputes that notion, arguing that post-1992 universities, with roots in technical and vocational education, are typically more focused on employability than pre-1992 universities. Boden and Nedeva (2010) echo this by noting that students at the University of Oxford gain broad-based knowledge and cultural capital, whereas developing the employability agenda is essential for post-1992 universities to attract student numbers.

In understanding the responsibility of the university for employability, we come full circle to the definition of employability from Cheng et al. (2021), given at the start of this chapter. They saw employability as multifaceted, depending on the capabilities of individuals, the labour market and social capital. They noted that students with lower social capital are less likely to have developed employability skills when entering university.

This suggests, therefore, that the university attitude to employability is going to be tailored by the demographics of students that they recruit. This supports the view by Boden and Nedeva (2010), that different universities need to view employability in different ways.

CONCLUSION

Employability is a complex mix of factors which come together to enable the individual to find meaningful employment. When students enter university, they will already have some of the components that go together to create these employability skills. However, there will be students entering university with low social capital, and limited work experience. Arguably, these students will need more support in developing employability skills.

Employers are clear that they want to recruit individuals who can make an immediate contribution to the workplace, but subject knowledge is not enough on its own. There is the expectation that employees will have a number of soft skills which enable them to work effectively. Once employed, the employee will be looking to the employer to enable the ongoing development of employability skills.

A lot of emphasis has been put on the role of the university in developing employability skills, but this causes a tension between the academic purpose of study and the measures of good graduate outcomes used by many external agencies to determine the worth of a course of study.

There is no one body that can make a student employable. Ultimately, the responsibility for employability is a shared responsibility.

REFERENCES

Argyris, C. (1960), *Understanding Organisational Behaviour*, London: Tavistock.
Boden, R. and Nedeva, M. (2010), 'Employing discourse: universities and graduate "employability"', *Journal of Education Policy*, 25(1), 37–54.
Brown, P., Hesketh, A. and Wiliams, S. (2003), 'Employability in a knowledge-driven economy', *Journal of Education and Work*, 16(2), 107–126.
CBI (1999), *Making Employability Work: An Agenda for Action*, London: CBI.
Cheng, M., Adekola, O., Albia, J. and Cai, S. (2021), 'Employability in higher education: a review of key stakeholders' perspectives', *Higher Education Evaluation and Development*, 16(1), 16–31.
Clark, G., Marsden, R., Whyatt, J. D., Thompson, L. and Walker, M. (2015), '"It's everything else you do...": alumni views on extracurricular activities and employability', *Active Learning in Higher Education*, 16(2), 133–147.
Collins, S. (2012), *What Are Universities For?* London: Penguin.

Conway, N., Guest, D. and Trenberth, L. (2011), 'Testing the differential effects of changes in psychological contract breach and fulfillment', *Journal of Vocational Behavior*, 79(1), 267–276.

De Weert, E. (2007), 'Graduate employment in Europe: the employers' perspective', in U. Teichler (ed.), *Careers of University Graduates*, Dordrecht: Springer, pp. 225–246.

Frankham, J. (2017), 'Employability and higher education: the follies of the "productivity challenge" in the teaching excellence framework', *Journal of Education Policy*, 32(5), 628–641.

Gedye, S. and Beaumont, E. (2018), 'The ability to get a job: student understandings and definitions of employability', *Education and Training*, 60(5), 406–420.

Hinchliffe, G. W. and Jolly, A. (2011), 'Graduate identity and employability', *British Educational Research Journal*, 37(4), 563–584.

Knight, P. T. and Yorke, M. (2003), 'Employability and good learning in higher education', *Teaching in Higher Education*, 8(1), 3–16.

Mason, G., Williams, G. and Cranmer, S. (2009), 'Employability skills initiatives in higher education: what effects do they have on graduate labour market outcomes?', *Education Economics*, 17(1), 1–30.

McCowan, T. (2015), 'Should universities promote employability?', *Theory and Research in Education*, 13(3), 267–285.

O'Connor, H. and Bodicoat, M. (2016), 'Exploitation or opportunity? Student perceptions of internships in enhancing employability skills', *British Journal of Sociology of Education*, 38, 435–449.

Pegg, A., Waldock, J., Hendy-Isaac, S. and Lawton, R. (2012), *Pedagogy for Employability*, York: The Higher Education Academy.

Roulin, N. and Bangerter, A. (2013), Students' use of extra-curricular activities for positional advantage in competitive job markets', *Journal of Education and Work*, 26(1), 21–47.

Rzemieniak, M. and Wawer, M. (2021), 'Employer branding in the context of the company's sustainable development strategy from the perspective of gender diversity of generation Z', *Sustainability*, 13(2), 828.

Schein, E. H. (1978), *Career Dynamics: Matching Individual and Organisational Needs*, Reading, MA: Addison-Wesley.

Siebert, S. and Wilson, F. (2013), 'All work and no pay: consequences of unpaid work in the creative industries', *Work, Employment and Society*, 27, 711–721.

Sin, C. and Neave, G. (2016), 'Employability deconstructed: perceptions of Bologna stakeholders', *Studies in Higher Education*, 41(8), 1447–1462.

Smith, S., Smith, C. and Caddell, M. (2015), 'Can pay, should pay? Exploring employer and student perceptions of paid and unpaid placements', *Active Learning in Higher Education*, 16(2), 149–164.

Stoten, D. (2018), 'Employability: a contested concept in higher education', *Journal of Pedagogic Development*, 8(1), 9–17.

Tholen, G. (2012), 'Graduate employability and educational context: a comparison between Great Britain and the Netherlands', *British Educational Research Journal*, 40(1), 1–17.

Tomlinson, M. (2008), '"The degree is not enough": students' perceptions of the role of higher education credentials for graduate work and employability', *British Journal of Sociology Education*, 29(1), 49–61.

Tymon, A. (2011), 'The student perspective on employability', *Studies in Higher Education*, 38(6), 1–16.

Walker, M. (2005), *Higher Education Pedagogies*, Maidenhead: McGraw-Hill Education.
Yorke, M. (2004/2006), *Employability in Higher Education: What It Is – What It Is Not*, York: The Higher Education Academy/ESECT.

REFLECTION

From a senior director of a major retail organisation

As both an employee and an employer, I see it as my primary purpose to coach others to deliver excellent results in their current role and to excel in their own career paths. I have focused on developing talent in a number of ways: by starting and developing a graduate programme in my function to bring in young talent, focusing on finding the right new recruits for the team and stretching existing colleagues within the team. Providing the right development opportunities for the right colleagues, and taking calculated risks within this, drives colleagues and the business forward.

I also use these focuses to balance skills and diversity in my team, which is important in order to build a sustainable team. I am only as good as my team, and doing all of these things has delivered a stronger, more resilient and higher performing function.

Over my career, I have learnt that communication is key, to tell stories in everything I speak about, with a start, middle and end. This drives honest and constructive conversations with colleagues that support them in growth. Occasionally, some colleagues can create blockage for others through poor performance, and therefore tackling these issues through support and honest conversations in my experience is also something I need to be aware of and equally focus on.

As I highlighted at the beginning, I see it as my job to do this; it's not just a meeting or a coffee, it's a way of life. Others look to me to understand how to coach and develop colleagues around me using a consistent and fair approach. So, this should be in everything I do, and I aim to lead by example.

2. Whose job is it to make a graduate employable?

Martin Edmondson

INTRODUCTION

It feels like there is a growing consensus that university graduates should emerge fully formed, perfectly skilled and immediately work ready. Take, for example, the recent study of HR leaders by Pearson (referred to in Baska, 2022) which made the point that 'nearly a fifth of graduates are not "workplace ready"'. Putting aside the slightly 'glass half empty' nature of this headline, whereby presumably over 80 per cent are work ready, it is not an unfamiliar narrative.

The phrase 'oven ready' graduates appears consistently, and tends to over-simplify what is ultimately a very complicated issue – how do you produce genuinely employable graduates, and match the supply of skills/people with the demands of the economy and employers, when all are moving targets?

When we examine this further, the real problem lies in the lack of a clear understanding of what an employable graduate is, and whose responsibility it is to make them employable.

Is it the role of the education system and teachers, employers, parents, the state more broadly, or the individual? Clearly all play a part, but the prevailing answers go a long way to solving skills supply/demand challenges, and to understanding the employability expectation disconnects that exist between graduates, employers and universities.

WHAT IS AN EMPLOYABLE GRADUATE?

Firstly we need to understand what an employable graduate is, and that should not be simply seen as one who has secured a job. In higher education (HE) in the UK, this confusion is not necessarily helped by using metrics (Graduate Outcomes Survey – GOS and the Longitudinal Educational Outcomes – LEO) that are very much 'employment' metrics, but they nonetheless do function as useful (if flawed) absolute and relative indicators of employability at an individual and institutional level. To this confusion we can also add the challenge of defining what a graduate job is, which remains an ongoing and unresolved challenge. As Charlie Ball puts it in the Universities UK publication, *Busting graduate job myths* (2022: 10), 'It's hard to tell how many graduate jobs there are or how many graduates are in graduate jobs, in part because it depends on how you measure what a graduate job is.'

This challenge doesn't mean we should not try to understand the definition of a graduate job. Indeed, although the primary HE metrics are employment metrics, they can still provide a useful or proxy indicator as to whether graduates are employable; but this is not the only definition.

It is perhaps then useful to define what employability is, and this in itself can be a challenge as there is no single definitive description. Perhaps the most common is that provided by Prof. Mantz Yorke (2004/2006): 'A set of achievements – skills, understandings and personal attributes – that make graduates more likely to gain employment and be successful in their chosen occupations, which benefits themselves, the workforce, the community and the economy.'

The more pithy definition, which is on the wall of the Gradcore office, is that given by Prof. Pete Hawkins in his book, *The Art of Building Windmills* (1999: 1): 'To be employed is to be at risk, to be employable is to be secure.'

Between these definitions we see the importance of employability as the development and usefulness of the whole individual on an ongoing basis, rather than as the fixed point of employment. One analogy is to see it like the relationship, in finance terms, between a profit and loss report and a balance sheet. The former shows ongoing movement and progression, and the latter is a picture of a fixed point in time.

WHOSE RESPONSIBILITY IS IT TO MAKE GRADUATES EMPLOYABLE?

Given this context, we will now explore the different roles and responsibilities played by the key actors in graduate employability – universities, employers and the graduates themselves. Clearly other stakeholders, such as parents and the government, play a role too – but this chapter focuses on the three primary parties.

Universities

Historically it has been the role of the careers service to deliver employability provision at universities. Careers services remain important, but on their own cannot deliver personalised employability provision at scale across a whole university. Their role is transforming from a student support service dispensing student guidance, to now being a consultancy practice with a key role in equipping academics with the tools to embed employability into curriculum. The nuts and bolts of recruitability – CVs, interview practice, job applications – can be primarily delivered digitally on demand, or increasingly by student peers trained in these fundamentals. The University of Liverpool has particularly pioneered this approach with its Career Studio (see Chapter 13), and the model is being regularly replicated elsewhere.

Alongside this shift in the role of careers services, academics in universities understand that it is part of their role to produce employable graduates, yet they are often untrained to do so, and in some cases reluctant. The curriculum is the primary place where graduate attributes can be developed and assessed, so there is a need to better equip academics to fully embed and integrate this development into teaching and assessment.

Institutional honesty of mission

One factor in the provision of appropriate employability support at a university is 'honesty of mission'. Universities are complex organisations, at one moment highly commercial corporations, at another charitable entities for public good, and in terms of classification, they can sometimes sit simultaneously as private, public and third-sector bodies. Layered on top of this operating complexity is the 'university class system', which comes from mission group classification and history, where status, course mix, and prestige play a major role in university identity and self-actualisation.

In that context it is perhaps no surprise that universities often have identity crises, struggling to develop a mission that is genuinely distinctive, and most importantly, true. This confusion could be said to have led to the real or perceived pre-Brexit detachment that universities were seen to have in their local communities, as cited by Professor Dame Nancy Rothwell (2017: 2): 'The vital work that universities undertake to improve the health, and the economic and cultural wellbeing of the UK, did not feature prominently in the debate prior to the recent EU referendum, nor did our many other contributions to widening access or working with local communities.'

In some academic circles the discourse around widening access, or employability impact, is dismissed as instrumentalist and diminishing to the true calling of HE. Stefan Collini (2012: xi), in his excellent book, *What Are Universities For?*, states:

> If we start from the current preoccupation with 'access', 'funding', 'impact': these three starting points – taken either singly or, more often, as a trinity signalling the realism and up-to-dateness of one's position – now utterly dominate the political and media discussion of universities in Britain. But these are secondary matters, and the last two, in particular, are merely transient formulae – clumsy articulations of aspects of social attitudes to which politicians find it expedient to appeal.

It is perhaps equally anti-intellectual to dismiss the real life-changing benefits of 'access' and 'impact' in careers and employability terms of HE as it is to state that universities should solely be focused on employability. Ultimately, whether it is seen as universally desirable or not, the number one reason students give for going to university is to develop or progress their career. This can be seen in many studies, including the 2020 Higher Education Policy Institute (HEPI) student survey where 'getting on the career ladder' was given as the number one reason by students for going to university.

In this context, employability provision should be closely linked to the psychological contract that is created between students (and staff) at any given university. This stems from the vision, mission and positioning of that university, and where that mission intersects with the individual goals and aspirations of the student. Gradcore has had the privilege of reviewing employability provision at dozens of universities over the last decade, and this emerges as a consistent challenge.

For example, where a university primarily serves a locally recruited, low social capital cohort, and is not particularly renowned for research; if it then chooses to position as a research-led institution, it will create patterns of activity and behaviour that support the research goals, but perhaps do not help it best perform its role as a key provider in a regional skills ecosystem.

This can be seen in hiring decisions, where staff are recruited and promoted on the basis of their research, but then perhaps asked to focus on embedding employability in the curriculum (or perhaps vice versa), which is a recipe for staff dissatisfaction as well as being unlikely to meet student expectations or needs. This is not to say that universities should not make the strategic choice to change or redefine their purpose, but in doing so should be honest to staff and students about the implications of those choices.

What gets me promoted round here?
One phrase that stuck out in researching this chapter was a comment from an academic at a mid-tier university who asked, 'What gets me promoted round here?' She outlined that all of the promotion mechanisms in the university were predicated on research performance, and to some extent teaching and the National Student Survey (NSS). There was no recognition or parity of esteem for an academic who successfully embedded employability into the curriculum, or significantly improved the GOS performance of their student cohort. It may perhaps be the case that the Office for Students (OfS)'s new regulation of student outcomes may change this, with the increasingly granular focus on outcome performance by course.

Towards institutional employability

If a university wishes to place employability at the heart of its mission, and to contribute in terms of delivering employable graduates into the economy, it must adopt an attitude of institutional employability. Institutional employability is where the development of employability is culturally understood to be something everyone in a university can contribute to. An example of this is York St John University, where the retail and hospitality provision was brought in house, enabling the university to have greater jurisdiction over the work experience opportunities that can be given to students in that area. Another example is Queen Mary University of London, where the estates team who are supporting the redesign of the careers service offices are designing the buildings and space to play a role in employability, through student familiarisation with environments typical of workplaces and recuitment/assessment centres.

Effective employability strategies

Part of my role is to lead overall reviews of employability strategies and provision at universities, and I have reviewed more than 30 universities across the UK and Europe in the last five years. The most successful and progressive universities in terms of employability are those which:

- seek to provide a personalised employability journey for every student;
- create work experience opportunities for all students;
- meaningfully embed employability in the curriculum via graduate attributes, and train their academic staff to deliver this in teaching and assessment;
- use data effectively to target high-value careers resources at those students who need the most help, in terms of low social capital, marginalised groups, etc.

Employers

Employer trajectory is increasingly veering towards hiring for skills, regardless of background, or at the very least regardless of subject or degree classification. The Institute of Student Employers (ISE) survey (ISE, 2021) shows that since 2018 there has been a drop from 66 per cent to 57 per cent of employers wanting a 2:1 degree or better in their selection process. In addition, recent data from *Harvard Business Review* and the Burning Glass Institute (Fuller et al., 2022) suggests that the requirement for a degree is starting to be taken away from job specifications and advertisements, in favour of the pursuit of specific skills. 'A person's educational credentials are not the only indicators of success, so we advanced our approach to hiring to focus on skills, experiences and potential,' says Jimmy Etheredge, CEO of Accenture North America, in a CNBC interview (Caminiti, 2022).

Clearly doctors will still be hired after taking degrees in medicine, but in many professions and recruitment pathways it will be about the capacity of an individual to demonstrate skills and attributes within the context of their employer (or their own business).

Employers further demonstrate their commitment to broad employability, and the importance of graduate attributes and competencies, in the way they recruit and develop people. Huge amounts of investment have gone into the design of assessment and ongoing continuing professional development (CPD) methodologies, which focus on drawing out the skills and potential of individuals. Factors such as course or degree classification may attract some credit in an application process, but the majority of effort and activity goes into measuring competencies and skills. This is primarily done by a series of applications, psychometric tests, interviews and assessment centres.

One area where employers could perhaps contribute more is how they can support graduates to become more employable when they choose not to hire them. There is a persistent complaint from graduates that they do not get feedback from employers when rejected. This situation is slowly changing, but if all employers adopted the mantra 'making everyone more employable even if they don't get the job' in their recruitment processes (as seen in the case study at the conclusion of this chapter), this would be beneficial to the graduates and also a positive marker for their brand as an employer – especially for those representing consumer-facing brands.

An area where employer activity has crossed over into HE, as a means of employability development, is the use of assessment centres. It is now commonplace to see universities deploying assessment centres as a way of gauging the current and real-time employability of their students (rather than waiting three to five years for the GOS data to emerge). Increasingly these are deployed within the curriculum, and in some cases at the beginning and end of academic programmes to measure distance travelled and learning gain. Universities such as Kingston, the University of Liverpool Business School and Manchester Metropolitan are all using assessment centres for large parts of their cohorts. Such events serve first as a practice and demystifying exercise for students, as well as helping them understand their current and potential graduate attributes. The aggregate data also allows universities to shape additional careers or curriculum provision around any skills deficits that emerge in the cohort.

Skills forecasting

Employers are increasingly hiring for skills, as noted above, yet it is incredibly difficult to accurately forecast skills needs in a company, region or country. I once attended a skills forecasting conference at the International Labour

Organization (ILO), led by the foremost global experts on skills forecasting. I was dismayed then to hear in the opening keynote that 'We have been trying to forecast skills needs for 50 years, and we still don't know how to do it.'

Disconnect between area or employer skills forecasting often leads to calls for more vocational degrees, even though we know, for example, that music graduates outperform business graduates in terms of graduate-level destinations. There is often rhetoric about being 'more like Germany' with their more integrated employment and education system – but even that is running into challenges. According to researchers at the Institute for German Economy (The Local, 2022), around 63,000 traineeship spots remained empty in 2021, accounting for around 12 per cent of available positions.

In the UK we should celebrate our non-linear labour market – where 71 per cent of graduate jobs are open to any degree discipline (Ball, 2014) – and the open-minded large graduate employers who increasingly seek to hire on skills rather than privilege or background.

Graduates

Graduates must increasingly own their employability, and take accountability for it, whether that be in terms of gathering work experience, or actively and consciously seeking to develop skills. However, for graduates this is not a level playing field and social capital plays a key role in the awareness an individual graduate has of the need and means for them to drive their own employability. Where universities are populated with large numbers of first-generation students, who tend to lack social capital, there is more need to help students and graduates realise the importance of employability development, and to lead them to a sense of ownership of their own employability.

Perhaps the two biggest barriers to this, as we deal with the impacts of the Covid-19 pandemic, are lack of confidence and loss of work experience opportunities. The Careerpass Network Temperature Check survey (Haththotuwa, 2022) showed that 55 per cent of graduates did not feel confident about securing their ideal graduate job, and 41 per cent did not feel they had the opportunity to gain any work experience during their time at university.

According to the HEPI student survey 2021, all the measures of student well-being have also dipped year on year for the last three years – which is bound to have a diminishing effect on confidence. In addition, we know that work experience makes a positive difference to graduate destinations metrics, and this can be seen in the view of employers – where 78 per cent of employers agreed that 'graduates who had completed an internship or work placement were more skilled than those who had not' (ISE 2021).

So, whilst it is clearly important in a HE environment for students to own their employability, just like they need to drive their own study, there is perhaps a greater weight than usual on universities (and employers) in the post pandemic economy to build student confidence and generate work experience opportunities.

CASE STUDY: CITY GRADUATE SCHEMES

One case study that does draw together many of these threads is the 'City Graduate Scheme' concept.

After our work on graduate utilisation with Regional Development Agencies in the 2000s, Gradcore came up with the idea of the 'City Graduate Scheme'. The concept was to turn a place into a graduate scheme – and to bring together clusters of small and medium-sized enterprises (SMEs) in that place to recruit from one cohort, providing the SMEs with the collective infrastructure and marketing reach of a graduate scheme which they would be unable to deliver alone. This had the benefit of better matching graduate skills with employer needs, converting SMEs into companies who hire graduates, and bolstering local university GOS performance.

This concept was first rolled out as RISE in Sheffield, and similar schemes have since been launched in Cardiff, Liverpool, Manchester and Nottingham. These collaborations are ones that bring the best of industry and HE together, delivering a gross value added (GVA) return of more than £5 for every £1 invested, and placing thousands of graduates in companies who might not have previously hired a graduate. The recruitment process for the jobs is also designed to provide each applicant with personalised employability feedback, so everyone is made more employable even if they do not get the job.

This type of approach helps foster employable graduates, match up skills supply and demand, build better understanding between universities and their communities and boost GOS data. It also offers principles that could be taken forward by all those responsible for making graduates employable.

CONCLUSION

At the macro-economic level, skills anticipation and matching are fraught with challenges. We should still aim to do this on a 'best guess' level regionally and nationally – but perhaps accept that it will be flawed, and that those flaws are best mitigated for individuals (and the overall system) by producing genuinely employable graduates in the broadest sense.

At the individual level this means providing personalised employability support and development, and at the university and employer systemic level, putting in place the training and data architecture to make personalised employability development possible. Whether training in the specific academic disciplines of music, medicine, teaching or art – or any others – we must seek to develop the whole student, and to overtly foster in them a range of graduate attributes that will make them employable whatever path they choose (or find themselves on).

Meaning, honesty of purpose, skills focus and personalised approaches – these things act as guiding principles for graduates, employers and universities, and when applied, meaningful and successful employability (and employment) will follow.

BIBLIOGRAPHY

Ball, C. (2014), 'What proportion of jobs for graduates do not require a specific subject?', *The View from HECSU*, 9 December. Available at: https://hecsu.blogspot.com/2014/12/ (accessed: 21 January 2023).

Ball, C. (2022), *Busting graduate job myths*. Universities UK. Available at: https://www.universitiesuk.ac.uk/what-we-do/policy-and-research/publications/busting-graduate-job-myths (accessed: 21 January 2023).

Baska, M. (2022), 'One in five graduates not "workplace ready", research finds', *People Management*. Available at: https://www.peoplemanagement.co.uk/article/1744896/graduates-not-workplace-ready (accessed: 21 January 2023).

Blackmore, P., Blackwell, R. and Edmondson, M. (2017), *Tackling Wicked Issues: Prestige and Employment Outcomes in the Teaching Excellence Framework*. HEPI. Available at: https://www.hepi.ac.uk/wp-content/uploads/2016/09/Hepi_TTWI-Web.pdf (accessed: 21 January 2023).

Caminiti, S. (2022), *No college degree? No problem. More companies are eliminating requirements to attract the workers they need*. CNBC Work. Available at: https://www.cnbc.com/2022/04/25/companies-eliminate-college-degree-requirement-to-draw-needed-workers.html (accessed: 21 January 2023).

Collini, S. (2012), *What Are Universities For?* London: Penguin.

Edmondson, M. (2019), *The Career Wiggly Line*. TEDx Keele University. Available at: Youtube.com. https://www.youtube.com/watch?v=iDF6QtClBxM (accessed: 21 January 2023).

Fuller, J. B., Langer, C., Nitschke, J., O'Kane, L., Sigelman, M. and Taska, B. (2022), *The Emerging Degree Reset*. The Burning Glass Institute. Available at: https://www.hbs.edu/managing-the-future-of-work/Documents/research/emerging_degree_reset_020922.pdf (accessed: 21 January 2023).

Haththotuwa, S. (2022), '41% of graduates don't feel confident about entering the workplace, survey finds', *Business Leader*, 25 April. Available at: https://www.businessleader.co.uk/41-of-graduates-dont-feel-confident-about-entering-the-workplace-survey-finds/ (accessed: 21 January 2023).

Hawkins, P. (2005), *The Art of Building Windmills*, Liverpool: University of Liverpool, Graduate into Employment Unit.

ISE (2021), *ISE Development Survey 2021*. Available at: https://ise.org.uk/page/graduates-lack-work-ready-skills-that-businesses-need-during-covid-era (accessed: 21 January 2023).

Rothwell, N. (2017), 'Public engagement must not be a soft option', in the University of Manchester (ed.), *On Brexit*, Manchester: University of Manchester, pp. 3–4. Available at: https://documents.manchester.ac.uk/display.aspx?DocID=32694 (accessed: 21 January 2023).

The Local (2022), *Germany struggling to fill tens of thousands of trainee jobs*. Available at: https://www.thelocal.de/20220426/germany-struggling-to-fill-tens-of-thousands-of-trainee-jobs/ (accessed: 21 January 2023).

Willetts, D. (2017), *A University Education*, Oxford: Oxford University Press.

Yorke, M. (2004/2006), *Employability in Higher Education: What It Is – What It Is Not*, York: Higher Education Academy.

REFLECTION

From a graduate recruiter

The intricacy of identifying and subsequently hiring the right talent is an ever-evolving model with layers of complexity perhaps not at first appreciated. From the student or graduate's perspective, they must successfully navigate their way through the ever-evolving range of psychometric tests before they are given the opportunity to demonstrate the alignment of their values with that of the organisation, which is commonly expected. To take it further, and for that individual to be able to demonstrate their technical ability based on not only academic knowledge, but also workplace experience, has become essential to the success of that candidate. In addition, it is also important how that individual 'competes' in an assessment centre environment and how they distinguish themselves from the other top talent present.

From the employer's perspective, how do we prevent ourselves time after time from hiring the same graduate who ticks all of the above boxes and has the most presence at the assessment centre? Employers are continually tasked with assessing who the perfect graduate is, the attributes they share, the skill set they come equipped with and the drive they continue to demonstrate. But they must balance this carefully so as not to churn out the same graduate repeatedly, but instead build into their graduate profile a sense of individualism and enthusiasm.

3. Employability: the student voice
Omolabake Fakunle and Yuchen Xiao

INTRODUCTION

A degree is an expected outcome of higher education and conceivable evidence that a graduate possesses certain skills, knowledge and the ability to perform designated role(s) in the workplace. However, the debate around the extent to which the degree prepares career-ready employable students remains unabated in existing literature. The debate revolves around two fundamental issues.

The first issue relates to the purpose of higher education, and contentions around its role of producing employable graduates. Such debates draw on postulations on the purpose of a university by Newman and Collini (McCowan, 2015) as an independent entity vested with knowledge creation and academic rigour versus a marketised university as an entrepreneurial and training institution (Tomlinson, 2018). This ideological argument is unlikely to subside (Atkins, 1999). Given the funding and regulatory role of government and the related emphasis on employability, scholars posit a balance instead of a dualistic polarising debate on the role of university in relation to employability (Knight and Yorke, 2003; McCowan, 2015).

The second issue pertains to the contested notion of employability as a concept. The seminal definition of employability by Hillage and Pollard (1998) as an individual 'being capable of getting and keeping fulfilling work ... depends on the knowledge, skills and attitudes they possess' (p. 2) underpins mainstream construction of employability from a skills-based and human capital perspective, with the onus on the individual to develop employability-related skills. This approach has, however, been criticised by scholars who contend that having employability skills does not automatically insulate an individual from the vagaries of the labour market (McQuaid and Lindsay, 2005; Tomlinson, 2008). Furthermore, Moreau and Leathwood (2006) argued that normative conceptions of employability neglect the impact of social inequalities, and that 'social class, gender, ethnicity, age, disability and university attended all impact on the opportunities available' (p. 305).

Drawing on extant literature, Fakunle and Higson (2021) put forward three conceptual categorisations of employability: outcomes, process and conceptual approaches. The first two approaches will be discussed briefly as they relate to this chapter (see Fakunle and Higson, 2021, for a full discussion). They outline how employability-related discourses from an outcomes approach focus on individuals' skills and knowledge, and their ability to secure and maintain employment.

The outcomes approach focuses on how employability is measured based on employment indices, captured, for example, in the UK Graduate Outcomes Survey (GOS), which collects data on graduates' employment 15 months after completing their studies. This approach neglects the student voice and the role of institutions in developing employable graduates.

A process approach focuses on how employability development opportunities (EDOs) are embedded within an institution. Drawing on Harvey (2005), a process approach consists of an employability audit that examines the effectiveness of EDOs within an institution and how these processes may be improved to enhance student employability. This is conceptually different from Holmes's (2013) notion of employability as processual, which centres around individual skills, attributes and identity. The observation that employability-related initiatives in universities are rarely subject to empirical exploration (Jackson and Bridgstock, 2020) points to the gap in this area. This chapter contributes to addressing this gap by adopting a process approach to examine student employability.

The two key debates in employability provide the background for this chapter. On the one hand, the wider debate relates to the benefit of a liberal arts education (including arts, humanities, and the social sciences) in a highly marketised and neoliberal-driven higher education system. On the other hand, there are questions around how a liberal arts education adequately prepares students in a technology-driven world. Chao et al. (2003) describe student employability as a long-standing challenge for liberal arts colleges and universities. They cite the 'widely held view that graduates in the liberal arts are at a disadvantage upon first entering the workforce ... as they lack appropriate information technology skills' (p. 332), to inform their research on the extent of the 'digital divide' between arts and non-arts students at three Canadian universities.

Another study conducted at the University of Minnesota-Twin Cities' College of Liberal Arts explored the career readiness of students based on their reflections on their liberal arts education (Stebleton et al., 2020). These studies attest to scholarly interest in the employability of liberal arts students across different global contexts. Yet Nicholas (2018) queries the lack of recent studies that focused on the perspectives of liberal arts students regarding career-related questions. This chapter contributes to this identified gap by drawing on findings from empirical research that explored liberal arts stu-

Programme Curricula

The participants articulated different employability-related skills they had developed on their degree: 'I found that my languages courses made me very analytic. I think the obvious skills [are] like working both independently and in teams, working to deadlines, and generally having a good critical analysis' (Nancy, Programme 1).

In Sarah's (Programme 3) opinion, taking a wide variety of courses 'adds a bit of an edge' to make her more employable or competitive.

Across all four programmes, participants discussed the importance of having a year abroad embedded in their liberal arts degree programme. For example, the experience of living and working abroad provided an intercultural experience, which contributed to developing employability:

> I think that [study abroad] is probably one of the most rewarding things I could have done in terms of putting myself out there into the game, and showing that I have more well-rounded education and instead of just staying at a room for four years ... maybe push me like an extra step further in terms of how I'm viewed on my CV. (Tess, Programme 4)

At the same time, the students talked about the impact of Covid-19 on their study experience, which Afra (Programme 1) describes as having a 'massive effect'. The impact of Covid-19 for most students meant a curtailing of the one-year overseas study time. Ella talked about the impact on her perceptions on developing employability skills:

> I studied in [the Middle East] as part of my degree, but obviously because of the pandemic, it was cut very short. I spent such a short period of time out there that I don't think I got out of it, what I would have done. But I think it would have been a very important thing to get the language to the level that would make it beneficial to employability, but unfortunately, that wasn't possible this year. (Ella, Programme 2)

Expressing keen interest in a career that is language orientated, Ella talked about her intention to attend language schools in the summer to further her language education. Also linked to the impact of Covid-19, some students, for example Afra, were pursuing Master's-level studies.

Work Experience

Echoing Tomlinson (2008), that the degree is not enough for employability development, students across different programmes restated the importance of work experience during degree studies:

> I thought that my degree would almost automatically make me employable. Because it would say [names University] on it, and it's a degree in Chinese. So the employer will see that I can speak several languages and that I have academic skills. But over my degree ... from what I've seen, [work] experience [is] valued more than grades, especially for humanities. (Sarah, Programme 3)

> As far as I know employers really value work experiences even more so than a degree, and it's really hard to get into any kind of job without some kind of work experience ... so I think there should be more encouragement towards doing those kinds of things while you're a student. (Jill, Programme 4)

Although work experience was not explicitly integrated into their programme, students were doing part-time work and volunteering during their degree, as in this account from Kate (Programme 3):

> This isn't related [to the programme] but I worked during my undergraduate degree, almost every year. And one of the things I did was student-led consulting in Edinburgh ... making a project for a real client that then used it. Because we worked for charity it was really important in developing more technical skills that employers like, you know, like researching and drafting and presenting and just like public speaking and being able to actually sell your idea to somebody.

Additionally, Tab (Programme 1) talked about working while studying abroad as part of his degree. Tab was able to relate his extracurricular activities as being part of a valued work experience:

> I've done things with a boxing club, which is on my CV, and have definitely come up in interviews that have helped my employability ... as the Social Media Manager for two years and I had to basically do all the digital marketing ... advertising on Instagram, Facebook, Twitter, Snapchat ... So that's sort of like a proven project delivery example that I have on my CV.

Tab acknowledged that his rounded experience had contributed to obtaining a job at a global financial company (to start after completing his degree).

However, a few students did not link their part-time work to employability-related skills. For example, Sarah did not consider her work experience in charity shops as being of interest to potential employers. This brings to the fore individual proclivities that may impact employability development, perhaps due to their previous experiences and socio-economic background. This raises the need for HEIs to develop employability initiatives to support all students.

Careers Service

All the participants talked about a range of careers services, including checking the website for job opportunities, speaking to a careers advisor and attending careers fairs. However, they stressed the need for a student to be proactive in engaging with the careers service.

> What I found with the Career Service was you have to reach out yourself, you know, you don't get what you don't ask for essentially, but they send out so many different emails with all sorts of different websites, and I found they were brilliant ... but again like I said, you have to be the one to ask for it and no one's going to force you to go down that path. (Cara, Programme 1)

Cara further stressed the need for careers support for liberal arts students:

> I think a general perception is that arts courses are far less employable and that makes people quite anxious when it comes to searching for jobs, so I found a lot of my friends and classmates towards the end of this year have been becoming more and more stressed at, you know, the idea of finding a job.

As an international student, Wen (Programme 1) talked at length about navigating the careers service:

> When I was a freshman, I went to the Career Service to confirm my future career path. I had a meeting with them, but it was useless. Because the teacher won't give you advice directly, he will give you advice according to your ideas, but I didn't have any ideas at that time, so it didn't help. And the Career Service has sent me a lot of emails about some job opportunities and positions in the final two years ... I'm always not qualified ... they require British nationality rather than international students, so I think the information is very inhumane.

Resonating with previous work with international Master's students (Fakunle, 2021) and Wen's quote above, Sarah (Programme 3) elaborated the need for the careers service to provide differentiated service for diverse students enrolled in the university:

> Careers services should be much more focused and expanded a lot more, to be able to cater to all sorts of different degrees. And different students that have different backgrounds and different goals ... When you go to the careers service they treat you all as if you're like a UK student ... that's much more complex for us ... And if you're European or if you're American, or even for Asian students, I doubt that they have much there to help you.

Elaine's positive experience further reiterates the value of the careers service and the need for all students to feel able to have a similar experience:

> I was quite surprised that both the careers advisors who I spoke to said that I should talk about my acapella, because we've been in, you know competitions we've won, like the Scottish championships and I was doing like musical director so I wrote music and things like that and I didn't consider that as something that would be relevant to employers, until I was told that it is something that then makes you stand out ... So I think that those things have been really useful, but I didn't realise. (Elaine, Programmes 1 and 2)

However, the students' perceptions were less positive regarding careers fairs:

> I was in contact with the Career Service recently, and with a CV advice thing and I thought that was very useful. I just wish the actual careers fairs were not as STEM and vocation orientated. (Ella, Programme 2)

Ella elaborated further:

> We're not the target for employers in the same way that Science, Technology, Engineering and Maths (STEM) students are. So like the careers fair, it's a lot of just STEM subjects that they're looking for and the company would maybe not seek out graduates from humanities subjects like LLC ... so it can be difficult to know what jobs are even available to you.

The quote below from Elaine highlights the 'disconnect' between the academic and the careers service, with a suggestion on how a connection may be fostered:

> I think if teachers just dedicated a class or two classes to talking about the careers department ... even if it's one in first year and then one in fourth year ... I think that would be more helpful because ... it's all been very optional, and you have to find out for yourself.

The research findings suggest that students need to be proactive to benefit from the expertise and help provided by careers services. Considering the benefits of one-on-one engagement between students and careers advisors, institutions can assess and improve on facilitating such connections. The careers fair also merits an employability audit (Harvey, 2005) to assess its benefits for all students.

CONCLUSION

This chapter demonstrates students' understanding of mainstream employability-related discourses as skills development. The chapter, however, further examines the skills development narratives (outcomes approach) within the context of the EDOs within an institution from a process approach. This demonstrates the interrelatedness of different employability constructs (Fakunle and Higson, 2021), and it shows how the student voice can provide HEIs with evidence for adopting a process approach to assess how their employability-related activities are afforded or not to students whilst enrolled on their degree.

In conclusion, the findings from our research with liberal arts students suggest that specific aspects of the curricula, including course work and overseas study opportunities embedded in the course, can help them to develop employability-related skills. Studying abroad also provided work opportunities which the students valued in relation to developing employability. Extracurricular work was seen as a positive signal to potential employers, with Tab articulating how his activities attracted the attention of employers.

The findings suggest that student experience whilst enrolled on a degree programme can adequately prepare students for post-graduation work. However, there are some caveats. Covid-19 was an unforeseen obstacle that impacted the cohort of students interviewed. For some students this led to plans for further study to delay entering the job market. The majority of the students found the careers service websites and one-on-one meetings with careers advisors to be helpful. Resonating with existing literature, the need for the careers service to cater for the diverse students recruited at the university was an issue raised by all the international students except Gale, who expressed his disfavour of employability as a concept. The findings show that the work of the careers service should be more visible to students at the start of their degree.

This chapter buttresses the applicability of utilising a process approach (Fakunle and Higson, 2021) in the form of an employability audit to 'identify the extent of employability development activity at the program and central levels' (Harvey, 2005: 18), ostensibly to review existing practice and make changes to adequately prepare students for living and working in a globalised world.

REFERENCES

Atkins, M. J. (1999), 'Oven-ready and self-basting: taking stock of employability skills', *Teaching in Higher Education*, 4(2), 267–280.
Braun, V. and Clarke, V. (2022), *Thematic Analysis: A Practical Guide*, Los Angeles: SAGE.
Chao, T., Butler, T. and Ryan, P. (2003), 'Providing a technology edge for liberal arts students', *Journal of Information Technology Education*, 2(2), 331–348.
Clarke, M. (2018), 'Rethinking graduate employability: the role of capital, individual attributes and context', *Studies in Higher Education*, 43(11), 1923–1937.

Fakunle, O. (2021), 'International students' perspective on developing employability during study abroad', *Higher Education Quarterly*, 75(4), 575–590.

Fakunle, O. and Higson, H. (2021), 'Interrogating theoretical and empirical approaches to employability in different global regions', *Higher Education Quarterly*, 75(4), 525–534.

Harvey, L. (2005), 'Embedding and integrating employability', *New Directions for Institutional Research*, 2005(128), 13–28.

Hillage, J. and Pollard, E. (1998), *Employability: Developing a framework for policy analysis*. Research Report RR85. Department for Education and Employment.

Holmes, L. (2013), 'Competing perspectives on graduate employability: possession, position or process?', *Studies in Higher Education*, 38(4), 538–554.

Jackson, D. and Bridgstock, R. (2020), 'What actually works to enhance graduate employability? The relative value of curricular, co-curricular, and extra-curricular learning and paid work', *Higher Education*, 81(4), 723–739.

Knight, P. T. and Yorke, M. (2003), 'Employability and good learning in higher education', *Teaching in Higher Education*, 8(1), 3–16.

Lincoln, Y. S. and Guba, E. G. (1985), *Naturalistic Inquiry*, London: Sage.

McCowan T. (2015), 'Should universities promote employability?', *Theory and Research in Education*, 13(3), 267–285.

McQuaid, R. W. and Lindsay, C. (2005), 'The concept of employability', *Urban Studies*, 42(2), 197–219.

Moreau, M. P. and Leathwood, C. (2006), 'Graduates' employment and discourse of employability: a critical analysis', *Journal of Education and Work*, 18(4), 305–324.

Nicholas, J. M. (2018), 'Marketable selves: making sense of employability as a liberal arts undergraduate', *Journal of Vocational Behavior*, 109(2018), 1–13.

Stebleton, M. J., Kaler, L. S., Diamond, K. K. and Lee, C. (2020), 'Examining career readiness in a liberal arts undergraduate career planning course', *Journal of Employment Counseling*, 57(1), 14–26.

Tomlinson, M. (2008), 'The degree is not enough: students' perceptions of the role of higher education credentials for graduate work and employability', *British Journal of Sociology of Education*, 29(1), 49–61.

Tomlinson, M. (2018), 'Conceptions of the value of higher education in a measured market', *Higher Education*, 75(4), 711–727.

REFLECTION

From a graduate who works for a national law firm

I had no idea what I wanted to do when I finished my undergraduate degree. I was almost certain I did not want to go into legal practice but wasn't really sure what other routes were available to me as a law graduate. Looking back, I wish I had sought out advice from the career service and sought more advice from my lecturers at my university. At the end of the day, they are all there to help.

You feel pressure coming to the end of your degree that you should know where you want to go in life and what you want to do, but in reality, you aren't alone if you have no idea, and the pressure I felt was almost certainly self-inflicted. I should not have worried that I did not know what to do and I'm glad I took the time to decide what I want to do for a career as I am now in a job I love.

PART II

What employers want from graduates

4. Creating a new university to meet the employability challenge

Ross Renton and Fiona McGonigle

INTRODUCTION

This chapter outlines the innovative approach used when creating ARU Peterborough, a new university for Peterborough, in the UK. It provides examples of the lessons learned, and the solutions identified, to improve employability for potential graduates, and how they were central to the design of the university.

In Peterborough, there is one of the most ambitious educational developments in the UK, which seeks to provide an approach where employers are immersed in the delivery of education and research with businesses locating their research centres on the campus. A brand-new university opened in 2022 – ARU Peterborough – backed by over £75 million of investment. The initiative, a partnership with the Cambridgeshire and Peterborough Combined Authority (CPCA), Peterborough City Council and Anglia Ruskin University, secured early-stage formative partnerships with several large local employers. The employer-focused university launched in September 2022 and the first dedicated on-campus Research and Design centre for local industry opened early in 2023.

CONTEXT

Peterborough is a city located approximately 100 miles from London, in the UK. It has over 204,910 inhabitants (Office for National Statistics (ONS), 2021b) within the local authority area and has previously been identified by the CPCA as one of the largest cities in England without a university. It began as a small Saxon settlement which expanded in the 18th and 19th centuries. It was designated as a New Town in 1967, enabling it to receive significant public investment in housing, infrastructure, and civic projects. In the 20th century, it experienced periods of both rapid population growth and industrial decline. In response, the UK government designated Peterborough and the adjacent

Fenland area as a 'levelling up' priority, a scheme designed to target funding at areas of social and economic deprivation.

ARU Peterborough opened its doors to students in September 2022 and a key priority from inception was to develop the university to meet the needs of industry. This is particularly important in creating a high-skilled economy within a higher education 'cold spot' with a range of social and economic challenges:

- Social deprivation is particularly high near the centre and south of the City of Peterborough (ONS, 2019b) and rates of unemployment are persistently higher than national averages.
- Child poverty is high, with 25 per cent of children in Peterborough living in poverty, compared to 17 per cent nationally (ONS, 2019a)
- Social mobility is low, with Peterborough ranked 191st and nearby Fenland ranked 319th out of 324 local authority districts (Social Mobility and Child Poverty Commission and Social Mobility Commission, 2016)
- Healthy life expectancy is below retirement age in parts of the north of the county (ONS, 2019c)

At the time when the university was being created, the UK government was particularly focused on measuring the outcomes of higher education within England, with a key regulatory emphasis being on the progress of students into employment. Whilst this desire is driven by a narrative of providing 'value for money' and addressing skills shortages, this measure highlights what can sometimes be a short-term and transactional relationship with employers.

In truth, the relationship between businesses and universities is far more nuanced and has been evolving slowly over the past decade. There needs to be a new compact between universities and businesses – in which the two parties are intertwined and evolve together rather than seeing each other simply as supply and demand partners.

Employee upskilling within the small and medium-sized enterprises (SME) sector still lacks sustained investment, and remains relatively undeveloped despite the evidence of the impact. The Higher Education Statistics Agency (HESA) Destinations of Leavers from Higher Education (DLHE) data consistently reported that less than a third of graduates secured work with an SME. The Wilson Review of business–university collaboration identified in 2012 that targeted government intervention was needed to support this work (Wilson, 2012). The planned lifelong loan entitlement (LLE), enabling learners/employees to access tuition loans for shorter courses for stand-alone qualifications, needs to be delivered in a way that benefits SMEs and supports their growth aspirations in partnership with universities.

Bringing into focus and aligning engagement strategies with emphasis on the Further Education (FE) White Paper, *Skills for Jobs: Lifelong Learning for Opportunity and Growth*, is essential (Department for Education, 2021). This reflects an ambition for universities, colleges, providers, and employers to work cohesively together to reinforce their pivotal role as anchor institutions. Driving up skills in Peterborough to increase productivity by developing a higher-skilled workforce is central to the purpose of the university. Alongside creating the university, there has been work collaboratively and proactively with employers, inward investment teams and government departments to attract new companies to the city, creating future job prosperity and improved education attainment for better employment outcomes.

WHY CREATE A NEW UNIVERSITY?

The top-line objectives for the new university are:

- Improve access to better quality jobs and improve access to better quality employment, helping to reverse decades of relative economic decline, and increasing aspiration, wages and social mobility for residents.
- Make a nationally significant contribution to government objectives for levelling up, increase regional innovation, and accelerate the UK's net zero transformation.
- Accelerate the renaissance of Peterborough. Translate the resulting increase in individual opportunity, prosperity, and social mobility into outcomes across well-being, health and healthy life expectancy from the programme, and on into people living happier, healthier lives.

CREATING A NEW CURRICULUM

Part of the journey to creating an employment-focused university, linked with local employers and high-skilled jobs, was the co-creation of an extensive new course portfolio. This involved gaining vital insight from businesses, education, stakeholders and member organisations from the Confederation of British Industry (CBI), Chamber of Commerce, Federation of Small Businesses (FSB), Construction Industry Training Board (CITB), Knowledge Transfer Network (KTN), Institute of Chartered Accountants in England and Wales (ICAEW) and Innovate UK. All of these member organisations represent large numbers of businesses, and as such lobby the UK government on their behalf about the skills shortages they face. This drives the skills agenda and the need to listen to industry and work hand in glove with them in developing courses that industry needs, and which students want to do, ultimately leading to graduate jobs.

Every new course developed has had industry consultation, which has resulted in the new curriculum that has been introduced. In some instances, thinking has been altered in line with feedback from businesses, on the types of courses and graduates produced that would meet their growth needs.

ARU Peterborough seeks to be a major contributor in influencing local and regional employers to create more opportunities for the student body, which will attract and retain graduates to live and work in the city and surrounding region. The new curriculum that has been developed aligns with transition pathways, linked to key industries, such as apprenticeships and T levels, for improved student outcomes with industry placements. Enhanced support via a central front door approach for local businesses and industry encourages local regeneration and skills sustainability in their future workforce.

Working collaboratively with employers in developing an extensive industry-focused portfolio, from degrees and apprenticeships to short courses and micro-credentials, is intended to increase student opportunities and ultimately sustained employment. Universities are fundamental to supporting the enhancement of commercial ambitions and retaining the talent in our local communities and regions, and in improving communities, so they thrive and succeed. Supporting local businesses and industry to grow, enabling local regeneration and growth through skills sustainability in businesses, is a key part of their purpose. Realising solutions to real-world problems such as climate change via live briefs (an embedded course activity) was incorporated to give employers the opportunity to help solve real-world challenges by bringing fresh thinking to their organisations.

In creating the university there has been consultation with over 170 businesses via business roundtables, education roundtables and a series of 12 sector interest groups (SIGs) (Anglia Ruskin University, Peterborough, 2021). This gained commitment on a range of collaborations, from the joint use of facilities and specialist equipment to employer involvement in industry talks and assessment. Two networks were also established, a Future Talent and Skills Network and an Agri-Food Tech and Sustainability Consortium – launched during the COP26 (UN Climate Change) conference, in November 2021, with a strong focus on the government agenda on becoming net zero. The model for engaging employers with lead academics has gained positive attention from other universities and across the other ARU campuses (Cambridge and Chelmsford).

The curriculum co-created with businesses and, in some instances, co-delivered through some industry-taught modules, will ensure the graduates are ready to meet the workforce needs of the region.

The ARU Peterborough model was designed to challenge the long-held perception that universities just supply the trained workforce, and businesses employ them in high-skilled jobs. The model moves away from reactive engagement to a relationship of co-creation and long-term joint planning.

The university continues to embrace the challenges that emerge as an institute for change in lifelong learning, and it will act as a landing-pad for people throughout their lives, dispersing the perceptions that 'universities are for other people'. Providing a new strategic service to employers across innovation and skills, and working with other local partners to support the development of connected and cohesive communities, are essential. Advancing economic growth and greater employment outcomes to enable better 'levelling-up' and a positive generational change for the City of Peterborough, the Fens and surrounding regions will enhance the local area.

WORKING WITH INDUSTRY

Businesses are being encouraged to utilise a strong university base through the two new networks: the Future Talent and Skills Network and the Agri-Food Tech and Sustainability Consortium. Two vibrant consortiums of businesses, academia, education, government and key stakeholders, with a drive to actively engage in national and local innovation systems to support growth, are required. This will be important in enabling the government, together with business and education, to deliver on its ambitions for the UK to be a global leader across many sectors. The Consortium has over 180 members and is still growing and will be the foundation for a potential new Agri-Food Technology Centre that will focus resources and stakeholders towards creating sustainable solutions.

The Future Talent and Skills Network, with over 200 members, is a combination of all the sector interest groups (SIGs); it is intended to create a space where businesses can collaborate across multiple sectors. Many businesses will have a mixture of requirements in many disciplines, thus being connected to all the faculties and research institutes at ARU, including further education colleges throughout the network.

The objective of the Consortium, the Future Talent and Skills Network and the sector interest groups is to give industry a voice, ensuring that businesses, their workforce, and the community receive the training, education, research, and innovation support they need to thrive under national, international, environmental, social and economic challenges.

These new university networks, alongside the 12 SIGs, have created a successful model in helping to advocate, broker and facilitate enhanced collaboration and collective delivery between businesses and education. They will stimulate opportunities across the wider university portfolio in all campuses in Peterborough, Cambridge, Chelmsford and London in innovation, research, placements, live briefs, upskilling, and talent generation.

ARU Peterborough is ambitious to invest further in the city and recognises this development as an ideal opportunity to promote economic development and tackle social inequalities across the region. It is already working with local NHS trusts and local hospitals and has ambitions to further develop the workforce to help address the health inequalities within the region. This includes ARU leading, in partnership, on the developments of a talent pillar to support the health and life sciences sectors.

ARU Peterborough is helping to shape the development of the talent pillar of the Cambridgeshire and Peterborough Life Sciences 2050 Vision Strategy, which is a partnership with Cambridge University Health Partners and a cadre of industry leaders. We have convened a series of workshops, bringing together employers, health organisations, stakeholders, and education providers across the health and life sciences sectors. The workshops explored and captured the current and future talent and skills needs across the ecosystem. Initial hypotheses have formed the starting points of these discussions, drawn from relevant strategy documents and reports already produced in this area, such as the *NHS People Plan 2020/21: Action for Us All* (NHS, 2020). These collaborations will ensure that Cambridge and the surrounding region stays globally competitive as a leader in health and life sciences, with ARU fully supporting the partnership.

A manufacturing employer who has supported the co-design of the course portfolio has said, by way of feedback:

> My career as a HR Professional has spanned 30+ years with over 20 of those being at a senior level. During that time, I have seen much economic change, experienced the rise of digitalisation and artificial intelligence and have seen change in the graduate employment market in both what graduates expect and what employers need! Over that time the employers I have worked with have experienced long term skills shortages and constant skills gaps in a number of vital areas such as engineering and have often been surprised that their future needs have not been met by higher education.
>
> As ARU Peterborough opens its doors and welcomes those who we hope will be our future generation of local employees, it is refreshing to have been part of a forum of like-minded Peterborough based employers who have worked with the Faculty Heads to outline what skills and talents are needed to support local business growth. With the mixture of full time and part time courses that are on offer, and the partnership approach, it feels like we are all putting in the effort and pulling in the right direction to effect real change. The major employers in Peterborough have not only been encouraged to build early relationships with the students (by offering visits, work experience, setting real life projects, etc.) but will hopefully be able to employ graduates as part of their strategy to sustain strong long term economic growth for the area.
>
> The collaborative approach to course design focused on creating a competent, adaptable, flexible and rounded workforce that meets the future needs of local employers. Together with the local employers' desire to offer high quality opportunities for those looking to be employed in the area post course completion, this will undoubtedly be a great strategic partnership that can only benefit the ARU students.

An early example of the success of this model is the relationship between ARU Peterborough and a global 3D printing business, with a base in Arizona, which is thriving in Peterborough, with 145 current staff (along with 210 new jobs planned) and is recognised for their innovation, having secured three industry awards. They will move their research and development facilities and staff to the ARU Peterborough campus, helping to form a new model of how businesses and universities are working side-by-side.

Through working closely with government departments and inward investment teams, there is a partnership model of collaboration and support. This model demonstrates the connectivity and ability that ARU Peterborough can deliver as a key education partner to those businesses relocating to the region. Strong links have also been formed with two global agri-food tech companies who have located their UK manufacturing facilities in Peterborough. One of the companies has already opened their facility and started recruiting their workforce, expecting to create 300 jobs. The other agri-food company is expected to open its UK headquarters in the second quarter of 2023, creating 200 jobs. It is anticipated that many of these jobs will be opportunities for students and graduates, including student placements to gain industry experience.

Businesses are already utilising the talent, knowledge, and expertise of the students, academics, and professional staff to grow their businesses. For example, a project has commenced with academics from ARU Peterborough and students from ARU's Cambridge campus, studying the Sustainable Land Management module. Students visited the new factory site and have been tasked with creating a two-minute promotional video explaining how biodiversity will be encouraged in the unused land around the factory site.

IMPACT

One of the key purposes of modern higher education is to develop human capital, where education increases the skills and productivity of the workforce, leading to increased economic growth. Covid-19 is likely to have had a medium-term impact on the opportunities for placements, internships and jobs for undergraduates and graduates, which is likely to have a negative impact on graduate outcomes nationally. This is one of the main drivers for ARU Peterborough, strengthening the engagement with businesses and involving them at every stage in the development of the curriculum, creating further opportunities for collaboration. Highlighting the importance and connectivity to businesses to ensure an interconnected relationship with ARU Peterborough as their first point of contact for access to talent and skilling their workforce is key.

There has been eager anticipation from many stakeholders and employers for a new university in the City of Peterborough. The expectation from employers is that the university will fill many of their skills and workforce shortages. Various companies will have jobs, placements, and projects that the university can support. A leading indicator of success will be the increase in skills levels in the city and surrounding region, which currently has lower skills levels in comparison to Cambridge, only 40 miles away. The attraction for companies relocating to the city, who will need to create an entire workforce, will also determine the impact a new university will generate, through the graduates and degree apprentices they employ.

Expansion of the education infrastructure within a cold spot region, such as Peterborough, will increase the numbers of graduates with improved skills. This anchors ARU Peterborough as a significant contributor in supplying and upskilling new talent in Peterborough and the surrounding region. This is particularly important as Peterborough is one of the UK's fastest growing cities, and a university will further support and increase that growth. A culmination of feedback from employers through the SIGs has found that improvement in soft skills, also known as 'power skills', such as, critical thinking, problem solving, public speaking, professional writing, teamwork, digital literacy, adaptability, leadership, professional attitude, work ethic, and intercultural fluency, will increase employability of graduates (these differ from hard skills, which are specific to individual professions). This improvement has been highlighted as fundamentally important to businesses looking to universities as 'talent generators' to resolve their rising skills and people shortages.

Assessing labour competencies from the viewpoint of employers has steered the future direction towards the types of courses that employers want to see, which crucially will lead to jobs and improved graduate outcomes. García-Álvarez et al. (2022) noted that many employers give more importance to transferable competencies than to professional competencies.

> In the hiring process, graduates' lack of professional experience, together with the skill mismatch between their education and the training needed for the job, mean that many highly qualified young people experience long periods of unemployment, find low-paying jobs, or face working with uncertain long-term prospects. Hence, for employers, 'being capable' (trained and skilled) and 'being someone' (with broad social networks and links) are inherent to the job, and are, therefore, fundamental to graduate employability.

These considerations have been factored into the new course portfolio.

Employers have stated they are keen to work closely with FE colleges and universities, which is why schools, colleges, and university partners were involved in the consultations to align progression routes and gaps in provision. There is ongoing consultation, review and development of many practically feasible solutions in the relationship between education and employability, to support and boost economic prosperity post-pandemic.

Significant cultural and structural barriers persist in the long-term planning of the East of England's regional workforce needs, leaving gaps in the skills supply chains post-Brexit. A sustainable model of planning, with the co-creation of provision with universities and colleges, is needed to mitigate future risks to the UK economy.

Universities are essential to the UK government's 'levelling up' goals. They need to re-energise employment, research, innovation, and communities. Businesses need universities, and universities need businesses – but there needs to be a greater osmosis.

We need change; radical solutions to power forward and set new goals for businesses and universities to reflect a post-pandemic, post-Brexit Britain.

CONCLUSION

The new University Quarter in Peterborough will deliver a platform for businesses to showcase new and exciting innovations within their companies, which can be profiled to our student body, encouraging workforce recruitment. Providing earlier access and connectivity to businesses will be a strong focus of the model we are creating. This model will enrich the industry experience and opportunities, and will be purposefully student-centric to improve employability. Exposing students to more than one industry sector, outside the sectors related to their degree, will enhance their employment opportunities.

Now is the right time to reimagine the model of collaboration between universities and business, to create institutions with greater levels of permeability and lasting integration, leading to jobs for our graduates.

BIBLIOGRAPHY

Anglia Ruskin University, Peterborough (2021), *Sector Interest Groups (SIGs) Futures Paper*. Unpublished document.

Department for Education (2021), *Skills for Jobs: Lifelong Learning for Opportunity and Growth* (White Paper, CP 338). London: HMSO.

Department for Levelling Up, Housing and Communities (2022), *Levelling Up the United Kingdom* (White Paper, CP 604). London: HMSO.

García-Álvarez, J., Vázquez-Rodríguez, A., Quiroga-Carrillo, A. and Priegue, D. (2022), 'Transversal competencies for employability in university graduates: a systematic review from the employers' perspective', *Education Sciences*, 12(3), 204. https://doi.org/10.3390/educsci12030204.

Lambert, R. (2003), *The Lambert Review of Business–University Collaboration*, London: HM Treasury.

NHS (2020), *We Are the NHS: People Plan 2020/21: Action for Us All*, NHS England.

ONS (2019a), *English Indices of Deprivation 2019: Income Deprivation Affecting Children Index*, 26 September. Available at: https://www.gov.uk/government/statistics/english-indices-of-deprivation-2019 (accessed: 22 January 2023).

ONS (2019b), *English Indices of Deprivation 2019: Index of Multiple Deprivation*, 26 September. Available at: https://www.gov.uk/government/statistics/english-indices-of-deprivation-2019 (accessed: 22 January 2023).

ONS (2019c), *Health and Life Expectancies 2016–18*. Available at: Health and life expectancies – Office for National Statistics (ons.gov.uk)

ONS (2021a), *National Life Tables – Life Expectancy in the UK: 2018 to 2020*, 23 September. Available at: https://www.ons.gov.uk/peoplepopulationandcommunity/birthsdeathsandmarriages/lifeexpectancies/bulletins/nationallifetablesunitedkingdom/2018to2020 (accessed: 22 January 2023).

ONS (2021b), *Population Estimates for the UK, England and Wales, Scotland and Northern Ireland: mid-2020*, 25 June. Available at: https://www.ons.gov.uk/peoplepopulationandcommunity/populationandmigration/populationestimates/bulletins/annualmidyearpopulationestimates/mid2020 (accessed: 22 January 2023).

Peterborough HE Property Company (2021), *A New University for Peterborough Phase 3: Business Case*. Unpublished company document.

Social Mobility and Child Poverty Commission and Social Mobility Commission (2016), *Social Mobility Index*, 31 January. Available at: https://www.gov.uk/government/publications/social-mobility-index (accessed: 22 January 2023).

Wilson, T. (2012), *Business–University Collaboration: The Wilson Review*. London: Department for Business, Innovation and Skills. Available at: https://www.gov.uk/government/publications/business-university-collaboration-the-wilson-review (accessed: 22 January 2023).

REFLECTION

From an employer in manufacturing

As an employer in the manufacturing industry, we've known for a long time that we need to attract and retain great people in our company to succeed and grow. We recognise, more than ever, that learning is not complete for our employees once they join us from formal education.

A culture that encourages continual learning and an enthusiasm to share knowledge is not only good for our business but good for our teams – we highly value employees who are willing learners and teachers. Consequently, encouraging the blending of work and learning is helpful both for attracting and retaining people and increasing performance for the business.

5. Developing employability skills through working in a law clinic

Kaye Howells and Sue Jennings

INTRODUCTION

This chapter seeks to explore, through the example of setting up a law clinic, how to ensure students are learning the skills that employers require from graduates. It will further address, in the context of clinical legal education (CLE), the impact of Covid-19, asking whether the skills employers require have changed as a result of the pandemic and looking at how this is being addressed by Derby Law School.

The Student Legal Advice Centre (the Centre) at Derby Law School opened in February 2019, 13 months before the Covid-19 pandemic. The purposes of the Centre are threefold:

(1) to provide students with the opportunity to gain real world experience, in the context of CLE;
(2) to provide a service to the community, aligning with the notion that law clinics have a place in social justice and enabling access to justice;
(3) to signpost to other providers where the Centre is unable to assist.

The focus within this chapter is on the provision of an opportunity for students to gain real-world experience, in the context of CLE and the extent to which Covid-19 has impacted the skillset required in the workplace. Whilst the times of crisis in the pandemic have passed, it is fair to say that the pandemic forced industry and the HE sector alike to take stock. Lessons learned during the pandemic, in terms of ways of working and skills required in industry, continue to shape the future ways of working.

CLINICAL LEGAL EDUCATION

There is no one definition of CLE. Thomas et al. (2018) suggest that CLE is the 'learning of the law and its implementation in the real world through action and reflection that has educational, public interests and employability benefits'. Lewis (2000) states that 'the main advantage of clinical education is that, compared to traditional teaching methods, it involves a different approach to the learning of law: it encompasses experiential learning, or "learning by doing"'. Student engagement within a clinic setting offers the opportunity for experiential learning. CLE can be delivered through simulated or real-world experience. From a law school's perspective and perhaps that of a prospective employer, nothing can equal the benefits of actual real-world experience, which include practising skills learned, practical understanding of knowledge learned and an insight into the realities of a legal career.

It is imperative to be able to maximise that opportunity for students. There is a place for simulation, but real-world learning is most impactful. Be it through simulation or real-world experience, both are examples of experiential learning and will benefit the students' learning and experience. Whilst there are advantages and disadvantages to both, arguably the real-world experience is more effective in terms of developing students' understanding of the true nature of the skills required in the workplace.

The notion of law schools being required to prepare students for their future roles in the legal profession and to do so by teaching beyond traditional classroom methods is not a new concept. Cantatore (2018) comments: 'A pivotal role of Law schools is to prepare students for their future roles as legal practitioners, which will require a wide range of skills, not all readily accessible through traditional classroom education.'

The emphasis in the Centre is around real-world learning, with opportunities for simulated experiences, as building blocks for scaffolded learning.

STUDENT LEGAL ADVICE CENTRE

When the Centre opened in February 2019 its initial provision was advice and assistance in respect of family law matters. Since opening, the Centre has expanded and in addition to its family law clinic, the following services are now provided: immigration family reunion clinic (whereby the clinic partners with the British Red Cross and Paragon Law), support at Court for Litigants in Person in family law matters, a Justice Project (tackling social justice issues) and a Policy Clinic. The Centre is currently developing its business clinic for new entrepreneurs. The Centre's development and growth are providing a diverse range of experiences for the students in terms of different areas of the law it covers and exposure to issues of social justice and the commercial realities within which the law operates.

Student engagement in the Centre is both curricular and extra-curricular. The journey for students begins in the first-year undergraduate programme, in which students can become involved in the Justice Project; in the second year they can be involved in the Policy Clinic and Immigration Family Reunion

Clinic; and third year students are able to enrol on the Clinical Legal Skills module, which is a year-long module (with a focus on the Family Law Clinic and support at Court for Litigants in Person). Volunteering opportunities are available across all clinics for postgraduate students. In both extra-curricular and curricular involvement, students undergo extensive training and reflective activities, supported by academics with practice experience.

Before Covid-19, the Centre's delivery was face-to-face from an office within the Law School, closely following how advice and assistance were delivered within the profession at that time. As a result of Covid-19, the Centre moved to online delivery through the use of MS Teams, aligning with how the legal profession was responding to the disruption caused by Covid-19.

Arguably, the Centre creates a work placement embedded into study during a student's journey at the Law School. It is an alternative to a more traditional placement. This has widened access to placements for students from all backgrounds as it is embedded within their studies. It is inclusive and accessible to all law students.

The Centre is led by a director who is also a law academic. Students (in pairs) meet with clients to take instructions, essentially carrying out a fact-finding interview. Supervision is provided by a supervising solicitor prior to and following the client interview. The students conduct research following the client meeting, draft an attendance note and, where required, a letter of advice, which is approved by the solicitor before being sent. The supervision aspect is not only to ensure the students understand the legal processes/areas of research required but also to provide an opportunity for reflection, which is key in clinical legal education, and key to becoming a reflective practitioner.

In planning the delivery of the Centre, a Management Board was convened, including a regional solicitor, with links to Derby and District Law Society. The Law School benefits from having academics who are experienced practitioners, who retain links with the legal profession and wider industry. This provides a channel to ensure the foundations and evolution of the Centre align (as far as possible) with the realities of legal practice.

In designing the delivery of the Centre's immigration family reunion clinic, the advice of the British Red Cross (BRC) around the practicalities for the delivery of such a service was crucial. Due to strict regulation of the provision of immigration legal advice, the Centre developed a collaborative partnering with an established firm specialising in Immigration Law. This has enabled students to collaborate in a tripartite working relationship and experience teamwork and professional relations with external parties in the third sector and industry.

SKILLS REQUIRED BY EMPLOYERS

Whilst conversations and collaboration with the legal profession are key to ensuring that students are provided with the skills required by the profession, the authors of this chapter were of the view that there was an opportunity, and arguably a necessity, to carry out research to consider what skills employers expect of law graduates and whether such skill sets have changed in light of Covid-19, to underpin the provision with research-informed practice.

The questions posed by the research were: are we preparing students for the demands of the legal world and, in doing so, have the needs of the profession changed in light of Covid-19?

Legal professionals across England were approached for views on the impact of real-world experience gained by students upon their employability and whether the impact of Covid-19 has altered the skill set required of graduates.

Twenty-eight responses to the questionnaire were received. The professionals were asked about their understanding of CLE, whether engagement with real-world learning is important from a prospective employer's perspective and whether the professional would be more likely to employ a graduate who had gained real-world experience during the degree or in postgraduate study. In respect of understanding of CLE, there was a mixed response, with 46 per cent demonstrating an understanding, 25 per cent with no understanding and 29 per cent who stated they understood what CLE is but when asked to define it, gave incorrect definitions.

When professionals were asked how important engagement with facilities such as the Centre is, no one suggested that it was not important; 18 per cent stated it was slightly important; 21 per cent, moderately important; 50 per cent, important; and 11 per cent, very important. This is suggestive and supportive of the assertion that the provision of real-world experience through law clinics is viewed as important by the profession. Even for those professionals who had no, or limited, understanding of CLE, working within facilities such as the Centre clearly was of significance to the profession and continues to have value.

When asked whether employers were more or less likely to employ a graduate who has gained real-world experience, 4 per cent said very unlikely, 4 per cent unlikely, 4 per cent possible, 36 per cent likely and 32 per cent very likely. This is again suggestive that the provision of real-world experience through law clinics is a significant factor for graduates when seeking employment.

Asking these questions of professionals is important to evaluate and evidence the necessity of the provision of facilities such as a law clinic; and important, furthermore, to be able to demonstrate the value added in terms of student experience and how it assists in enhancing employability.

The questionnaire then moved on to discuss more specific skills, with professionals being asked: which skills/experience are essentially to be gained through the engagement with real-life experience? The key themes from this question were:

- communication
- listening skills
- drafting
- research
- problem solving.

Having considered these themes, it was important to consider whether students are given the opportunity to develop such skills through their volunteering in the Centre.

It was then significant to consider whether the provision is providing the opportunity to develop the necessary skills in light of Covid-19. The professionals were asked: 'Businesses have been required to change ways of working as a result of Covid-19. Can you identify any new skills/experience you require in a graduate?'

The themes that emerged were:

- IT/video conferencing
- working independently/self-motivation
- resilience
- flexibility
- ability to integrate with a team remotely.

Some interesting points were raised. Eleven per cent suggested that although the way we interact has changed, the skills are the same. Communication skills are heightened. There needs to be awareness/sensitivity of different opinions regarding Covid-19 and the measures to be taken to accommodate client needs.

Perhaps this is where a hybrid model for a clinic setting is appropriate, thus enabling an opportunity for students to gain experience of the provision of legal services both online and face to face. Thanaraj (2017) comments that 'technical, theoretical and practical knowledge gained from the experience of learning through the VLC (Virtual Law Clinic) about matters such as handling client confidentiality and the communication, storages and security of client data are absolute core requirements of a digital lawyering curriculum'.

Arguably, whilst the provision of the Centre online has been, and continues to be, successful considering the skill sets identified by the employers in the research carried out, there is some need for face-to-face experience for the students as well. McFaul et al. (2020) comment that 'There are some areas of legal work and some clients where advice in person is the preferred option, so while a virtual law clinic is not a replacement for face-to-face advice, it can work to enhance the provision of legal support.' This, arguably, prepares students for the reality of the provision of legal services.

In considering some of the additional comments professionals made within the research questionnaire, one professional commented 'recruiting for paralegals, many of the applicants with clinic experience have scored higher in shortlisting', thus evidencing the positive impact of students engaging in real-world experience.

A less positive comment was: 'I honestly believe that the only beneficial skills learned in such environments are people skills. The skills learned are often not conducive to private practice and there is a need to retrain the graduate.' Albeit only one comment from the sample, it raises the question as to whether employers view the clinic setting as part of the students' education journey or as work preparation.

The authors of this chapter have very similar memories of their first days qualifying as a solicitor, being handed a number of files and being sent off to Court with little to no experience of a court setting/advocating. Perhaps the phrase 'a rabbit in headlights' is apt! Providing students with the opportunities of real-world experience through 'working' within the Centre is arguably a stepping stone towards being in practice and the authors of this chapter are both of the view it is a stepping stone that is part of the student's educational journey with an element of work preparation but not with the expectation that a student will be work ready.

One response from a professional stated 'working in this type of environment [as in a clinic] may help but may also hinder because the student will expect to continue in a similar capacity during training, whereas I tend to find that they are sometimes used to too much independence and aren't as good as they've been told'. Is the onus on educators to manage the expectations of students in terms of the differences between experience in a clinic setting and what to expect in practice? This is a question the authors are reflecting upon.

CONCLUSION

To ensure we continue to provide opportunities to develop the skills required by employers, our provision must be in line with developments in the legal world and be reflective of the fluid approach to working. The authors of this chapter are of the view that collaboration with the industry is key as a means of ensuring that as educators, we are providing opportunities for students to develop the skills employers want.

It is noted within the HM Courts and Tribunals Service Reform Programme guidance (2021) that 'the case for continued modernisation is more compelling than ever'. In respect of reform, digitalisation of the courts, remote hearings, and so on, students need to be upskilled to conduct themselves in line with the developing profession and accordingly, HE providers need to make provision either through curricular or extra-curricular work to ensure students are equipped to be innovators and contributors to this evolving workplace.

Clark (2021) states:

> Quite simply, law firms need to become 'future flexible' in every way ... The pandemic has forced through 20 years of change in just 6 months. Law firms must now reflect on their 2020 experiences, revisit their priorities and plan for the future. All of this requires firms to see changes as a process rather than a destination and to embrace the new opportunities ...

Arguably the same can be said for HE providers – embrace change, revisit priorities and plan for the future. Furthermore, ensure HE providers are developing in line with how the profession is changing, to enable students to develop the skills required in employment.

As Thanaraj (2017) comments, 'Universities are in an influential position to bridge the gap between what the employment industry requires and the academic skills, practical skills and personal values they instil in their graduates.' There is a clear onus on HE institutions to deliver on this. Arguably there is a requirement for HE providers to enable students to be 'future ready' and equipped with the necessary skills that employers want.

It is important to highlight that whilst this chapter approaches what employers want from the perspective of CLE, this discussion is not limited to CLE or a law school but is transferable into other disciplines within HE. Having a clinic setting enables providers of HE to develop students' skills and simulate the evolution of the workplace, to be reactive and in line with industry, as evidenced through the Centre's response to Covid-19. Examples of the response include use of MS Teams; risk assessments for remote working by students; accessing case management system remotely; establishing a client rapport in a virtual setting; and so on.

It is imperative that HE providers keep abreast of developments in the legal world. In doing so, it is essential that providers ensure methods of teaching and provisions, both curricular and extra-curricular, are regularly reviewed to ensure they align with the developments of the industry. For students to gain the skills required by employers, HE providers have a responsibility to keep abreast of such developments to ensure curricular and extra-curricular provisions are current, future focused and innovative.

BIBLIOGRAPHY

Cantatore, F. (2018), 'The impact of pro bono clinics on employability and work readiness in students', *International Journal of Clinical Legal Education*, 25(1), 147–172.

Chambers Student Guide (2021), *Trends affecting the legal profession*. Available at: https://www.chambersstudent.co.uk/where-to-start/trends-affecting-the-legal-profession (accessed: 22 January 2023).

Clark, A. (2021), *Five ways in which the legal office is changing*. Available at: https://communities.lawsociety.org.uk/coronavirus-managing-in-a-recession/five-ways-in-which-the-legal-office-is-changing/6001581.article (accessed: 22 January 2023).

HM Courts and Tribunals Service (2021), *The HMCTS Reform Programme*. Available at: https://www.gov.uk/guidance/the-hmcts-reform-programme (accessed: 22 January 2023).

Lewis, R. (2000), 'Clinical legal education revisited', *Dokkyo International Review*, 13, 149–169.

McFaul, H., Hardie, L. Ryan, F., Bright, K. and Graffin, N. (2020), 'Taking clinical legal education online: songs of innocence and experience', *International Journal of Clinical Legal Education*, 27(4), 6–38.

Seiler, D. (2021), *Building workforce skills at scale to thrive during and after the COVID 19 crisis*. Available at: https://www.mckinsey.com/business-functions/people-and-organizational-performance/our-insights/building-workforce-skills-at-scale-to-thrive-during-and-after-the-covid-19-crisis?cid=eml-web (accessed: 22 January 2023).

Thanaraj, A. (2017), 'Making the case for digital lawyering framework in legal education', *International Review of Law*, 2017(3), 1–21.

Thomas, L., Vaughan, S., Malkani, B. and Lynch, T. (2018), *Reimagining Clinical Legal Education*. Oxford: Hart Publishing.

REFLECTION

From a law graduate

I am a Solicitor with a firm based in Derbyshire/Nottinghamshire. I have experience of Law Clinics both from my time as a student and also from the point of view of an employer interviewing graduates.

In my very first interview for a Paralegal role I was asked by the very interested interviewer all about the Law Clinic I was involved with at University. This was the first question they asked. The interviewer was so impressed with the work of the Law Clinic and the skills I had gained from my time in the Law Clinic. We spoke about this for some time. Now, cut to 12 years later and I have just interviewed somebody for a role working alongside me and they had undertaken the same Law Clinic module at University. I knew they would be coming to me with communication skills, the ability to work in a team, experience interviewing clients, drafting documents and then also, importantly, client confidentiality skills, ideas on file set ups and to some level case progression.

6. Problems delivering the skills employers want? Creativity – a case in point

Elaine Clarke

INTRODUCTION

We seem to have a problem with creativity. To begin with, a sprinkling of evidence: the World Economic Forum (2016, 2018 and 2020) and QS Employer (2020) show creativity as being a key skill that employers state they need for the future. McKinsey (2021), in a report based on a survey of 18,000 people in 15 countries, set out 'Distinctive Elements of Talents' (DELTAs), skills and attributes which, regardless of sector or occupation, should enable individuals to (i) add value beyond automation, (ii) operate in a digital environment, and (iii) continually adapt. Creativity and imagination feature as DELTAs. We see, therefore, a strong message from global surveys of the need for creativity. Bakshi et al. (2017), as part of a partnership between Nesta and the Oxford Martin School, produced a report on the Future of Skills Employment in 2030. This emphasises the importance of higher-order skills, and places originality and fluency of ideas in the top ten skills of the future.

At an organisational level, in an attempt to inform our own practice, the author and a colleague, Chris Wilson, undertook a survey on creativity with a broad range of employers in 2019. Looking at whether we have a problem with creativity, our survey indicated the answer could well be 'yes'. Results confirmed the importance of creativity, yet revealed a very low level of strategic focus on it across organisations, evidenced through the lack of mechanisms in place to identify or reward creativity (less than 25 per cent agreement that either existed). Almost half of respondents said they had had *no creativity training* in the last five years, and only a further 12 per cent had had *one day's* training in the same period. The survey also revealed similarly low levels of employers who include some rating of candidates' creativity in their recruitment processes. We therefore have a contradiction between our respondents' acknowledged need for creativity, and their moves to recruit for it, develop it, or encourage latent creativity.

At an individual level, Hopkins (2019), based on insights from wide-ranging interviews, writes of the erosion of our imaginations, exacerbated by school curricula that drive conformity, our reduced engagement with nature, art and play, increasing distractions and demands on our attention, and distant actors who use the unprecedented amount of data they have on individuals to influence daily behaviour, reducing our ability to imagine alternatives.

What of the higher education sector's role? The QS report of 2020, mentioned above, asked employers not only which skills they view as being the most important but also how satisfied they are with the skills they see. Problem-solving, resilience, communication, creativity and flexibility were the skills that showed the largest gaps between their perceived importance and the satisfaction employers stated with those skills in recent graduates, ranging from a 33 per cent to a 23 per cent difference, and indeed those gap scores had worsened slightly since the same survey was undertaken in 2018. Our own survey also revealed a low level of satisfaction (less than 25 per cent) with students' being able to demonstrate or articulate their creative skills. This indicates that we, in higher education, have a problem. We appear not to be helping our graduates to develop and demonstrate skills deemed important by employers for the future. Those of us who are advocates for developing greater creative thinking might also maintain that the other skills showing large gaps (complex problem-solving, for example, or communication) could be enhanced with a greater ability to think and act creatively. Likewise, many of the DELTAs identified by McKinsey (2021) (such as agile thinking, problem-solving, asking the right questions, synthesising messages, courage and risk-taking, driving change and innovation, breaking orthodoxies, coping with uncertainty), could be enhanced through greater creative thinking abilities. This makes it all the more important that we, as educators, not only increase creativity in the learning experience, but also ensure that students are comfortable demonstrating their abilities and talking about them. This is what this chapter aims to address.

ARE THERE PARTICULAR DIFFICULTIES WITH CREATIVITY?

It could be that creativity itself is perceived as a particular problem, due to:

- a lack of recognition of the importance or relevance of creativity, or it being seen as a distraction from serious business (a 'messy, unpredictable, potentially uncontrollable, frivolous and unprofitable use of time (Hopkins, 2019: 13));

- the concept itself being misunderstood, or the notion that only a minority of people can be creative, and we can do nothing to change that;
- there being thus no cross-organisational leadership;
- the feeling that it is someone else's responsibility;
- the perception that it is difficult to judge the quality of creativity in student work;
- fearing it goes against processes and systems and can't easily be accommodated;
- having not been trained in it ourselves, we feel poorly qualified to help students;
- our having grown risk averse in an environment under constant scrutiny and measurement.

The following sections address the above, but first...

A PAUSE TO ENSURE WE AGREE ON OUR TOPIC

We need a broadly agreed view of creativity if we are to act. The literature has converged over time on the view that creativity involves producing ideas, processes, or objects that are not only *novel* (unique, original, atypical, cutting-edge) but also *appropriate* (relevant, useful, applicable, fitting, effective) (Hallman et al., 2016). It often involves combining or synthesising existing ideas in new ways, so it need not invoke fear of having to create something out of nothing. In a comprehensive updating of Amabile's 1988 model of creativity and innovation, Amabile and Pratt (2016) reminds us that creativity at the level of the individual enables the exploration of new perspectives, pivoting among different ideas, thinking broadly, and making unusual associations. It also includes self-efficacy, risk-taking and the avoidance of conformity (Amabile and Pratt, 2016).

In addition to the insights that I and my colleague gained on what happens within organisations, we also asked practitioners for their understanding of creativity and the characteristics of creative people, so that we could target improvements in practice. Net agreement scores of between 60 per cent and 80 per cent indicated the top five characteristics to be that (i) creativity is about flexibility of thinking and (ii) questioning assumptions, (iii) it means different things in different contexts, (iv) it involves going beyond boundaries, and (v) that a person is more creative when they mix with people who are different from themselves. There was 60 per cent net agreement that creative people (i) are open to new experiences, (ii) are inquisitive, (iii) enjoy challenge, (iv) want to overcome obstacles, (v) cope well with novelty, and (vi) take more risks.

On the basis of the accepted definition, insight into employers' views of creativity and the nature of creative people, and the possible difficulties postulated above, we proceed to look at how higher education can play its role in expanding students' creative abilities.

Creativity IS Relevant and Serious

When such wide-ranging surveys as those quoted above all emphasise the importance of creativity, then we as educators need to take it seriously. The widely agreed definition of it being useful as well as novel (another often-used term is 'task-appropriate') also speaks to its relevance. We need to focus on bringing it up to a strategic level within higher education, ensuring that leaders encourage and support creativity through (a) the allocation of time and resources to projects, (b) the development of staff to become facilitators of creativity, (c) signalling its importance in reporting processes, and (d) in recognition and reward for bringing about change.

Are We Imagining Constraints and Barriers that Don't Exist?

The developed world in higher education has coalesced around some variation of building credits towards qualifications, and in order to gain those credits, students must study for a given number of hours and/or carry out assessment tasks. This much we cannot change in the short term. I would urge us, however, to look carefully at what the real – and not the imagined – boundaries of those constraints are, and to creatively work at changing what we can change. The skills and attitudes that contribute towards creativity are not themselves subject-specific, although individual activities designed for students might well be. We can think creatively around structures and across boundaries, for example in allowing students across disciplines, backgrounds and stages of study to work creatively together, and still fulfil challenging assignments that can be fitted into the particular demands of their subject.

Creativity IS Our Responsibility

We don't need to wait for anyone else to act, we can all be leaders in creativity. Our ability to make a difference depends on our own level of *commitment* and our perception of our ability to make a difference (*agency*). We are fortunate in higher education that designing learning is an ongoing activity for academic staff; therefore we do have agency, at whatever level we operate. We can change what we do in our own modules and courses, even as we influence senior leadership to take on a more strategic approach. Elements of the creative process can be built into what we do on a daily basis with our students, and shared with our colleagues, probably in forums that already exist. All we need is the will and ongoing commitment to do it.

Sharpening Our and Our Students' Skills

Contrary perhaps to the perceived wisdom that creativity is the domain of a minority of people, academic literature broadly acknowledges both the desirability and the possibility of training individuals and teams in both skills and processes of creativity. In addition, the majority of respondents in our survey deemed that creativity can be improved over time, and that it is possible to train people to be creative. Training helps to overcome resistance and bring about behaviour change (Clarke, 2019). When training students or staff to work creatively in teams, many of the skills involved do overlap with those associated with effective teamwork itself: goal setting, time management, listening, supportive communication, consensus building and implementing action. In addition to these skills, those that are conducive to creative thinking are, 'belief in the value of diversity and an openness to experience, divergent, convergent and associative thinking, developing an explorative mindset, evaluating ideas positively, perspective-taking and a willingness to change perspectives' (Clarke, 2019). Specific training should be sought and offered in the latter group, in particular.

Judging Quality – Nothing a Little Imagination Couldn't Solve

One of the possible reasons as to why there is a skills gap in creativity could lie in the perceived difficulty of being able to assess it. Many writers acknowledge that measures of creative output are subjective; 'the creative process, for any learner, is unpredictable and difficult to capture' (Cowan, 2006). Bearing in mind the multitude of skills and attitudes that are applied and developed during the creative process and that 'often it is in the experiences of failure and frustration that the creative ability is honed and developed' (Cowan, 2006), we ought to be thinking about how we assess the process as much as the outputs themselves. Hopkins (2019) writes of the need to rewire our brains and learn to switch off the internal censor that is frightened of giving a wrong answer, or trying to anticipate what the tutor wants to hear. He refers to this as the fallacy of the correct answer.

Assessment *for* learning is about learning from the process in order to enhance both cognitive and behavioural skills – an ideal vehicle in which to embed creativity. How often, however, in assessment for learning, do we assess the output to the detriment of the process? Why not include in our assessment criteria elements of the process, such as the exchange of and building upon ideas, recovering from setbacks, the ability to change minds to reach common ground, the formation of coalitions with people who are different, the extent to which students feel they have grown in potential ... as well as the quality of ideas, ideas taken forward, implementation plans and so forth, as outputs.

Cowan (2006) suggests that the learners themselves choose the criteria against which their creative processes, thinking and outcomes will be judged, so that students may explore, experience and develop creativity in the context of their own field of study. In this context, the tutor is there to create the appropriate climate and conditions, and to help students develop their capability in recognising, representing and evaluating their own creativity.

What Does This Mean for What and How Our Students Learn?

The possible lack of exposure to creative practices and the perceived difficulties could be lessened if we were to break down the elements of creativity into actionable parts, and to ensure our students know that this contributes to creativity. Drawing from the elements of creativity and creative individuals identified above, we find that they can be clustered into those that relate to the learning environment, and those that relate to activities in which we can engage our students.

The learning environment we seek means:

- mixing students with people who are different to themselves;
- facilitating a supportive environment;
- allowing freedom and risk-taking.

Diversity is a key contributing factor to creativity in both face-to-face and virtual teams. Technology has been identified as both an inhibitor and an enabler in working in virtual teams; something we find ourselves doing much more these days. It inhibits when it is unreliable, or becomes quickly obsolete, or when team members have different levels of proficiency. It enables through its versatility, mobility, and the capacity for sharing ideas, documents and information (Han et al., 2017). Tutors should facilitate the positive use of technology to serve the creative process, as its role in teamwork becomes more prominent and accepted. Within teams of any nature, therefore, we should seek the access to different knowledge and perspectives that diversity brings. This is why we should proactively find ways in which our students can work with people who are different to themselves.

Diversity can relate to age, gender, occupation, knowledge, skills, background, geography. Li et al. (2015) demonstrated that diversity within a team positively relates to team and individual-level creativity through information sharing and evaluation. We need to be aware, however, that although diversity is overwhelmingly acknowledged as a positive contributor, there can be pitfalls. Harvey (2013) in his work on 'deep level diversity' (underlying perspectives) claims that where diversity might improve divergent processes in a group (those that lead to more ideas and originality), those different perspectives might get in the way of *converging* around those ideas and finding a solution.

The literature shows widespread agreement on the importance of a supportive environment, freedom, and a low aversion to risk. This applies both to the environment within which the tutor operates and to the learning environment the tutor creates for the students. A supportive climate is one in which participants are motivated by mutual effort, sharing of ideas and information; where they engage in constructive debate, filter and refine each other's ideas, and mistakes are tolerated. There is active support for creativity, the nurturing of new ideas and knowledge, helping to build the confidence and resilience of participants. Perceived psychological risk is therefore reduced through trust in the intentions of others, rendering participants more willing to be vulnerable and to take risks (Clarke, 2019). Creating a supportive environment within the classroom, discussing the ethos with students, and spending time helping them to create supportive environments within their own teams should be a priority, to bring about creative thinking. A word of caution, however, in that low psychological risk, while generally demonstrated to be a precursor to positive team creativity, could be counterproductive if it lowers team members' expectations.

As part of a supportive environment, participants need to spend time developing their confidence and trust in each other. There is broad agreement for the need for a process of socialisation, exploring each other's differences and perspectives, breaking down reservations and potential bias, and building enthusiasm. Tutors therefore need to acknowledge this need and actively build in time and guidance for it to happen. A willingness to invest time in improving creative thinking extends beyond the early stages of the process. Learning to exercise creative thinking takes practice, as well as teams needing to mature to be fully effective. Hallman et al. (2016) maintain that multiple interventions over time have more chance of bringing about change than short-term, one-off interventions, although the latter can be useful for teaching specific creativity skills.

An effective creative team is likely to have a commonality of purpose, values and beliefs – a shared mental model. A team's shared mental model will evolve with time and provided the team remains open to difference, to external influences, and to a dynamic and evolving process, that shared mental model acts as an encouragement to creativity. Shared mental models, however, become counterproductive and reduce the potential for creative solutions when they lead to the team being unreceptive to challenge and input that does not initially fit. Our role as educators would be to encourage the development of an initial shared mental model (examples include allowing teams to choose names, design and explain a logo/slogan/coat of arms for itself), and ensure constant questioning as to whether that model continues to be conducive to creative endeavours.

Facets of creativity and of creative people provide the following themes that should inform the activities we design for our students:

- exploring contexts, making the creativity context-specific;
- going beyond boundaries;
- providing new experiences/novelty;
- encouraging inquisitiveness;
- bringing about flexibility in thinking;
- providing challenges and obstacles to overcome
- questioning assumptions.

All of the above can be built into the learning experiences we design. Problem-based, or curiosity-based, or challenge-based learning lends itself to creative thinking in involving multiple stakeholders, perspectives and implications, and in allowing the replication of real-life dilemmas. It provides richness of detail into which challenges and obstacles can be built. Design thinking as an approach is growing in influence outside the sphere of design and is shown to help increase students' creativity. It involves solving ill-defined problems through collaboration. The key is to take a human-centred or end-user approach and to engage in framing or reframing of the problem, recognising divergent perspectives and collecting evidence around alternative proposals (Guaman-Quintanilla et al., 2022). Not only do these approaches provide a vehicle for creative thinking, they also support development of many other future skills, not least of which is complex problem-solving. We also need our students to question assumptions, and for this they need to be taught how to do so.

In bringing about inquisitiveness, new experiences and flexibility of thinking, we should look to engage more of our students' senses in the learning process – smell, touch, sound, taste – and emotion. The appeal of serious play has soared in recent years. Educators of adults have recognised the benefits of play, which was educated out of us as we moved through school. Play teaches social skills, co-operation, creativity, conflict resolution, resilience, empathy, risk-taking, and makes us better at finding solutions (Hopkins, 2019). Looking back at the desirability and possibility of training for creativity, play might prove a liberating starting point in that journey.

FINAL THOUGHTS

We might take issue with the notion that there is a problem with our engendering creativity in our graduates – although we would do well to pay attention to repeated messages from employers to that effect; however, we cannot ignore the strength of the message about its importance. We need to look at the constraints we place upon ourselves and question whether we have moved too far in our own aversion to risk. Or indeed, looking at the elements that contribute towards creativity and the ease with which they can be built into the curriculum, pedagogy and assessment, question whether it would actually be that much of a risk to embrace the challenge and bridge the gap.

REFERENCES

Amabile, T. M. and Pratt, M. G. (2016), 'The dynamic componential model of creativity and innovation in organizations: making progress, making meaning', *Research in Organizational Behavior*, 36, 157–183.

Bakshi, H., Downing, J. M., Osborne, M. A. and Schneider, P. (2017), *Future of Skills Employment in 2030*. London: Pearson and Nesta.

Clarke E. L. (2019), 'Team creativity', in M. Peters and R. Heraud (eds), *Encyclopedia of Educational Innovation*. Singapore: Springer.

Cowan, J. (2006), 'How should I assess creativity?', in N. Jackson, M. Oliver, M. Shaw and J. Wisdom (eds), *Developing Creativity in Higher Education: An Imaginative Curriculum*. Abingdon: Routledge.

Guaman-Quintanilla, S., Everaert, P., Chiluiza, K. and Valcke, M. (2022), 'Impact of design thinking in higher education: a multi-actor perspective on problem solving and creativity', *International Journal of Technology and Design Education*. doi: https://doi.org/10.1007/s10798-021-09724-z.

Hallman, S. K., Wright, M. C. and Conger, A. J. (2016), *Development and Assessment of Student Creativity*. Occasional Paper No. 33. Center for Research on Learning & Teaching, University of Michigan.

Han, S. J., Chae, C., Macko, C., Park, W. and Beyerlein, M. (2017), 'How virtual team leaders cope with creativity challenges', *European Journal of Training and Development*, 41(3), 261–276.

Harvey, S. (2013), 'A different perspective: the multiple effects of deep level diversity on group creativity', *Journal of Experimental Social Psychology*, 49, 822–832.

Hopkins, R. (2019), *From What Is to What If – Unleashing the Power of Imagination to Create the Future We Want*. London: Chelsea Green Publishing.

Li, C. R., Lin, C.-J., Tien, Y.-H. and Chen, C.-M. (2015), 'A multilevel model of team cultural diversity and creativity: the role of climate for inclusion', *Journal of Creative Behavior*, 51(2), 163–179.

McKinsey and Company (2021), *Defining the Skills Citizens Will Need in the Future World of Work*. Available at: https://www.mckinsey.com/industries/public-and-social-sector/our-insights/defining-the-skills-citizens-will-need-in-the-future-world-of-work?cid=other-eml-alt-mip-mck&hdpid=b8fa5a7b-9f0e-4549-9fe1-8166a75a9b39&hctky=12109167&hlkid=89ebe66e8b49410d9bd4084d0388536d# (accessed: 22 January 2023).

QS Employer (2020), *Insights Report 2020*. Available at: https://info.qs.com/rs/335-VIN-535/images/QS-Employer-Insights-Report.pdf (accessed: 22 January 2023).

World Economic Forum (2016), *The Future of Jobs Report*. Available at: https://www3.weforum.org/docs/WEF_Future_of_Jobs.pdf (accessed: 22 January 2023).

World Economic Forum (2018), *The Future of Jobs Report*. Available at: https://www3.weforum.org/docs/WEF_Future_of_Jobs_2018.pdf (accessed: 22 January 2023).
World Economic Forum (2020), *The Future of Jobs Report*. Available at: https://www.weforum.org/reports/the-future-of-jobs-report-2020 (accessed: 22 January 2023).

REFLECTION

From a senior manager in manufacturing

When I attend a graduate assessment centre I try to imagine what the student will be like in two years' time, and five years' time. Yes, I have an immediate need for a student to join the organisation and make a contribution. However, I want a student who will develop and grow and be able to take a senior role in the future.

To me, being employable is not just about having the right fit for the current job. It is about having the skills and abilities to grow, and be the employee of the future. That is difficult to assess, and there is certainly some subjectivity in the process. I use my experience of seeing successful and unsuccessful graduates over many years and from that experience I think I can spot a future star when I see one, even if I can't explain exactly what it is that I am looking for.

7. Mind the gap: employers' and students' perceptions of skills and knowledge needed by accounting graduates in Greece

Efimia Anastasiou, Siobhan Neary and Alison Lawson

INTRODUCTION

Technology and the increasing globalisation of work are significantly changing many professions, including the accounting profession (Pincus et al., 2017). This has inspired a plethora of education studies aimed at identifying or embedding in the curriculum experiences that will provide students with the opportunity to acquire the necessary knowledge, skills and attributes that are required to function in today's diverse business environment (Berry and Routon, 2020).

The current debate on the development of graduates with the necessary professional skills is not entirely novel. A key starting point in these studies is derived from Becker's fundamental Human Capital Theory (Becker, 1964). The core assumption of the concept rests on the idea that an individual can acquire skills and attributes in order to make themself more attractive and successful in the labour market (Yorke and Knight, 2006). Indeed, one only has to see university entrance web pages regarding the statistics of the employment rates of recent graduates implying that there is a direct relationship between the learner's attainment of skills and the subsequent rewards (in a sense that acquiring a set of skills facilitates the obtainment of employment). These required professional skills centre on communication, teamwork, problem solving, and technology use. In the framework for this study, the terms 'professional skills' and 'attributes' are perceived 'as being the skills, knowledge and abilities of university graduates, beyond disciplinary content knowledge, which are applicable to a range of contexts' (Barrie, 2004: 262).

However, despite widespread initiatives by educators to embed professional skills in the curriculum, it seems that educational reforms have not been fully achieved and gaps between graduates' performance in the workplace and employers' expectations persist. Related research in Greece has revealed a mismatch between market needs and newly recruited applicants (Asonitou and Hassal, 2019). In a study by the Hellenic Federation of Enterprises (SEV), 36 per cent of the firms interviewed stated that they were dissatisfied with recent hires, and the main reason (46 per cent) was that graduates did not possess the required skills for the job (Ioannou, 2019). Asonitou (2022) found that accounting teachers, students and professionals thought that the greatest barrier to skills development was the lack of effective partnerships between higher education institutions (HEIs) and industry.

The human capital perspective of employability has been heavily contested by some authors (Bennett et al., 2019; Tomlinson, 2017). Alternative approaches suggest an increasing prevalence of identity-based views of employability, arguing that graduates must act in ways that lead others to ascribe to them the identity of a person worthy of being employed (Holmes, 2015). Holmes (2013) describes the iterative approach to employability development as processual (the *process* by which the graduate's employability is built over time) and differentiates this from possessional and positional approaches. In the possessional approach, for example, the focus is on graduates possessing the skills, abilities or characteristics required for work. The positional approach highlights the social and cultural capital in the graduate labour market. Whilst the human capital approach views employability as the individual's responsibility to increase his or her employability-enhancing activities, the labour market is an arena where individuals and groups are in competition that does not relate to skills or work-related capacities (Tholen, 2015). Employers further reinforce this selective advantage by recruiting from prestigious universities (Holmes, 2013; Tomlinson, 2012).

As a contribution to this debate, this chapter reports findings of a study that examined the perceptions of employers in Greece of the skills and attributes that accounting graduates are expected to bring to the job in order to be hired, as well as which of these skills employers believe students should have acquired during their tertiary education. Since the 'problem' begins with equipping students with the 'right' skills and attributes to perform in a changing work environment, it stands to reason that no study is complete if it does not include the other important stakeholder, namely the students. Furthermore, as this research was conducted in the insecure job environment being faced by Greek students after the first austerity measures were passed in 2011, the study was interested in students' perceptions regarding their tertiary education in relation to employability. Besides focusing on students' perceptions of the skills and attributes that can be acquired though their formal education, the study also looked at why they thought these skills could not be developed through HEIs. The chapter presents the research methods, followed by an interpretation of results. It concludes with a discussion of findings and recommendations for practice.

METHODOLOGY

A total of 42 interviews were conducted. Thirty of those were conducted with students and graduates recruited from the three largest public universities and one private institution, situated in Athens and Piraeus. The students and graduates were selected as they were representative of all the main disciplines in their HEIs that included accountancy, such as Business Administration with an emphasis in Accounting and Finance, and Banking and Financial Management. At the time of the interview, students were either currently studying for their final year, recent graduates, or graduates who had completed their degrees up to 18 months previously. The 12 employers recruited reflected a range of employer types, size and sectors, such as the Big Four (PwC, KPMG, Deloitte and EY), consulting (private and banking), but also a range of industries that provide work opportunities for the accounting graduate, such as in software, manufacturing and retail companies. The criteria used for the selection of employers was that participants were holding central positions in the firm as well as being in charge of recruitment.

Interviews were conducted face-to-face over a six-month period using a semi-structured interview schedule. The study first sought to understand how students perceive their future work, and *then* to gauge what knowledge and skills are perceived as necessary to perform in this job.

UNDERSTANDING WHAT MAKES AN ACCOUNTANCY GRADUATE DESIRABLE TO EMPLOYERS

In order to gain insightful perspectives on the value of a degree, employers were asked how important a degree is in their recruitment decisions for accountancy positions. Employers cited the importance of a university degree, regardless of the subject studied. Besides acting as a threshold entry to the workplace, employers inferred that graduates who have acquired a degree possess certain abilities or traits, such as processing and presenting data, working in teams, flexibility and so forth. In terms of specific technical skills, employers responded that a good knowledge of basic accounting, including principles and concepts, was sufficient. Moreover, accountancy was viewed as a *learned* professional occupation in which competency is gained in the workplace:

> ... the most important thing for me is on the job training ... I'm not expecting the graduate to have technical knowledge. I know they don't have it. I want someone who is clever, understands and is easy to work with. (CFO – Manufacturing)

However, two employers representing the investment banking services sector believed that graduates should possess more technical knowledge. Thus, it seems that the extent of knowledge specialisation can be seen as context-specific or dependent on the kind of occupation being considered. In this case, specific technical knowledge was considered more important for the finance area.

A second key theme emerging from the data was that personal attributes were emphasised more often than skills requirements. It is not that employability skills were not considered, but that the focus was on the graduate being able to demonstrate a certain behaviour or portray a certain attitude. Furthermore, the closer the graduate's behaviour was to the organisation's culture, the more successful the hiring.

The most commonly mentioned attributes were:

- willingness to learn;
- adaptability;
- initiative;
- reflectiveness.

Furthermore, employers were asked which skills and attributes could be taught or acquired at university. The skills and attributes most frequently identified were:

- ability to work under pressure and self-management;
- communication skills;
- analytical and critical thinking skills;
- team-working attitude;
- business awareness.

It should be noted that personal attributes deemed necessary at appointment, such as 'business etiquette', 'hard-working', 'can fit with organisation ethos', were not mentioned as expected to be developed by universities. This does not necessarily demonstrate that employers think that these attributes cannot be developed at university, but they may be perceived as being more difficult to include in the curriculum since they relate more to the specific context within which graduates will be hired. As far as 'willingness to learn' and 'initiative' are concerned, these attributes are initiated by the student, as opposed to being academic led, since it is the student who is responsible for when to study and so forth. This is interesting, because employers considered personal attributes as important for selection.

STUDENTS' PERCEPTIONS

Students envisioned their future career aspirations and described the tasks they imagined they would be performing differently, although they came from a similar disciplinary background. Students were categorised into three cohorts:

- accounting – those who mentioned practical tasks relating to accounting in firms, controllership and/or internal auditing;
- finance – those with career aspirations to be analysts, traders, working in investment banks and insurance;
- managerial/entrepreneurship – those who saw themselves progressing into management positions or owning their own business.

Having identified the students for each of the three cohorts, the study set out to code the competencies perceived by students as necessary to perform in their job role. The necessary skills and attributes perceived by students were categorised into five areas: disciplinary understanding, IT (information technology), communication skills, analytical and critical thinking skills, and personal capacities and attributes.

1. Disciplinary Understanding

Students believed that the primary benefit of a degree was the specific knowledge learned. Thus, if one did not possess this knowledge, one was seen as not being able to perform in this specific job role. 'You must understand what you have in front of you, for example the accounts. You can't have a history degree and do entries' (Accounting student 7).

Although all three cohorts recognised that their future jobs required a developed understanding of their discipline, the accounting cohort referred more to this than the other two cohorts. This is strengthened in their responses, as they did not suggest the need for complementary bodies of knowledge, such as economics or management, while the other two cohorts did see the need to capitalise on other disciplines.

2. Skills: Information Technology, Communication and Analytical/Critical Thinking Skills

The accounting cohort referred to communication and technological competencies as necessary to perform in their jobs to a greater extent than the other two cohorts, whilst the finance cohort placed a greater value on analytical and problem-solving skills. Both accounting and finance tracks need to use software, spreadsheet models or technology to analyse and present data. However, the accounting cohort saw it more as a necessary requirement to operate and apply 'packaged software' whilst the finance cohort saw it more as a tool in order to analyse data to report on, or the need to take decisions from this data, hence the value placed on 'analytical and critical thinking'. 'I envision my job being related to problem-solving ... this intrigues me because you have to think in order to find a solution ... finance is creative' (Finance student 16).

3. Personal Attributes

The managerial cohort placed less value on skill requirements and viewed personal attributes and competencies as necessary. Different emphases and understandings in perceptions among the three groups further illustrate the contextual element. For example, only the managerial/entrepreneurial cohort referred to being a risk-taker. The finance cohort focused on intellectual ability, flexibility and adaptability, since they saw themselves working in fast, dynamic sectors; while the accounting cohort focused on attributes such as conducting oneself in a professional manner, confidence and teamwork as being more important, as they envisioned themselves being entrusted with valuable information regarding the company. Lastly, the managerial/entrepreneurial cohort referred to a greater number of attribute items; for example, they perceived that their jobs were related to a wider environment and noted that they should be aware of changes in the economy: 'It's not only what you do here [the student was referring to the university] you have to be aware of what's going on out there' (Managerial student 27).

For students it was not an either/or situation, whether a university education could develop skills and attributes beyond disciplinary understanding, since individual responses included too many attitudes all at once. For example, the following extract from a student's response indicates this: 'Yes ... but I think it's a bit hard. You can develop someone only if they want to be developed ... but I don't think it's easy ... you can teach the necessary skills but that doesn't make someone into a leader ... though you should be motivated by the university' (Finance student 2).

Although there was considerable overlap in the respondents' own answers, the analysis of the responses focused on 'what' knowledge, skills and attributes, and for those students whose answers contained ambivalence in this regard, 'why' they thought they could not be developed through their university education.

Students believed that 'disciplinary knowledge', 'communication skills', 'business awareness', 'team-work', 'research, analytical and critical thinking skills', and 'professional conduct and working within deadlines' could be developed through their HE experiences. Interestingly the students' cohorts that saw the skills as being necessary in their future roles were also aware that they were developed through their education. For example, the managerial cohort who mentioned 'business awareness' second, after disciplinary understanding, were more aware of its development in a university setting: 'also universities connect students with businesses or invite employers to come to the university in order for students to meet or to start having a feeling about businesses' (Managerial student 12).

Among the 30 students, 23 noted some uncertainties about whether professional skills and attributes could be developed in a university setting. The perceived barriers were coded as: personality traits, practical difficulties, and the importance of 'learning on the job'. Personality traits highlight the issue of characteristics, such as 'leadership', 'motivation' and 'hard-working', which are difficult to develop in a university context since they are determined by early experiences and are deeply rooted in one's personality (Tymon, 2013).

The second category, 'practical difficulties', refers to students' views on barriers related to large student numbers found in a university setting, the difficulty of teaching attributes in practice, and the nature of the bachelor's degree.

Another fundamental issue raised by some respondents was that in accountancy, skills and personal attributes are developed by job experience. Students viewed their degree as a basis of knowledge, but recognised that they had to 'practise' what they learnt *in situ* – on the job:

> No, a university cannot develop personal attributes because I don't think you can develop personal attributes in a schooling environment ... because you are in a safe environment you are not exposed you are protected ... outside you have to challenge yourself to face different experiences which you have to deal with by yourself. (Managerial student 27)

Although these responses can be read as students letting HE 'off the hook', or could be attributed to contextual differentials such as Greece having a higher percentage of small firms in relation to other EU countries, another reason could be that when the question is directed to an individual, the student feels responsible for the answer. Furthermore, personal attributes could be perceived as inherent, whereby students feel that being willing to work hard and persevere is an intrinsic factor of their own effort and not that of an HEI.

CONCLUSION

While a degree does open a gateway to the labour market as employers' comments suggest, what makes an applicant desirable is more complicated than just acquiring skills. The analysis reported here reinforces the importance of an applicant's possession (or lack thereof) of various personal attributes and dispositional traits. This presents a challenge to HEIs since the focus has stayed firmly on the development of students' skills – measures underlying the human capital view of employability, such as communication and critical thinking, rather than their capability to 'act' or 'behave' in a professional way. Thus, while employability models have contributed to a conceptual theoretical background, a graduate's success in attaining employment is not entirely based on their possession of necessary skills.

The study highlights the importance of contextual aspects, such as the economic environment in Greece and the actual or perceived work environment. Employers attributed a higher level of importance to HEIs developing students with the ability to work 'under pressure' and with 'self-management'. Since employers had to work under very volatile conditions themselves, the economic environment influenced how employers perceived and attributed value to the specific desired attribute and teaching this to students was of top priority. This adds an interesting perspective to the complexity of employability discourse, since what employers are looking for from graduates might shift according to the needs of the market. Also, since there was no strong agreement among employers on a specific desired skill, this implies that required skills and attributes are influenced by the broad understanding employers hold on the position they were thinking of when replying, albeit all in the accounting sphere.

Furthermore, the philosophy underpinning the study was that, if we truly want to develop the employability of HE students and better prepare them for the world of work, then we have to understand and account for students' views. Although all students had some form of accounting in their background, the study identified that their career aspirations and the way they envisioned their career post-HE differed. The three student cohorts, divided into accounting, finance and managerial, derived their understanding of the various professional skills in relation to their perception of the application of these skills in their future perceived job. For example, the need for a broader disciplinary understanding, including knowledge of management, communication and technological competencies, analytical and critical thinking skills, were perceived in varying ways. Such factors need to be understood in order to make sense of employability and prepare students for employment. Employability agendas should not homogenise students (Barrie, 2007).

The argument proposed is that instead of approaching employability by fragmenting it into a set of skills or attributes, a more comprehensive framework is needed that can enhance students' employability, acquired through both formal and informal experiences geared towards improving graduate work-readiness. Many universities are now including work-integrated learning programmes and experiential learning in their curriculum with the aim of enhancing graduate employability. Furthermore, a majority of students noted some barriers to the development of employability through HEIs. An emphasis on employability training by higher education is unlikely to be successful without the motivational engagement of the student. Overall, there seems to be a consensus in the education literature on the importance of student engagement and active learning models (Pincus et al., 2017). However, much of this research is related to the importance of student engagement and active learning models and their effect on learning and performance outcomes in assessments. Thus, despite the attention received, further research is warranted on student activity and the enhancement of employability skills. This could also help to reduce the divergence in perceptions between students and employers on the importance of the HEI role in developing individual attributes and dispositions.

REFERENCES

Asonitou, S. (2022), 'Impediments and pressures to incorporate soft skills in Higher Education accounting studies', *Accounting Education*, 31(3), 243–272.

Asonitou, S. and Hassall, T. (2019), 'Which skills and competences to develop in accountants in a country in crisis?', *International Journal of Management Education*, 17(3), 1–19.

Barrie, S. C. (2004), 'A research-based approach to generic graduate attributes policy', *Higher Education Research & Development*, 23(3), 261–275.

Barrie, S. (2007), 'A conceptual framework for the teaching and learning of generic graduate attributes', *Studies in Higher Education*, 32(4), 439–458.

Becker, G. S. (1964), *Human Capital*, Chicago: University of Chicago Press.

Bennett, D., Knight, E., Divan, A. and Bell, K. (2019), 'Marketing graduate employability: the language of employability', in J. Higgs, W. Letts and G. Crisp (eds), *Education for Employability (Volume 2): Learning for Future Possibilities*, Leiden: Brill, pp. 105–116.

Berry, R. and Routon, W. (2020), 'Soft skill change perceptions of accounting majors: current practitioner views versus their own reality', *Journal of Accounting Education*, 53. doi: https://doi.org/10.1016/j.jaccedu.2020.100691.

Holmes, L. (2013), 'Competing perspectives on graduate employability: possession, position or process?', *Studies in Higher Education*, 38(4), 538–554.

Holmes, L. (2015), 'Becoming a graduate: the warranting of an emergent identity', *Education + Training*, 57(2), 219–238.

Ioannou, C. A. (2019), *Business, Human Resources and Education System: Research in Industrial Enterprises, Findings and Policy Proposals* (in Greek), Athens: Hellenic Federation of Enterprises (SEV).

Pincus, K. V., Stout, D. E., Sorensen, J. E., Stocks, K. D. and Lawson, R. A. (2017), 'Forces for change in higher education and implications for the accounting academy', *Journal of Accounting Education*, 40, 1–18.

Tholen, G. (2015), 'What can research into graduate employability tell us about agency and structure?', *British Journal of Sociology of Education*, 36(5), 766–784.

Tomlinson, M. (2012), 'Graduate employability: a review of conceptual and empirical themes', *Higher Education Policy*, 25(4), 407–431.

Tomlinson, M. (2017), 'Forms of graduate capital and their relationship to graduate employability', *Education + Training*, 59(4), 338–352.

Tymon, A. (2013), 'The student perspective on employability', *Studies in Higher Education*, 38(6) 841–856.

Yorke, M. and Knight, P. (2006), *Embedding Employability into the Curriculum* (Learning and Employability Series, No 3), York: Higher Education Academy.

REFLECTION

From an accounting graduate

Definitely... the degree does give you skills that are useful in your job. Yes, absolutely yes. But a degree on its own is not enough.

I think critical thinking is more in the hands of the professor to develop, by asking questions and encouraging students to challenge their understanding. Setting tough questions which require a lot of critical thinking in order to be solved is helpful, and one will fail if one can't do this.

I think hard-working is inherent. I don't think you can learn this from school and I don't think the university can teach you. I think you can achieve this at an early age. However, after someone is about ten years old they are either hard working or not. You don't have any hope in changing someone who wants to be lazy.

PART III

Employability and the curriculum

8. Employer input to curriculum and assessment

Gillian O'Brien and Darren Siggers

Embedding interaction with employers into the curriculum has been a hot topic in the higher education (HE) and graduate recruitment sector for many years. Exposing students to employer priorities and decision-making during their studies has been shown to have a positive effect on their employability prospects (Mason et al., 2009). It can help students, whatever their subject of study, to identify the links between their education and their employability. It is no surprise then that this is where many careers professionals are starting to dedicate more of their time.

The University of Liverpool Careers and Employability team prioritise the development of curricular embedded employability, enabled through the introduction of a student-led peer-to-peer frontline service (see Chapter 13). As a result of this prioritisation, 49 per cent of undergraduate courses now have employability embedded within them, enabling the introduction of employers to students and facilitating connection with them in a variety of ways. This approach is also reflected in the employer engagement strategy, which focuses on building mutually beneficial partnerships and creating innovative and relevant opportunities that expose the students to industry connections throughout their university journey.

A FRAMEWORK FOR EMBEDDING EMPLOYERS

A range of opportunities for embedding employers in the curriculum has been developed, which are centred on students' active participation in immersive work-based experiences, self-reflection, self-awareness, and peer learning. The main aim is to develop students' employability skills by giving them the opportunity to apply their academic skills to industry-related tasks. Employers are key to making this happen. The range of opportunities available to employers to engage with the curriculum includes:

- *Employer-led challenges*: collaboration with employers to set real-world projects for students, relevant to their sector and the students' discipline.

- *Embedded internships*: work-based learning opportunities undertaken as part of a module.
- *Employer perspective on modular activities*: industry representatives provide a contextual framework around activities and assessments within the curriculum (this might be subject-specific or may focus on cross-cutting themes such as sustainability, inclusion and ethics). This can also involve employer representatives acting as independent consultants via industrial liaison boards.
- *Skills development*: employer-led skills development within modules, helping students achieve intended learning outcomes and skills gains (either in line with corresponding assessments, or as stand-alone activities). This may also involve employers providing insights into recruitment processes to enhance the recruitment skills of students.

ENHANCING TEACHING, ENABLING INCLUSION AND CREATING INDUSTRY CONNECTIONS AT SCALE

For students, academics, careers professionals and employers, there are significant benefits from involving employers within the academic curriculum.

Embedded employability enables career messaging to be scaled to large numbers of students in a place that makes sense to them and removes the requirement for students to opt in to extra-curricular employability activities. Engaging employers as part of this links students with industry connections from the comfort of their compulsory academic modules. It allows careers teams to focus on developing high-impact employer activities which can provide all participating students with the opportunity to develop, practise and articulate the skills we know graduate recruiters demand.

'Widening participation' groups spend less time engaging in university-linked extra-curricular initiatives than students who are not from disadvantaged backgrounds, and these initiatives are things which employers identify as important in their shortlisting (Stuart et al., 2011). Embedding employability within a degree programme makes it accessible to all; so engaging employers in large-scale modules ensures that all students benefit. This in turn provides employers with exposure to a diverse talent pool that does not ordinarily attend their university-led extra-curricular activities (Stuart et al., 2011) and is therefore otherwise hard to reach, which in turn supports organisational priorities such as achieving diversity. This approach also provides employability support and connections to those students who need it most.

Embedding employers into the curriculum can help students make the links between their education and their employability. An employer-informed approach to any curriculum design or delivery can support universities in ensuring that teaching remains relevant to the world of work. Students can hear an employer's perspective at first hand, acting as a reinforcement of key messages provided by careers teams and academics. Chadwick et al. (2012) suggest that to develop work-related skills beyond a baseline, universities require realism and authenticity, and that authenticity is provided principally by employer engagement (in all its forms).

From an employer's perspective, this is a more targeted approach to engaging with students outside traditional campus activities. Depending on the nature of the employer input, this can also provide them with an extra resource dedicated to a real business issue. Following the restrictions of the Covid-19 pandemic, employer guides to campus engagement, from organisations such as the Institute of Student Employers (Hooley, 2020), listed employer involvement in curricular work as one of the few ways employers could promote themselves to students. Continuing pressures on universities to demonstrate how students are supported to enhance their employability and achieve successful graduate outcomes has made embedding employability a priority within HE (Tibby and Norton, 2020). It is expected that this increased exposure of employers to curricular activity, coupled with these pressures within HE, mean it is likely employers will increasingly look to capitalise on these opportunities as a key avenue within their campus attraction strategies.

CONSIDERATIONS AND CHALLENGES

At the University of Liverpool, a holistically redesigned approach to the careers and employability offer enables it to achieve scale in employability delivery and in turn, increase student and employer engagement. However, the success of embedding employers in the curriculum requires careful module design and a collaborative effort between academics, careers and employability professionals and industrial partners.

To embed employers effectively, consideration needs to be given to the degree programme (and what that already offers in terms of wider skills and experience), the students in question (and their place in the student journey), the module (percentage of cohort and learning outcomes) as well as the delivery style. Beyond this, employability development requires students to be aware of what they are learning and why (Knight and Yorke, 2003), taking care to embed employer activity in such way that students explicitly see the discipline-specific relevance of the skills developed. Some students can find it difficult to make the connection between an experience, employability development and the professional applications of their learning. The embedding of meaningful pedagogical processes for employability development, such as the SEAL (situation, effect, action, learning) reflective process proposed by Reid et al. (2021), is of vital importance.

Whilst bringing employers into the curriculum is a great way to add value to what is already there for students, it requires practitioners to think and work in new ways. This can be a challenging and complex process that all stakeholders need to navigate. Embedding employability will require academics, careers staff and industry partners to think about alternative methods for engaging students. This could go against the grain of what a 'traditional' module and 'traditional' careers service offer may look like.

A good partnership with industrial contacts is needed to bring together the nature of the discipline and the reality of working within the discipline in industry. Once an opportunity for collaboration has been identified, the opportunity for the appropriate inclusion of employer partners must provide for mutual benefit. It can be time-intensive to engage the right employers at the right time, so employer engagement professionals should be utilised by academics to support this process.

EMPLOYERS IN THE CURRICULUM – IN PRACTICE AT THE UNIVERSITY OF LIVERPOOL

Case Study 1: An Example of Embedded Real-World Employer Projects

The 'Professional Projects and Employability in Mathematics' final year module, developed in a Department of Mathematical Sciences and Careers and Employability collaboration, embeds three real-world mathematical group projects (designed and delivered in collaboration with employers) as the main assessment tool. This provides students with a range of opportunities to enhance their skills for graduate employment; this is reflected in the module learning outcomes, authentic assessments, reflective writing pieces, and an individual employability skills portfolio. Reflective activities were important in the module design as employability development requires students to be aware of what they are learning and why (Knight and Yorke, 2003).

It is important that from the outset (and throughout) effort is put into engaging the students with the purpose of the module and the use of non-standard teaching methods, as this module has a different style and focus to more traditional mathematics modules (Russell and Rowlett, 2018). An application process was designed as part of module registration; students write a short 'application', outlining their motivations for choosing this module.

Module teaching engages students with project briefings and activities on specific skill areas, such as presentation skills, commercial awareness, video interview techniques, and report writing for a client, taking an active learning approach. These sessions are delivered and designed by careers staff. In addition, laboratory sessions are used for in-depth group project work.

The three real-world group projects each have a slightly different focus and are designed in partnership with industrial partners to provide students with genuine problems which mathematicians face within graduate-level employment. This explicit embedding approach aims to engage students by developing skills through work on discipline-specific projects. Here, students appreciate the additional considerations required to complete mathematical work for a specific audience (the employer) and commented that they viewed this as important in their development as mathematicians (Russell and Rowlett, 2018).

The group-project outputs (written reports and group presentations) are assessed using a grade-based marking scheme (Russell, 2019). Input on the reports and presentations (particularly the Q&A section of the presentations) is provided by the industrial partners who designed the projects. This provides additional realism for students, an additional check that students are addressing the 'client' concerns (from the brief), and highlights to students the potential impact of their mathematical analysis on the organisation and sector concerned. Reflection forms a key element of the module. Short reflective pieces are completed frequently as part of the module assessment, with students considering their approaches to the tasks and the skills they have developed through participation in module activities.

The impact

The module learning outcomes are skills-based and emphasise the importance of conducting thorough mathematical investigations and communicating results to client audiences in group presentations and written reports. The group projects and module sessions provide opportunities for students to explore their own professional competencies. Students' assessments of their own skills over the course of this module have demonstrated positive change; at the beginning and end of the module a survey was distributed, asking students to rate their competence in 12 professional skills. Median scores for several of the skills increased in the second self-assessment compared with the first (Russell and Rowlett, 2018).

When reflecting on their module experience, students identified the benefits of studying this module (compared to more traditional mathematics modules they have studied). A recurrent theme within module reflections is the positive benefit of the module activities on student confidence and preparedness for graduate employment. The focus on skills development was aided by the mathematical (subject) content, with feedback highlighting how direct employer involvement added a relevance to the project work (Russell and Rowlett, 2018).

Success story from an employer's perspective

One project was designed in collaboration with Very Group. The analytics department within this organisation provided real data from customer interactions with their website. Students were tasked with analysing this data, identifying trends in behaviour and developing recommendations on how Very could create more high-value customers.

The group deemed to have delivered the best presentation were invited to visit Very Group HQ. This visit introduced students to people in a range of roles (many of which they never knew existed), with students encouraged to consider the variety of career areas they could go into with a maths degree.

For the Very Group, this opportunity provided them with guaranteed exposure to a talent pool of students who do not ordinarily attend their campus events, whilst also providing an extra resource dedicated to a real business issue.

Case Study 2: An Example of Embedded Employer-Led Skills Development

In response to digital technologies becoming the norm for hiring and selection (Hooley, 2021) and evidence from the Institute of Student Employers (2020) showing that one of the biggest skills employers feel graduates lack is commercial awareness, the School of Life Sciences (SoLS) and Careers and Employability re-imagined how we should develop and assess employability skills across the School. Whilst reviewing the curriculum, there was a recognition that students do gain the key subject-specific skills required by industry; however, improvements could be made in supporting students with commercial awareness and recruitment skills. A cross-School second-year module was identified as an appropriate place to address these needs; these could be linked to student learning outcomes, module assessment could be utilised, and it would engage all students within the School.

A particular challenge was how a task could be designed that would feel relevant to a group of students with diverse career interests; there are about 430 students within each year group of the School, split across 12 degree programmes (ranging from Anatomy and Human Biology to Zoology). Aligning with an existing extra-curricular employability activity that involves employers was identified as the best approach. For a number of years, the extra-curricular Life Science Employability Week initiative provided opportunities for students to network with employers, attend industry talks, and participate in employability workshops. Typically, about 20 per cent of the undergraduates within SoLS would attend an activity during this week. Aligning curricular activity to this initiative would offer several mutual benefits; most significantly, it was anticipated that there would be improved student engagement across the week (as it would become part of the module's teaching) which in turn would provide a more attractive opportunity for employers to engage with.

The activity – commercial awareness video interview assessment

Students chose one of seven potential future employers to research during Life Science Employability Week. They then completed an asynchronous video interview using video interview software, answering four questions relevant to their chosen employer. This accounted for 12.5 per cent of the module mark. All assessments were marked by academics using an assessment rubric created by the careers team.

From a teaching perspective, the careers team delivered lectures covering an introduction to commercial awareness, the application process, digital interviews, and researching an employer. A tutorial (delivered by academic advisors) supported student understanding of these topics and provided a practical exercise to familiarise students with self-reflection and articulating themselves within the recruitment process. All students had access to a formative assessment opportunity, utilising the artificial intelligence-based feedback system within the video interview software.

Employer input was light touch. By aligning to an existing activity, there was only a small time commitment required from the participating employers. All employers provided online talks and Q&As during Life Science Employability Week (as in previous years); however, now they also included insights and learning points for students in relation to their industry and relevant transferable skills to support students' wider understanding of their business. In addition, each employer filmed an interview introduction and interview questions to be used for the assessment, to ensure students had an authentic interview experience.

The impact

Employers were brought into the curriculum by aligning an existing careers event to the module and using digital interview technology to develop digital fluency and commercial awareness in order to raise student confidence and enhance employability skills. The design of the activity and use of digital interview technology enabled the development of an authentic assessment that was scalable for about 430 students. Students engaged directly with scientific and non-scientific employers, carried out research to develop their sector knowledge and then completed a digital video interview that replicated part of the recruitment experience.

The assessment provides clear links between the core module content/ assessment and the extra-curricular employability week. Linking the employability week to the assessment made the week unmissable for students. Of the 430 students registered for the module, 395 students completed a digital video interview and 329 students connected with employers during Life Sciences Employability Week (a 62 per cent increase on those that attended in previous years without an attached assessment). Student confidence in completing a video interview increased by 44.6 per cent and in demonstrating commercial awareness by 30 per cent.

CONCLUSION

It is reasonable to assume that given current challenges within HE, alongside the clear benefits of embedding employers within the curriculum, this approach is likely to continue to increase in use in the coming years. The development of more success stories, similar to those included in this chapter, evidencing how this works in practice as well as showcasing the benefits for all parties, will support the evolution of this approach.

The success across the sector of more embedded employer activity in the curriculum will also require careful module design and, in most cases, improved collaborative effort between academics, careers and employability professionals and graduate recruiters.

Investment in this approach is something that we at Liverpool would highly recommend because when we get it right, embedded employer-connected employability activity is difficult to fault.

REFERENCES

Chadwick, E., Waldock, J., Bradshaw, N., Orpin, L., McNulty, D., Singh, M., Haydock, T., Ellis, C., Rowlett, P. and Steele, N. (2012), 'How realistic is work-related learning, and how realistic should it be?', in J. Waldock and P. Rowlett (eds), *Employer Engagement in Undergraduate Mathematics*, Birmingham: The Higher Education Academy, and Maths, Stats and OR Network, pp. 47–51.

Hooley, T. (2020), 'What are employers looking for? Student recruitment in the 2020s', *Institute of Student Employers Graduate Employability Conference 2020*. Available at: https://adventuresincareerdevelopment.wordpress.com/2020/06/26/what-are-employers-looking-for-student-recruitment-in-the-2020s/ (accessed: 22 January 2023).

Hooley, T. (2021), 'Bouncing back: graduate recruitment after the pandemic'. *Prospects Luminate*. Available at: https://luminate.prospects.ac.uk/bouncing-back-graduate-recruitment-after-the-pandemic (accessed: 9 January 2023).

Institute of Student Employers (2020), *It's virtually autumn*. ISE Webinar. Available at: https://www.youtube.com/watch?v=5ChYYJQGOtQ (accessed: 22 January 2023).

Knight, P. T. and Yorke, M (2003), 'Employability and good learning in higher education', *Teaching in Higher Education*, 8(1), 3–16.

Mason, G., Williams, G. and Cranmer, S. (2009), 'Employability skills initiatives in higher education: what effects do they have on graduate labour market outcomes?', *Education Economics*, 17(1), 1–30.

Reid, A., Richards, A. and Willox, D. (2021), 'Connecting experiences to employability through a meaning-making approach to learning', *Journal of Teaching and Learning for Graduate Employability*, 12(2), 99–113.

Russell, E. J. (2019), 'Making the grade: supporting mathematics students in understanding the use of grade-based marking criteria for assessments', *MSOR Connections*, 17(2), 68–74.

Russell, E. J. and Rowlett, P. (2018), 'Professional skills development for mathematics undergraduates', *Higher Education, Skills and Work-Based Learning*, 9(3), 374–386.

Stuart, M., Lido, C., Morgan, J., Solomon, L. and May, S. (2011), 'The impact of engagement with extracurricular activities on the student experience and graduate outcomes for widening participation populations', *Active Learning in Higher Education*, 12(3), 203–215.

Tibby, M. and Norton, S. (2020), *Essential frameworks for enhancing student success: embedding employability. A guide to the Advance HE Framework*. York: AdvanceHE.

REFLECTION

From an HR director in service banking

Besides knowledge of the subject area, students need to have analytical capacity, be adaptable, have a good demeanour and be able to work in a team with other colleagues.

I believe these skills can be developed while at university.

They can work together in team projects, and one can help the other. Also, another important factor is to be able to work under pressure. In our market we have to be able to respond to cut-off times which you cannot lose, so I'm looking for people who can respond quickly and be responsible, you cannot say 'I'll do it later' – this might result in losing a deadline. The picture the client has of us is very important. We are client focused. Obviously, we are being evaluated by the client since we are a service agent transaction bank which makes the client our top priority. We offer them top services, especially since our clients are foreign so we have to be able to compete with other investment bankers, so we give extra attention to our personnel to have a good training and being able to work under pressure, and to have team spirit.

9. Real work opportunities in the curriculum: three different approaches

Charles Hancock, Tracy Powell, John Day and Alison Lawson

INTRODUCTION

Employability is becoming ever more important in higher education, with universities seeking to equip their graduates with the skills, knowledge and behaviours needed for successful careers. Academics are seeking to embed employability in their teaching in a variety of ways, to avoid a stand-alone skills-focused module tailored to specific subject areas or careers, which can be perceived by students as off-topic and dull. This chapter presents three ways in which employability has been embedded in the curriculum at Derby Business School at the University of Derby. Each has been successful and has not only embedded the necessary learning but has fully engaged the learners such that they enjoyed the learning and understood the benefits.

CASE STUDY 1: FOSTERING ALUMNI-ENGAGED STUDENT PROJECTS

Derby Business School enhances employability through using live project briefs where possible. This case study concerns a live project in the Agency Executive module, which is a core module for 2nd year Marketing students. The module has hosted alumni-derived real-world projects, including working with local car dealerships, breweries and other SMEs as well as large international companies based in the region. A result is that the module is particularly well received by students and employers. It enjoys great feedback year on year with high participation rates and very high-quality work produced.

This student success is delivered by the model shown in Figure 9.1. The Alumni Engaged Student Projects (AESP) process starts by using the LinkedIn platform to identify various settled alumni in their chosen career pathway, normally two years after graduation. The choice of alumni and their employer must be carefully matched to ensure an interesting project can be defined which provides sufficient employability skill development, academic challenge, and enjoyment. Once a suitable alumnus is identified, stage 2 (the development stage) can commence. Professional contact must be made, to include establishing the purpose of the working relationship with both the alumnus and the host organisation. Stage 3 is the creation of the live brief, which must be relevant for both the host employer and the students' learning outcomes. The project should have real purpose for the organisation and inspire students to fully engage with it. A defined brief is further developed to include a live launch by the alumnus and specific grading criteria to reflect the project's nature. This stage takes time, so is best scheduled a month or two before the teaching commences.

The engagement stage, stage 4, is very important for both students and the employer, as the students should relate to the alumnus briefing them on the project. This approach has been particularly successful as students are inspired to see that previous graduates are successful when they leave university and find meaningful careers in their respective academic disciplines. This creates an instant connection between the alumnus, the students, the employer and the project.

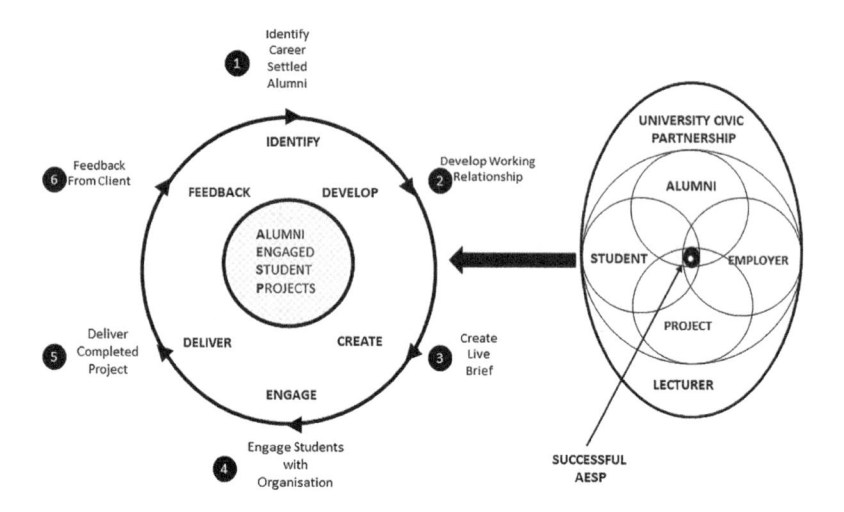

Source: Charles Hancock.

Figure 9.1   Model for fostering alumni engaged student projects

To realise the most from the engagement stage, students are encouraged to participate in a live question and answer session, firstly in relation to the brief and then also with reference to the alumnus' career success and their journey to securing employment. The alumnus provides their contact details to students for follow-up questions regarding the live brief. In addition, part way through the process the alumnus may provide some initial feedback on the progress of part 1 of the project, normally a stage for pitching ideas. Additional activities are also used, such as live video call Q&A sessions, and/or a physical event or a visit to the employer to further enhance the project engagement.

For example, during a recent project, students were invited to attend a collaborative enterprise venue where they participated in a sensory live brewing and tasting experience provided by a local brewery to fully immerse themselves in the project. One student said, 'This live event brought the whole assignment to life and really provided an understanding of marketing in a real-world setting.'

The project outcomes can be delivered to the alumnus and employer (stage 5). This can be achieved in several ways, such as through poster presentations, formal presentations, video pitches or electronic brochures; the latter two are particularly useful during remote learning or if the employer is based some distance away.

The key to delivering the project brief is to ensure that clarity is first established for the students when designing the brief, ensuring that the organisation knows what it wants to achieve and to create something which is realistic and achievable in a set time frame. An alumnus recently involved in the module said:

> Working with students is so useful for us as an organisation, as it enabled us to see different solutions which we hadn't considered or our consultants hadn't come up with, it's been so helpful to see the ideas through many different eyes and these are our future professionals and perhaps customers too.

The final stage in the process is feedback to students (stage 6). This is an important stage as it enables the alumnus and the employer to feed back directly to students on their ideas and solutions. It enables the module team to reflect upon the success of the brief and whether students have learned the relevant skills during the project.

Employability Benefits of Alumni-engaged Projects

The AESP should offer:

- an opportunity to improve professional communication with a live client;
- inspiration and aspiration for a graduate career choice;
- time management skills by working to client deadlines;

- group working by delegating tasks amongst a team;
- creative skills in coming up with real solutions;
- a continuing relationship with alumni so students can network;
- an opportunity to apply research to current and topical business issues.

In conclusion, AESP are beneficial to all parties: the alumni, the students, the employer and the module team. A real-world live brief set by an alumnus creates credibility and better engagement with current students due to relatedness with someone who has recently been through the university programme and successfully engaged on their career journey.

CASE STUDY 2: USING SOCIAL MEDIA IN AN ASSESSMENT TO BUILD STUDENT EMPLOYABILITY

A desire for students to be fully prepared to embark on a placement or internship was the starting point for a new module with a creative assessment. The aim was to develop the 'set of achievements, skills, understandings and personal attributes – that make graduates more likely to gain employment' (Yorke, 2004/2006). Delivering the module at level 4 (first year undergraduate) would maximise the benefit of their learning, so that they could apply for internships and placements with confidence.

A further aspiration was to support small organisations and charities in the local community who are often challenged with small budgets and limited capabilities, especially in marketing and social media. The module structure was designed so that it would enhance the company's social media campaigns and enable students to showcase their capabilities, knowledge and skills to a national (and sometimes international) audience.

The Task

Working in small groups, students were assigned a case-study organisation and used their theoretical learning within the classroom, and their own independent research, to develop engaging content to be published on Twitter. They were left in charge of tweets for their organisation for a total of four to six weeks. Tweetdeck was used to schedule tweets appropriately and to allow them to be checked by the organisation before publishing. Key features of the assessment were as follows.

- A selection of organisations was offered to students so they could choose one that they felt most interested in or passionate about – this resulted in students quickly developing a passion for their respective organisations.

- Students met the companies to discuss and develop their understanding of the brand and culture.
- Students developed SMART objectives with company representatives.
- Students implemented the campaign using classroom learning.
- Students used a professional platform to communicate with each other and the organisation (e.g. Microsoft Teams).
- Soft skills such as communication, professionalism and working effectively in teams were linked to learning outcomes (Finch et al., 2013).

To ensure engagement and the constant progression of the Twitter campaigns, continuous assessment was used. This took two forms.

1. The Twitter page itself: students had to meet criteria agreed with the organisation, such as a minimum number of tweets per week including video or animated tweets, photo tweets and hashtags to be used. Evidence of the tweets, the content calendar produced and the communication between the students and the organisation were captured on the Microsoft Teams site and milestones had to be met. Other software could be used to do this, including Blackboard and Moodle.
2. Students presented their critical evaluation of the theories used to develop their content at several points during the semester. Presentations were assessed in front of the whole class to simulate a real business scenario.

Tips for Success

The background planning to this module assignment is imperative for success. Key points for success were as follows.

- Using business development managers and local charity liaison officers can help to reach out to local companies and pitch the project.
- The initial meeting between organisations and students was overseen by the module team so that good foundation principles were laid. Students were encouraged to prepare for their meeting by preparing questions based on their research about the organisation.
- Some time was needed in the seminars for students to write their tweets following the learning from that session. This ensured that progress continued to be made and checked understanding.

Adaptation to Other Subject Areas

The focus was on the content of the posts. The act of putting the content on social media meant that students needed to make their topic interesting to others, take pride in their work and really demonstrate what they were learning at university. One student said: 'Working with you has helped us to develop our existing skills and knowledge whilst managing a professional Twitter account.'

Other examples of using social media teaching and learning could include:

- Using LinkedIn, for an engineering firm, might include references to theory about why or how a certain product works. This in-depth knowledge would give other companies viewing the post confidence in the product and could generate sales for the organisation.
- Facebook can be used to give information to the public in a special interest group around the subject area.
- Instagram could be used to get students to use pictures that tell a story of a historical chapter, or the development of mathematical formulae.

Outcomes

This was an important project for the students as they learnt to turn their social media skills to use in a business context, learning the appropriate language and tone for organisations and understanding how different business-to-consumer communications are from chatting with friends. Using the medium of social media, and asking students to display their content on an international forum, meant that students gained confidence in their ability and knowledge. The students really saw an outcome of their work and the importance of being thorough and accurate. One student said: 'We are proud of our work and happy to tell you we have gained you 144 followers, helped you post over 180 tweets and upped engagement levels on your page.'

Organisations involved in this project were delighted that their online presence had been much improved. For example, one charitable organisation said:

> ... the team have consistently kept in touch, delivered a consistent message, used their own initiative to maximise the impact in a fun and light-hearted way. We have never had an enquiry via social media before, but we have now, which demonstrates their impact, I hope all those involved enjoyed it as much as I did.

The organisations that worked on this project were so impressed by the work output that three internships were created. There were 19 companies involved in this project, extending the reach of the university, as many of these were new relationships.

CASE STUDY 3: WORKPLACE DEVELOPMENT

The Workplace Development Module (WDM) is a 2nd year module in the BSc (Hons) in Logistics and Supply Chain Management. It is an applied module with the main purpose of allowing students to work on projects within an external logistics organisation and to begin to understand the links between the theory they have learned in the classroom and practice in the real world.

From pre-validation discussions with potential employers, a number of key areas were identified as attributes that would be valued in graduates. Amongst these the ability to work on projects within diverse groups and to be able to present findings and recommendations were the most frequently identified. An understanding of the practicalities of the workplace or 'real world' was also prominent in discussions. Whilst students can clearly perform group work and presentations within the classroom, it was felt that the best way to emulate 'real-world' situations would be to set them in the workplace.

The module is a 40-credit through module, i.e., taught throughout one academic year. Typically, students spend eight or nine full days (one day per week) within a logistics organisation. At the end of this period, they will present their findings and recommendations to key managers at the organisation.

The other time in the module is allocated to briefings, linking theory with practice and assessment preparation.

The assessment has three key components:

1. Literature review. Students identify an area they have observed during their time in the organisation and write a 2000-word literature review. In essence they must discuss what the theory tells them about the area.
2. A report that compares the main findings of the literature review with the practice they observed during their projects. The report must include key recommendations for the organisation and/or similar organisations.
3. A 500-word reflective document on how they operated as a group. Students are asked to analyse their contribution to the group and what key learning points they will take from the experience.

A number of organisations have been involved, including warehousing and distribution centres for international logistics organisations, offering students the opportunity to work with companies in sectors such as groceries, automotive and clothes retail. All the organisations have both warehouse and transport functions, giving students a good overview of key logistics activities. The projects assigned to students by these organisations have included the following:

1. Groceries distributor
   - transport – review the current tote returns process and understand/assess the efficiencies or savings if we added an extra layer of totes on the vehicle;
   - warehouse – complete a review of beer/wines/spirits pick performance rates/manual chamber and present your findings/recommendations for improvements.
2. Automotive logistics
   - planning and processing of reverse logistics;
   - capacity planning and the effects on financial performance;
   - review and make recommendations for warehouse layout after reduction in space.
3. UK distribution centre for fashion retailer
   - possible use and application of radio frequency identification (RFID) technology;
   - optimising container shipments to UK from India;
   - improving employee on-site communications;
   - reducing waste incurred from reverse logistics (returns).
4. UK distribution for fashion retailer
   - reducing waste on site;
   - optimising use of agency labour;
   - new developments in order-picking technology and possible applications.

Projects with a broader specification tend to work better than those with more detail. These give students a wide scope of reference and tend to take advantage of two key attributes which they bring to the organisation, namely a fresh pair of eyes and no preconceptions. Projects which are highly detailed obviously limit scope but also tend to be seeking recommendations and justification for the project proposers' ideas.

Group Dynamics and Learning

The module has proven extremely valuable in developing students' understanding of all the key elements and dynamics involved in group work, often through things going wrong. Examples include allocation of tasks that don't match students' skills, e.g. data collection and analysis, vital tasks given to a single individual who does not complete on time, and managing group members' absence.

When looking at the reflective element of the assessment, it is clear that this has been the single largest learning area to the point where there appears to be better learning within groups that experienced and overcame issues rather than those which worked well from the outset.

Success Stories

There have been many examples of students' recommendations being implemented. One of the most notable is from a fashion retail distributor. The project brief was to investigate the possible use and application of RFID technology. Given a brief that said no more than 'How can we use RFID?', students researched and recommended a number of applications which were subsequently presented to the organisation's board and then implemented in full.

The Director of Logistics at the organisation emailed the module leader to compliment the student group. Having presented the students' ideas to the board in the form of a business plan, the Director was given the go-ahead for implementation straightaway. The students had made such a strong case that the board was able to give a very quick decision and the steps for implementation had already been set out – a company was approached for the tags and another for the hardware and software. This was an example of a student project leading to clear improvement in business processes for a large organisation.

Another successful project for one organisation was considered so impressive by the client that they entered it as a project in the National Logistics Awards in 2019. They won the Future Skills Award in recognition of the work done with students on this module. This recognition of the impact of projects completed in the Workplace Development module is excellent reinforcement for the students that their skills and knowledge are applicable, well regarded and sought after in professional practice.

SUMMARY AND CONCLUSION

The three case studies presented here embed employability skills in three very different ways – one through working with a client organisation following a brief, one working together with a client organisation to manage a specific function for a period of weeks and one in which students work one day a week at an organisation while working on a live project to solve a problem on site. The skills built through working on these projects are not only the subject-specific technical skills required in the roles, but general transferable skills such as group working, presentation, data collection and research, analysis, communication and planning. Coupled with the theoretical underpinning delivered in the classroom alongside the client projects, this gives the students a great opportunity to apply theory in practice. Knowledge of the subject develops and deepens alongside knowledge and experience of professional practice, with skills woven into the projects rather than taught separately. Having had a taste of real-world learning, students are better equipped and more enthusiastic about applying for internships, placements and graduate roles.

REFERENCES

Finch, D. J., Hamilton, L. K. Baldwin, R. and Zehner, M. (2013), 'An exploratory study of factors affecting undergraduate employability', *Education + Training*, 55(7), 681–704.

Yorke, M. (2004/2006), *Employability in Higher Education: What It Is – What It Is Not*, York: Higher Education Academy.

REFLECTION

From a Biomedical Science student

The course I am currently studying, is all science core subjects and is helping me to understand basic principles of health and medicine. I am genuinely enjoying this course, including all practical aspects in the laboratory, where I performed well and gained valuable experience and skills, such as meticulous attention to detail, teamworking, analytical thinking, communication, and time management. During my academic year, the university added a personal professional development module. This module gives me academic and co-curricular activities, extra-curricular activities, and employability activities. This whole aspect of this specific module is very beneficial to building career opportunities and accumulating a wide range of skills.

The realisation of multiple options after the first year of my degree has broadened due to seminars and workshops the university organised for students. Attending the seminars and workshops opened up an employability opportunity that encouraged me to apply to be a student ambassador. This gave me the confidence to speak with others, whilst earning money gave me a self-reliable and positive attitude while studying. I recently started working as a community engagement coordinator, at the university, organised by the university, which has enhanced my IT skills. This demonstrates my willingness to dedicate my passion for learning, developing various new skills, which are essential for my future career aspirations.

10. Using a professional skills module to develop student confidence

Parminder Johal and Ruth Smith

INTRODUCTION

In this chapter the approach taken to embed employability within the BA (Hons) Accounting and Finance programme in the Derby Business School (DBS) at the University of Derby will be explained. Employability will be viewed from the perspective of pre-professional identity (PPI) formation. PPI relates to an understanding of, and connection with, the skills, qualities, conduct, culture and ideology of a student's intended profession. It is 'the sense of being a professional' (Paterson et al., 2002: 6) and 'work-related disposition and identity' (Tomlinson, 2012: 409).

Within higher education (HE) the Graduate Outcomes (GO) metric is, today, a key performance indicator across all UK universities. In percentage terms the GO survey measures graduates in employment or further study 15 months after they have graduated. This measure is now commonly known as the GO record and was implemented in the academic year 2017/2018 (HESA, 2022). GO data is now a component of yet another metric, introduced by the Office for Students (OfS) in the UK, which measures the 'projected completion and employment for students from the point of entry' (acronym: Proceed) (OfS, 2021). Such metrics, which form the basis for performance indicators, continue to emphasise the need for universities to address the 'employability' agenda.

In addition to the OfS, employability is also a key concern for students who see university as a route to employment. The consideration of employability is not a new phenomenon to HE or to the student body (Fallows and Steven, 2000; Yorke and Knight, 2004; Pegg et al., 2012; Tibby and Norton, 2020; Advance HE, n.d.), but the changing landscape in HE has resulted in universities prioritising and pursuing a number of options to address employability, with an overall aim to improve the GO metric. This improvement includes demonstrating that students are receiving value for money and that higher education institutions (HEIs) contribute to the local communities and national economy.

These varied approaches include embedding employability at programme level, either through the whole curriculum, the core elements of the curriculum, work-based learning relevant to individual components within the curriculum or modules specifically addressing employability. It is also embedded in parallel but external to the programme curriculum, through the career services available to students (Yorke and Knight, 2004; Bradley et al., 2022). In addition, HEIs have been supported and guided in their approach to addressing employability by organisations such as Advance HE (formerly known as the Higher Education Authority) through their 'framework for embedding employability' (Advance HE, n.d.) and bodies such as the Quality Assurance Agency (QAA), an independent body responsible for the quality of education in the UK (QAA, 2017).

The various approaches to employability recognise that a 'one size fits all' approach to employability would not be appropriate for all HEIs. At DBS a stand-alone module, titled 'Professional Development for Accounting and Finance Graduates' (PDAFG), is used as the anchor within an undergraduate degree programme, to embed, connect and develop employability skills throughout the programme curriculum. Although the module is a stand-alone module, it is designed with consideration for its fit, not only with the wider programme, but also with the parallel provision of the Careers Employment Service (CES), amongst other stakeholder groups. Being part of a well-designed programme curriculum helps to scaffold learning and contribute to developing the student's skill set for employability in a more holistic manner.

A NEW MODULE – A REVISED APPROACH

Prior to the PDAFG module, a generic 'employability' module was common across all the undergraduate programmes; thus, DBS appeared to be pursuing a 'one size fits all' approach to addressing employability, or as suggested by Cranmer (2006), a 'bolt-on' approach, also referred to as an 'embedded approach', whereby employability is limited to only one or two modules in the programme. However, following feedback from students on the Accounting and Finance degree programme, it was highlighted that students felt this module did not adequately reflect the accounting and finance profession, the link to the profession was lacking and the focus on employability was too generic. This feedback reflected the need to develop a connection with the students' intended profession: to develop a pre-professional identity (Jackson, 2016).

Whilst it is appreciated that employability skills are transferable (Sithole, 2015), it is also recognised that employers look for technical competence specific to the profession and these technical skills should not be put second to the non-technical, soft skills (Rebele and St Pierre, 2019). In response to the module feedback, a review of the module took place to ensure that it provided students with relatable examples for their intended career, the opportunities to develop their technical and non-technical skills and greater awareness of the culture and ideology of the finance profession. The review and revisions to the module were informed by reports from organisations such as Advance HE, employability frameworks, and consultation with the CES and graduates. The outcome of the review resulted in abandoning the generic single module and instead replacing it with a new, revised module, namely PDAFG, designed to ensure it was specific to the student's programme of study and career aspirations. Although one module was replaced with another, DBS moved away from the 'bolt on' approach (Cranmer, 2006) to a combination of 'bolt on' and the 'parallel' approach. The latter approach addresses employability through the universities' CES and is a popular approach amongst many universities (Bradley et al., 2021). However, in isolation, this approach does not always capture and/or engage the majority of students. For this reason, the combined approach required the PDAFG module and the CES to work closely together.

The PDAFG module was created without using existing materials to ensure its content was relevant to enhancing skills relevant to the profession; to enhance familiarity with the accounting jargon and to build confidence. It also included content to better prepare the students for the recruitment process, developed with employers seeking graduates for an accounting and finance-based role. Therefore, the module familiarised the students with the 'recruitment journey' that lay ahead, providing students with the opportunity to identify their skills gaps, which they could then address through a personal action plan.

The module takes the student through a personal development journey, during which students assess their values, interests, skills and career aspirations and use this information to prepare the process of developing their accounting and finance graduate identity. To this end a range of key transferable skills expected of accounting and finance graduates are explored, such as leadership and enterprise capabilities, supporting talent development, commercial awareness, professional scepticism, communications, report writing, presenting skills, coaching and emotional intelligence (Aryanti and Adhariani, 2020). These skills are addressed within the context of the technical capabilities required of the profession. Students use their learning from other modules in the same year and from the previous year to recognise and further practise problem solving and decision making, using analytical modelling tools such as spreadsheets, advanced Excel, and using accounting software commonly used by employers. Central to their learning is the need to explore appropriate behaviours and a positive attitude (accaglobal, 2022).

PDAFG MODULE CONTENT AND STRUCTURE

The module learning outcomes were revised so that on successful completion of the module, students will be able to:

1. Understand the graduate accounting and finance skills and competencies required by either the accounting and finance function of organisations or in professional practice.
2. Articulate an understanding of the area of professional practice and body relevant to your career aspirations.
3. Reflect upon and evaluate your capabilities in relation to the skill requirements of your area of professional practice/body.

The PDAFG module is delivered in the first semester of the second year of the Accounting and Finance degree. This timing was based on careful consideration of the design of the whole programme. Throughout their first year the students are introduced to the different professional accounting bodies so that they can begin to formulate a picture for themselves of what a career in the finance profession would look like for them. The importance of integrating student membership of a professional body into the programme is that it enables students to identify, early on in their programme of study, with the career that they have chosen (Mistry, 2021). Students can begin to form a PPI (Jackson, 2016). This knowledge creates a powerful context for the PDAFG module.

Students are also required to draw on their learning from their first-year modules: for example, the academic skills module, which is not a prerequisite to the PDAFG module, helps students to reflect, research and articulate their learning. In addition, towards the end of their first year the students are invited to apply for an industrial placement year which, if the application is successful, they would commence after completion of their second year of study. This experience is a feed into the second year PDAFG module, which exposes the student to the world of applications, psychometric tests, interviews, assessment days, situational judgement scenarios and an awareness of gaps in their skill set and/or CV. It creates an eagerness to engage with extra-curricular activities to fill these gaps, and to practise and learn about how to prepare for employment in their chosen discipline area. This learning is relevant both for students seeking a placement year as part of their degree programme and/or graduate roles at the end of their degree programme.

The module content typically follows a schedule of delivery as outlined in Table 10.1 below. This is revisited every year following changes in the sector which are picked up through attendance at professional body and other rele-

Table 10.1 Schedule of delivery: professional development for Accounting and Finance graduates

Week	Lecture	Seminar
1	Introduction to module	Defining your career, personal branding and work-ready virtual experience
2	CV writing	Job market and applying for roles
3	Volunteering, internships and placements	CV workshop
4	How to prepare for online videos	Working online, meetings and online interview experience
5	Online and psychometric tests	Reflections and preparation for assessment centre
6	Online assessment centre	Questions and support with assessment
7	Commercial awareness	Use of accounting software (Sage)
8	Cover letters and business games	Use of accounting software (Sage)
9	LinkedIn	Spreadsheets
10	Ethics	Spreadsheets
11	Leaders and managers, motivation and appraisals	Spreadsheets
12	Time-controlled assessment	Drop-in session – poster guidance

vant conferences/webinars and through consultation with the DBS network of employers and other stakeholder groups.

Students are given the opportunity to practise and develop different skills through a variety of different activities, on a weekly basis. These include an accounting-based escape room, drawing on their accounting knowledge, problem solving and team working skills; reflective practice; mock interviews; CV writing; and drawing on peer review. Students are placed in different teams every week for the different tasks to simulate a more real-life experience within the workplace. A combination of the technical and non-technical skills is further put into practice as students progress to year three modules, which engage employers and real-world applied learning.

The module benefits from the support provided by the CES, which is aligned to the module delivery. Sessions on CV writing are introduced by the CES in a PDAFG session. This familiarises the students with the CES through an initial introduction so that they are more confident in approaching the CES for further support, particularly when it comes to psychometric tests and more practice for assessment centres.

Figure 10.1 illustrates the interaction between modules in years one, two and three. This demonstrates how the structure of the programme helps to scaffold the students' technical/non-technical skills, which are then fed into the PDAFG module for students to apply and include in their reflection. For example, the knowledge and learning on double entry from the Introduction to Financial Accounting module is applied in PDFAG when students learn how to use the Sage accounting software. This practice enables students to articulate their technical abilities and knowledge more confidently in an interview/assessment centre situation.

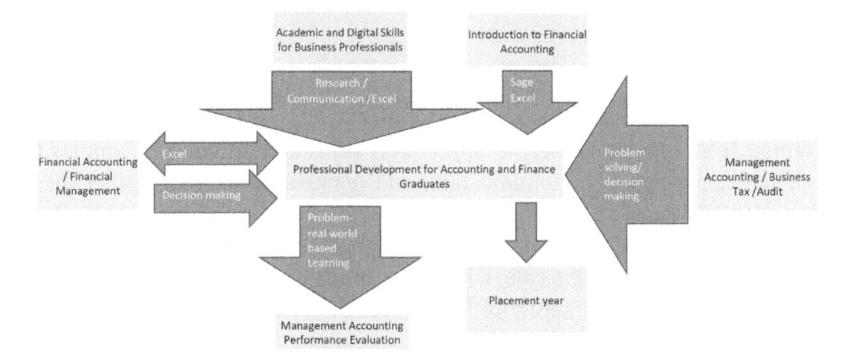

Figure 10.1   Professional development for Accounting and Finance graduates module structure

ASSESSMENT STRATEGY

Assessment on the PDAFG gives students the opportunity to benefit from formative feedback and to showcase the different skills they have developed and/or learned. The module is assessed through two pieces of summative coursework. Coursework one requires the students to build a digital portfolio. Students are required to identify and apply for an advertised placement or graduate role; submit their CV, which they have developed within the module through guidance from the CES; produce a two-minute video 'selfie' as part of the application, to demonstrate their digital communication skills, which is a vital component of the world we are now living in; attend a mock assessment centre, led and run in conjunction with employers to provide a real-life experience and complete an individual and a group problem-solving task, similar to those expected in a real-life assessment day. Students reflect on their experience, and module feedback has noted how students feel more prepared to apply for placement roles and how much more aware they are of the full process. The final component is a personal development plan, enabling students to reflect on their current skills, plan what they want to achieve and to focus on skills they still need to develop.

The second piece of coursework continues to develop skills and PPI formation. Students explore career aspirations relevant to accounting, they research various roles, e.g., auditor, management/financial accountant, forensic investigation, sustainable finance, and tax roles, amongst others. This research is a useful preparation for the modules that will be studied in the next semester. In addition, students work in groups, to practise negotiation through teamwork, and to complete a spreadsheet-based task, requiring them to analyse large data to make recommendations.

CONCLUSION

As students progress through this module, they constantly draw on their learning from other modules, to apply their skills and articulate examples of leadership, resilience, communication, and teamwork. As they gather these examples and practise applying for roles, they begin to identify both their strengths and areas for improvement. Having gone through the process of applying for a placement role within the module, they are not only more confident to continue to apply for 'live' roles but also more willing to engage with the CES, professional body content, recruitment agencies, LinkedIn, etc. During the module, through exposure to guest speakers from industry and practice, the professional body representations and real-world applied learning via live briefs and company visits (see Figure 10.1), the students enhance their understanding of the profession, and they demonstrate greater clarity around the various roles and career progression routes available to them. The active learning approach undertaken in the module has contributed to developing the student employability skill set, in particular student confidence and self-awareness. The programme has experienced an increase in the number of students applying for placement opportunities. Informal feedback suggests this is partly through exposure to and familiarity of the recruitment process, knowing more about the profession, being more self-aware and a greater feeling of confidence through PPI formation.

REFERENCES

accaglobal (2022), *What Do Employers Look For?* Available at: https://www.accaglobal.com/an/en/student/sa/professional-skills/what-do-employers-look-for-.html (accessed: 9 January 2023).

Advance HE (n.d.), *Framework for embedding employability in higher education.* Available at: https://www.advance-he.ac.uk/knowledge-hub/framework-embedding-employability-higher-education (accessed: 23 January 2023).

Aryanti, C. and Adhariani, D. (2020), 'Students' perceptions and expectation gap on the skills and knowledge of accounting graduates', *Journal of Asian Finance, Economics and Business*, 7(9), 640–657.

Bradley, A., Quigley, M. and Bailey, K. (2021), 'How well are students engaging with the careers services at university', *Studies in Higher Education*, 46(4), 663–676.

Bradley, A., Priego-Hernandez, J. and Quigley, M. (2022), 'Evaluating the efficacy of embedding employability into a second-year undergraduate module', *Studies in Higher Education*, 47(11), 2161–2173.

Cranmer, S. (2006), 'Enhancing graduate employability: best intentions and mixed outcomes', *Studies in Higher Education*, 31(2), 169–184.

Fallows, S. and Steven, C. (2000), 'Building employability skills into the higher education curriculum', *Education + Training*, 42(2), 75–82.

HESA (2022), *Graduate Outcomes*. Available at: https://www.hesa.ac.uk/innovation/outcomes (accessed: 9 January 2023).

Jackson, D. (2016), 'Re-conceptualising graduate employability: the importance of pre-professional identity', *Higher Education Research & Development*, 35(5), 925–930.

Mistry, U. (2021), 'Enhancing students' employability skills awareness through the accounting professional body on an undergraduate accounting degree', *Accounting Education*, 30(6), 578–600.

OfS (2021), *New measure shows substantial differences in likely job and study outcomes for students*. Available at: https://www.officeforstudents.org.uk/news-blog-and-events/press-and-media/new-measure-shows-substantial-differences-in-likely-job-and-study-outcomes-for-students/ (accessed: 9 January 2023).

Paterson, M., Higgs, J., Wilcox, S. and Villeneuve, M. (2002), 'Clinical reasoning and self-directed learning: key dimensions in professional education and professional socialisation', *Focus on Health Professional Education*, 4(2), 5–21.

Pegg, A., Waldock, J., Hendy-Isaac, S. and Lawton, R. (2012), *Pedagogy for Employability*, York: Higher Education Academy.

QAA (2017), *How universities and employers can work together to improve graduate outcomes: evidence from QAA reviews*. Available at: https://www.qaa.ac.uk/docs/qaa/about-us/qaa-viewpoint-improving-graduate-outcomes.pdf?sfvrsn=8f3df681_4 (accessed: 9 January 2023).

Rebele, J. E. and St Pierre, E. K. (2019), 'A commentary on learning objectives for accounting education programs: the importance of soft skills and technical knowledge', *Journal of Accounting Education*, 48, 71–79.

Sithole, S. T. M. (2015), 'Information technology knowledge and skills accounting graduates need', *International Journal of Business and Social Science*, 6(8), 47–52.

Tibby, M. and Norton, S. (2020), *Essential frameworks for enhancing student success; embedding employability*. Guidance notes. Advance HE.

Tomlinson, M. (2012), 'Graduate employability: a review of conceptual and empirical themes', *Higher Education Policy*, 25(4), 407–421.

Yorke, M. and Knight, P. (2004), *Embedding Employability into the Curriculum*, York: Higher Education Academy.

REFLECTION

From an Accounting and Finance student

In my second year as an Accounting and Finance student, I undertook a 12-week Professional Development module. The purpose of the module was to improve my employability skills to become a more well-rounded graduate to future employers. I already had up to seven years of work experience at Sky, with a secured placement role between my second and final years. Therefore, I went into the module questioning its benefit, but after discussing it with my lecturer, I tried to have an open, albeit sceptical, mindset.

The module was split into multiple employability topics. I particularly enjoyed learning how to write a CV. Despite having experience in face-to-face interviews and completing job application forms, I surprisingly had no up-to-date CV or clue on how to create one. I knew that I would have put off creating my CV until I was looking for graduate roles. I was relieved knowing that I could spend more time on my dissertation and applying for jobs rather than building a CV from scratch.

I benefited from learning how to create a personal development plan. I have always found it challenging to identify my strengths, most likely due to my imposter-syndrome personality. However, my lecturer pointed out that my time management from juggling university and part-time work, as well as leadership experience from working at Sky, are stand-out strengths and should be honed in on. As a result, I felt more confident and set SMART targets to help secure a placement year, which in turn settled my nerves.

Looking back, the module provided me with the opportunity to add value to my future degree that goes beyond my grades. All students have an opportunity to obtain technical skills, but on reflection, I ask, 'Is this enough to make a student stand out from the crowd?'

11. Developing an ecosystem: employability skills and authentic assessments
Sarah Montano

INTRODUCTION

Employability skills and graduate outcomes are often seen to be the purpose of a higher education institution (HEI), yet HEIs are continually criticised for graduates emerging without the skills needed to be successful employees. In 2015, the then Minister of State for Universities and Science in the UK stated that universities and their teaching were not delivering employment-ready graduates (Department for Business Innovation and Skills, 2015). In particular, employers were saying that they needed graduates with 'human skills' such as creativity (Fahey, 2021). Creativity (see Chapter 6) is increasingly desired by employers as innovations directly contribute to organisational value and success (Ma et al., 2018) and advanced digital skills. It is often argued that despite being 'digital natives', university students lack the workplace digital skills that are vital as the world has become increasingly technology-based (Centre for Economics and Business Research (CEBR), 2018; Langley, 2019) and HEIs themselves are urged to consider how they can use technological opportunities to resolve these challenges (Barber et al., 2013).

Whilst the reasons for this lack of skill development are complex, three reasons may be that:

- Firstly, employability skills are not always embedded within modules ('employability' may be seen by students as part of extracurricular activities).
- Secondly, assessments are not reflective of industry practice.
- Thirdly, even when assessments are industry-based, skill development is not recognised by students and so they are unable to articulate their new-found skills to employers and, to take us back to the start, this results in employers criticising graduates for not having the required skills.

This chapter explains a postgraduate retail marketing authentic assessment, as an exemplar, to illustrate how HEIs need to refine their approach to employability skills and create experiential learning-based authentic assessments that will enable students to gain valuable skills, recognise their own employability skill development and demonstrate such skills to employers within the competitive marketplace (Fuller, 2021). The chapter also shows how an integrated institutional approach is needed and that authenticity will be redundant if students cannot demonstrate their skills to their chosen industry that the assessment claims to support.

EMPLOYABILITY CONTEXT AND GRADUATE EMPLOYABILITY SKILLS

As Jackson argued in 2013, HEIs, and in particular business schools, have been focussed on trying to embed employability skills into curricula. Yet there does not seem to be much positive change as employers and employer bodies report that students still lack employability skills. For example, QS (2019) and WEF (2020) identified that graduates do not have sufficient work-ready skills. To further complicate matters, as we contemplate the Fourth Industrial Revolution, employers require graduates to emerge with the aforementioned desirable skills, such as advanced digital skills and creativity. HEIs are therefore in the ideal position to try and resolve this continued problem and take responsibility (Somerville, 2019). However, it is not as simple as just 'giving' students employability skills, as HEIs need to create an ecosystem whereby students can acknowledge that they have gained the desired employability skills and can demonstrate these to their future employer (Jackson et al., 2013; Succi and Canovi, 2020).

AUTHENTIC ASSESSMENTS AS A SOLUTION

Concurring with Cheng et al. (2022) that any response to these problems must be collaborative and requires engagement with invested stakeholders, one solution to these problems is the use of authentic assessments that will enable a redesign of modules and programmes to focus on employability skills (Sin and Neave, 2016; Villarroel et al., 2018). By bringing in industry expertise and the careers service, ways can be found to enable students to both gain and, crucially, demonstrate the development of employability skills.

Authentic assessments (Sotiriadou et al., 2020) are a valuable solution as they enable students to engage in common industry tasks such as store design, writing blogs or creating adverts. The Institute of Student Employers (ISE) (2021) also supports authentic assessment design as a way of enabling students to gain much-needed skills. The core principle is that any assessment that is 'authentic' replicates work tasks (Wiggins, 1990) that enable students to understand the complexity of work, develop the missing employability skills and offer opportunities for reflection on their own skill development (Ashford-Rowe et al., 2014). Such authentic assessments must engage students but also be academically rigorous and be facilitated by a collaborative learning environment (Robinson and Hullinger, 2008) and offer an engaging learning experience (Kennedy et al., 2008).

The underpinning pedagogy of authentic assessments being experiential learning is a long-standing approach (Burch et al., 2019). Experiential learning is an under-utilised strategy, yet offers us a considered and evidence-based solution. Fundamentally, an experiential learning pedagogy offers students a learning experience that is grounded in reality and aims to give students 'an experience' within the safe confines of a module or programme (Kolb and Kolb, 2009). Specifically, within marketing, Kumar and Bhandarker (2017) argue that students can only learn a business subject by 'doing' and engaging in experiential learning (Greene, 2011). Yet business schools often do not adopt such an approach (McMurray et al., 2016).

Furthermore, Villarroel et al. (2018) found that authentic assessments have three key characteristics: realism, cognitive challenge, and evaluative judgement:

- Firstly, realism, whereby authentic assessments mirror industry practice and ask students to replicate common tasks. In the exemplar stated below students are asked to design their own concept store, which is common practice in retail design (Ma et al., 2018).
- Secondly, cognitive challenge, whereby students need to develop the human skills that are much in demand, such as the aforementioned digital and creative skills (Langley, 2019). Students can be imaginative and develop new ideas and also gain life-long skills (Frederiksen and Knudsen, 2017; Rawson et al., 2013).
- Thirdly, evaluative judgement, whereby students are able to more objectively try and assess their own work and identify areas for improvement and development.

However, it is argued that the authentic assessment cannot end here, and an ecosystem needs to be created so that students can demonstrate these skills.

THE AUTHENTIC ASSESSMENT

The assessment in this example is the group assessment for an elective MSc Marketing module. The students are required to design their own concept store and create an eight-minute digital presentation which is submitted via the virtual learning environment (VLE). Students must design a completely new concept store and brand (so, for example, they could not create a new Nike store). There are a number of key requirements that students must consider and present, such as location, target customers, brand concept, product range, floor plans, customer experience and the use of new technologies. Students design their stores using a range of software, embedded videos, gaming platforms or PowerPoint. It is key to note that students are not graded on the technicalities of the presentation but on the store concept and explanation of their design. Students are not required to be visible in the presentation, rather they include a voiceover that narrates their store vision.

The assessment is authentic, as it enables students to mirror current industry retail practice and supports students to recognise that they have gained valuable marketing and retail industry employability skills. The first element of authenticity is that retail industry professionals talk to the students around current retail industry innovations. The second element is that concept design mirrors innovative retail space design such as, for example, Amazon Go; Brown's East; Burberry; Glossier and Selfridges' immersive spaces. Students work in groups as quasi 'retail consultants' to create their store and make key decisions, for example on location, that directly reflect industry considerations. The focus on creating this assessment was to ensure that there was a way in which students could develop the very skills that employers argue students lack. The final authentic element, which creates the ecosystem, is that careers professionals are involved in the module and deliver lectures and other sessions to support the students, to recognise the new skills that they have gained, and how to showcase these skills to the very industry professionals that are also engaged with the module.

OUR ECOSYSTEM

As has been demonstrated, 'authenticity' helps students to understand the complexity of work and to contextualise their skills, and allows students to develop missing employability skills (Ashford-Rowe et al., 2014). Importantly, when reflecting industry practice, assessment content can be used as part of their application (Herbert et al., 2020) to showcase skills to future employers (Tomlinson, 2010). However, this is where a problem can occur as an ecosystem also needs to be created whereby students are supported to understand that skill development is not siloed within modules, but rather their assessment is integral to demonstrating that they have the skills that are needed in a competitive graduate market (Fuller, 2021), in which students have to have something 'different' on their CV to help them stand out.

Responding to Jackson et al. (2013) and Succi and Canovi (2020), the approach in this example supports students' needs to become aware of skill

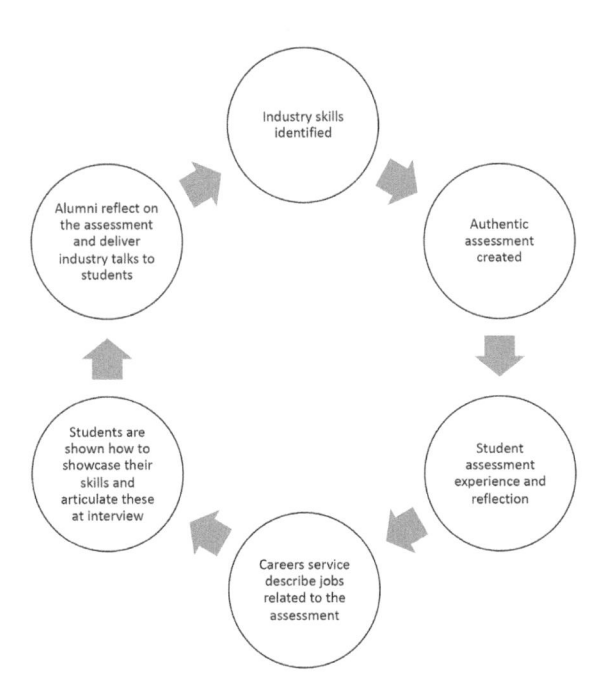

Figure 11.1   The assessment and employability skill ecosystem model

development and ensure that an authentic assessment fulfils its ultimate aim. By bringing in the careers service and industry speakers and offering a 'joined up' and collaborative approach, students are supported to articulate their new 'high-demand' skills but also to visualise inspirational careers where these skills can be used, thus understanding the relationship between the module, industry, and their own careers. Via the cognitive challenging aspect of the authentic assessment, students are also better able to understand that they have developed the mindset required to manage their future career. Finally, as some students may not have work experience (Holt-White and Montacute, 2020), by offering industry-reflective assessments, students can gain skills in areas they previously have not experienced, which offers them new opportunities. The authentic assessment infrastructure allows students to showcase high-demand skills (e.g. digital, curiosity and learning agility).

CONCLUSION

In conclusion, authentic assessments are an important development and the way forward to closing the enduring gap in graduate employability skill development. Importantly, HEIs must take a holistic and team approach and build in stakeholder support so that students can articulate and demonstrate their newly developed industry-ready skills. Even with authentic assessments that are designed to mirror industry practice, there is no automatic transfer of skills gained (Jackson, 2013). This is particularly important when we consider industry needs and how students need to offer more than just learnt theories.

REFERENCES

Ashford-Rowe, K., Herrington, J. and Brown, C. (2014), 'Establishing the critical elements that determine authentic assessment', *Assessment & Evaluation in Higher Education*, 39(2), 205–222.

Barber, M., Donnelly, K. and Rizvi, S. (2013), *An Avalanche Is Coming: Higher Education and the Revolution Ahead*, London: Institute for Public Policy Research.

Burch, G. F., et al. (2019), 'A meta-analysis of the relationship between experiential learning and learning outcomes', *Decision Sciences Journal of Innovative Education*, 17(3), 239–273.

CEBR (2018), *The Economic Impact of Digital Inclusion in the UK*. A report for Good Things Foundation. Available at: https://www.goodthingsfoundation.org/insights/economic-impact-digital-inclusion/ (accessed: 9 January 2023).

Cheng, M., Adekola, O., Albia, J. and Cai, S. (2022), 'Employability in higher education: a review of key stakeholders' perspectives', *Higher Education Evaluation and Development*, 16(1) 16–31.

Department for Business Innovation and Skills (2015), *Fulfilling Our Potential: Teaching Excellence, Social Mobility and Student Choice*, London: HMSO.

Greene, H. (2011), 'Freshman marketing: a first year experience with experiential learning', *Marketing Education Review*, 21(1),79–87.

Fahey, S. J. (2012), 'Curriculum change and climate change: inside outside pressures in higher education', *Journal of Curriculum Studies*, 44(5), 703–722.

Frederiksen, M. H. and Knudsen, M. P. (2017), 'From creative ideas to innovation performance: the role of assessment criteria', *Creativity and Innovation Management*, 26(1), 60–74.

Fuller, G. (2021), 'Covid economic fallout leads to rise in postgraduate applications', *The Guardian*, 16 February. Available at: https://www.theguardian.com/education/2021/feb/16/covid-economic-fallout-leads-to-rise-in-postgraduate-applications (accessed: 9 January 2023).

Herbert, I., Rothwell, A., Glover, J. and Lambert, S. (2020), 'Graduate employability, employment prospects and work-readiness in the changing field of professional work', *International Journal of Management Education*, 18(2), 1–13.

Holt-White, E. and Montacute, R. (2020), *COVID-19 and Social Mobility Impact Brief #5: Graduate Recruitment and Access to the Workplace*. The Sutton Trust. Available at: https://www.suttontrust.com/wp-content/uploads/2020/07/Access-to-the-Workplace-Impact-Brief.pdf (accessed: 9 January 2023).

ISE (2021), *ISE Student Development Survey*. Available at: https://ise.org.uk/page/ISEPublications (accessed: 9 January 2023).

Jackson, D. (2013), 'Business graduate employability – where are we going wrong?', *Higher Education Research & Development*, 32(5), 776–790.

Jackson, D., Sibson, R. and Riebe, L. (2013), 'Delivering work-ready business graduates – keeping our promises and evaluating our performance', *Journal for Teaching and Learning for Graduate Employability*, 4(1), 2–22.

Kennedy, G., Judd, T., Churchward, A. and Gray. K. (2008), 'First year students' experiences with technology: are they really digital natives?', *Australasian Journal of Educational Technology*, 24(1), 108–122.

Kolb, A. Y. and Kolb D. A. (2009), 'Experiential learning theory: a dynamic, holistic approach to management learning, education and development', in S. J. Armstrong and C. V. Fukami (eds), *The SAGE Handbook of Management Learning, Education and Development*, Thousand Oaks, CA: SAGE, pp. 42–68.

Kumar, S. and Bhandarker, A. (2017), 'Experiential learning and its relevance in business school curriculum', *Developments in Business Simulation and Experiential Learning*, 44, 244–251.

Langley, E. (2019), 'This is how the UK can stay ahead of the game with digital skills according to an expert', *Evening Standard*, 18 June.

Ma, X., Yuanyuan, Y., Wang, X. and Zang, Y. (2018), 'An integrative review: developing and measuring creativity in nursing', *Nurse Education Today*, 62(March), 1–8.

McMurray, S., Dutton, M., McQuaid, R. and Richard, A. (2016), 'Employer demands from business graduates', *Education and Training*, 58(1), 112–132.

QS (2019), *Global Skills Gap Report*. Available at: https://www.qs.com/portfolio-items/the-global-skills-gap-report-2019/ (accessed: 9 January 2023).

Rawson, K., Dunlosky, J. and Sciartelli, S. (2013), 'The power of successive relearning: improving performance on course exams and long-term retention', *Educational Psychology Review*, 25, 523–548.

Robinson, C. and Hullinger, H. (2008), 'New benchmarks in higher education: student engagement in online learning', *Journal of Education for Business*, 84(2), 101–109.

Sin, C. and Neave, G. (2016), 'Employability deconstructed: perceptions of Bologna stakeholders', *Studies in Higher Education*, 41(8), 1447–1462.

Somerville, S. (2019), *Taking Responsibility for the Graduate Skills Gap*. Prospects Luminate. Available at: https://luminate.prospects.ac.uk/taking-responsibility-for-the-graduate-skills-gap (accessed: 9 January 2023).

Sotiriadou, P., Logan, D., Daly, A. and Guest, R. (2020), 'The role of authentic assessment to preserve academic integrity and promote skill development and employability', *Studies in Higher Education*, 45(11), 2132–2148.

Succi, C. and Canovi, M. (2020), 'Soft skills to enhance graduate employability: comparing students and employers' perceptions', *Studies in Higher Education*, 45(9), 1834–1847.

Tomlinson, M. (2010), 'Investing in the self: structure, agency and identity in graduates' employability', *Education, Knowledge & Economy*, 4(2), 73–88.

Villarroel, V., Bloxham, S., Bruna, D., Bruna, C. and Herrera-Seda, C. (2018), 'Authentic assessment: creating a blueprint for course design', *Assessment and Evaluation in Higher Education*, 43(5), 840–854.

WEF (2020), *The Future of Jobs Report*, Geneva: World Economic Forum. Available at: http://www3.weforum.org/docs/WEF_Future_of_Jobs_2020.pdf (accessed: 9 January 2023).

Wiggins, G. (1990), 'The case for authentic assessment', *Practical Assessment, Research & Evaluation*, 2(2), 28–37.

REFLECTION

From a Costume Design graduate

I pursued my studies as a passion, not necessarily as a job. I had spent a lot of time training as a dancer, and so costume design was something that I was always interested in from that. I suppose that I had understood it as a user rather than a maker. I knew that self-employment was probably what I would have to do going into the degree, and that is what I am doing now.

Thinking back, I wish there was more on the business side of things for becoming an entrepreneur and starting your own business. The degree was great in preparing me for the costume side of things, and for the project planning side of things, but not so much the ins and outs of marketing, business admin, etc. These are things that I have learnt on the fly as I have gone along.

PART IV

Innovative approaches to career guidance

12. Using career pathways to tailor and personalise employability activities

Rebekah Marangon

INTRODUCTION

Whilst research suggests that students are increasingly recognising the need to stand out to employers (Tomlinson, 2008), engagement with employability provision within HE remains low (Knight and Yorke, 2004; Jackson and Tomlinson, 2022). Generally, this low level of engagement is attributed to low motivation on the part of the student body (Rae, 2007). Whilst students are motivated to obtain a job after their degree, students' employability strategies are often dominated by achieving a high grade in their degree, rather than attending soft skills careers and networking sessions (Bennett, 2018). Career planning and employability activities are often viewed as 'less important' when compared to the 'main subject' of their course (Rae, 2007: 609). A student cannot always see the immediate value of attending a careers session, when compared, for example, to preparing for an assessment due in a few weeks' time. As their academic study takes priority, engaging with employability can often be put to one side as there is no immediate reward attached to attendance. Furthermore, add in further obligations such as caring responsibilities (Bathmaker et al., 2016) and part-time jobs (Clegg et al., 2010), and attending careers sessions can fall even further down the list of students' priorities (Thompson et al., 2013).

This lack of immediate value must be tackled if there is to be wider engagement with careers programmes. The sessions require an inherent value to be attributed to them, so that students recognise their importance and feel motivated to participate and to prioritise attendance/engagement over their other responsibilities.

This chapter seeks to explore how effective curriculum design processes can be used to encourage engagement with employability throughout a student's programme of study. This will be considered within the context of the Career Pathway Scheme at Derby Law School (where the author previously worked), a careers programme based on constructive alignment principles.

CORRELATIONS BETWEEN APATHY IN EMPLOYABILITY AND LEARNING GENERALLY

As demonstrated above, a key factor underpinning why students are apathetic to employability sessions relates to the lack of perceived inherent and immediate value within the sessions themselves. In this context, parallels can be drawn with students who adopt surface approaches to their learning more generally.

Students who adopt surface approaches to learning tend to engage in tasks with the view of doing the bare minimum needed to achieve the course requirements (Biggs and Tang, 2011). They are primarily motivated by the content of any assessments attached to their course (Prosser and Trigwell, 1997), often only attending those sessions relevant to passing their assessment (Rust, 2002). Compare this to a student who adopts a deep learning approach. These students want to gain an 'in-depth understanding of high-level concepts' (Floyd et al., 2009: 182), attributing value to, and therefore attending, all classes regardless of whether they concern topics covered within their assessment.

Comparisons can therefore be drawn between students who do not see the immediate advantage in attending careers sessions and those who adopt a more surface approach to their learning. In both instances, the student is prioritising short-term goals over long-term ones. They are strategic, with the student engaging in surface learning prioritising information relevant to their upcoming assessment over broad subject knowledge, and the student engaging in a surface approach to employability prioritising studies or outside commitments over their long-term graduate prospects.

Given the similarities identified above, this chapter considers whether the widely researched techniques for tackling surface approaches to learning can also be applied in the context of employability.

CONSTRUCTIVE ALIGNMENT

One approach advocated to help transition students from surface to deep learners is constructive alignment. Constructive alignment is the process of informing students what they should learn and how they should evidence this learning before teaching begins (Biggs, 2014). It requires lecturers to 'identify clear learning outcomes', 'design appropriate assessment tasks that will directly assess those learning outcomes', and 'design appropriate learning opportunities', which enable students to undertake the assessed tasks (Rust, 2002: 148).

By placing learning outcomes at the heart of the curriculum design process, constructive alignment encourages deep learning. Through constructive alignment, clear links are established for students between learning outcomes, the assessment and the recommended learning activities. Students are therefore able to see the importance of what they are being asked to do (namely due to its relevance to an assessment), thus increasing the likelihood that they will be motivated to engage with the activity in question (Rust, 2002). Constructive alignment makes succeeding at their assessment (a motivation the student often intrinsically holds) an extrinsic motivation for participating and engaging with planned learning activities.

Applying this in the context of employability, constructive alignment can be used to draw to students' immediate attention the links between employability and engaging with employability activities, with some form of assessment used to extrinsically motivate the students to prioritise attending planned employability sessions.

This was the approach taken within Derby Law School's Career Pathway Scheme. The Career Pathway Scheme introduced five career pathways to the students: Solicitor, Barrister, Further Research, Non-Legal, and Don't Know. Students were then invited to choose a pathway, considering their own goals, and attend events designed for them. In terms of constructive alignment, the pathways themselves were used to integrate intended learning/career outcomes, the career events constituted the learning activities, and the Law School's employability blog was used as the method of assessment. Each of these elements will now be discussed in turn.

INTENDED CAREER OUTCOMES AND THE CAREER PATHWAYS

The first requirement of successful constructive alignment concerns the creation of clear intended learning outcomes. An intended learning outcome is a statement of 'what a learner is expected to know, understand and/or be able to demonstrate at the end of a period of learning' (Adam, 2007: 2). When effectively drafted, learning outcomes can enable lecturers to incorporate additional skills, beyond subject knowledge, into the educational process (Maher, 2004). If improperly drafted, however, learning outcomes can have the opposite effect. If drafted too specifically, learning outcomes risk leading to 'rigidification of teaching' (Hill, 2012), stifling creativity and harming the idiosyncratic nature of learning by being too impersonal (Jervis and Jervis, 2005). This is particularly significant when drafting intended career outcomes given the personal nature of the employability process. For example, in the context of legal education, it would be over-restrictive if the outcomes were limited to 'traditional' legal roles of 'lawyers', especially considering the fact that each year many law graduates gain employment in non-legal sectors (Chowdrey, 2014).

In the Career Pathway Model, intended learning outcomes were embedded within each pathway, taking the form of a list of goals attached to both the specific activities within the pathway and more generally to the pathway itself. For example, whilst a broad goal may ask a student to 'consider and appraise' their employability skills within a chosen pathway, a more specific sub-goal may ask them to 'evaluate' how a skill developed in a particular session might help them carry out a task more effectively. By attaching different outcomes to all five pathways, and by combining general and more specific outcomes, a personalised approach can be achieved, with students offered freedom and flexibility to achieve the outcomes however they wish.

There are various considerations when drafting effective learning outcomes, from general matters such as considering what exactly needs to be assessed (Biggs and Tang, 2011), to technical points such as using action verbs (Kennedy, 2006), and using approaches such as Bloom's taxonomy to classify learning objectives according to complexity and specificity (Bloom et al., 1956). To satisfy the first element here, consideration must be given to what employability skills encompass. It is only when it is understood what employability skills entail that, as Biggs and Tang suggest, the intended career outcomes to be assessed can be identified.

According to Helyer and Lee (2014), employability skills can be described as not only those skills that are 'essential to obtaining a job, such as interview techniques, job searching skills and those required to create a professional curriculum vitae', but also as including 'skills needed to carry out a job effectively' including generic abilities such as communication skills, and personal attributes, such as attention to detail and self-confidence (2014: 351). Subsequently, these can be further supported by 'specific/subject abilities', such as the skills that are explicit to law, like drafting and advocacy (Soares et al., 2017).

These three elements of employability were embedded in the intended career outcomes of the Pathway Scheme. For example, the Solicitor Pathway required students to 'evaluate skills gained in a workshop on negotiation' and thus assess attainment in a specific/subject activity, whilst also asking them to 'consider how those skills might help them obtain a role and effectively carry out the role of a solicitor', requiring an assessment of the skills needed to both obtain and carry out a job effectively. Finally, analysing the examples above, the words 'consider', 'appraise' and 'evaluate' can be seen as examples from Bloom's taxonomy, hitting the markers of an effective learning outcome from a technical requirements perspective.

ASSESSMENT AND THE LAW SCHOOL'S BLOG

Just as assessment can be used to drive student engagement within taught modules, assessment can also be used to motivate learning within employability; for example, acting as a motivator for students to develop 'specific employability attributes' (Pegg et al., 2012: 33). Given the importance of assessment on engagement, the assessment methodology within the Career Pathway Scheme was vitally important. It was the assessment method that provided the extrinsic motivator that incentivised student engagement.

For the purposes of the Career Pathway Scheme, a broad interpretation of assessment was used, focussing on the role assessment plays in providing proof of achievement (Boud and Falchikov, 2006). Consequently, rather than assessing through a summative approach (Malott et al., 2014), the focus was on developing a method that allowed students to creatively demonstrate achievement in the intended career outcomes in a way that was visible to prospective employers. This led to the creation of the Derby Law School Career Blog.

The blog allowed students to post summaries and reviews of the various careers events run by the Law School. It offered a platform for students to share any success they experienced either directly relating to, or by virtue of, the Career Pathway Scheme, allowing the students to evidence to themselves and lecturers the employability skills they had gained. Furthermore, as the platform was externally facing, students could share any blog posts they wrote with potential employers. This provided an additional advantage and incentive to engage with the Pathway Scheme. Research suggests that the incentive to engage with careers activities increases wherever there is 'prominent job market signalling value' (Jackson and Tomlinson, 2022). In allowing students to promote their abilities, through social media platforms like LinkedIn, direct to employers, the blog provided that signalling value.

LEARNING OPPORTUNITIES AND CAREERS EVENTS/ ACTIVITIES

Finally, the learning opportunities element of constructive alignment was achieved through careers events and activities. For the Career Pathway Scheme, these included events specific to obtaining a job (for example CV writing and Applicant Day training), events specific to carrying out jobs effectively (such as presentation skills, and 'life as a lawyer' type sessions), and events specific to subject abilities (such as drafting and negotiation); reflecting the definition of employability posited earlier.

Crucially, for learning activities to be effective within constructive alignment it is vital that students recognise what they have been learning (Knight and Yorke, 2003). Consequently, it is equally vital that for these careers activities, students recognise the employability skills that they have gained from engaging with the careers activity. Because of this, the Career Pathway Scheme coded all careers events with the pathway they corresponded to, and with the specific learning outcomes they could be used towards. Reminders of the 'assessment' method were then provided at the end of each careers activity to reinforce the extrinsic motivation to attend future sessions.

Student Viewpoint

Student feedback and engagement with the Career Pathway Scheme proved positive. Pre-pandemic attendance at careers events was up on previous years, with students reporting positively about the blog, in particular. One third year student wrote:

> The Derby Law School Blog has been a crucial port of call for myself, as well as a number of other students seeking to enhance their employability within the legal sector. The blog supplies a platform in which students can gain a thorough insight into the ways in which they can acquire the experience, skills and qualities, which are commonly desired by the legal profession. Most crucially, the blog provides a 'vehicle' in which students can receive first-hand advice from other alumni, along with a platform in which the successes of current or former students can be recognised and celebrated.

Employer Viewpoint

The blog has also been positively received by employers. One employer wrote:

> Students should be aware that prospective employers are increasingly looking at all available resources, especially online resources, for clues as to an applicant's attitude and aptitude. Willingness to create content and participate in marketing activities from an early stage at university through the blog is definitely a positive indicator for employers.

CONCLUSION

Whilst apathy for improving employability is nothing new, nor is the potential solution advocated by this chapter. This chapter has aimed to demonstrate that curriculum design principles such as constructive alignment can be effectively used to tackle lack of engagement in careers, just as they are used to tackle students who take a surface as opposed to a deep approach to learning. The approach undertaken by Derby Law School illustrates how constructive alignment can be embedded into a careers programme successfully, with the door open for further integration of curriculum design principles in the future.

REFERENCES

Adam, S. (2007), 'An introduction to learning outcomes'. Available at: https://is.muni.cz/do/1499/metodika/rozvoj/kvalita/Adam_IH_LP.pdf (accessed: 9 January 2023).

Bathmaker, A. M., Ingram, N., Abrahams, J., Hoare, A., Waller, R. and Bradley, H. (2016), *Higher Education, Social Class and Social Mobility*, London: Palgrave Macmillan.

Bennett, D. (2018), 'Graduate employability and higher education: past, present and future', *HERDSA Review of Higher Education*, 5, 31–61.

Biggs, J. (2014), 'Constructive alignment in university teaching', *HERDSA Review of Higher Education*, 1, 5–22.

Biggs, J. and Tang, C. (2011), *Teaching for Quality Learning at University*, 4th edn, Maidenhead: Open University Press.

Bloom, B. S. et al. (1956), *Taxonomy of Educational Objectives: The Classification of Educational Goals*, New York: David McKay.

Boud, D. and Falchikov, N. (2006), 'Aligning assessment with long-term learning', *Assessment and Evaluation in Higher Education*, 31(4), 399–413.

Chowdrey, N. (2014), 'Guardian students: I'm studying law – but I don't want to be a lawyer', *The Guardian*. 30 May.

Clegg, S., Stevenson , J. and Willott, J. (2010), 'Staff conceptions of curricular and extracurricular activities in higher education', *Higher Education*, 59(5), 615–626.

Floyd, K. S., Harrington, S. J. and Santiago, J. (2009), 'The effect of engagement and perceived course value on deep and surface learning strategies', *Informing Science: The International Journal of an Emerging Transdiscipline*, 12, 181–190.

Helyer, R. and Lee, D. (2014), 'The role of work experience in the future employability of higher education graduates', *Higher Education Quarterly*, 68(3), 348–372.

Hill, R. (2012), *Whackademia: An Insider's Account of the Troubled University*, Sydney: NewSouth Publishing.

Jackson, D. and Tomlinson, M. (2022), 'The relative importance of work experience, extra-curricular and university-based activities on student employability', *Higher Education Research & Development*, 41(4), 1119–1135.

Jervis, L. M. and Jervis, L. (2005), 'What is the constructivism in constructive alignment?', *Bioscience Education*, 6(1), 1–14.

Kennedy, D. (2006), *Writing and Using Learning Outcomes: A Practical Guide*, Cork: University College Cork.

Knight, P. and Yorke, M. (2003), *Assessment, Learning and Employability*, London: Society for Research into Higher Education and Open University Press.

Knight, P. and Yorke, M. (2004), *Learning, Curriculum and Employability in Higher Education*, 1st edn, London: RoutledgeFalmer.

Malott, K. M., Hall, K. H., Sheely-Moore, A., Krell, M. M. and Cardaciotto, L. (2014), 'Evidence-based teaching in higher education: application to counselor education', *Counselor Education and Supervision*, 53(4), 294–305.

Maher, A. (2004), 'Learning outcomes in higher education: implications for curriculum design and student learning', *Journal of Hospitality, Leisure, Sport and Tourism Education*, 3(2), 46–54.

Pegg, A., Waldock, J., Hendy-Isaac, S. and Lawton, R. (2012), *Pedagogy for Employability*. Available at: https://www.advance-he.ac.uk/knowledge-hub/pedagogy-employability-2012 (accessed: 9 January 2023).

Prosser, M. and Trigwell, K. (1997), 'Relations between perceptions of the teaching environment and approaches to teaching', *British Journal of Educational Psychology*, 67(1), 25–35.

Rae, D. (2007), 'Connecting enterpise and graduate employability: challenges to the higher education culture and curriculum', *Education + Training*, 49(8/9), 605–619.

Rust, C. (2002), 'The impact of assessment on student learning: how can the research literature practically help to inform the development of departmental assessment strategies and learner-centred assessment practices?', *Active Learning in Higher Education*, 3, 145–158.

Soares, I., Dias, D., Monteiro, A. and Proenca, J. (2017), 'Learning outcomes and employability: a case study on management academic programmes', in *Proceedings of 11th International Technology, Education and Development Conference*, Valencia: INTED 2017, pp. 6588–6594.

Thompson, L., Clark, G. and Walker, M. (2013), '"It's just like an extra string to your bow": exploring higher education students' perceptions and experiences of extra-curricular activity and employability', *Active Learning in Higher Education*, 14(2), 135–147.

Tomlinson, M. (2008), 'The degree is not enough: students' perceptions of the role of higher education credentials for graduate work and employability', *British Journal of Sociology of Education*, 29(1), 49–61.

REFLECTION

From a Psychology graduate

It has been three years since I graduated from psychology, and I now work at a university facilitating employability and career development workshops. To be honest, it feels pretty ironic teaching students about career development, even though I am at the beginning of my own career journey. I have heard people, students and staff, label me as the 'career development expert'. As if in just 25 years of life I could absorb all the information on every career, and every job application process, and predict what it would be like in the future?

As a student, I used to think that 'career experts' existed. I thought that if I could just talk to one for five minutes they could solve my identity crisis on what to do after university. I often think back to that version of me, and I ponder, what did she need? Perhaps it may have helped if career development was embedded across her university experience, rather than it being just an extra-curricular support. Perhaps it may have helped if career development was scaffolded across her degree, rather than just a support for her final year. Perhaps it may have helped if someone had explained to her that there was no such thing as a career expert and that every person in her university journey was capable of contributing to her understanding of the professional self.

And then I realise, I was a student three years ago, and even within that short amount of time so much has changed. I should also be asking my students, right now, what do they need? I should invite them to the collaboration table, to take the time to listen to their experiences, and together develop ideas to enhance career development learning for the students experiencing university today.

13. The Career Studio: peer-to-peer support

Emma Moore and Paul Gratrick

INTRODUCTION

There are just under 30,000 students at the University of Liverpool across 35 academic departments, representing a diverse cohort at various stages in their career planning, experience and goals. In 2018, the University of Liverpool holistically redesigned its careers and employability offer to achieve scale in employability delivery and to increase student engagement. One element of this transformational project was the introduction of the UK's first student-led frontline service, known as the Career Studio.

Before 2018, the Careers Service at the University of Liverpool was designed around the traditional delivery model adopted by most university careers teams. Information, advice and guidance was delivered to students primarily through booked appointments lasting either 20 or 50 minutes. All appointments were delivered by qualified careers advisers. The team also delivered a workshop programme and a wide range of on-campus employer-led events. All careers support was delivered in the extra-curricular space apart from a couple of careers modules supporting year-in-industry programmes. Through this traditional model the Careers Service reached 10 per cent of students.

The new model inspired by the University of Nevada (Calhoon, 2018) centres around a peer-to-peer frontline space called the Career Studio, and a team of 20 coaches who are recruited from the existing student population to enable this. Recruitment is by personal statement, video interview and full assessment centre. Every time recruitment occurs the process is refined. Every new cohort of coaches takes part in a bespoke, immersive two-week long training programme (delivered primarily by the careers team) where they learn how to co-explore career ideas with their peers. Every coach is mentored, observed and given fortnightly feedback from a member of the professional team to ensure quality and enable continuous improvement. These paid student career coaches work as part of the careers team and staff the space on a rota, 10 a.m. to 5 p.m. each day. Students can drop in to work with a career coach to co-explore career options, find work experience, or get support with applications. This co-exploration model removes the need for career coaches to have extensive knowledge about career sectors. Having a student-led frontline frees up the rest of the team to deliver careers and employability support through the curriculum. In the academic year 2021/2022, the careers and employability team have reached 49 per cent of students this way and have strong ambitions to increase this reach.

This chapter summarises the peer-to-peer theory underpinning the Career Studio before providing an overview of how this looks in practice, and the impact that it is having.

PEER-TO-PEER IN THEORY – A BRIEF LITERATURE REVIEW

In designing the Career Studio, the principles of peer mentoring were adopted and applied to the university's employability context. To operate the Career Studio, 20 current students are employed as career coaches and they embody 'peer support', defined by Byrom (2018) as 'support provided by and for people with similar experiences'. At its most basic level, peer mentoring enables students to discover resources and information from their peers (Clark and Crome, 2004). In the Career Studio the career coaches focus primarily on the peer mentoring aspect of peer support, breaking the student client's career journey down into small manageable steps and then supporting them to take incremental actions, rather than trying to solve everything at once.

Peer-to-Peer and Well-Being

Improvements in mental well-being (Glaser et al., 2006; Jacobi, 1991) can be achieved by the implementation of peer-to-peer models. Stress and anxiety, and its relationship with peer mentoring, are also explored by Tremblay and Rodger (2003), and their data found that students with high levels of anxiety showed reduced anxiety levels in a peer mentoring group. An explanation for this may be the 'alleviation of anxiety' through peer mentors sharing their experiences of their studies, academic results and examples of persistence.

Peer-to-Peer and Integration

Improving retention (via increased integration) is a significant requirement for institutions and peer mentoring can support this (Treston, 1999), as well as increasing a sense of belonging and supporting new students to make social connections with others (Pargetter et al., 1999; Pope and Van Dyke, 1999). The results from a number of academic studies (Borden et al., 1997; Carter,

2000; Gardner et al., 1999; Muckert, 2002; Pike et al., 2000; Pope and Van Dyke, 1999; Treston, 1999; Webb, 1999) all discuss the value of peer-to-peer models in assisting students with their adjustment to university life, their academic performance, and persistence decisions (Fowler and Muckert, 2004). Collings et al. (2014) also found that peer mentored individuals showed higher levels of integration to university. Their study found that four times as many non-peer mentored students had seriously considered leaving university compared to peer mentored students. Students can often feel they are leaving their known support system when they go to university and must start again (Collings et al., 2014; Earwaker, 1992). Interestingly, the research also demonstrated that non-peer mentored students had a 'lower level of perceived support from their university friends than their peer mentored counterparts' (Collings et al., 2014).

Peer-to-Peer and the Benefits to the Mentor

Using peer-to-peer mentoring in a nursing centre in Canada provided benefits to both students and peer mentors (Dennison, 2010). Students were recruited and paid to assist skills practice, develop new learning opportunities, and organise this Canadian centre. They assisted students with materials and supported open and comfortable learning (Dennison, 2010). As a consequence, the peer mentors were expected to have diverse skills sets (both clinical and academic), good organisation, communication and leadership potential. Critically in this context, they were not expected to know all the answers but were trained in how to seek resources (Dennison, 2010). This research demonstrates how peer mentors develop an increased sense of confidence in their skills as well as their leadership and teaching abilities.

Peer Mentoring and Employability

Jones et al. (2012) researched the specific employability benefits of a peer-to-peer model in the context of a support service for postgraduate students. This support service worked alongside a Careers Service and was focussed on the assessment of graduate attributes, the development of new skills, and acted as a place for students to find information and training. In this context student ambassadors 'serve as advocates and nurturers of their peers' career and skills development' (Jones et al., 2012). These ambassadors were selected based on the skills they can offer their peers and learn themselves through intensive training over a 15-week period. The benefits of peer-to-peer in this environment are to build a learning and knowledge community (Devenish et al., 2009), develop transferable skills and promote students' professional networks and for peers to learn from each other (Boud and Lee,

2005) whilst 'empowering ownership of the learning process' (Jones et al., 2012; Packham and Miller, 2000).

PEER-TO-PEER IN PRACTICE – CREATION OF THE CAREER STUDIO

Considering the literature above and internal factors, the Career Studio delivery model was created in 2018 and has developed from there. Internally, this significant change was in response to a perfect storm of poor metrics, dwindling student interactions and low levels of engagement with the service.

A New Employability Ecosystem and Scalability

University leadership called for transformational change around employability delivery and the benefits of that are now coming to the fore. The leadership wanted a move away from the pure career guidance model that was engaging only 10 per cent ($c.2,000$ students) of the undergraduate student body, who arguably were the most motivated, career-ready students. Alongside enabling the benefits of peer-to-peer models previously highlighted, the aims were to be innovative with the new approach to careers and employability, and to achieve scale.

To this end a dramatic increase in student engagement has been observed since the Career Studio first opened. In year one 18 per cent of the undergraduate student body (3,623 students) visited the Career Studio compared to the 10 per cent achieved via the previous model.

By creating the studio, it has been possible to divert resources to curriculum development work. Three years on, 49 per cent of undergraduate students are experiencing careers and employability support through the curriculum. Academic colleagues view the careers team as credible partners and demand for support to deliver active learning, authentic assessment and confidence through the curriculum is growing at pace, taking it ever closer to the goal of 100 per cent reach.

The student career coaches inform and support curricular delivery and they become a sounding board for curricular ideas and assessments and come into lectures/workshops to deliver recruitability content. Whilst technically still students, the career coaches are part of the careers team and so it is possible to have open conversations with them as colleagues and to hear that perspective. One of the academic colleagues recently fed back:

> The careers team are great at planning suitable interventions in the curriculum. The team listen carefully to departments and understand that there is no 'one size fits all' approach. The team listens to new ideas and values the input from academic

colleagues. It feels good to be working together with passionate individuals who are very responsive to new ideas.

Inspiring Action and Increased Integration

As one route to see if the known benefits of peer-to-peer models are happening in the Career Studio, on the Friday of each week following a student's visit to the studio they are emailed a survey. This asks them a range of questions, including if, and which, actions they have taken following their visit. From this it can be seen that career coaches prompt 81 per cent of student visitors (from the 267 survey responses) to take a singular, or small number of actions. This stops them being overwhelmed, and encourages them to undertake practical actions which will have an immediate impact, such as creating a CV in order to apply for jobs, or organising a mock interview for an upcoming real one. These interactions replace a traditional careers consultation interview, but are supported by ongoing curriculum work, where Faculty-facing teams deliver in-curriculum sessions. In this way, students are 'nudged' from a number of angles. In addition, from the survey it can be seen that 77 per cent of student visitors noted that they were 'likely' or 'very likely' to 'engage with other areas of the university' following their visit to the studio, which supports wider efforts to increase retention and a sense of belonging with the university.

Improved Well-Being and Networks

A central space has been created on campus where students can go and speak to students just like them and this contributes to a student's sense of belonging. The peer-to-peer benefit of reducing anxiety also comes through. Via the aforementioned Friday follow-up surveys for Career Studio visitors, it was observed that prior to visiting, 40 per cent of students felt anxious or very anxious about their career plans. After visiting, this reduced to 9 per cent, showing a marked improvement in anxiety levels. Creating and developing a network is a key ingredient to students enhancing their graduate prospects and so by developing peer mentoring in an employability context it provides an additional route for these networks to be cultivated.

Mentor Benefits and a Talent Pipeline

Over 50 students have been a career coach, and 31 have now graduated. All the career coach alumni were in high-skilled employment or further study 15 months after graduating (Graduate Outcomes Survey data) and many cite their career coach role as instrumental in securing their future roles. It is not just the wider student body who benefit from the career coach model; as coaches, they themselves develop a wide variety of skills not available through other on-campus roles.

One aim in developing the career coach position was to create a talent pipeline into the sector, using the career coach role as an inspiration for a long-term career in employability. This pipeline has become a reality as many career coach alumni are now working in a variety of HR, talent management, higher education, and employability roles, providing a pipeline that has advantages for the careers team too. The career coach alumni who are now working in roles across the sector have enhanced the existing network and opened new partnerships to develop.

CONCLUSION

Pivoting to a new peer-to-peer model has made all these benefits and positive impacts possible. It has helped strike the perfect balance between frontline and curricular delivery and it has created a new employability ecosystem at Liverpool, which continues to thrive. Student engagement with the Career Studio and associated research tell us the Liverpool peer-to-peer model works and an increasing number of services across the UK are adopting very similar models or incorporating students as partners somewhere else within their offer.

After the Covid-19 pandemic, the Career Studio is still the 'jewel in the crown'. It is helping to buck the negative trend in student engagement. Having provided a virtual drop-in Career Studio on Zoom during the Covid-19 pandemic, it reopened on campus in May 2021, and since then has continued to offer both services in parallel to students. In semester one of 2021/2022, students voted with their feet, with 90 per cent of interactions happening in the on-campus Career Studio, meaning frontline engagement was back at 75 per cent of pre-Covid levels.

Conversations in the Career Studio also sounded quite different post-Covid. Something the career coaches always did well was to establish rapport using shared experiences. The shared experience of career exploration and job searching in Covid times comes through in almost every interaction. Career coaches empathise with their peers in an authentic way, reducing anxiety and building confidence. This is something that cannot be created and it only happens when peers connect with peers, in a place where they feel inspired and supported. This space is the peer-to-peer Career Studio.

REFERENCES

Borden, V. M. H., Burton, K. L., Evenbeck, S. E., and Williams, G. A. (1997), 'The impact of academic support programs on student performance and persistence', *Research Brief*, 4(4), 1–14.

Boud, D. and Lee, A. (2005), '"Peer learning" as pedagogic discourse for research education', *Studies in Higher Education*, 30(5), 501–516.

Byrom, N. (2018), 'An evaluation of a peer support intervention for student mental health', *Journal of Mental Health*, 27(3), 240–246.

Calhoon, M. (2018), 'The studio method', *NACE Journal*, 1 February. Available at: https://www.naceweb.org/career-development/organizational-structure/the-studio-method (accessed: 10 January 2023).

Carter, J. A. (2000), 'Empowerment groups: a creative transition and retention strategy', in J. A. Chambers (ed.), *Selected Papers from the 11th International Conference on College Teaching and Learning*, Jacksonville, FL: Florida Community College at Jacksonville, pp. 43–50.

Clark, W. A. and Crome, W. W. (2004), *Personalising the Transition Experience: Induction, Immersion or Intrusion?* Auckland: University of Auckland.

Collings, R., Swanson, V. and Watkins, R. (2014), 'The impact of peer mentoring on levels of student wellbeing, integration and retention: a controlled comparative evaluation of residential students in UK higher education', *Higher Education*, 68, 927–942.

Dennison, S. (2010), 'Peer mentoring: untapped potential', *Journal of Nursing Education*, 49(6), 340–342.

Devenish, R., Dyer, S., Jefferson, T., Lord, L., van Leeuwen, S. and Fazakerley, V. (2009), 'Peer-to-peer support: the disappearing work in the doctoral student experience', *Higher Education Research and Development*, 28(1), 59–70.

Earwaker, J. (1992), *Helping and Supporting Students: Rethinking the Issues*, Buckingham: Open University Press.

Fowler, J. and Muckert, T. (2004), 'Tiered mentoring: benefits for first year students, upper level students and professionals', in *Transforming Knowledge into Wisdom, Proceedings of the 27th HERDSA Annual Conference*, Miri, Sarawak, 4–7 July. Milperra: Higher Education Research and Development Society of Australasia, pp. 155–163. Available at: https://citeseerx.ist.psu.edu/document?repid=rep1&type=pdf&doi=9e7f3858ffaf45ef7e4e37f64bf5f04940042b4e (accessed: 10 January 2023).

Gardner, J., Kendall, D. and Kendall, L. (1999), *University of Tasmania Mentor Scheme: An evaluation*. Unpublished.

Glaser, N., Hall, R. and Halpern, S. (2006), 'Students supporting students: the effects of peer mentoring on the experiences of first year university students', *Journal of the Australian and New Zealand Student Services Association*, 27, 4–17.

Jacobi, M. (1991), 'Mentoring and undergraduate academic success: a literature review', *Review of Educational Research*, 61(4), 505–532.

Jones, N., Torezani, S., Luca, J. (2012), 'A peer-to-peer support model for developing graduate students' career and employability skills', *Intercultural Education*, 23(1), 51–62.

Muckert, T. D. (2002), *Investigating the student attrition process and the contribution of peer mentoring interventions in an Australian first year university program*. PhD thesis. Griffith University.

Packham, G. and Miller, C. (2000), 'Peer-assisted student support: a new approach to learning', *Journal of Further and Higher Education*, 24(1), 55–65.

Pargetter, R., McInnis, C., James, R., Evans, M., Peel, M. and Dobson, I. (1999), *Transition from Secondary to Tertiary: Performance Study*, Canberra: DETYA – Higher Education Division.

Pike, L., Pooley, J., Young, A., Drew, N., Haunold, S. and O'Donnell, J. (2000), *An Evaluation of the Peer Mentoring Program*. School of Applied Psychology, Edith Cowan University.

Pope, G. and Van Dyke, M. (1999), 'Mentoring ... value adding to the university', *Journal of the Australia and New Zealand Student Services Association*, 13, 15–27.

Tremblay, P. F. and Rodger, S. (2003), 'The effects of a peer mentoring program on academic success among first year university students', *Canadian Journal of Higher Education*, 33(3), 1–17.

Treston, H. (1999), 'Peer mentoring – making a difference at James Cook University, Cairns, It's moments like these you need mentors', *Innovations in Education and Training International*, 36(3), 236–243.

Webb, C. (1999), *Academic Development Unit. The first two years. A report on activities: 1998–1999*. Academic Development Unit, Centre for Higher Education Development, University of Western Sydney, Hawkesbury.

REFLECTION

From a public sector senior manager

Having recruited over 10,000 graduates over the past 20 years for leading public sector employers I have seen trends come and go, suppliers come and go, employers come and go, and student aspirations, motivations and behaviours evolve, especially during and now post Covid, but one thing has never changed – that take up of careers support is NOT equitable in the UK.

The 'keeny beanies' as I call them get involved in everything, they attend sessions, connect with employers, get every badge on offer to show they have developed their skills and guess what? They go on to work with leading employers post university, however this group is not that large and often come from middle class backgrounds and have been socialised to know what they need to do to deliver successful employability. The students that I care most about are the 'lost souls', those first generation students going to university, those from low socio-economic backgrounds and other protected characteristics and I am convinced the ONLY way to ensure ALL students leave their university with a solid understanding of the graduate job market, the concept of transferable skills, their own strengths and weaknesses and an understanding of what sectors and potentially what employers are of interest to them is by embedding employers into the curriculum.

14. Supporting employment outcomes for students from Asia
Louise Nicol

INTRODUCTION

The UK's international student body has been dominated by students from China for many years. In recent times the number of students from elsewhere in Asia has increased; for example, India has become a dominant source of international students and makes up the majority of students in emerging study destinations such as Canada.

International students go overseas to study because they want to improve their career prospects. In this chapter we explore what support international students need to achieve great graduate outcomes. We explore what international students go on and do when they leave university, and what they need from a university to help them achieve their ambitions.

MAJORITY GO HOME

According to the UK's Migration Advisory Committee (2018), prior to the reintroduction of post-study work in the UK, 96 per cent of international students returned to their home country after graduation. In 2018, at the height of international student recruitment in Australia, only 50,000 of a total international student population of 350,000 students stayed on in Australia to take up the opportunity of post-study work, which equates to just 14 per cent, according to the Australian Department of Home Affairs (Department of Home Affairs, 2022).

Having the ability to work in the country where students go to study is part of the decision-making process when choosing where to study. Back in 2012, the UK government stopped the post-study work visa for international students, meaning that the right to stay in the UK and work for up to two years was removed. In 2011, under the previous Tier 1 Post-Study Work Visa, the numbers of students transferring into work visas was 46,875. Following the 2012 changes, that fell in 2013 to just 6,238 (O'Malley, 2019). Then, in

September 2019 the UK government announced the return of the post-study work visa from 1 July 2021, meaning that international students can stay in the UK to work for up to two years.

Following the reinstatement of post-study work in the UK, UK Visas and Immigration data suggests that in 2019/2020, 12,484 out of the 556,625 students that were studying in the UK had applied for the graduate visa. This represented 7 per cent of international students, compared to 4 per cent prior to the reinstatement of post-study work rights in the UK.

Although the ability to stay and work in the UK is certainly appealing to many international students, there are still a significant number of students wanting to return to their home country to work after their studies. In 2019, in the report 'Powering the Asian Century', the Asia Careers Group analysed 34,955 individual graduate destinations of students, the majority of whom graduated in 2015–2020 (Asia Careers Group, 2019). Fourteen per cent of the UK graduates worked in just 20 companies, of which eight were founded in Asia. Comparable data for Australian graduates shows 13 per cent of students working for the same 20 companies (the eight that were founded in Asia (Asia Group) and the remainder, which were founded in the West (West Group)). Figure 14.1 shows the destinations of these 34,955 students, with the y axis showing the number of students entering each company.

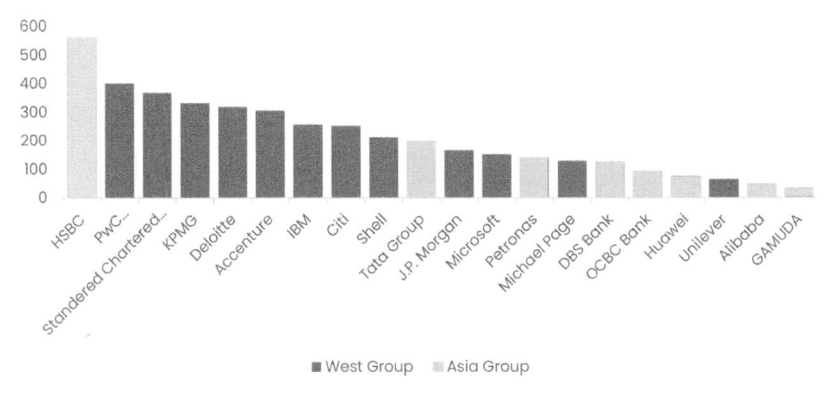

n = 4,248

Figure 14.1   Number of 2015–2020 graduates entering the top 20 companies

Taking just two of the countries, India and Malaysia, we see different sectors dominating the job opportunities for graduates (Figures 14.2 and 14.3).

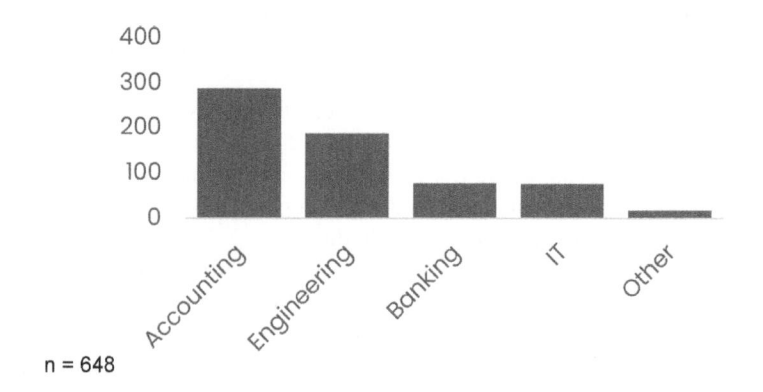

Figure 14.2   Graduate employment sectors, India

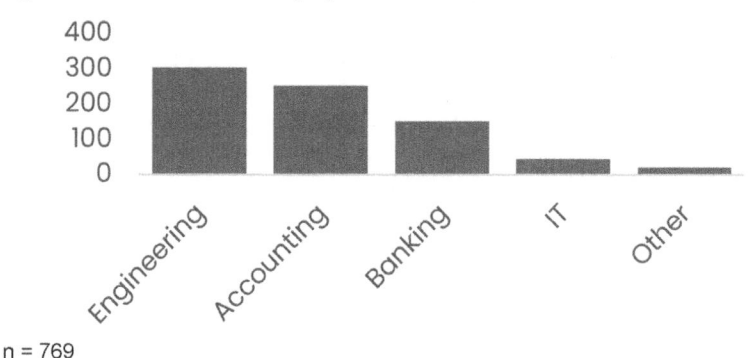

Figure 14.3   Graduate employment sectors, Malaysia

The first trend emerging is that of an Asian Century, when economic activity has pivoted eastwards. Ten years ago, the most desirable companies for graduates to work for would be based in the Western advanced economies, for example the Big Four accounting firms, major banks and oil and gas companies. Although these companies are still taking a significant number of graduates in Asia, we increasingly see students looking to support their home economies and the desire to work for Asian-founded businesses has increased.

According to data from Universum (https://universumglobal.com/rankings/malaysia/) of the ten most desirable companies to work for among Malaysian graduates only one is a Western based multinational company, in this case Google, whose parent company is Alphabet.

This brings us to the next trend, the rise of tech. If we look back a decade, we could not have expected the prolific rise of FAANG (Meta – formerly known as Facebook, Amazon, Apple, Netflix, and Alphabet – formerly known as Google), and the way that these companies continued to thrive during the Covid pandemic (Pisal, 2021). The US is not alone in this; there has also been a proliferation of tech giants in Asia, for example Huawei, JD.com, China Mobile, Alibaba, and Tencent.

As noted by Verhoef et al. (2021) none of these companies were in the ascendency a decade ago, but now it is hard to imagine life without them. According to Mearian and Gruman (2022) all these companies have numerous employees, all need talent, and most are actively recruiting all year round. In the US, technology companies added 22,800 net new workers in May 2022.

CAREERS SUPPORT FOR INTERNATIONAL STUDENTS

Understanding the likely destinations of international students is crucial to determining the careers support that they will need. So much has changed and so much will change. Without robust global graduate destinations data, it is impossible for any higher education institution to embark on an informed international employer engagement strategy, through which they impact the international employability of their students.

Job-seeking behaviour varies in different countries and support for students will determine the market that they intend to work in. For example, if a student is looking to return to China following their studies, it is unlikely they will ever need to write a CV or attend an interview. CV workshops and mock interviews are irrelevant for this group of students. Instead, it is far better that their time is spent on learning how to complete an application form, that will make it through the complex online screening processes used by the majority of Chinese employers to filter and evaluate graduate applications.

When it comes to India, the world's second largest market for international student mobility, those students opting to study overseas often do so because the competition to attend India's prestigious IITs (Indian Institutes of Technology) is fierce. According to Ghosh (2021), the IITs are among the most difficult schools in the world to get into. He says:

> The University of Oxford accepts one out of five applicants. IITs take in just one out of 50. So it is little wonder that for any Indian child with ambitions of becoming an engineer, getting into an IIT looks like the pinnacle of achievement. Many gifted students have no option but to complete their higher education elsewhere.

Historically, Indian IITs have been recruitment hothouses for India's leading firms, the likes of Tata Consultancy Services (TCS), Infosys Technologies Ltd, ICICI Bank Limited, etc. Every year leading Indian employers attend the IITs with the express purpose of recruiting India's brightest and best minds. In fact, in 2021 there was a 15–25 per cent increase in firms participating in campus recruitment at IITs. Therefore, attendance at an IIT pretty much guarantees Indian students a job, hence the competition to be admitted. Many high-calibre Indian students attending university overseas expect the same, that leading companies will come to leading Western universities and will recruit them on the spot. They do not expect to have to go through the involved processes of careers fairs, generic applications, selection centres and interviews.

Given the challenges facing the global economy following the worldwide pandemic, a pivot to Asia in terms of economic growth and the rise of technology companies and digitisation, careers information advice and guidance will no doubt experience significant change and disruption. Kettunen (2021) carried out a study of change in careers provision, interviewing designated governmental and non-governmental representatives from 33 countries attending the International Symposium for Career Development and Public Policy. Respondents were asked about the innovations that they saw as important for careers services, and their responses were collated into four different categories of innovation:

- initiating services – the need to promote the value of career development and engaging with careers services;
- developing demographic-based programmes – the importance of developing careers programmes that meet the specific needs of different groups of people;
- professionalising the sector – having recognised professional training and qualifications for careers advisers in the different countries in which they were operating;
- exploiting cross-sectoral synergies – finding new ways of providing careers support and using new technologies such as artificial intelligence.

Whilst the author of this study acknowledges that the data might not represent the critical factors for the entire careers service across all countries, there are some important messages that emerge. There is a need to innovate and find new ways of providing careers advice that fits with the individual needs of students, and the job markets that they intend to enter.

4i CAREERS EDUCATION

Reflecting the innovation which is needed to support international students in their quest for graduate level employment, the Asia Careers Group SDN BHD has created 4i Careers Education – the four essential components of a new era of careers information advice and guidance (CIAG).

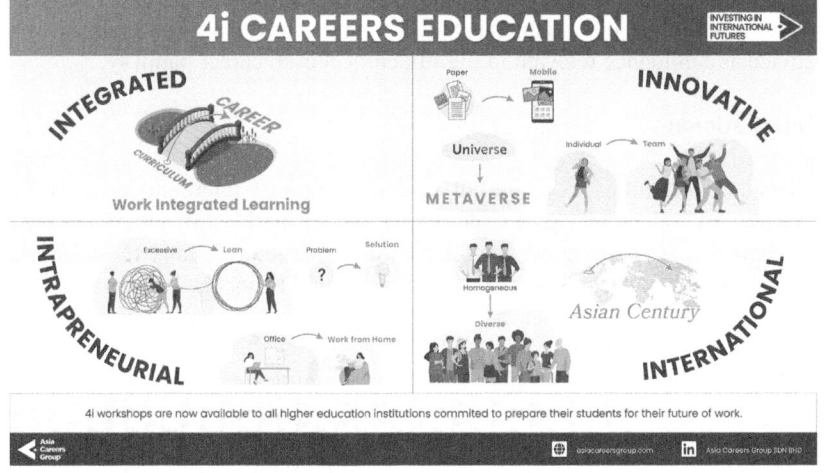

Supporting employment outcomes for students from Asia 141

Source: Asia Careers Group SDN BHD.

Figure 14.4   4i Careers Education

The principles of the approach are:

International	Informed by robust, representative domestic and international graduate outcomes data, providing international opportunities for both domestic and international students
Innovative	CV workshops, mock interviews and careers fairs both in person and online have their place but team building, problem solving, resilience and creativity are now far more relevant for the volatile, uncertain, complex and ambiguous (VUCA) world we find ourselves inhabiting and in which these students will be searching for jobs
Intrapreneurial	Looking to create job makers (not job takers), whether a student wishes to work within an organisation or start a business, supporting entrepreneurship and giving students opportunities to invent, create and express themselves
Integrated	Work integrated learning (WIL) and careers advice delivered to students where they are, through their course of study and university life

APPLYING THE 4i MODEL

At the heart of the 4i model sits data; robust, representative data on international graduate outcomes in their country of study for post-study work, but far more importantly, country-specific graduate employability and leading graduate destinations data for those students that return to their home country for their early careers. Without a road map to inform careers information advice and guidance for international students it is very difficult for careers services based in a country other than the student's own to provide careers information advice and guidance relevant to the student's chosen career pathway.

International

Global opportunities exist for all students, not just international students. Without an understanding of wider global labour markets, it is hard to advise students that are looking outside their locality and home country to find work. If the world continues to pivot eastward, there will be increasing opportunities for graduates to expand their horizons and take advantage of significant skills shortages further afield.

The first thing to make clear is that opportunities exist outside students' home countries in the wider region. Indeed, a good example of this is the ability for individuals with an ASEAN passport to work across countries within the block. Whilst opportunities could be limited in a student's home country, they could be numerous if they are encouraged to look outside their home country. The UN DESA Global Migration Database in Huelser and Heal (2014) indicates there are significant opportunities for students to work in Thailand and Singapore within ASEAN, with over 3,000 and 1,000 individuals respectively migrating from the wider ASEAN region to Thailand and Singapore to find work.

An understanding of labour markets and graduate destinations in both Thailand and Singapore specifically would be of interest to all students studying overseas who have a passport from within the ASEAN region.

Innovative

Team building, problem solving, resilience and creativity are all key skills that universities can instil within their graduates. Group careers counselling sessions are a first step to team building. Thought should be given to the make-up of groups to ensure they reflect different course and nationality backgrounds to encourage diversity of thought and productive sharing.

Problem solving is something that is very much integrated into students' university courses and learning. However, in a careers context it is very much about encouraging students to 'think outside the box'. In many ways job hunting is all about problem solving: a graduate is unemployed and wishes to be employed. How will they go about it? What steps will they take? If plan A does not work, what is plan B?

An example could be of a student wishing to work in a Big Four accounting firm but their applications to the graduate schemes are all rejected. Where do they look next? Do they look to leverage personal contacts within firms they may have access to? Do they shift their search to accounting and finance functions at other well-known multinational companies? Do they decide to do a postgraduate qualification to make future applications more attractive to prospective Big Four accounting firms? Careers services can provide a key role in encouraging students to think around the challenges of their job search and provide their own solutions.

When it comes to resilience, most international students studying overseas for the first time have had to be resilient from the outset, but many disassociate their personal experiences from 'professional skills'. They are in fact one and the same. Our experiences shape us both personally and professionally, and students need to be taught how to reflect on their experiences so that they can communicate them in their job search.

It is often the case that whilst students have had to be resilient throughout their studies, many do not understand how that experience can be applied within a job application form and/or interview situation. It is the role of the careers service to reinforce the value of those experiences and support students to frame them in a professional context.

Creativity is probably the most challenging element to bring to bear, particularly when supporting international students whose upbringing and culture may be more disposed to more prescribed thinking. It is well known that in Asia many parents want their children to enter 'the professions', i.e. doctor, lawyer, accountant, etc. Thinking creatively when it comes to employment for many students is a new concept. If I study engineering, I must become an engineer. This of course is not the case; many students with engineering degrees work in other disciplines, for example consulting, sales, product design, etc. This ability to think creatively when it comes to planning one's career is essential as many career paths are now 'non-linear' and individuals may in fact have numerous careers within their lifetime. It is down to careers services to highlight that fact to students and reinforce that decisions are not binary and that looking creatively at careers is very much part and parcel of 'the future of work'.

In addition to the support that careers services can provide in a one-on-one or group setting with students, many universities have embraced career preparedness platforms and online courses to equip students for their transition to the workforce. There are examples of countries and institutions going further and implementing virtual reality as part of careers education.

Intrapreneurial

An understanding of start-up ecosystems overseas and support available to returning graduates can provide graduating students returning home with a significant advantage when looking to start a business. For example, Cradle, based in Malaysia, aims to create an ecosystem that supports a strong and innovative business-building environment for technology entrepreneurs and innovators through the Cradle Investment Programme (CIP). Established in 2003 with a mandate to fund high-calibre technology, Cradle has supported over 1,000 Malaysian technology-based companies across multiple sectors and holds the highest commercialisation rate amongst funding agencies in the country. Working closely with universities and start-up incubators, Cradle's programme offerings are not restricted to monetary aid, but also include commercialisation support and various other value-added services to accelerate growth.

Another example is the AirAsia Innovation and Entrepreneurship Centre at Asia School of Business, which runs the ASB101K Entrepreneurship Competition annually, aimed at building a dynamic entrepreneurial ecosystem in South East Asia (SEA). This is open to teams of tertiary students and early-stage start-ups from around the region. On top of gaining exposure to coaching and bootcamps delivered by mentors from ASB and the regional start-up and venture capitalist ecosystem, teams vie for the total prize money of over US$50,000, and additional benefits from competition partners, including Microsoft.

Integrated

Finally, as noted by Vu et al. (2022), it is widely recognised that international students may face additional challenges when it comes to WIL, but this should not prevent universities addressing this issue when it comes to enhancing the employability of their international student population. International employer engagement is the key, with a target list of leading graduate destinations by country. Universities, through their faculty structures and careers services, are often in a strong position to set up work-based learning opportunities with companies worldwide. This, however, is only possible if universities are able to target specific employers, ideally those where alumni are presently working.

If a university has access to the top five employers by country, this provides a starting point from which they can better target employer engagement overseas and then expand to related companies and sectors to widen their overseas employer network.

There are also specific examples in Asia where universities are working hand in hand with employers to provide opportunities for their students and graduates. Ericsson, Universiti Teknologi Malaysia (UTM) and Digital Nasional Berhad (DNB) have announced their collaboration to launch a 5G education initiative in Malaysia that will help educate over 1,000 Malaysian students on 5G and emerging technologies.

Ericsson will open its Ericsson Educate platform to UTM students to provide access to learning material on key technologies including: 5G networks, artificial intelligence, machine learning, automation, blockchain, cloud computing, data science, the Internet of Things and telecommunications. The collaboration provides both students and lecturers with access to quality digital learning resources that draw on Ericsson's 145-year experience in telecommunications and ICT. It has been reported that content from the Ericsson Educate portal will be provided at no cost and will be integrated to complement UTM's online-based degrees and micro credentials programmes.

A further example includes a collaboration between INTI International College Subang and IBM, where INTI students were asked to develop a public relation strategy for IBM's Shared Services, a connected enterprise that serves IBM's business needs worldwide.

> Through this collaboration, our students had to work on a real case and provide a valid solution, to one of the leading IT companies in the world. The students worked really hard on this project and the end product of their work is really impressive – we are extremely proud of them. (Rohayu Kosmin, Senior Lecturer at INTI International College Subang)

Around 30 INTI Marketing students took part in the project, which ended with a final presentation to the representatives from IBM Malaysia.

CONCLUSION

Understanding how international students transition to the workforce will be even more critical following the 'great global reset' as a result of the pandemic and the economic transformation brought about by technology. It is clear that significant disruption provides an opportunity for significant change. The future graduate labour market will not be an exception, and harnessing the great innovations from careers services is key to the future employability of international students. Access to international graduate outcomes data and 4i Careers Education represents one model which can be adopted by universities to facilitate and underpin a strategic change to further strengthen and enhance the employability of all students, including those from overseas.

REFERENCES

Asia Careers Group (2019), *Powering the Asian Century*. Available at: https://asiacareersgroup.com/news?article=powering-the-asian-century (accessed: 10 January 2023).

Department of Home Affairs (Australia) (2022), *BP0019 Number of Temporary visa holders in Australia at 2022-11-30*. Available at: https://data.gov.au/dataset/ds-dga

-ab245863-4dea-4661-a334-71ee15937130/distribution/dist-dga-54b2d02b-45bf -4c2d-a2bd-d9a9064f365c/details?q= (accessed: 10 January 2023).

Ghosh, D. (2021), '15–25% rise in firms participating in campus recruitment at IITs', *The Hindu Business Line*, 17 December. Available at: https://www.thehindubusinessline.com/news/national/15-25-rise-in-firms-participating-in-campus-recruitment-at-iits/article37971226.ece (accessed: 10 January 2023).

Huelser, S. and Heal, A. (2014), *Moving Freely? Labour Mobility in ASEAN*. Asia-Pacific Research and Training Network on Trade, Policy Brief. Available at: https://www.unescap.org/resources/moving-freely-labour-mobility-asean-apb-no40 (accessed: 23 January 2023).

Kettunen, J. (2021), 'Careers experts' conceptions of innovation in career development', *International Journal for Educational and Vocational Guidance*, 8, 1–16.

Mearian, L. and Gruman, G. (2022), *How many jobs are available in technology?* Computer World. Available at: https://www.computerworld.com/article/3542681/how-many-jobs-are-available-in-technology.html (accessed: 10 January 2023).

Migration Advisory Committee (2018), *Impact of international students in the UK*. Available at: https://assets.publishing.service.gov.uk/government/uploads/system/uploads/attachment_data/file/739089/Impact_intl_students_report_published_v1.1.pdf (accessed: 10 January 2023).

O'Malley, B. (2019), *Government drops post-study work visa restrictions*. University World News. Available at: https://www.universityworldnews.com/post.php?story=20190910232257848 (accessed: 10 January 2023).

Pisal, S. (2021), *Rise of Facebook, Amazon, Apple, Netflix, Google during Covid 19 Pandemic*. MSc dissertation. California State University, San Bernardino. Available at: https://scholarworks.lib.csusb.edu/cgi/viewcontent.cgi?article=2460&context=etd (accessed: 10 January 2023).

Verhoef, P., Broekhuizen, T., Bart, Y., Bhattacharya, A., Dong, J., Fabian, N. and Haenlein, M. (2021), 'Digital transformation: a multidisciplinary reflection and research agenda', *Journal of Business Research*, 122, 889–901.

Vu, T., Ferns, S. and Anantham, S. (2022), 'Challenges to international students in work-integrated learning: a scoping review', *Higher Education Research & Development*, 41(7), 2473–2489.

REFLECTION

From a Geography graduate working in a major retailer

When I applied to university, I decided to just choose a subject I enjoyed. I loved my Geography degree, and the success of just going with what sounded interesting was something I have carried with me to where I am now. I applied for the graduate scheme I am on now because it sounded interesting. Now, nearly two years in and reaching the end of the scheme, I am looking for jobs that excite me.

I have never had a 'career plan', and I don't think I ever will. It's not for me. However, I have learnt how important it is to have a development plan; it helps me to push myself towards a goal, whatever it may be. By focusing on behaviours and skills, what my strengths and weaknesses are, and what is important to me, I can grow without having a specific job or responsibility in mind.

For me, having a job I am interested in and that challenges me is the most important. I know that my organisational and communication skills are strong, but that I need to work on adaptability and influencing skills. Therefore, my development plan focuses on these goals. Wherever this takes me in my career, I am ensuring that I am happy and that I never stagnate in a job.

PART V

Practical examples of employability activities

15. Using social action to support skill development

Fiona Walsh

INTRODUCTION

Student Hubs has been working in partnership with universities across England since 2007 to deliver social action activities for students, with our origins as a charity stemming from students studying at the University of Oxford, who wanted to do more to bridge the gap between their university life and the community they lived in. As a charity, we occupy a unique space sitting across the higher education sector and the youth social action sector, meaning our approach has always been shaped by learnings and development in both areas.

Using social action as a vehicle to support students' skill development, networks and learning about the social issues and communities they live in has always been central to what we do. However, with an increased focus on employability for students, and with universities developing civic agendas, an approach which embeds social action in student life has never been more important. This chapter will explore what social action is, present case studies of how Student Hubs have supported students to take part in social action activities which develop their employability skills, and give examples of what this practice can look like for others in the sector.

Our mission at Student Hubs is to mainstream student social action, and we are excited to see more universities in the sector continuing to adopt social action practices in their strategic approach on employability and civic engagement for their student cohorts. This chapter will explore what the benefits are of an approach to employability shaped through socially active programmes for students, and how this format impacts students' understanding of their professional skills.

WHAT IS SOCIAL ACTION?

There are various definitions of social action. In a government policy paper from 2016, social action was described as being 'about people coming together to help improve their lives and solve the problems that are important in their communities. It can include volunteering, giving money, community action or simple neighbourly acts' (Centre for Social Action, 2016).

For another perspective which has shaped our work, we can look to the #iwill Campaign. The #iwill Campaign was set up through the organisation 'Step Up to Serve' in 2013 (Prime Minister's Office, 2013), backed by cross-party political collaboration and the then Prince of Wales, to encourage 10–20-year-olds to get involved in youth social action in their local communities. Key aims of the campaign included reaching young people, especially from low income and ethnic minority backgrounds; supporting young people to shape decisions in the public, private and voluntary sectors; for more organisations to demonstrably take action to grow the power of youth; and to shift public perception on the role of young people in society.

Their definition of youth social action is: 'Youth social action refers to activities that young people do to make a positive difference to others or the environment.' The resulting research from the #iwill Campaign established six principles of youth social action (#iwill Campaign, 2022), which we continue to embed in our development of programmes and activities. These principles include 'be youth led', 'be challenging', 'be reflective', 'be embedded', 'be progressive' and 'be socially impactful'.

In recent years the #iwill Campaign itself has shifted, with the #iwill Movement, which focuses on an increased age demographic, engaging 10–25-year-olds in their work. The campaign still has much to offer in terms of shaping and sharing practice of how activities in higher education could be designed and delivered.

SOCIAL ACTION THROUGH STUDENT CONSULTANCY PROJECTS

Whilst the origins of Student Hubs' work started through practical volunteering projects, within a few years our work as a charity diversified to placements. Our placements have been structured work experience opportunities involving community partners working in social action and social impact, but typically only six to eight weeks in length, across a term or during the summer. Placements through Student Hubs' delivery have been primarily voluntary opportunities, with support for any associated travel costs or expenses.

Our flagship programme as part of this placement offering, called the Social Innovation Programme, started at the University of Cambridge in 2013 and has been running in various Hub university partner locations ever since including the University of Bristol, University of Winchester and Kingston University, representing its flexibility and appeal as a format to various student cohorts and demographics.

The Social Innovation Programme (SIP) is a termly programme which recruits interdisciplinary teams of students to engage in a free consultancy project for a local organisation across a term. Whilst many universities have similar programmes, we believe a focus specifically on small community groups and socially impactful organisations rather than businesses or corporate organisations makes a big difference in the way we can reach marginalised student groups, and supports our university partners' strategic aims with both employability and civic engagement.

We recruit students and community partners to participate and match student teams and organisations at a launch event, where students discover the challenge brief their organisation is presenting to them. They conduct research or practical activities for the organisation, before submitting a report and taking part in a showcase presentation at the end of the project. Throughout the term, the student participants take part in weekly training sessions delivered by Student Hubs staff, which are mandatory as part of the programme.

THE BENEFIT OF TRAINING EMBEDDED IN CONSULTANCY PROJECTS

Another key difference in how we deliver the programme is a focus on how students are supported, with key time set aside across the entire delivery for students to focus on developing core skill areas in a focused space with their peers. Providing additional training as part of our programmes allows us to fully embed the ethos and framework of social action into our activities. It provides an additional opportunity to bring students together to discuss their community's challenges and to network outside their set teams; it enables us to bring in the #iwill Campaign's principles such as embedding activity, being reflective and being challenging for our students; and it develops positive habits for students in sharing challenges and experiences, and engaging with others they may not know.

Our weekly training includes taking part in:

- information about the social impact sector;
- leadership development for group team leaders;
- training on research skills;
- action learning sets;
- data collection;
- how to write a report.

These training sessions implicitly support the students to develop and refine the skills required and practised during their project, but they also enable students to have a reflective space to share, to network with their peers and teams, and to ask questions in a supportive environment.

In some formats of the programme, we also work in partnership with corporate organisations, members of which act as mentors for the student teams. This adds a further level of support and additional spaces where students can reflect on and ask questions which hone their employability skills, as well as the benefits of accessing training from employers, being mentored by an industry professional, and developing their connections to local businesses.

In our 2020–21 case studies, a student said about their involvement:

> I feel that I have developed my consultation skills throughout this process. The large-scale email campaign we conducted enabled me to improve my written communication skills, and I am now more confident liaising with companies and charities. Furthermore, Bristol Hub and [law firm] Burges Salmon [our corporate partner] hosted a range of training sessions on a range of skills from 'how to present' to research methods. These sessions were incredibly valuable, and I hope to use these skills in future projects.

THE BENEFIT OF A COMMUNITY-LED APPROACH

Many students are drawn to the concept of supporting their local community and engaging in a placement-style programme, but may face challenges around low confidence and a lack of belief in their abilities. Looking ahead to the future and the impact of the pandemic on students, as a sector we need to deliver activities to students who may face these barriers. A report released by the Sutton Trust in February 2021 found that 76 per cent of students 'were worried about being able to gain the skills and experience needed for employment' (Sutton Trust, 2021), with 47 per cent of students surveyed also not taking part in any 'wider enrichment activities' that term.

Whilst circumstances have progressed significantly since then, it is important to recognise the legacy that the lack of experiences will be leaving on students, and how this impacts their confidence and initiative to set up their own employability-based experiences, such as year-long placements or work experience. For students who face these concerns, an approach to work-based placements where the emphasis is on students to find a placement partner, approach them directly, or take part in a placement with no additional training or university-based support, can appear frightening and lead to a lack of engagement.

A mentor for students, from our corporate partner working with a 2020–21 cycle of the Social Innovation Programme, said: 'One of my students that I was mentoring suffered from anxiety and it was great to see her confidence grow during the whole process, she was able to present confidently at the end presentation and showed great leadership skills.'

We see our approach through social action and student consultancy projects as a way to foster confidence, help students better understand and articulate their skill sets, and build evidence and enthusiasm for employability-based experiences which they can use to go onto the next step, and links with the 'progressive' principle of the #iwill Campaign's work. This might include students booking an appointment with their careers and employability team, or signing up to another work-based learning opportunity through their faculty, all of which are actively encouraged throughout their time on the Social Innovation Programme.

SUPPORTING STUDENTS' OVERALL SKILLS

Finally, through our consultancy projects, students themselves talk about the impact that the activity had, not only on their immediate experience during the programme, but on how the activity continued to shape their skills following the end of the programme.

One student shared about their experience of the programme in 2020–21: 'I have gained confidence in my abilities within projects but also in my daily life [as a result of taking part in the Social Innovation Programme]. I find myself better able to face challenges due to the project challenging my ability to balance and organise tasks.'

Looking at other data from our 2020–21 Impact Report (Student Hubs, 2022), from our Social Innovation Programme we reported that:

- 97 per cent of students agreed they developed professional skills from this activity;
- 97 per cent of students agreed that they better understand how to use their skills to support local organisations;
- 95 per cent of students agreed that they gained a useful insight into a socially impactful organisation and/or the social impact sector.

In addition, where corporate mentors were involved with the programme, 100 per cent of students agreed the mentors provided the support they needed, and 93 per cent of students agreed their mentors' skills and expertise improved the quality of their report and presentation.

SOCIAL ACTION IN THE CURRICULUM

Student Hubs began delivering Service Learning in 2017 in our Kingston Hub in collaboration with Kingston University, as a natural leap from our extra-curricular offering. Building in elements of community service to students' academic experience enabled us to address further barriers that many students faced, whilst also integrating our social action approach into the curriculum itself.

THE BENEFIT TO THE ACADEMIC COMMUNITY

In partnership with academics, we source and support community partners in the social action space (e.g. charities, social enterprises and local organisations) who can provide briefs and practical opportunities to deliver course-based assessments. Our approach has added capacity to the academics, who may not have established community networks or the capacity to give the community partner the level of support they required to work well as a partner, and delivers both what the students and the teaching and learning experience needed.

The benefit of this approach is that learning experiences can be unique. Projects are centred on what the community partner needs, aligning with the already existing assessment methods within the course to ensure it does not need to be revalidated, and projects can range from teams taking part in individual briefs to whole module cohorts focused on one brief. Projects are typically research, consultancy or practical in nature, with students participating in specific functions or activities required by the community partner, e.g. marketing and communications, data analysis or design.

An academic partner said:

> The initiatives have been really great for the students. They have introduced real world learning into their programme and have enabled us to deliver a more diverse and authentic learning experience. They have also given us the opportunity to bring new faces (as in people from the community/industry) into the classroom thus giving the students a better experience and a better awareness of their employability skills. They have also benefited from the fact that their efforts are contributing to wider communities. Students said in their feedback that contributing to the community made their activities meaningful.

EMPLOYABILITY DELIVERED ACCESSIBLY

By embedding social action directly in the curriculum, we were able to tackle the barriers that even our extra-curricular opportunities could not. We reached students in the spaces they were most engaged, and crucially, we came to them. Some work-based learning approaches at universities provide travel expenses and have the expectation that students will go to an employer to participate in that activity (which often the student has had to coordinate themselves, or with some support from their university). We know from our volunteering experience that even travel reimbursement can provide a barrier to opportunity for some students, both in the upfront costs required from them with a delay in getting reimbursed, and with the administration involved in reclaiming this money.

Therefore, taking an approach where the community partner either connects with the students remotely or comes to the classroom itself, instead of requiring students to travel to the partner and outside the classroom, is important for retaining the accessibility of the Service Learning module. This also benefits the community partner and their learning about their local institutions, as it enables them, if they choose, to enter the university space, which they may otherwise not get access to.

THE LIVE BRIEF EXPERIENCE

From the *Kingston Hub Impact Report 2020–21* (Student Hubs, 2021), examples of projects we have delivered at Kingston University include:

- Graphic Design students working with the Rio Ferdinand Foundation and Caius House to help design activities and facilities which better engaged with young people locally;
- Geography students working with a local organisation, the Community Brain, to use their academic skills relating to human demographics and research skills to reimagine usage of local community spaces;
- International Business students consulting for local organisation, the Baytree Centre, to adapt their marketing, outreach and other programme delivery to reach a wider pool of service users in their local area;
- Working with Children & Young People: Social Pedagogy students collaborating with Kingston Libraries' children and family unit to design and deliver activities for young people locally.

Through these projects, students benefit not only from the live brief experience, which supports their employability experiences, but also in how they develop key skills such as stakeholder management, critical thinking, communication and teamwork. They also get to apply their learning in a practical way, which supports them translating their theoretical work into their future workplace experiences.

A Service Learning participant in our 2020–21 case study said:

> [Service Learning] has been extremely beneficial, mainly because it has given me practical experience in learning more about different cultures. The fact that in this case my team and I were able to deal with issues related to the module whilst being able to communicate with the client directly helped to make a lot of theories and topics come into practice. It has been very inspirational to work directly with a community partner as it allowed me to actually understand the reality behind how some members of society are being integrated and given me insight into details to

take into consideration in a professional environment to communicate with clients with confidence and competence.

CONCLUSION

Overall, we think social action as a focal point for student projects, placements and in-curriculum learning can provide a unique opportunity to engage cohorts of students who might not otherwise have participated; to develop students' skills, employability and professionalism in support of a meaningful cause; and to reach and impact local organisations, allowing students to have a leading part in the university's civic engagement work.

This is also the direction of travel many students want to see. Students care more about their communities, social issues, and belonging than ever before, as well as participating in jobs that they see as meaningful, and universities should be capitalising on this engagement to encourage students to take part in employability-focused activities in new and exciting ways. With recent research suggesting that '51% of graduates in the UK remain local to their university after graduation' (Bridge Group, 2021), these types of experiences which are locally rooted support students to build key links and connections with a community which they may continue to serve and support upon graduation, as well as supporting their overall feelings of belonging and connection.

For us at Student Hubs, social action is the core way in which we can drive change with a dual benefit, both on a personal level for the students who participate, and for the communities in which they engage through their activity.

REFERENCES

Bridge Group (2021), *Focus on salaries undermines retaining graduates locally.* Available at: https://www.thebridgegroup.org.uk/news/bg-upp-report-2021 (accessed: 10 January 2023).

Centre for Social Action (2016), *Social Action Policy Paper.* Available at: https://www.gov.uk/government/publications/centre-for-social-action/centre-for-social-action (accessed: 10 January 2023).

#iwill Campaign (2022), *About Us.* Available at: https://www.iwill.org.uk/about-us (accessed: 10 January 2023).

Prime Minister's Office, 10 Downing Street, Deputy Prime Minister's Office, Cabinet Office, The Rt Hon David Cameron, the Rt Hon Nick Clegg (2013), *Step Up to Serve: making it easier for young people to help others.* Available at: https://www.gov.uk/government/news/step-up-to-serve-making-it-easier-for-young-people-to-help-others (accessed: 10 January 2023).

Sutton Trust (2021), *Covid-19 and the University Experience.* Available at: https://www.suttontrust.com/our-research/covid-19-and-the-university-experience-student-life-pandemic/ (accessed: 10 January 2023).

Student Hubs (2021), *Kingston Hub Impact Report 2020–21.* Available at: https://www.kingstonhub.org/about (accessed: 10 January 2023).

Student Hubs (2022), *Impact Report 2020–21.* Available at: https://www.studenthubs.org/impact-2020-21/ (accessed: 10 January 2023).

REFLECTION

From a graduate

Volunteering made me understand what I wanted to do. It made me realise what I wanted to do in my life and my purpose – giving back to communities and being an active citizen. I'm always doing something ... Throughout uni I was studying full time, working part time and volunteering – it was a busy schedule. I got into the schedule of that and even now I have a full-time job, I volunteer on the side and I'm looking for other things to do. It's one of those things that I am realising more and more, there are limitless opportunities to be an active citizen no matter what you want, need and can do. There are limitless options and I want to do all of them. Being an active citizen is actually not a difficult thing to do, it's not difficult at all ... If you want to do it, you can do it, you just need to find the time to do it ... I just think no matter what you want to do, no matter what skills you want to gain, no matter how much time you have or what resources you have, whether it's online or in person, there are limitless opportunities to get involved with. People always underestimate volunteering as they think to gain a skill they need to get it in a job. They don't – volunteering gives you those skills – it's completely free, there is possibly less interview process, it's less lengthy and the impact you will have is much greater. You will learn and give back too. Being an active citizen is simple, you just have to look for it.

16. The Big Challenge: interdisciplinary development of employability skills

Valerie Derbyshire, Laurice Fretwell and Caroline Harvey

INTRODUCTION

Just before the Covid-19 pandemic, students at the College of Life and Natural Sciences (CLANS) at the University of Derby took part in an interdisciplinary challenge, termed 'The Big Challenge', alongside academics in their subject specialities and several leading industry professionals. This challenge aimed to support the development of key employability skills and was staged as part of a knowledge exchange activity to encourage mutual learning for both the academics and the employers involved (Reed, 2018). The challenge also aimed to provide an opportunity for experiential learning through deep involvement for the students, creating a more effective and long-lasting form of learning via meaningful experience (Beard and Wilson, 2013). The event formed part of an enhancement week of activities for students and was not a compulsory part of in-curriculum learning. The Careers and Employment Service assisted the college in designing and implementing the Big Challenge. At the time of the challenge, the college incorporated students from a diverse range of courses including Biomedical Health, Human Biology, Psychology, Forensic Science, Zoology, Geography, Geology, Sport, Outdoor and Exercise Science and Environmental Assessment.

The Big Challenge provided the first opportunity for students across these diverse courses to work together in interdisciplinary teams with their peers, to solve a problem they might encounter in the real world. The project aimed to provide several outcomes including increased confidence across teamworking; project management; working in an interdisciplinary manner; leadership; negotiation skills; time management; communication; and presentation skills. These skills have been identified by a number of research studies as being lacking in the UK workforce, creating hard-to-fill vacancies (Winterbotham et al., 2020). The project also allowed students to understand the complicated nature of a real-world challenge and the necessity of working cohesively to address any issues they might encounter as they approach their graduate careers.

Career professionals have long recognised the importance of employer engagement in career effectiveness (Hambly and Bomford, 2019). Hambly and Bomford describe the skills that students will require to equip them for the world of work as resilience, the ability to upskill, face uncertainty, market their skills and find a network in which they belong. All of these skills contribute to the ability to manage an effective career. The Gatsby Benchmarks, as outlined in the Gatsby Foundation's report (2013), argue that students, from school age onwards, should have a variety of opportunities to learn from employers, enhancing their knowledge about work and employment, and developing employability skills which are valued in the workplace. The authors go on to suggest that employer engagement has an impact on students' future prospects and earning potential. For example, research from the Education and Employers Taskforce (Huddleston, 2020) demonstrates higher labour market returns for individuals who had greater contact with employers and engaged with careers talks from external speakers and employers. The work of the Taskforce demonstrates that these interactions with employers broaden students' horizons, raise aspirations and challenge stereotypical views often held about the jobs people do based on gender, ethnicity and social background (Huddleston, 2020).

Similarly, Binnie (2020) reaches the same conclusions in relation to university students, arguing that employer engagement is a vital element of the university experience. Not only does engaging with employers during their time at university enhance graduate transitions into employment, but it also supports improved engagement and attainment whilst at university. This report also highlights the value placed by employers on engaging with university students, demonstrating the significance of employer/student engagement events for both parties. Furthermore, Kuijpers (2019) argues that these employer engagement opportunities are essential for students to develop a clear image of an occupation, a realistic picture of the world of work and for them to project their 'possible selves' into these roles. Additionally, Cranmer (2007) argues that such learning cannot effectively take place in the classroom but needs to be delivered with employer involvement.

Clearly, research suggests that employer/student engagement is beneficial, but not all students are taking the opportunities provided by higher education institutions to engage with employers. Binnie's (2020) report notes that 30 per cent of employer engagement opportunities are extra-curricular and this was the case with the Big Challenge. The event was open for all students from CLANS, who could register to take part. The challenge met the requirements of our Access and Participation Plan (University of Derby/Office for Students, 2019), in that it aimed to improve equality of opportunity for all groups of students, empowering them to succeed and progress from higher education to graduate-level employment or further, higher-level study. Since the success of the staging of the Big Challenge, there is now an appetite to embed student engagement in development opportunities through work experience and impactful relationships with employers within the curriculum (Wheldon and Morrison, 2019). The university recognises that many students, however, do not have the confidence to engage and network efficiently with employers, but that student confidence, knowledge and the skills most sought by employers as graduate attributes can increase as a result of targeted employer relationships (Thompson, 2017). Indeed, lack of confidence in employer engagement is recognised as a common issue for students in career coaching. Hambly and Bomford (2019) argue that many clients require help in developing the confidence to engage effectively with employers, yet this ability to network proficiently is key to the success of meaningful employer engagement with students. They go on to contend that career effectiveness requires the five Cs of concern, control, curiosity, commitment and confidence, and it is confidence – or lack thereof – that has long been an issue in this type of engagement, forming a significant barrier in the success of employer engagement opportunities for a proportion of students. However, networking is a key skill and one which students need to develop in order to create career success as graduates.

Hambly and Bomford (2019) suggest that students may find approaching an employer directly very intimidating, and one way in which confidence can be developed is through facilitating a warm introduction to employer engagement. Students often have a deep-seated fear of rejection by employers, which can lead even the most proactive students to refuse to engage with employers (Hambly and Bomford, 2019). The Big Challenge effectively provided a warm introduction to employers, enabling student–employer engagement in a more relaxed environment. The event, from the beginning, aimed to imbue students with the courage of confidence which, as Hambly (2009) argues, is so essential in career interactions.

INTRODUCING THE BIG CHALLENGE

In order to cover all of the very diverse subjects that the students from the College of Life and Natural Sciences represented, the Big Challenge itself focused on an analysis of sports facilities in Derby and set students the task of developing a new sporting facility for the city. This involved consideration of a wide range of factors that might impact on the development of the facility. For example, students were asked to consider the siting of the facilities, planning requirements, psychological benefits of the facility, if any environmental assessment was required, any impact on crime and disorder in the local area and the need to ensure accessibility to the facility for all. Industry experts from a variety of relevant companies took part and were available throughout the day to provide advice and support to students. This included employers from nine different organisations, including one large international corporation, two charities, two public sector organisations and four small and medium-sized enterprises (SMEs).

At the beginning of the day, a lead industry professional introduced the challenge to the students. Other industry experts then introduced themselves to students in the familiar forum of the lecture theatre, sharing how their individual input could support the students as they addressed the requirements of the challenge. Academic and career professionals were also on hand to facilitate engagement between students and the industry professionals, fostering that atmosphere of warm introduction (Hambly and Bomford, 2019). Students were then allocated to interdisciplinary teams with approximately one representative from each discipline area in each team. Most of these students were not known to each other prior to the event. Before they embarked upon their task, they were advised that they would need to present their findings to the industry professionals at the end of the day, and that a variety of prizes would be on offer including: the best employability skills exhibited by individual teams; the best academic performance; the team with the most sustainable solution to the challenge; the team that worked together most effectively; and a best Geotechnical prize.

During the day, the challenge was enhanced by 'real-time' issues that may arise in a large and complicated project of this nature, with the intention of testing how students and their teams coped with these difficult and unexpected demands. For example, two hours into the challenge an email was sent out to the teams announcing that 'Great crested newts have been found on the site. What mitigation do you need to put in place?' An hour later, a further email was issued which read: 'The NHS are very interested in your leisure facilities. Can you help them contribute to community health? What classes/facilities can you provide?' These purposeful disruptions reflected the rapidly changing nature of a project, and how urgent issues may need to be addressed to successfully progress a project in the workplace.

At the conclusion of the event, the students seemed noticeably more confident and all of them reported enjoying the challenge and gave positive feedback. This was supported by the industry professionals who commented how they had enjoyed the event and were extremely impressed by the innovative and well-presented solutions individual teams had found. From the feedback presented about each other, teams seemed to have found a way to work together quickly and stayed together even after the event was over. Many reported that they would continue to stay in contact in the future, thus developing their network across disciplines in the college.

FOLLOW-ON RESEARCH PROJECT

Whilst the overall project was deemed to be a success by the participating students and the university, as Binnie (2020) argues, there can be a mismatch between how universities and employers measure the effectiveness of employer engagement. A considerable body of research analyses the work of careers and employability services within higher education. In addition, there is extensive work on how this translates to graduate transitions into employment, and it is clear, as argued earlier, that students do benefit from engaging with employers whilst they are in higher education. However, there is less research analysing these issues from the perspective of employers (Binnie, 2020). With this in view, it was felt that during the follow-up research project, the employer viewpoint should be sought, in order to provide some insight into an under-researched area. Furthermore, as Tymon (2013) argues, despite this ongoing debate as to the value of these exercises, the undergraduate viewpoint is equally little understood, although they are the recipients of this employability development. Therefore, the follow-up research project also aims to assess whether the impact of the challenge had any long-term beneficial effects upon students in terms of increase of confidence and attaining highly skilled graduate outcomes.

STUDENT VIEWPOINT

Within the online questionnaire and through the focus group discussions students will be asked about their engagement with employers during the challenge and about any effects on their own confidence across a range of employability skills. This will include a focus on skills identified by Crowley and Jeske (2020) as those most desirable in graduates, and include teamworking, project management skills, research skills, time management, communication and presentation skills. They also include some of the soft or transferable skills that Succi and Canovoi (2020) argue are considered by employers as essential graduate attributes, such as leadership, negotiation and planning. The development of these skills will enable students to progress to more confident career-building and self-management tools, of the type Bridgstock (2007) refers to in her discussion of graduate attributes. The questionnaire and focus group will allow for greater insight into the impact of the challenge on skills development.

EMPLOYER VIEWPOINT

Initial feedback from focus group discussions with employers highlights an overwhelmingly positive experience from working to support the students through the challenge. Employers were impressed with the way that the students were open to discuss their projects and take advice from the professionals. They felt the challenge was relevant and presented issues which students would encounter in the workplace. They also felt it was important to be able to share their experiences from the workplace with students and that this type of 'real world' learning could also benefit themselves as employers, given it might provide an opportunity for them to employ a graduate who had actual experience of this type of problem resolution to build upon. Finally, they also commented on how the event had reminded themselves of what it was like to be a student and how confidence needs to be developed in students in order for them to successfully progress to graduate careers.

CONCLUSION

In conclusion, initial feedback indicates that the approachability of the employers and their willingness to share their expertise, skills, time and knowledge with students, and the ability of students to develop teamworking skills rapidly in the face of the Big Challenge, empowered the students to develop new employability skills and confidence. Students enjoyed working in an interdisciplinary manner and learning more about alternative professions and opportunities. Both students and employers felt the value of the Big Challenge and it had clear impacts in that students were then able to identify the skills they had developed and use these as evidence in future job interviews. The experience of the challenge was also positive from the employers' point of view and has enhanced employer relationships with the university, as employers enjoyed the experience and expressed a willingness to support future events of this nature.

The initial concept for the challenge was inspired by the Pearson and Nesta report, *The Future of Skills: Employment in 2030* (Bakhshi et al., 2017) which highlighted a growing need for employees to be capable of working across disciplines in the future workplace. The challenge permitted students to see beyond the niche of their academic studies and begin to appreciate that many professionals work in an interdisciplinary manner and that opportunities exist for those who can work flexibly and effectively across teams and disciplines. As the event progressed, student confidence and the enthusiasm for the challenge grew, enabling students to engage positively with the employers, breaking down barriers and starting to build a professional network. Speaking with the employers enabled them to see beyond the logical professions linked with their academic studies and broaden their horizons to embrace new possibilities which they came to understand were open to them by discussing the career pathways of the professionals. The professionals had studied the same degree courses as the students, but by working in an interdisciplinary manner and focusing on developing transferable skills such as teamworking, problem solving and communication skills, they were able to progress to high levels in a diverse range of roles. This served as a locus of inspiration for the students.

REFERENCES

Bakhshi, H., Downing J. M., Osborn, M. A. and Schneider, P. (2017), *The Future of Skills: Employment in 2030*, London: Pearson and Nesta.

Beard, C. and Wilson, J. (2013), *Experiential Learning: A Handbook for Education, Training and Coaching*, London: KoganPage.

Binnie, G. (2020), *Evaluating the Effectiveness of Employer Engagement: A Report by the AGCAS Employer Engagement Task Group*, Sheffield: AGCAS.

Bridgstock, R. (2007), 'The graduate attributes we've overlooked: enhancing graduate employability through career management skills', *British Journal of Guidance & Counselling*, 28, 31–44.

Cranmer, S. (2007), 'Enhancing graduate employability: best intentions and mixed outcomes', *Studies in Higher Education*, 31, 169–184.

Crowley, L. and Jeske, D. (2020), 'Recruiter perceptions and expectations of desirable graduate attributes and fit', *British Journal of Guidance & Counselling*, 49, 78–89.

Gatsby Foundation (2013), *Good Career Guidance*, London: The Gatsby Charitable Foundation.

Hambly, L. (2009), 'The courage of confidence: the role of faith' in H. Reid (ed.), *Constructing the Future: Career Guidance for Changing Contexts*, Stourbridge: Institute of Career Guidance.

Hambly, L. and Bomford, C. (2019), *Creative Career Coaching: Theory into Practice*, Abingdon: Routledge.

Huddleston, P. (2020), *A Short History of Employer Engagement: Once More Round the Buoy or Set Fair for a Better Voyage?* London: Education and Employers Taskforce.

Kuijpers, M. (2019), 'Career guidance in collaboration between schools and work organisations', *British Journal of Guidance & Counselling*, 47, 487–497.

Reed, M. S. (2018), *The Research Impact Handbook*, 2nd edn, Huntly: Fast Track Impact Limited.

Succi, C. and Canovi, M. (2020), 'Soft skills to enhance graduate employability: comparing students and employers' perceptions', *Studies in Higher Education*, 45, 1834–1847.

Thompson, H. (2017), *Work Experience Policy and Quality Assurance Guidelines*, Derby: University of Derby.

Tymon, A. (2013), 'The student perspective on employability', *Studies in Higher Education*, 38, 841–856.

University of Derby/Office for Students (2019), *Access and Participation Plan 2020–21 to 2024–25*, Derby: University of Derby.

Wheldon, J. and Morrison, S. (2019), *Strategy for Highly Skilled Graduate Outcomes*, Derby: University of Derby.

Winterbotham, M., Kik, G., Selner, S., Menys, R., Stroud, S. and Whittaker, S. (2020), *Employer Skills Survey 2019: Research Report*. London: Government Social Research/Department for Education.

REFLECTION

From a manager in an SME

For me, I think it's really valuable for students to work together in an interdisciplinary way. In my profession, we have to work with lots of different disciplines on a daily basis and so to know how to interact and do that work as a wider team is a really useful skill. I was also really surprised with how well they all engaged and took on feedback and used our expertise. Students from quite different courses worked together to come up with some really good ideas. It's been a while since I've been at university and I wasn't quite sure what to expect from them, but actually overall I was really impressed with what I saw, and it did make me think as employers we sometimes get graduates who haven't got the necessary skills in a professional manner; I think it just made me understand a little bit where they're coming from.

17. Modifying the journey to graduate employment through changes to work-based learning
Catherine O'Connor

INTRODUCTION

For more than three decades, university graduates have been identified as having a positive impact on economic productivity with an ever-sharper focus from government ministers on ensuring that a degree should mean transition to highly skilled employment. This chapter explores the drivers for an institutional change project at Leeds Trinity University (LTU) around its placements and work-based learning against the backdrop of the wider policy agenda and a regulatory environment setting down performance baselines around graduate outcomes. It also considers key literature that can support approaches to graduate employment in the context of an evolving labour market.

POLICY AND LABOUR MARKET CONTEXT

The link between higher education, skills and economic productivity has long been made (Robbins Report, 1963; Dearing Report, 1997) but since the turn of the millennium, there has been a clear legislative and policy trajectory which has emphasised the importance of human capital to support economic advancement. This was reinforced in the UK in late November 2021 with the announcement that universities would be asked to rewrite their access and participation plans with a shift in focus 'from intakes to outcomes – real social mobility' (Department for Education and the Rt Hon Michelle Donelan, 2021). In early 2022, the Office for Students consulted on numerical thresholds for student outcomes, a mechanism for holding institutions to account for performance around continuation, completion and progression to highly skilled outcomes and billed as a means to 'crack down on poor quality courses' (Office for Students, 2022).

The equation of being a graduate and achieving a highly skilled outcome is, however, not as straightforward as it seems. Recent research shows two things; that graduates from poorer backgrounds are less likely to be in top-level jobs in their 20s (Duta et al., 2021); and that graduates from poorer backgrounds earn half as much as more privileged peers in their first job after graduating because they do not put themselves forward for as many roles and do not have the family connections and financial support to search for top jobs (Hall, 2021). Such evidence is highly relevant to LTU, which has a significant widening-access focus.

As an anchor institution, LTU also draws on local labour market data to understand trends, gaps and requirements. This includes engaging with Leeds City Council's growth agenda and data published by West Yorkshire Combined Authority and Leeds City Region Enterprise Partnership. The significance of digital skills – and the connection between education and employment – was identified in the 2021 West Yorkshire Combined Authority and Leeds City Region Enterprise Partnership Employment and Skills Framework. But the digital skills gap is not specific to 'specialist' organisations; gaps relating to computer literacy and basic IT skills exist across all organisations, in lower skilled roles and managerial roles. There is also a need to improve problem-solving skills among workers in higher skilled management professional and associate roles (West Yorkshire Combined Authority, 2021).

ACADEMIC APPROACHES TO EMPLOYABILITY

A wealth of literature addresses both the concept and components of employability (Hillage and Pollard, 1988; Harvey, 2001; Brown et al., 2003; Yorke, 2006) as well as the impact of the higher education (HE) performativity agenda (Ball, 2003, 2012; Avis, 2011) and employability on the very nature of university education and its graduates (Boden and Nedeva, 2010). The challenge and complexity of understanding employability from the perspective of attributes is illustrated through systematic reviews, including a 2016 study by Williams et al., which considered 16 conceptualisations of employability and 88 different components before detailing how these feed into human, social, cultural and psychological capital (Williams et al., 2016). These capitals were also the focus of Tomlinson (2017), who viewed them as being acquired through graduates' 'lived experiences' (p. 340) and emphasised the importance of accessing experience and presenting the value in it as part of the journey to being a graduate.

This more human dimension of employability was central to the work of Bennett (2012) who critiqued the way learning, identity and work are discussed in academia. She noted students need a future vision of self, motivation and self-esteem in order to develop their identities and asserted that there was a growing demand for graduates who can manage change, have an entrepreneurial outlook, can contribute creatively, are engaged in learning as a lifelong activity and who can 'transform information and content into strategies and tools, and transform themselves from receivers of knowledge into participatory learners' (p. 36). This notion of the participatory learner can be aligned to Donald et al. (2018) who noted the importance of student voice in the labour market and as part of an interconnected 'career ecosystem' (p. 514). For Bridgstock and Tippett (2019), a connected approach to learning focuses on partnerships, groups, communities and networks. While recognising that the language of skills and attributes is likely to always have a place within graduate employability discourse, the Change Project outlined in this chapter focused on supporting students to develop their place and voice within this agenda through evolving networks and connections.

DRIVERS FOR CHANGE

Placements at LTU are delivered in partnership with a network of more than 3,000 employers, with a focus on students as individuals. They help to develop a wide range of skills and behaviours but, more importantly, provide a clear process (Holmes, 2013) for students to go through to build these attributes with a concomitant impact on their graduate capitals (Tomlinson, 2017). For an institution in which more than 60 per cent of students are the first in their family to attend university, the development of social, cultural and identity capitals is of particular significance.

The LTU 2021–2026 strategy positions the institution as career-led, with a clear aim to have graduates leave with a career passport to support them in their graduate journey. Along with this, there were three further drivers for this change project:

- Institutional data, feedback and experience which highlighted that a significant number of Level 4 (first year undergraduate) students found engaging with the first placement challenging, either because of uncertainty about their career pathway or because of lack of confidence. The institution's dedicated placements team measured engagement with the confirmation of placements and, through direct interaction with students, they accumulated evidence and information which shone a light on the reasons for lack of engagement.
- The 'gap' at Level 6 (final year undergraduate) in terms of work–place connectivity, learning and development for students who did not undertake the work-based project originally offered as an optional module. This was viewed as significant and as a 'break' in the pathway to graduate outcomes.

- Feedback from employers about the benefits of, and preference for, being able to work with final year students who can contribute more to the workplace and gain greater value from the experience.

The Change Project was discussed at various levels within the institution, including with Student Union representatives, before it was formally approved through the Learning and Teaching Committee, which includes student members.

INSTITUTIONAL CONTEXT

LTU is a Catholic Foundation university with 4,700 students on its Horsforth, Leeds, campus and around 5,500 franchise partnership students. Its development stems from two teacher training colleges and, thanks to this heritage, has always embedded credit-bearing placements within undergraduate (UG) degrees, with students traditionally going out to the workplace at the end of their first and second years of study, as well as having the option for a final year work-based project. The Change Project involved making the Level 4 placement optional and shorter and framing it as an introduction, and making the Level 6 work-based project a core module for all students, whilst keeping a six-week placement at Level 5 (Table 17.1). These changes built work-based learning and connectivity into every level of study, providing a strong transitional journey into the labour market. Students are supported to take greater ownership of how they map their employability journey, have a means to address workplace confidence at Level 4 and will further develop their networks and employability through the compulsory Level 6 work-based project.

Table 17.1   Institutional Change Project summary

Study level	Framework for entrants up to September 2020	Framework for entrants from September 2021
Level 4	Two-week work placement launch programme, plus five-week placement	Choice of two-week placement or institution-wide professional challenge project
Level 5	Six-week work placement	Six-week work placement
Level 6	Optional work-based professional learning through work project	Core work-based professional learning through work project

In undertaking placements, students receive support from both their academic personal tutor and the university's placements team. The placements team deliver some embedded content in the modules within which placements are situated, plus additional events, and meet with students to support applications for and engagement with placements. All placement opportunities are advertised and competitive so the process of securing a placement is similar to applying for a job. Embedding this professional approach is seen as significant in supporting understanding that every aspect of getting into and taking part in a placement genuinely matters, not just the completion of one. Academic personal tutors are expected to meet with their tutees prior to them going out on placement, keep contact during placement and speak with employers to check that workplace activity is progressing satisfactorily.

In the final year of study, the work-based project, which has moved from being optional to core as part of this Change Project, means that not only are academic staff supervising a capstone project with a work-based focus, they also have the opportunity for regular interactions to prompt on career interactions and career readiness. This provides an opportunity for information sharing and joined-up approaches across academic staff and the graduate employment team. The work-based project has been an optional module in some programmes for a number of years and we are aware that it has supported students in developing further work with their Level 5 placement provider, with some going on to highly skilled employment with their employer upon graduation. One of the objectives of this Change Project was to develop this journey at institutional scale.

THE VALUE OF CHOICE AT LEVEL 4

In making this change, LTU has provided for Level 4 students who *are* ready for an external placement; equally, it has ensured that students who are not ready have the opportunity to develop their networks, attributes and apply knowledge through the completion of a professional challenge project. This engages them with the United Nations Sustainable Development Goals (UNSDG), focusing on deprivation, inequality and environmental issues (United Nations, n.d.), and providing a key platform to address issues of social justice and community agendas in the Leeds City Region. Students choose two from four challenges offered and work in small groups with the support of a coach, who is either an academic or professional services member of staff.

The project sought to engage students with many of the same skills and behaviours as a placement – teamworking, communication and consideration of how discipline and broader skills can be applied – but all the work linked to the project was undertaken on campus in collaboration with peers and university staff. Students also had agency through elements of co-creation and choice. Importantly, it allowed students to explore skills and issues in a broader context, moving them away from feeling like they have to 'fix' on a particular placement or pathway at the start of their degree, even if they are not ready. With its focus on issues and challenges which exist in the Leeds area, but which are relevant to the UNSDG, the project sought to support students in authentic and connected learning. The aim was to ensure the range of opportunities included would support an increased understanding of broad opportunities for graduate career pathways and inspire students to be active and impactful citizens.

Whether students decided to undertake an industry placement or the professional challenge project, they were able to draw together and apply their learning from their first year of study, laying the foundations for professional development through their Level 5 placement and, eventually, their final year 'professional learning through work project'.

FINAL YEAR AGENCY AND OWNERSHIP

By shifting to a professional learning through work project for all students at Level 6, the university is situating this as the capstone in all UG degrees, with final year students required to:

- negotiate a specific project with an employer or other relevant organisation, the objectives of which are approved by the university, and which is researched, delivered and evaluated by the student;
- identify the intended outcomes for the project, along with the methods and approach for delivering them;
- situate the project in the context of professional good practice and relevant literature;
- evaluate the final project against the agreed objectives and consider lessons learned, and recommendations for future projects.

In this regard, the professional learning through work project can be regarded as the culmination of a personalised approach which seeks to develop graduate capital incrementally. It speaks to key aspects of the connectedness learning model developed by Bridgstock and Tippett (2019) in that it involves authentic work-based learning through real professional contexts that require students to interact with professionals, and to take responsibility through co-design and for the delivery of a 'product'. At the heart of the model are five connectedness capabilities which range from building a connected identity through public-facing profiles, through to what the authors refer to as 'social network literacy' (p. 26), an ability to understand and analyse professional networks and utilise this for professional purposes. The LTU Change Project is viewed as supporting the development of these capabilities but, most significantly, allowing students to negotiate their entry point and initial development aligned with their personal reflections and readiness during their first year of study, while supporting all students to a final capstone to provide a gateway to graduate employment.

CONCLUSION

As the Change Project rolled out during 2021–22, the staff team monitored and evaluated the changes to consider engagement and feedback, points of success and areas for enhancement. This evaluation will reflect on the two key strengths this Change Project was considered to have.

Firstly, there is a perceived advantage in providing a supportive framework to understand and accommodate student perceptions of their readiness for the workplace through either the Level 4 optional placement, or the professional challenge project.

Secondly, the Change Project provides an opportunity for Level 6 students to be immersed in authentic employer-driven, real-world projects through a final capstone module with flexible assessment.

Evaluating key touchpoints across all three levels of all UG programmes will allow us to track and review the journey to graduate outcomes throughout every year of each degree. It will provide us with an evidence base to enhance embedded placements and careers-related content, which will need to be designed to engage students with the changing nature, composition and requirements of the labour market. Most importantly, the Change Project and associated ongoing evaluation will facilitate LTU in providing its students with an incremental, integrated and personalised graduate employability journey which is mapped, scaffolded and developed across levels, as well as addressing the related policy and audit agendas.

REFERENCES

Avis, J. (2011), 'More of the same? New Labour, the Coalition and education: markets, localism and social justice', *Educational Review*, 63(4), 421–438. doi: 10.1080/00131911.2011.616633.

Ball, S. J. (2003), 'The teacher's soul and the terrors of performativity', *Journal of Education Policy*, 18(2), 215–228. doi: 10.1080/0268093022000043065.

Ball, S. J. (2012), 'Performativity, commodification and commitment: an I-spy guide to the neoliberal university', *British Journal of Educational Studies*, 60(1), 17–28. doi: 10.1080/00071005.2011.650940.

Bennett, D. (2012), 'A creative approach to exploring student identity', *International Journal of Creativity & Problem Solving*, 22(1), 27–41.

Boden, R. and Nedeva, M. (2010), 'Employing discourse: universities and graduate "employability"', *Journal of Education Policy*, 25(1), 37–54, doi: 10.1080/02680930903349489.

Bridgstock, R. and Tippett, N. (2019), 'Connectedness capabilities', in R. Bridgstock and N. Tippett (eds), *Higher Education and the Future of Graduate Employability:*

A Connectedness Learning Approach, Cheltenham, UK and Northampton, MA, USA: Edward Elgar Publishing, pp. 22–29.

Brown, P., Hesketh, A. and Williams, S. (2003), 'Employability in a knowledge-driven economy', *Journal of Education and Work*, 16(2), 107–126. doi: 10.1080/1363908032000070648.

Dearing Report (1997), *Higher Education in the learning society: Report of the National Committee of Inquiry into Higher Education*. London: HMSO. Available at: http://www.educationengland.org.uk/documents/dearing1997/dearing1997.html (accessed: 23 January 2023).

Department for Education and the Rt Hon Michelle Donelan MP (2021), *Higher and Further Education Minister speech at Times Higher Education event*. Available at: www.gov.uk/government/speeches/higher-and-further-education-minister-speech-at-times-higher-education-event (accessed: 11 January 2023).

Donald, W. E., Ashleigh, M. J. and Baruch, Y. (2018), 'Students' perceptions of education and employability: facilitating career transition from higher education into the labor market', *Career Development International*, 23(5), 513–540. Available at: https://doi.org/10.1108/CDI-09-2017-0171 (accessed: 11 January 2023).

Duta, A., Wielgoszewska, B. and Iannelli, C. (2021), 'Different degrees of career success; social origin and graduates' education and labour market trajectories', *Advances in Life Course Research*, 47(2021), 100376. doi: 10.1016/j.alcr.2020.100376.

Hall, R. (2021), 'Disadvantaged graduates earn half as much as privileged peers in first job', *The Guardian*, 12 November. Available at: www.theguardian.com/money/2021/nov/12/disadvantaged-graduates-earn-half-as-much-as-privileged-peers-in-first-job (accessed: 11 January 2023).

Harvey, L. (2001), 'Defining and measuring employability', *Quality in Higher Education*, 7(2), 97–109. doi: 10.1080/13538320120059990.

Hillage, J. and Pollard, E. (1998), 'Employability: developing a framework for policy analysis', Research Brief No. 85, Department for Education and Employment, London. Available at: https://www.academia.edu/23029127/Employability_developing_a_framework_for_policy_analysis (accessed: 11 January 2023).

Holmes, L. (2013), 'Competing perspectives on graduate employability: possession, position or process?', *Studies in Higher Education*, 38(4), 538–554. Available at: https://doi.org/10.1080/03075079.2011.587140 (accessed: 11 January 2023).

Office for Students (2022), 'OfS sets out plans to crack down on poor quality courses'. Office for Students, 20 January. Available at: https://www.officeforstudents.org.uk/news-blog-and-events/press-and-media/ofs-sets-out-plans-to-crack-down-on-poor-quality-courses/ (accessed: 11 January 2023).

Robbins Report (1963), *Higher Education: Report of the Committee on Higher Education*. London: HMSO. Available at: http://www.educationengland.org.uk/documents/robbins/robbins1963.html (accessed: 23 January 2023).

Tomlinson, M. (2017), 'Forms of graduate capital and their relationship to graduate employability', *Education + Training*, 59(4), 338–352. doi: 10.1108/ET-05-2016-0090.

United Nations (n.d.), *The 17 Goals*. Available at: https://sdgs.un.org/goals (accessed: 11 January 2023).

West Yorkshire Combined Authority (2021), *Local Skills Report: Leeds City Region*. Available at: https://www.westyorks-ca.gov.uk/media/6033/local-skills-report-final.pdf (accessed: 11 January 2023).

West Yorkshire Combined Authority and Leeds City Region Enterprise Partnership (2021), *Employment and Skills Framework*. Available at: https://www.westyorks-ca

.gov.uk/media/6573/employment-skills-framework-final.pdf (accessed: 11 January 2023).

Williams, S., Dodd, L. J., Steele, C. and Randall, R. (2016), 'A systematic review of current understandings of employability', *Journal of Education and Work*, 29(8), 877–901. doi: 10.1080/13639080.2015.1102210.

Yorke, M. (2006), *Employability in Higher Education: What It Is – What It Is Not*, York: Higher Education Academy. Available at: https://www.advance-he.ac.uk/knowledge-hub/employability-higher-education-what-it-what-it-not (accessed: 11 January 2023).

REFLECTION

From a student studying to be a teacher

For many students in teacher-training programmes, internationalisation and out-of-school working experiences are rare phenomena during their education. Thus, it was important for me to get insights into the working environment in education but outside of the classroom. I sought working practices from outside of school to acquire skills and gain cultural experiences, important for the cultural awareness and international experiences of teachers. Therefore, I organised an internship abroad, at the International Office of a middle-sized university, to work in education, internationalisation, and administration. The aim was to receive a multi-perspective view on organising, realising, and evaluating activities for international exchange students. I was able to improve skills such as organising large-scale activities, reflecting on the activities and the observed procedures as well as evaluating them in writing, proposing improvements and providing criticism to supervisors. Looking back on the internship, it has helped me to hone important skills for my future career.

Internships allow students to get to know the working environment in detail, create vital networking opportunities and thus help everyone still indecisive of their career paths. Having an internship abroad adds important sets of skills, such as the ability to communicate confidently in a foreign language environment or a multi-perspective approach towards problem-solving and decision-making, or communicative skills with cultural awareness, which is particularly valuable in today's society. Reflecting on these aspects, I have come to realise that not only my language skills have improved – which is especially important for language teachers – but I have also broadened my cultural horizons by living in a foreign country and being part of a culturally different social environment. In conclusion, an international internship does not only improve your working and social skills or your language skills, but it also allows you to see and experience the world from different and new perspectives.

PART VI

Enterprise/entrepreneurial opportunities

18. 'One for all and all for one': the 3Es (employability, enterprise, and entrepreneurship)
Emily Beaumont

INTRODUCTION

Employability, enterprise, and entrepreneurship (commonly referred to as the 3Es) are topics firmly established in the rhetoric and practice of the higher education (HE) sector and higher education institutions (HEIs) in the UK and beyond. It has been suggested that due to the recent global pandemic, now more than ever, there is a 'renewed recognition, and indeed emphasis, on positively supporting student trajectories through and beyond university by enhancing a range of activities linked to the 3Es' (Norton and Sear, 2021). However, the 3Es are frequently addressed 'as distinct, if not mutually exclusive concepts' (Dean, 2010: 21), existing in silos, with employability regularly separated from enterprise and entrepreneurship, the latter two being habitually 'lumped together' because they appear akin (an approach the author has reluctantly taken within this chapter). Evidence of this can be seen in a survey of 100 AGCAS members, where 65 per cent of non-Russell Group respondents stated that they had a separate enterprise and/or entrepreneurship specialist unit to their careers and employability service (Hook, 2020). Even Norton and Sear of Advance HE (2021), despite their call to enhance the range of activities linked to the 3Es, present an 'Advance HE Guide to the Framework for Enterprise and Entrepreneurship Education' as their solution, curiously omitting employability. Subsequently, in trying to positively support student trajectories through and beyond university, we are currently offering students two distinct and mutually exclusive pathways, employability and/or enterprise and entrepreneurship. This chapter aims to explore why the siloed approach to the 3Es exists and considers its consequences. As a result, an alternative [re]freshed approach which suggests the 3Es should be addressed collectively as one concept is presented, proposing the significant impact that adopting this approach could have.

THE DOMINANCE OF EMPLOYABILITY

In the past 30 years, HE has experienced an employability agenda that has advanced both in terms of knowledge and understanding, but also in significance, making employability a priority for universities (Quinlan and Renninger, 2022). According to Dean (2010) this can be attributed to a number of factors:

- the then Department for Innovation, Universities and Skills commenting that 'We want to see all universities treating student employability as a core part of their mission' (Department for Innovation, Universities and Skills, 2008: 6);
- employability growing in strength by incorporating concepts such as key skills and career development learning;
- the belief that some students are attracted to 'safe' options and subsequently the language of employability, over the portrayal of enterprise and entrepreneurship as 'risky';
- and the growing presence of proxy measures for employability featuring strongly in external metrics and reporting (such as university league tables and graduate destination data and starting salaries).

At the same time, there has been a global increase in the provision of enterprise and entrepreneurship in HE (Bae et al., 2014; Nabi et al., 2017) and yet it has failed to match the magnitude of the employability agenda. Whilst all of the above are potential reasons for this, cynics may suggest that employability's presence and prominence in published league tables such as The Complete University Guide, The Guardian University Guide, and The Times League Table are the most pervasive and persuasive of reasons for employability's dominance over enterprise and entrepreneurship in HE. For ease of use by such publications, employability is reduced to a proxy measure extracted through the Graduate Outcomes Survey (GOS).

The Higher Education Statistics Agency (HESA) has been surveying the employability of graduates in the UK since 1994 through the Destination of Leavers from Higher Education (DLHE) survey. HESA has evolved DLHE into the GOS to allow a longer period between a student's studies and the survey (from 6 to 15 months), whilst enabling what they described as a richer insight into outcomes through more meaningful subjective questions (HESA, 2022). Whilst both the DLHE and the GOS are repeatedly argued against as being valid measures of employability ('employability is not something that can be quantified by any single measure'; Cole and Tibby, 2013: 6), HESA continues to operate such instruments, the results of which feed into external-facing university league tables.

University league tables are now a common feature of HE and, despite a multitude of criticisms, are widely accepted as a helpful resource for stakeholders, such as prospective students (when considered alongside other sources of information). The research group YouthSight created a perception of reputation index that illustrates a close relationship between league table scores and the perceptions that students have about university reputation (Catchside, 2012). Additionally, Chevalier and Jia (2015) found a positive (albeit rather small) effect of league table score on the number of applications received by a university. Consequently, 'in spite of the controversial nature of rankings, there seems to be a persistent desire on the part of universities to assert their international rank by the position they clinch on league tables' with institutions increasingly using rankings for goal-setting purposes (Salmi and Saroyan, 2007: 22).

Like employability, proxy measures for enterprise and entrepreneurship also exist, yet they are limited to a reliance on venture creation as an outcome and proxy measure of impact. Despite criticism of this approach, venture creation data has been routinely collected (annually) for policy-driven metrics such as the Higher Education Business and Community Interaction survey (HE-BCI). Yet this data does not feature in any of the three prominent university league tables, and Smith et al. (2020) note that the graduate spin-out data collected as part of HE-BCI does not contribute to the formula for calculating the Higher Education Innovation Fund pot for each HEI, subsequently limiting a university's 'interest' in enterprise and entrepreneurship as a vehicle for venture creation. There is potential, however, for the Knowledge Exchange Framework (KEF) to change this and include a ratio of the number of new start-ups created by student full time equivalent (FTE) for the institution (Smith et al., 2020: 10). Given the significance this could have to the KEF rating, it could be suggested that HEIs will take an increased interest in enterprise and entrepreneurship in the context of venture creation. However, the weighting of this ratio will no doubt impact the level of interest.

At present, HEI's subservience to proxy measures related to the 3Es, and the university league tables that subsequently rate them, leads many HEIs to take a reductionist outcome-focused approach where employability equals employment (preferably in a managerial position), and enterprise and entrepreneurship equal venture creation. Due to the significant impact employability proxy measures have on league table position in comparison to their enterprise and entrepreneurship equivalent, it is clear why employability maintains the spotlight from which enterprise and entrepreneurship currently cannot distract.

TIME FOR A (RE)FRESH PERSPECTIVE

Whilst we might not agree with the current reality of the 3Es, it is perhaps understandable given the various external influencing factors at play. However, is it possible to find a fresh perspective to the 3Es which understands and appreciates the broader perspective and value of employability, enterprise and entrepreneurship, recognising the relationship between them, and yet still delivering on the proxy measures that will inevitably influence HE and HEIs for the foreseeable future? In short, yes, but it is not necessarily a 'fresh' approach, but an existing one in need of a (re)fresh.

There is a well-developed body of literature in employability, enterprise and entrepreneurship that over time has explored, and in some cases defined, elements such as the knowledge, skills, characteristics, behaviours, attributes and competencies, etc. that are required to enhance one's employability or enterprise and entrepreneurship capabilities. This approach considers a more rounded definition of employability, enterprise and entrepreneurship than the proxy measures allow us. Employability is awash with models, each with the intention of unpacking employability to reveal its building blocks. The most notable are Hillage and Pollard's (1998) employability framework, the USEM model (Yorke and Knight, 2004), and the CareerEDGE Model (Dacre Pool and Sewell, 2007) highlighting a similar range of elements, each with their own justification for inclusion. In enterprise and entrepreneurship, this approach is commonly related to the entrepreneurial mindset; 'a set of characteristics, behaviours and skills that drive [entrepreneurial] action' (Network for Teaching Entrepreneurship, 2017: 2). The European Commission's Entrepreneurship Competence Framework, EntreComp, is the best example of this approach, identifying 15 competencies over three key areas that define what it means to be entrepreneurial (Bacigalupo et al., 2016). It is worth noting, however, that due to the nature of the elements that exist within these models (e.g. skills, attributes, etc.), the models often become 'stuck' in the political, societal, economic, and technological space they were created in. Consequently, they are in danger of ageing, risking their current and future relevance.

Despite the existence of separate models or frameworks of employability to enterprise and entrepreneurship, it is within this approach that we begin to see a balanced perspective to the 3Es, with recognition of a relationship between them and an acknowledgement that one can, in turn, enhance the other(s) (Bauman and Lucy, 2021; Chandler and Broberg, 2019; Decker-Lange et al., 2022; Dhaliwal, 2017; Gibb, 1996; Nabi et al., 2018). Not only can they enhance one another, but there is recognition of an overlap between the skills, attributes and competencies of employability, and enterprise and entrepreneurship (Decker-Lange, 2021; QAA, 2018); so much so that 'over the last five years, there has become more of a blurring rather than distinction between the two: the components of enterprise are fundamental to the components of employability and vice versa' (Norton, 2019). This is visible in existing independent frameworks where we see self-awareness and/or self-efficacy within Hillage and Pollard's (1998) employability framework, the USEM model (Yorke and Knight, 2004), the CareerEDGE Model (Dacre Pool and Sewell, 2007) and the EntreComp framework. Further to this, Walmsley et al. (2022) noted 'substantial overlap' in the skills that are deemed critical to both entrepreneurship and employability, highlighting in particular creativity, innovation, passion, perseverance, resilience, leadership, planning and problem-solving skills, collaboration and communication (Decker-Lange, 2021). The 3Es share DNA and building blocks, revealing that they are more closely related than current discourse and practice in the HE sector may have us believe. It is therefore suggested that there could be value in a single model or framework for the 3Es, one that should be revisited to evolve over time, maintaining its relevance and currency to the stakeholders it serves.

Dean (2010) went so far as to present a continuum of enterprise and employability in which not only are enterprise skills viewed as employability skills, but the binary options and outcomes associated with employability to enterprise and entrepreneurship, propagated by the proxy measures utilised by university league tables, are instead replaced with a spectrum of opportunities. At one end of the continuum is the enterprising entrepreneur/portfolio worker, moving through to the job crafting intrapreneur, and finally on to the employable employee and everything else in between. By adopting an approach where the 3Es are 'all for one and one for all', Dean (2010) believes that we are not only 'doing right' by our students, but ultimately benefitting the economy as a whole (Dean, 2010).

To summarise, the current climate the 3Es exist within propagates a siloed approach to employability, enterprise and entrepreneurship in HEIs, existing to serve university league tables, which subsequently give prominence to employability. Adopting a broader perspective of the 3Es, considering the knowledge, skills, characteristics, behaviours, attributes and competencies, etc. that exist as building blocks for employability, enterprise and entrepreneurship creates a levelling-up process across all 3Es. It also removes the potential emphasis on the binary outcomes of employment or venture creation, and offers a spectrum of positive opportunities for graduates whilst delivering on proxy measures that will inevitably continue to exist in the world of HE.

CONCLUSION

So what are the steps for an HEI to adopt this 'broader perspective'? Whilst it is clear that further enquiry into this topic is required, even at this preliminary stage there are some recommendations that can be made to HEIs wanting to adopt this approach. For example, HEIs can reflect on existing frameworks of employability, enterprise and entrepreneurship and situate this in the current context of a range of factors significant to the HEI and its key stakeholders, such as political, economic, societal, technological and environmental factors. This can then support the choice and prioritisation of their own building blocks for the 3Es as a single concept in their HEI. In light of the above, HEIs should then review their employability, enterprise and entrepreneurship offer and consider how their current structure and operations may not be conducive to an effective 3E approach. Finally, an HEI needs to consider this as a live process that will change and evolve over time, subsequently building in a continual process of review of the 3Es to remain relevant and effective to all key stakeholders.

So, who will take up the mantle to further define such an approach, what will it look like, and when will this happen are questions unanswered and therefore posed by the author to members of the HE community. More pertinently, who will adopt it? Embedding such an approach would involve radical changes in an HEI's structure, operations, and culture, a move not for the faint hearted. In short, this chapter exists as a call to action for the continued work (both research and practice) to be done in the 3E space.

REFERENCES

Bacigalupo, M., Kampylis, P., Punie, Y. and Van den Brande, G. (2016), *EntreComp: The Entrepreneurship Competence Framework*. Luxembourg: Publication Office of the European Union.

Bae, T. J., Qian, S., Miao, C. and Fiet, J. O. (2014), 'The relationship between entrepreneurship education and entrepreneurial intentions: a meta-analytic review', *Entrepreneurship: Theory & Practice*, 38(2), 217–254.

Bauman, A. and Lucy, C. (2021), 'Enhancing entrepreneurial education: developing competencies for success', *International Journal of Management Education*, 9(1), 100293 doi: https://doi.org/10.1016/j.ijme.2019.03.005.

Catchside, K. (2012), 'What do universities actually gain by improving league table performance?', *The Guardian*, 16 March. Available at: https://www.theguardian.com/higher-education-network/blog/2012/mar/16/league-table-performance (accessed: 11 January 2023).

Chandler, G. N. and Broberg, J. C. (2019), 'Using a new venture competition to provide external assessment of a university entrepreneurship program', *Entrepreneurship Education and Pedagogy*, 2(2), 96–122.

Chevalier, A. and Jia, X. (2015), 'Subject-specific league tables and students' application decisions', *Manchester School*, 84(5), 600–620.

Cole, D. and Tibby, M. (2013), *Defining and Developing Your Approach to Employability: A Framework for Higher Education Institutions*. York: The Higher Education Academy.

Dacre Pool, L. and Sewell, P. (2007), 'The key to employability: developing a practical model of graduate employability', *Education + Training*, 49(4), 277–289.

Dean, L. (2010), 'Enterprise and employability: to conflate or not to conflate?', *Assessment, Teaching & Learning Journal* (Leeds Met), 8(Spring), 21–23.

Decker- Lange, C. (2021), 'Three reasons why we should think about employability in entrepreneurship education', *Centre for Innovation in Legal and Business Education (SCiLAB)*, 8 March. Available at: https://www.open.ac.uk/scholarship-and-innovation/scilab/blog/three-reasons-why-we-should-think-about-employability-entrepreneurship-education (accessed: 11 January 2023).

Decker-Lange, C., Lange, K., Dhaliwal, S. and Walmsley, A. (2022), 'Exploring entrepreneurship education effectiveness at British universities – An application of the World Café method', *Entrepreneurship Education and Pedagogy*, 5(1), 113–136. doi: https://doi.org/10.1177/2515127420935391.

Department for Innovation, Universities and Skills (2008), *Higher Education at Work: High Skills: High Value*. London: DIUS.

Dhaliwal, S. (2017), *The Millennial Millionaire. How Young Entrepreneurs Turn Dreams into Business*. London: Palgrave.

Gibb, A. A. (1996), 'Entrepreneurship and small business management: can we afford to neglect them in the twenty-first century business school?', *British Journal of Management*, 7(4), 309–321.

HESA (2022), *Graduate Outcomes – About the Survey*. Available at: https://www.graduateoutcomes.ac.uk/about-survey (accessed: 11 January 2023).

Hillage, J. and Pollard, E. (1998), *Employability: Developing a Framework for Policy Analysis*. London: Department for Education and Employment.

Hook, H. (2020), 'AGCAS Enterprise and Entrepreneurship Task Group', *Phoenix*, 159, 22.

Nabi, G., Liñán, F., Fayolle, A., Kreuger, N. and Walmsley, A. (2017), 'The impact of entrepreneurship education in higher education', *Academy of Management Learning and Education*, 16(2), 1–23.

Nabi, G., Walmsley, A., Liñán, F., Akthar, I. and Neame, C. (2018), 'Does entrepreneurship education in the first year of higher education develop entrepreneurial intentions? The role of learning and inspiration', *Studies in Higher Education*, 43(3), 452–467.

Network for Teaching Entrepreneurship (2017), *Entrepreneurial Mindset: On Ramp to Opportunity*. New York: Network for Teaching Entrepreneurship.

Norton, S. (2019), 'Enterprise: an approach to enhancing employability'. Available at: https://www.advance-he.ac.uk/news-and-views/enterprise-approach-enhancing-employability (accessed: 11 January 2023).

Norton, S. and Sear, L. (2021), *The '3Es' – Enterprise, Entrepreneurship, Employability*. Available at: https://www.advance-he.ac.uk/news-and-views/3es-enterprise-entrepreneurship-employability (accessed: 11 January 2023).

QAA (2018), *Enterprise and Entrepreneurship Education: Guidance for UK Higher Education*. York: Quality Assurance Agency.

Quinlan, K. M. and Renninger, K. A. (2022), 'Rethinking employability: how students build on interest in a subject to plan a career', *Higher Education*, 84, 863–883. doi: https://doi.org/10.1007/s10734-021-00804-6.

Salmi, J. and Saroyan, A. (2007), 'League tables as policy instruments: uses and misuses', *Higher Education Management and Policy*, 19(2), 31–68. doi: https://doi.org/10.1787/hemp-v19-art10-en.

Smith, K., Bozward, D., Draycott, M., Mave, M., Curtis, V., Aluthgama-Baduge, C., Moon, R. and Adams, N. (2020), *Assessing the Impact of Enterprise and Entrepreneurship Education: Literature and Policy Project Report*.

Walmsley, A., Decker-Lange, C. and Lange, K. (2022), 'Conceptualising the entrepreneurship education and employability nexus', in G. J. Larios-Hernandez, A. Walmsley and I. Lopez-Castro (eds), *Theorising Undergraduate Entrepreneurship Education: Reflections on the Development of the Entrepreneurship Education*. Cham: Palgrave Macmillan, pp. 97–114.

Yorke, M. and Knight, P. T. (2004), *Embedding Employability into the Curriculum*. York: Higher Education Academy.

REFLECTION

From an Economics and Politics graduate

I was an international student in the UK where I studied accounting at a top ten UK university according to the Times Higher Education rankings. I remember this being such a wonderful time in my life and being very confident that I would have a lot of job opportunities after graduation. I remember one of the main reasons I could convince my parents to pay for the high costs involved was the university's marketing material about how successful their graduates where.

Unfortunately securing a graduate job was quite difficult. I looked on my university's job board and there were only a few job options available, I applied to all of them and then applied to over 200 other jobs in the UK online and received no responses or invitations to job interviews. I asked career services at my university for help and all they could do was offer to review my CV.

I realised I would have to start looking for a job back in my home country and this was even more daunting as I had no one I knew back there who could offer me any support. Luckily my old high school teacher friend (who had also studied abroad) introduced me to a network of people who I was able to meet when I returned home and I was able to secure a job (that was not advertised online). It took me several months after graduating to realise it was not enough to have top grades from a top overseas university to get a graduate job. It was as important (if not more so) to have a strong network who could help introduce you to job opportunities.

19. BSEEN: extra-curricular enterprise and entrepreneurship support

Carolyn Keenan

INTRODUCTION

Birmingham Skills for Entrepreneurship and Employability (BSEEN), a student and graduate start-up support programme, was established in 2009, in the aftermath of the financial crisis. At launch its principal objectives were:

- to improve support for small business and entrepreneurship in the West Midlands region;
- to better support growth and economic impact and the longevity of start-ups;
- to increase the level of business skills in the students and graduates on the programme and invest in their employability at a time of high graduate unemployment.

In addition, the programme helped encourage more graduates to remain in the region rather than move away to secure jobs in London or the south-east.

SUPPORT OFFERED BY BSEEN

The award-winning BSEEN programme is the final stage in the support for student and graduate entrepreneurs at Aston University and facilitates new student and graduate businesses to register and launch. The project has received two awards: in 2011 it was the winner of the Association of Graduate Careers Advisory Services (AGCAS) Entrepreneurship Award and in 2016 the programme won the National Centre for Entrepreneurship in Education Award in the HE Team Enterprise category. It is led by Aston University in collaboration with Birmingham City University, University College Birmingham, and Newman University, and is in its 12th year of operation. During this time over 1200 students and graduates have joined one of the 28 bootcamps where over 700 businesses have been created. The programme has been supported since 2012 via match funding from the European Regional Development Fund.

The programme is available to students and graduates up to five years after graduating from one of the four partner universities, plus graduates from any university who have graduated within the last five years and live in the Birmingham area. It is promoted widely by each of the partner universities to their students and graduates via social media, newsletters, careers and placement departments, student unions and through supportive academics. BSEEN has a dedicated website which houses an online application form. Each university selects their own entrepreneurs to attend one of the three bootcamps that take place each year in April, June and September. They all use the same process to evaluate the students or graduates, which involves a six-minute pitch of their business idea followed by a question-and-answer session. The panel evaluates the viability of the business as well as the drive and passion of the student or graduate to make it happen. Applicants that are not successful are generally offered support in other ways and encouraged to reapply if appropriate.

The support offered by the programme kicks off with a five-day intensive start-up bootcamp held at one of the partner institutions. This training is delivered by practitioners with experience of running their own business and includes two who have been through the BSEEN programme themselves. They cover all the start-up essentials including business planning, finance, digital marketing, storytelling, pitching and sales and getting into the founder's mindset. They are interactive and designed to provide the participants with the skills, knowledge, and latest tools to use in running their business.

After the bootcamp, participants receive free office space for 12 months, which provides somewhere to register the business and hold client meetings, and they also gain peer support from fellow founders, along with the ongoing support from the BSEEN team. A small grant of around £500 is available to cover some of the initial start-up costs such as business insurance, equipment, training, marketing materials or attendance at trade fairs. A business mentor is offered to each founder from a pool of around 50 active mentors supporting the programme on a pro bono basis. They come from a wide range of backgrounds and include university and BSEEN alumni, as well as current and former businesspeople, and industry and investment experts.

In 2022 the need for a start-up support programme is still there, albeit for different reasons. As stated by Mark Hart, Professor of Small Business and Entrepreneurship at Aston Business School and leader of the Global Entrepreneurship Monitor (GEM) UK team: 'Entrepreneurial attitudes and behaviours will be as critical for the recovery after the pandemic as they were after the Great Financial Crisis over a decade ago.'

The ever-evolving labour market for new graduates is being affected not just by the recent pandemic but also by the Fourth Industrial Revolution, with digitisation and new technologies such as artificial intelligence, augmented and virtual reality leading to an increasing demand by employers for graduates with 21st-century skills (Fahey, 2012). The Nesta report, *The Future of Skills: Employment in 2030* (Bakhshi, 2017) maps out how employment is likely to change in the future, including the implications for skills required.

It finds that workers will need a mix of social and cognitive skills, including the social skills of teaching (instructing), adjusting to others' actions (co-ordination), assessing others' performance (monitoring) and providing motivation (management of personnel resources), and the cognitive skills of coming up with multiple ideas (fluency of ideas), deriving novel solutions (originality) and understanding new information (active learning). Enterprise and entrepreneurship education has huge potential to positively impact the career outcomes of the learner. It provides them with 'an enhanced capacity to generate ideas, and the behaviours, attributes and competencies to make them happen' (QAA, 2018).

The future employability of graduates will depend heavily on how adaptive, resilient and innovative they are, so that they can navigate their way through the new career paths of the future. Universities, therefore, must do all they can to equip their students and graduates to become job makers by offering training on commercial creativity, business planning and financial awareness and one way of doing this is through enterprise education. Jones (2011) makes a clear connection between this approach and graduate employability.

Figures from the 2019/20 Graduate Outcomes Survey (GOS) released by HESA show that over 67,500 graduates, 15 months after graduating, were self-employed, running their own business or developing a portfolio (HESA (Higher Education Statistics Agency), 2022). Starting a business while studying at university or shortly after graduating is an ideal time. The majority of graduate founders have little in the way of responsibilities and through their exposure to a range of ideas and opportunities are inclined to develop innovative business ideas and are well-placed to meet likeminded co-founders. However, the GEM report also found that whilst 61 per cent of respondents believed there were good opportunities to start a business in their area, 52 per cent of these people cited fear of failure as a reason for not starting a new business in the next three years. Universities are ideally placed to help their graduates overcome this fear of failure by offering access to training, mentoring, networks, funding, and office space through start-up programmes like BSEEN.

ENTREPRENEURSHIP AND ASTON UNIVERSITY

Aston University is situated in Birmingham, which has long been heralded as the most entrepreneurial city in the UK outside London, with the highest number of new start-up businesses in 2021 for the seventh year running, according to the annual survey by the Centre for Entrepreneurs (Centre for

Entrepreneurs, n.d.). Younger people aged 18–29 are the most likely to start their own business according to the 2021/22 Global Entrepreneurship Monitor (GEM) report (Global Entrepreneurship Monitor, 2022).

Aston University's commitment to nurturing entrepreneurs is engrained in its culture and is evident through the extensive range of practical, innovative entrepreneurial programmes taking place across the university. Most importantly, it is written into the Aston University Strategy 2018–2023 (Aston University, n.d.), so it receives full commitment from the University Executive. The strategy defines key entrepreneurial outcomes for the university's three beneficiary groups:

- For students: 'Students will be highly skilled in their discipline and have a global and entrepreneurial mindset.'
- For business: 'We will link businesses, the professions and other organisations to graduate employees and entrepreneurs.'
- For our region and society: 'Our research, innovation and enterprise activities will enhance the economy and improve quality of life in the West Midlands and beyond.'

Aston Enterprise offers a variety of extra-curricular activities and support to students and recent graduates and has a mission to help curious students explore, experiment, and launch new ideas. This is whether they are looking to learn more about self-employment, start up a business or develop the enterprising skills needed to have impact on their career and on the world around them. There is a focus on giving real-life insights from entrepreneurial people in a range of sectors, opportunities to work with other engaged students to learn in a practical way and to encourage students to think differently. The programme of activities enables students to explore the world of entrepreneurship and self-employment as a career through the popular 'How to' series of events. Panel sessions are held on how to start a food, fashion, or tech business or social enterprise, using fireside chats to introduce students to a wide range of relatable but aspirational role models who run their own ventures. For example, at the How to Start a Food Business event, two Aston alumni who founded food businesses supported by BSEEN (Reena Salhan, co-founder of The Green Sisters, an Indian inspired plant-based food business and Chukwudi Ononye, founder of Chefiesta, a catering and meal prep company specialising in African and Caribbean cuisine), gave very honest accounts of their entrepreneurial journeys and gave some sound advice to the student audience.

Those students who want to start experimenting with their own business ideas can enter the annual pitching competition, to win seed funding for their business along with feedback from a panel of expert judges. They can also apply to take part in Apollo, a six-week mini accelerator, which inspires entrepreneurs to develop business ideas through a mix of interactive masterclasses, lessons from real-life guest entrepreneurs, and practical group learning supported by mentors from the business community. Apollo fills a gap in provision between students developing an enterprising mindset and starting their business. Over 200 students have participated in the four years it has been running, and 28 businesses have gone on to launch with the support of the BSEEN programme. All of the students who take part in the programme, irrespective of what career path they take afterwards, learn to identify and solve problems, to work in interdisciplinary teams, and to communicate effectively with a range of people including the business mentors and facilitators involved in the programme. They learn to look outside the university to the local region and in doing so, broaden their network. One participant, a Product Design final year student, said of the programme:

> Apollo firstly helped me shape my final year project and gain substantial knowledge on what was needed and would work in the real world. I got a job in a start-up right after the end of the programme and again here, I was able to flaunt my experience and skills gained from Apollo and my previous leadership roles in Enactus.

BSEEN'S IMPACT

Research has shown (Hassan, 2020) that university incubators contribute to regional economic growth, productivity and innovation. The most recent independent evaluation of the BSEEN programme, which ran from 2016 to 2019, reported that projects such as BSEEN are investments in the future and are not necessarily expected to have an immediate economic impact. Nevertheless, there are early indications of economic impact. Of those businesses started from 2016 to 2019:

- 86 per cent of those who had started a business were either trading or intended to start trading in the next 12 months.
- These trading businesses were turning over an aggregate of around £2.5 million per annum and cautious two-year forecasts were for turnover to have reached over £8.5 million.
- In addition, 23 per cent of trading businesses had two or more employees.
- When those with trading businesses were asked about the impact of BSEEN on business development, 70 per cent reported that they would have made less progress without BSEEN support.
- 44 per cent of the BSEEN founders said they saw themselves running a business in Birmingham in five years' time.
- 37 per cent of BSEEN participants believed themselves to be much more enterprising because of BSEEN and 29 per cent, much more employable.

- When questioned about the skills and attributes developed through participation in BSEEN, 59 per cent said their ability to pitch business ideas to others had improved a lot; 51 per cent said the same for their ability to turn an idea into a business proposition; and 48 per cent said they had improved considerably their ability to identify a market for a business.

The West Midlands has a firm focus on business growth and job creation and the evaluation found evidence from its findings that BSEEN is creating jobs and generating young businesses with potential to grow. The evaluation also found that BSEEN is highly likely to contribute to the growth of existing firms in the region through supporting graduates to be more employable and enterprising and more likely to stay in the area after graduation than they would have been had they not participated in BSEEN. The region also has innovation at its centre and BSEEN has contributed a number of innovative businesses. For example, Petalite, a green tech business, is revolutionising electric vehicle fast charging technology. WEST CIC have a vision of engineering a more diverse and inclusive culture in Science, Technology, Engineering and Mathematics (STEM) and VOILO have developed an innovative QR payment system making the most of banking technology to empower ailing High Street shops.

Individual entrepreneurs have benefitted in different ways from taking part in the BSEEN programme. Examples include a food technology business which was acquired by a global tech giant for an undisclosed sum, which was a positive outcome for the founder and the 30 plus people employed in the start-up. Another example is the business graduate who co-founded a food start-up and used the experience to differentiate herself when being interviewed and subsequently securing a graduate role with one of the world's largest food and drinks companies. A further example is the tech start-up founder who networked extensively and gained exposure to the tech ecosystem and has recently been appointed as Head of Innovation for a national tech network.

The co-founder of the Birmingham Enterprise Community (BEC), who was on the BSEEN programme with a previous business in 2018, found that it is the rich combination of BSEEN support that provides the value:

> BSEEN is an incredibly valuable space for student entrepreneurs, providing access to network, mentoring and meaningful connections. It opens their eyes to new opportunities, and they can go forward with confidence as they know that the BSEEN team is always available to go to and ask for help. I joined BSEEN in 2018 and it was the perfect kick off into Birmingham's vibrant entrepreneurial community.

The founder of Unlimited You, a subscription-based fitness app for people with disabilities, found the most important element of BSEEN was the mentoring:

> I was matched with someone who has both business and sport experience as he sold a commercial cleaning company and is now on the board of a local cricket club. The networking has also been really great as being part of BSEEN means you are not alone as you mix with others who understand your challenges.

The higher education sector benefits from BSEEN and programmes like it. In the BSEEN evaluation, senior representatives of the partner universities involved in BSEEN report that it enables them to strengthen and extend their student and graduate enterprise offer which, in all cases, is strategically aligned with their institutional priorities. The project funding increased their capacity to deliver but will also have a longer-term impact as a result of the capability being developed within enterprise teams. The universities have achieved additional impact through the BSEEN collaboration, enabling them to exchange good practice related to enterprise with colleagues across the city. The collaboration has clear benefits through knowledge sharing at the operational level but is also important strategically as it has enabled senior staff from four distinctly different institutions to get to know one another better and to be in a position to explore future collaborations beyond BSEEN itself.

As more young people are becoming entrepreneurial (Global Entrepreneurship Monitor, 2022), they are increasingly researching the support offered by different universities when deciding which university to attend. Extra-curricular enterprise and entrepreneurship programmes enhance the student experience, and the students and graduates involved in enterprise and entrepreneurship activity, including venture creation, provide multiple PR opportunities for the institution. University alumni departments welcome the chance to engage with a range of alumni by asking them for their expertise and time as business mentors, and similarly it is a good way to increase engagement with professional services organisations, banks and investors and the start-up and SME community.

CONCLUSION

In conclusion, the impact of student and graduate start-up programmes like BSEEN is far-reaching and beyond just the numbers of start-ups launched. It is key that in order to remain effective, the programmes must be properly resourced and have the full backing of the university's executive team. Knowledge exchange is a key priority for universities and offering a wide range of enterprise and entrepreneurship education and start-up programmes such as BSEEN is a good way for them to demonstrate their strengths and successes in this area.

BIBLIOGRAPHY

Aston University (n.d.), *The Aston University Strategy 2018–2023*. Available at: https://www.aston.ac.uk/about/our-values/strategy (accessed: 11 January 2023).

Bacigalupo, M. et al. (2016), *EntreComp: The Entrepreneurship Competence Framework*. Luxembourg: Publications Office of the European Union.

Bakhshi, H., Downing J. M., Osborn, M. A. and Schneider, P. (2017), *The Future of Skills: Employment in 2030*, London: Pearson and Nesta. Available at: https://futureskills.pearson.com/assets/pdfs/technical-report.pdf (accessed: 11 January 2023).

BSEEN Final Evaluation and Summative Assessment, conducted by Kate Beresford and Associates and QA Research for Aston University, April 2019.

Centre for Entrepreneurs (n.d.), *The CFE Business Startup Index*. Available at: https://centreforentrepreneurs.org/cfe-research/business-startup-index/ (accessed: 11 January 2023).

Fahey, S. J. (2012), 'Curriculum change and climate change: inside outside pressures in higher education', *Journal of Curriculum Studies*, 44(5), 703–722.

Global Entrepreneurship Monitor (2022), GEM *2021/2022. Global Report: Opportunity Amid Disruption*. London: Global Entrepreneurship Research Association.

HESA (2022), *Graduate Outcomes 2019/20: Summary Statistics – Summary*. Available at: https://www.hesa.ac.uk/news/16-06-2022/sb263-higher-education-graduate-outcomes-statistics (accessed: 23 January 2023).

Hassan, N. A. (2020), 'University business incubators as a tool for accelerating entrepreneurship: theoretical perspective', *Review of Economics and Political Science*. doi: https://doi.org/10.1108/REPS-10-2019-0142.

Jones, C. (2011), *Teaching Entrepreneurship to Undergraduates*, Cheltenham, UK and Northampton, MA, USA: Edward Elgar Publishing.

QAA (2018), *Enterprise and Entrepreneurship Education: Guidance for Higher Education Providers*. York: Quality Assurance Agency for Higher Education.

REFLECTION

From a graduate entrepreneur

I've wanted to be an entrepreneur for as long as I can remember. My Dad's a plasterer, so watching him start his own business must have had an impact on me. At eight years old, I sold bags of apples (yes, apples) to our neighbours for extra pocket money, before moving on to the more lucrative world of washing cars. It was a lot of fun!

At 15, I bizarrely studied for not just one, but two Business-related GCSEs, before leading a Young Enterprise team selling handmade jewellery in 6th Form. Following a gap year spent selling bathroom suites over the phone for an Internet startup, I started at university.

Fast forward to 30 and I'm confident my time at university led to where I am today.

On paper, I'm perhaps the perfect output for a degree in International Business and Spanish. Since graduation, I've launched and grown my own company – one which now enjoys a 7-figure turnover and a 150-strong team – and I run it all from an office in sunny Spain.

But it's not books and PowerPoint presentations alone that got me here.

My time at university saw me meet a girl who I'm now proud to call my wife and business partner, make lifelong friends, inspire people to start their own businesses as President of the Entrepreneurs Society, and surround myself with talented, driven entrepreneurs through the university's startup programme.

I learned a lot about myself, the world and, most importantly, the people that live in it.

I now know university taught me what truly matters: *to do what makes you happy.*

PART VII

Widening participation

20. Employability monsters: breaking barriers to employability for widening participation students

Dawn Lees and Kate Foster

INTRODUCTION

Students from under-represented and disadvantaged groups often face barriers in developing their employability that impact them as they transition (a) into university and (b) into their post-graduation destinations. The global pandemic may create an even bigger gap for these students as 'the majority of students have had a prolonged period of time outside of education ... with the largest impacts felt by those from the poorest backgrounds' (Montacute et al., 2021). This uncertainty is likely to disproportionally impact students from under-represented groups.

Tomlinson (2017) set out five types of capital that confer benefit and advantages to the individual – namely, social, cultural, human, identity and psycho-social dimensions – and noted that these are acquired through formal and informal experiences. Research by upReach (2019) echoes this, suggesting that students from less privileged backgrounds will often have more limited access to careers advice at school, are less likely to have completed professional work experience and lack useful social networks. The impact of the recent disruption to education is likely to continue for years as primary children are reported to have lower levels of oracy, literacy and numeracy (Newton, 2021). This impact could continue as they progress through secondary education to higher education.

Graduates who are from lower socio-economic groups have lower graduate destination outcomes (a difference of −3.1 per cent at the University of Exeter), and earn on average 10 per cent less than their more advantaged counterparts on graduation (Britton et al., 2016). Students from less affluent backgrounds are less likely to enter key professions; 74 per cent of judges, 71 per cent of barristers and 51 per cent of journalists went to private schools, which educate only 7 per cent of the population (Montacute et al., 2021).

For students who disclose a disability, the difference in graduate outcomes and unemployment rates is even greater than for those from lower socio-economic groups. In 2018, 15 months after graduation, there were proportionally fewer disabled graduates in full-time education than non-disabled graduates, a difference of 7.4 per cent (Allen and Coney, 2021).

The graduate outcomes for care-experienced and estranged students are also lower than for the wider student population. Harrison et al. (2020) explored the graduate outcomes for 1010 care-experienced graduates in 2016–17. The results showed that 63.7 per cent of care-experienced graduates were in professional roles compared with 68.5 per cent for non-care-experienced graduates.

There was a similar situation for the graduate outcomes of BAME students graduating in 2016–17 (acknowledging that this is a contested term). Black Caribbean graduates were 3–4 per cent less likely to be employed than white British graduates; but for Pakistani and Bangladeshi graduates, as well as Chinese male graduates, this difference was 10–16 per cent (Zwysen and Longhi, 2018).

However, the Office for Students (OfS, 2021) reported that mature graduates continue to do slightly better than young graduates in terms of graduate outcomes. Seventy-seven per cent of mature graduates are in highly skilled employment or further study compared with 73 per cent for younger graduates.

The research explained in this chapter emerged as the University of Exeter was acutely aware of the variations in graduate outcomes across the population of widening participation (WP) students compared with non-WP students. Students from WP backgrounds reported that they felt there was a lack of inclusivity and access and that they 'did not belong'. Some WP students also felt they were less likely to be resilient and confident with job applications, career progression and seeking support. Whilst the university already had a rich portfolio of support, something was obviously going wrong as some students either did not feel entitled to access it, or there were not the correct interventions in place to make a material difference to those students.

METHODOLOGY

The Career Zone at the University of Exeter secured funding from the Centre for Social Mobility (https://www.exeter.ac.uk/research/socialmobility/). The 'Employability Monsters' project aimed to explore the challenges and barriers that students from under-represented and disadvantaged groups face with the development of their employability and to identify how these students could be better supported to become equipped to overcome these challenges.

Liminality methodology was adopted to explore challenges to progression utilising research by Hawkins and Edwards (2015, 2017). Liminal moments are those during which transition occurs, transporting an individual from one state of being to another (Turner, 1969; Van Gennep, 1960). Experiencing liminality in a workshop through experiential activities, e.g., modelling monsters using Lego Serious Play (Kristiansen and Rasmussen, 2014) offered students the opportunity to explore challenges and barriers, try out new ideas and identities and reflect on their experiences of liminal passage.

The approach taken is in line with Exeter's ambition to become a 'Playful University', where learning is created through joy and engagement and where learning to solve problems and overcome obstacles is a reward in its own right (Koeners and Francis, 2020).

The aim was to recruit 100 students who identified with one or more WP marker identified as target groups in the university's Access and Participation Plan. These are Black and Minority Ethnic (BAME), disabled, mature, care leavers/experienced or estranged students and students in receipt of an 'Access to Exeter' (AtE) bursary. Seventy-one registered an interest; 32 students were recruited, including eight first or second years and 24 final year students. These students were from a wide range of disciplines. Participants were asked to report which WP marker they identified with most, along with secondary characteristics (Table 20.1). Among the participants, 56 per cent (18) identified with one marker, 34 per cent (11) with two markers and 6 per cent (2) with three or more markers. The small size of the sample does need to be taken into consideration when analysing the results of the project.

Table 20.1   Breakdown of participants' WP markers

Marker	Primary Characteristic	Secondary Characteristics	Total
BAME	9	2	11
Care Leavers/Estranged	1	1	2
Disabled	8	1	9
Bursary	10	7	17
Mature	4	3	7
Grand Total	32	14	46

Participants were compared to their career registration data (Gilworth and Cobb, 2019). This identifies three stages of career readiness; 'Decide', 'Plan' or 'Compete' utilised in Exeter's online registration questions.

- 'Decide' refers to students who have yet to consider their career or are exploring ideas.
- 'Plan' refers to students who are seeking out relevant experiences or have an idea of their career goal, but are not certain how to achieve it.
- 'Compete' refers to students who are in the process of applying for graduate employment or postgraduate study opportunities.

Confidentiality was discussed and agreed to by each group of participants, ensuring that a safe space was created and enabling sensitive issues to be discussed.

Qualitative and quantitative data were recorded during two online, facilitated workshops using Padlets, photos and a Zoom poll. Using Lego® Serious Play® methodology, participants were guided by a trained facilitator to use Lego® to build models that represented the 'barriers and challenges they faced in their employability' enabling the researchers to explore their liminality. Participants were asked to share their model with the group and describe what it represented.

For example, in response to the prompt 'build a model that represents the barriers and challenges you face in your employability', a participant described their model as follows: 'The red block represents stress. The green represents money. The arch shows how there are not a lot of jobs near home, so I would have to move out. The figure is me, surveying everything and looking nervous, and the yellow piece on top represents the Corona Virus.'

In the second workshop, participants were asked to create a model 'to represent what would support you with your career decision making and employability'. After feeding back on their models individually, participants undertook a 'group build', choosing the most important aspects of their individual models. This methodology enabled the participants to further develop each other's ideas, to co-create and collaborate as part of the exploration process, and conclude with an agreed representation of the support that would help them.

Participants were invited to complete an online questionnaire after attending the first workshop, to enable the team to explore if a student felt supported to engage with the Career Zone activities. It also gave the team the opportunity to ascertain levels of engagement and other support students would benefit from. Partnering with social mobility charity upReach, participants were invited to complete their graduate employability framework (GEF) (upReach, 2020). The online questionnaire consisted of 40 multiple-choice questions that enabled participants to reflect on their level of leadership, communication, teamwork, resilience, self-awareness, problem solving/creativity, career knowledge, application and interview skills, work experience, and professionalism. The team received an anonymised summary of these data plus results from the following markers: final vs first year, AtE bursary vs non-AtE bursary, BAME vs non-BAME, mature vs non-mature and disabled vs non-disabled participants, and a discipline breakdown. None of the respondents identified as care leavers/ care experienced or estranged.

OUTCOMES

Key themes emerged from the research. Participants identified developing their employability as 'challenging' in the workshops. As expected, first year students had a lower overall percentage GEF employability score than final year students. First year students were also at earlier stages of career readiness (Decide and Plan) than final year participants.

In the workshops, participants also highlighted the competitive nature and their lack of knowledge of the graduate recruitment process as a challenge. Work experience, application, and interview skills scored low across all discipline areas in the GEF. It may therefore be useful to explore how the Career Zone can further explicitly promote developmental opportunities such as skills sessions, society committees and employability awards through 'Create Your Future', which is mandatory for all first years. The overall employability average score for AtE bursary students in the GEF (60.5 per cent compared to 68 per cent for non-bursary students), also reinforces the university's need to target activity and reduce the graduate outcome gap for AtE recipients in the Access and Participation Plan.

According to the Bridge Group (2017),

> Students from lower socio-economic backgrounds participate less in activities that have greatest currency amongst employers. This includes extracurricular activities (leadership roles in sports and societies, for example); work experience that contributes to career aspirations; internships amongst competitive employers; international opportunities to study and work; and access to postgraduate education.

The researchers would like to further understand WP participation rates in extra-curricular opportunities in addition to work experience, international activities and progression onto postgraduate study.

In the online questionnaire, participants highlighted that finance was a barrier to accessing opportunities, along with the time to engage with initiatives due to part-time work commitments. Funding would potentially enable them to access longer-term internships and contribute to other costs, such as travel to recruitment activities. Research demonstrated that '20% of working class graduates [who] did not take up a work experience placement during university could not afford to because of a need to spend the time in better paid employment or due to the cost of commuting. This compared to 15% of better-off graduates' (Montacute et al., 2021).

Although the Career Zone offers opportunities to interact with professionals through alumni Q&A schemes, mentoring and funded internships, multiple participants cited the lack of opportunity to network with professionals as a barrier to moving forward with their career planning. They also thought it would have more benefit if these professionals had similar lived experiences and were at early stages of their career. At the time of the research, a pilot peer-mentoring scheme was being offered in partnership with upReach, with upReach students mentoring AtE students. Peer mentoring, from students with similar 'lived experiences', was suggested as potentially providing support to overcome barriers, which reassured us we were taking provision in the right direction.

Participants discussed how opportunities were marketed: the channels used, accessibility and quantity of information received. Although students recognised the importance of gaining work experience, these opportunities were the initiatives least accessed, with only three of the 32 participating in funded internship programmes aimed at WP students. Students suggested that clearer messaging and signposting were required to raise their awareness of all employability opportunities. This could be through the use of Instagram, clearer information for WP students on a web page and in a variety of formats, including videos. Some participants mentioned that having a 'named' person (in the form of the Employability and Careers Consultant dedicated to WP students), really helped them feel supported and able to navigate the information available and support their career decision making. Evidence suggests that 'that the provision of effective career guidance within higher education can contribute to social mobility, improved retention, attainment and progression to employment as well as to enhanced career management skills' (Webb et al., 2017).

Key outcomes based on the research include the launch of a dedicated employability-focused web resource for WP students, and the continuation and development of the peer-mentoring programme for AtE recipients, working closely with upReach. The project continues into its next phase, enabling the team to reconnect with previous participants and recruit a new cohort of students to further explore the barriers and challenges faced, and to consider how Career Zone can further develop support for these students.

CONCLUSION

Using a play-based approach helped us to have a more honest and open discussion with students than perhaps the traditional focus group approach would have done. Through these discussions the researchers have a better idea of how to support these students and modify the service provided, as they transition from school to university, and then into the world of work.

REFERENCES

Allen, M. and Coney. K. (2021), *What Happens Next? 2021: A Report on the Outcomes of 2018 Disabled Graduates*. Available at: https://www.agcas.org.uk/write/MediaUploads/Resources/Disability%20TG/AGCAS_What_Happens_Next_2021_-_February_2021.pdf (accessed: 12 January 2023).

Bridge Group (2017), *Social Mobility and University Careers Services*. Available at: https://upp-foundation.org/wp-content/uploads/2017/05/1714-Social-Mobility-and-University-Careers-Services-report-Digital.pdf-.pdf (accessed: 12 January 2023).

Britton, J., Dearden, L., Shephard, N. and Vignoles, A. (2016), 'How English domiciled graduate earnings vary with gender, institution attended, subject and socio-economic background', IFS Working Paper W16/06, Institute for Fiscal Studies. Available at: https://ifs.org.uk/publications/how-english-domiciled-graduate-earnings-vary-gender-institution-attended-subject-and (accessed: 12 January 2023).

Gilworth, B. and Cobb, F. (2019), *Careers Registration Practical Guide*. London: The Careers Group, University of London. Available at: https://www.london.ac.uk/sites/default/files/uploads/TCG%20Registration%20Guide%20A5%20Final%20Version.pdf (accessed: 12 January 2023).

Harrison, N., Baker, Z. and Stevenson, J. (2020), 'Employment and further study outcomes for care experienced graduates in the UK', *Higher Education*, 83, 357–378.

Hawkins, B. and Edwards, G. (2015), 'Managing the monsters of doubt: liminality, threshold concepts and leadership learning', *Management Learning*, 46(1), 24–43. doi: 10.1177/1350507613501736.

Hawkins, B. and Edwards, G. (2017), 'Facing the monsters: embracing liminality in leadership development', in S. Kempster, A. Turner and G. Edwards (eds), *Field Guide to Leadership Development*, Cheltenham, UK and Northampton, MA, USA: Edward Elgar Publishing, pp. 203–217. Available at: https://www.researchgate.net/publication/320057373_Field_Guide_to_Leadership_Development (accessed: 12 January 2023).

Koeners, P. M. and Francis, J. (2020), 'The physiology of play; potential relevance for higher education', *International Journal of Play*, 9(1), 143–159. doi: https://doi.org/10.1080/21594937.2020.1720128.

Kristiansen, P. and Rasmussen, R. (2014), *Building a Better Business Using the LEGO® SERIOUS PLAY® Method*. Hoboken, NJ: Wiley.

Montacute, R., Holt-White, E. and Gent, A. (2021), *The University of Life: Employability and Essential Life Skills at University*. London: The Sutton Trust. Available at: https://www.suttontrust.com/wp-content/uploads/2021/02/The-University-of-Life-Final.pdf (accessed: 12 January 2023).

Newton, P. (2021), *Learning During the Pandemic: Quantifying Lost Learning*. Ofqual. Available at: https://www.gov.uk/government/publications/learning-during-the-pandemic/learning-during-the-pandemic-quantifying-lost-time--2 (accessed: 12 January 2023).

OfS (2021), *Differences in Student Outcomes*. Available at: https://www.officeforstudents.org.uk/data-and-analysis/differences-in-student-outcomes/degree-outcomes-overview/ (accessed: 12 January 2023).

Tomlinson, M. (2017), 'Forms of graduate capital and their relationship to graduate employability', *Education & Training*, 59(4), 338–352.

Turner, V. (1969), *The Ritual Process: Structure and Anti-Structure*. London: Routledge.

upReach (2019), *Impact Report 2018–2019*. Unpublished report.
upReach (2020), *Annual Report*. Unpublished report.
Van Gennep, A. (1960), *The Rites of Passage*, London: Routledge.
Webb, O., Wyness, L. and Cotton, D. (2017), *Enhancing Access, Retention, Attainment and Progression in Higher Education: A Review of the Literature Showing Demonstrable Impact*. York: Higher Education Academy.
Zwysen, W. and Longhi, S. (2018), 'Employment and earning differences in the early career of ethnic minority British graduates: the importance of university career, parental background and area characteristics', *Journal of Ethnic and Migration Studies*, 44(1), 154–172. doi: https://doi.org/10.1080/1369183X.2017.1338559.

REFLECTION

From a mature student

The decision to apply to university as a mature student was one that was not taken lightly, taking into account my caring responsibilities as a single mother.

Considering myself an organised person, I generally pride myself on my time management skills. However, with university commencing mid pandemic and the children being required to home school, time management took on a whole new meaning!

With my first year dominated by distance learning the focus in the home was very much on academic pursuits, for myself and the children. With the distractions limited, the primary focus was on assignments and the select extra-curricular activities participated in alongside overseeing the children's learning schedules.

In my second year, teaching returned to campus, with the commute and on-campus activities offering a new challenge regarding time management. The added impact of the additional time taken to commute to campus combined with extra-curricular responsibilities created additional pressure to ensure I maintained my standard of work.

The extra-curricular activities that I have taken on to enrich my university experience have added to the time constraints that I have faced this year, especially in relation to study time as deadlines across projects, assignments and extra-curricular endeavours all compete for my attention.

Throughout the course of this year, I have found that the additional pressures have helped me to realise my threshold for productivity, allowing me to consider more carefully the supplementary activities that I engage with. I have become more adept at scheduling days and weeks to ensure that my time is managed effectively, while also allowing time for myself and my children. I believe this will stand me in good stead moving forward, for both final year and the graduate world of work beyond.

21. Supporting 'first in family' students: My Generation Career Coaching Programme

Heather Pasero

INTRODUCTION

My Generation Career Coaching programme was launched in 2019 at the University of Southampton as a pilot project to support students who are the first person in their immediate family to attend university. The project aims to address unique challenges that first-generation university students face, enabling them to be better prepared for transitioning towards the graduate labour market and their individual career goals. The programme was developed by the careers department and funding was agreed for a pilot year covering marketing, coaching materials, books, events and student items such as interview attire. The joined-up working came from collaboration with the Widening Participation and Social Mobility Team to implement a four-stage marketing plan focusing on targeting first-generation UK domiciled undergraduate students from all year groups via positive action marketing.

BACKGROUND

The expansion of higher education since the late 1980s has so far disproportionately benefited those from more affluent backgrounds (Blanden et al., 2005). Concerned with this trajectory, the Higher Education Funding Council for England (HEFCE) and the Office for Fair Access (OFFA), now Office for Students (OfS), developed a national strategy for student access and success in higher education in 2014 with the laudable vision 'that all those with the potential to benefit from Higher Education have equal opportunity to participate and succeed' (HEFCE and OFFA, 2014: 7).

The recognition of a higher education system designed for those from higher income backgrounds to access and succeed (OFFA, 2015: 3) was a positive step forward. With this refreshed focus on those from lower income backgrounds as having a lower chance of attending university, graduating from university and gaining professional employment after graduation, new national, regional and institutional initiatives were funded with the aim of closing the gap.

Students' knowledge of higher education is still deeply situated within the familial context (Wainwright and Watts, 2021), and for many potential students, universities are still considered privileged spaces.

The vicarious learner (Bandura, 1978; Bandura and Walters, 1963) pays attention to the role model and this is a critical factor in this kind of learning. Support from a 'trusted' role model is important, not least because they are able to share concerns about their own lack of confidence and how common it is to have difficulties in particular areas. Family background, working-class status, location and cultural capital combine to assert a sense of 'strangeness' and not 'fitting in' with the HE system (Reay et al., 2010: 107); 'This sense of being an outsider reproduces a more diffused family learning effect with initial limited slipstream effect' (Wainwright and Watts, 2021: 120).

In addition to the recommendation for more 'joined-up services' from the Higher Education Careers Service Unit (HECSU)-funded research in 2016 and the report 'Talkin' 'Bout First Generation', the latter report also identified the need to nurture 'career vision via cultural capital practices' (Pasero, 2016: 33). These findings were taken on board to develop first the idea and then the plan for 'My Generation Career Coaching'.

The graduate destinations statistics in the higher education sector for first-generation students have consistently indicated a disadvantage gap of up to 5 per cent in relation to professional employment after graduation. For those who do not know if their parents participated in higher education, the gap is wider at 10 per cent. It is with this mindset that, following the 2019 pilot year, the My Generation Career Coaching programme eligibility criteria embrace both groups in line with the University of Southampton Access and Participation plan, which states: 'For progression, not knowing whether your parents had higher education seems to be a factor for lower employment, but more investigation is necessary to understand who these students are.'

IMPLEMENTATION

It was very quickly determined that measuring impact was key to understanding if, how and to what extent the My Generation Career Coaching programme could effectively support students towards reaching their career goals. It was decided to measure some 'hard' success factors, such as engagement with student societies or part-time work, as well as 'softer', but key, success factors such as self-confidence and self-awareness. Tracking data for all success factors was collated at the end of each individual coaching appointment and recorded on the service's customer relationship management (CRM) system.

My Generation students also took the career-readiness test (Tomlinson et al., 2021) at the start, and then again at the end, of the programme. The career-readiness test is a self-assessment tool to ascertain levels of graduate capital on the graduate capital scale developed by Dr Michael Tomlinson in the School of Education at the University of Southampton.

All My Generation coaches were qualified/experienced career consultants who, in order to commence coaching, attended a two-hour training session to introduce the project and learn about a carefully thought out and designed My Generation Career Coaching delivery framework. Peer supervision sessions ran monthly in small groups of three or four consultants and were useful for group reflection on the practice and development of skills and confidence in coaching work.

Before commencement of the programme, students were asked to agree to the following commitments, when applying via MyCareer:

- attend a one-hour coaching training session;
- attend at least four 60-minute support sessions with their coach between January and December;
- complete the Career Readiness Test twice, once in January, then again in December.

After each one-hour coaching session students were given a clear timebound action plan and success factors are recorded as part of this process.

Funding was offered to students to cover travel to or accommodation for interviews/work experience and/or interview attire in order to support their journey towards their goals and remove any element of money-related stress that may have been creating a small or large barrier to moving forwards.

MEASURES AND OUTCOMES

The measures and outcomes for the 2019, 2020 and 2021 My Generation Career Coaching student cohorts in aggregate, with a sample size of 60 students, are set out in Figures 21.1 and 21.2.

Success Factors Part 1

Students completed self-assessment related to the quality of their LinkedIn profile, self-awareness, self-confidence, career activism and career vision. These success factors were determined from findings gained via student interviews during the HECSU-funded 'Talkin' 'Bout First Generation' research project (Pasero, 2016). Students answered using a six-point scale, ranging from 'not at all confident' (1) to 'very confident' (6). Data was collected at each coaching interaction from the student and was entered into the CRM system.

On the left-hand side of Figure 21.1 are the start scores from the initial assesment and on the right-hand side we have the end scores from the final assessment, with the incremental increases labelled in the middle. Overall the part 1 success factors have increased by 39 per cent on average, as well as factors increasing at each stage of the programme.

Success Factors Part 1: January - December

Success factors	JAN	APR	AUG	DEC	Final
LinkedIn	2.5	0.8	0.5	0.2	4.0
Self-Awareness	4.0		0.4	0.5	0.1	5.1
Self-Confidence	3.4		0.7	0.5	0.2	4.7
Career Activism	3.7		0.6	0.7	0.3	5.3
Career Vision	3.8			0.4	0.3	0.1	4.7

Student self-assessment [Scale 1-6]

■ JAN - Initial assessment ■ APR - Follow-up ■ AUG - Follow-up ■ DEC - Final assessment

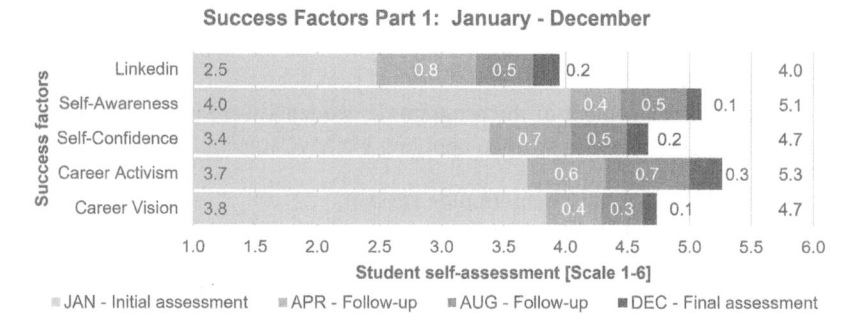

Figure 21.1   Success factors

Success Factors Part 2

During each coaching interaction, student engagement with employment-enhancing activities (listed from a to i in Table 21.1) was collected and entered into the CRM system. The overall beginning-to-end engagement impact was almost double, increasing from 34 per cent to 65 per cent on average (Figure 21.2).

Success Factors Part 2: January - December

Activity	Beginning	End
a	52%	77%
b	43%	68%
c	30%	57%
d	27%	60%
e	32%	67%
f	32%	55%
g	27%	55%
h	32%	57%
i	37%	88%

Unique activity type

■ Beginning of programme   ■ End of programme

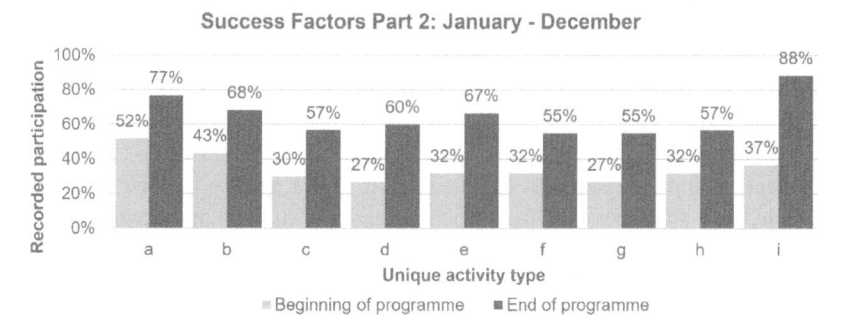

Figure 21.2   Employment-enhancing activities

Table 21.1   Activity types

a	Active member of societies and clubs
b	Attended Careers Fair
c	Attended employer event
d	Attended networking event
e	In part-time work
f	Involved in volunteering
g	Participated in/due to participate in work experience
h	Completed/has secured external work experience
i	Applied for/applying for opportunity

Graduate Career Readiness

The Career Readiness Test is an online test developed at the University of Southampton, through which students are able to assess their career readiness in line with the graduate capital scale learning outcomes. It is intended that this test will help students to identify specific action in support of their career planning. The Career Readiness Test reports on how developed the individual is against five key psychometric capitals. These are classified as human, social, cultural, identity and psychological metrics.

Students completed the test both at the start of the coaching programme and at the end to assess their levels of career readiness as they progressed on the graduate capital scale. From the start, the test revealed that the average My Generation Career Coaching student systematically scores below the average UK-domiciled undergraduate group (referred to as the 'norm group') in the first four capitals (Figure 21.3). The gap is 5–8 percentage points in the scale of

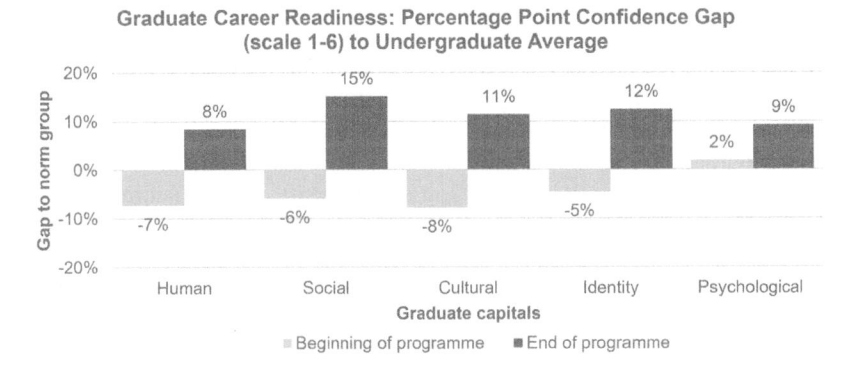

Figure 21.3   Graduate career readiness

measurement, but the scores are marginally higher in the psychological capital, at 2 percentage points. At the end of the year, My Generation students scored themselves higher in all capitals, and significantly higher than the norm group in all capitals, by 9–15 percentage points.

CONCLUSION

The key metric from the My Generation Career Coaching Programme was to measure the impact of one-to-one career coaching on the student participants. This has succeeded in terms of three key measurements: (1) self-confidence, (2) engagement with employment-enhancing activities, and (3) use of psychometric analysis (career readiness). All three measurements indicate significant improvement over a timescale of one year:

(a) self-confidence factors (part 1 success factors) increased by 39 per cent;
(b) engagement factors (part 2 success factors) almost doubled from 34 per cent to 65 per cent;
(c) the career readiness increase was 9–15 percentage points higher than the norm group.

This evidence shows that the My Generation Career Coaching Programme works to provide first-generation students with the support needed as they identify career goals and move towards the graduate labour market to succeed in higher education and beyond. Further evidence will be sought through the Graduate Outcomes Survey (GOS) data in the future.

Given the positive outcomes for the students on the My Generation Career Coaching Programme, it now operates as a 'business as usual' activity in the Careers, Employability and Student Enterprise department at University of Southampton.

Declarations and ethics statement
Student Success Factors part 1 and part 2 data was collated via the student CRM system. Students signed a GDPR-compliant consent form stating: 'Data will be anonymised and may be published in publications such as professional journals, conference communications, research papers or professional body articles.' (Career Readiness Test – University of Southampton Ethics Approval: Career Readiness Test (ERGO Number, 27201.A1))

REFERENCES

Bandura, A. (1978), 'Self-efficacy: toward a unifying theory of behavioural change', *Advances in Behaviour Research and Therapy*, 1(4), 139–161. Available at:

https://www.sciencedirect.com/science/article/pii/0146640278900024?via%3Dihub (accessed: 12 January 2023).

Bandura, A. and Walters, R. H. (1963), *Social Learning and Personality Development*, New York: Holt Rinehart and Winston.

Blanden, J., Gregg, P. and Machin, S. (2005). *Intergenerational Mobility in Europe and North America: A Report Supported by the Sutton Trust*. London: Centre for Economic Performance. Available at: https://www.suttontrust.com/wp-content/uploads/2020/01/IntergenerationalMobility.pdf (accessed: 23 January 2023).

HEFCE and OFFA (2014), *National Strategy for Access and Student Success*. Available at: https://www.gov.uk/government/publications/national-strategy-for-access-and-student-success (accessed: 12 January 2023).

OFFA (2015), *OFFA Strategic Plan 2015–2020*. Available at: https://www.offa.org.uk/wp-content/uploads/2015/03/OFFA-Strategic-Plan-2015-2020.pdf (accessed: 12 January 2023).

Pasero, H. (2016), *Talkin' 'Bout First Generation: An investigation into the needs of, and challenges face by first generation University students at the University of Southampton*. Southampton: University of Southampton. Available at: https://luminate.prospects.ac.uk/challenges-faced-by-first-generation-university-students (accessed: 12 January 2023).

Reay, D., Crozier, G. and Clayton, J. (2010), '"Fitting in" or "standing out": working class students in UK higher education', *British Educational Research Journal*, 36(1), 107–124. Available at: https://www.tandfonline.com/doi/full/10.1080/01411920902878925 (accessed: 12 January 2023).

Tomlinson, M., McCafferty, H., Port, A., Maguire, N., Zabelski, A. E., Butnaru, A., Charles, M. and Kirby, S., (2021), 'Developing graduate employability for a challenging labour market: the validation of the graduate capital scale', *Journal of Applied Research in Higher Education*, 14(3). doi: https://doi.org/10.1108/JARHE-04-2021-0151.

Wainwright, E. and Watts, D. M. (2021), 'Social mobility in the slipstream: first-generation students' narratives of university participation and family', *Educational Review*, 73(1), 111–127.

REFLECTION

From a career coach

As a coach, my approach is heavily focused on enabling students to identify for themselves what they want or need to do and how to do it. Often, students would require some positive affirmation and reassurance that what they were thinking of doing was the right thing for them. A reflection from my professional work as a whole (and not just working with students), is that students often require or expect permission or reassurance from a professional. There may be underlying beliefs such as there is an objective 'right way' and a 'wrong way' and that an 'expert' will tell them this. Whereas, in practice, it is more someone such as myself assisting them to recognise it is about taking the option that is right for them, in that instance and feeling confident to own that.

22. Unlocking the potential of under-represented students
Iwan Williams and Pamela McGee

INTRODUCTION

One of the true, fundamental purposes of a university careers team is to help every student, no matter their background, to have a fair and equal chance at pursuing personal success. But even this, the most honest and virtuous of aims, is not simple to achieve. Taking the complexity of an individual's social capital, ethnicity, disability, confidence level and financial status, and adding in factors such as location, and political and economic influences, can create a 'playing field' that is neither fair nor equal. The reality is that, for some of our students, things are just more difficult. At the University of Liverpool, the challenge has been tackled head on, with the Careers and Employability team refusing to allow external factors to dictate student success. It is through this commitment that the 'Unlock Your Potential' (UP) programme was created in 2019.

UP is a wide-ranging programme of careers and employability support, offering bespoke opportunities for students who are, traditionally, under-represented in higher education. The programme takes many forms, from financial support to intensive skills-building programmes, access to ring-fenced opportunities, networks, toolkits and training.

The University of Liverpool is well versed in the challenges faced by disadvantaged students, with many of the students recruited from a widening participation (WP) background (a measure of participation in higher education by those with specific background characteristics). Currently, 6,000 of the students recruited by the university are eligible for the 'Liverpool Bursary', which is assigned based on household income and designed to support those who might encounter financial hardship. As a Russell Group university, the University of Liverpool ranks sixth in the UK when it comes to intake of undergraduate students who reside in the first quintile of the Participation of Local Areas (in higher education) POLAR4 measure. POLAR4 measures student participation rates in HE by postcode and highlights neighbourhoods where university attendance is commonplace or less frequent. Although context needs to be applied, POLAR4 can be used to identify those students who might be arriving at university with lower levels of confidence and increased barriers to success compared to those from neighbourhoods with higher attendance rates.

The University of Liverpool is located in one of the most deprived regions in the UK; five of the six city boroughs score above the national average for school students claiming free school meals, and in one of the boroughs (Knowsley), it is over twice the national average. This local context is compounded by the national picture; the challenges faced by graduates from diverse backgrounds when accessing high skill opportunities are evidenced by the need for the 'progression' strand of the Office for Students' Access and Participation Plan (APP). For example, research conducted by Debut (a graduate recruitment service) has indicated that Black, Asian and ethnic minority students are applying for 45 per cent more jobs than white students – something that clearly highlights the challenges that ethnic minority graduates face (Frobisher, 2020). These differences in outcomes become acute where protected characteristics intersect with the low socio-economic backgrounds which prevail in the Liverpool City Region.

Acceptance of this reality only provides the first tentative step to tackling the issues; but what can be done about it? How do we drill down to the specific groups that most need help, and develop interventions that have sufficient impact? How do we create an offer that supports all 10,000 students at the university who fall within Office for Student's 2020 definition of being 'unheard and underrepresented'? This needs more than a superficial approach. It needs resource, fresh ideas and, most importantly, impact.

THE 'UNLOCK YOUR POTENTIAL' PROGRAMME

With the context established and the size of the challenge acknowledged, the UP programme was devised to attempt to make things better. The starting point was to analyse internal and external datasets to identify which students face the biggest barriers. Next, a digital platform was created, using Handshake (our online career-management platform) and Microsoft Teams, which provided those students with responsive, personalised and opt-in information and support. Insights into the experiences of under-represented students were gained through direct engagement with student leaders, strengthening partnerships with the Student Union, student societies and other networks, not merely to pay lip service, but to encourage students to be active in the creation and delivery of this support. The programme development also involved direct engagement with employers on equality, diversity and inclusion (EDI) related issues, and saw a range of employer-led events offered to students. Finally, this overarching, baseline offer was combined with a series of highly targeted, highly impactful, and highly resourced activities that sought to address the needs of individuals and small groups who needed the help most. While these activities can take time to plan, every meaningful intervention pays this back a hundredfold later down the line.

So, who is an UP student? It was agreed that the offer should be open to as many students as possible and that there should be broad eligibility criteria. The base level of support offered by UP is designed to be scalable, accessible and have community-building benefits. The higher-intensity and targeted activities come later and can be planned and analysed using cohort data and other relevant information. To identify the range of eligible students there were two primary sources; firstly, the criteria mirrored the student groups that the university's WP and recruitment team work with pre-entry. This enabled a seamless transition for students who are about to join the university and helped new students to feel confident that systems are in place to help them with their future and career progression. Secondly, the criteria identified by the Office for Students as 'unheard and underrepresented' were used to underpin the approach and ensure that all student voices are heard. This approach recognised that there can be changes at a national level that are yet to impact at an institutional one, and so it was important that the Careers and Employability team aligned their work with the national picture, to reflect the ever-changing dynamics of student recruitment profiles.

Combined, the complete eligibility list is:

- Black, Asian and Minority Ethnic groups;
- disabled students;
- disrupted education – this is an internal descriptor that includes any students who may have encountered disruption to the statutory schooling, such as care experienced students, young adult carers, estranged students and asylum seekers/refugees;
- POLAR4 quintile one (a governmental measure that identifies students who reside in neighbourhoods that send the fewest number of students into higher education);
- Liverpool Bursary holders (additional grants for those from families with less than £25,000 annual income);
- LGBTQ+ students;
- first-generation students;
- students who reside in a travel-to-work area (often referred to as 'commuter students').

In terms of numbers, there are $c.20,000$ undergraduate students at the University of Liverpool. Once the eligibility criteria are applied, the total number of students who can register for the UP programme is around 8,000. The largest individual groups are commuter students ($c.3,300$), those with a disability ($c.2,500$) and those from the lowest participation neighbourhoods in England (POLAR4 quintile 1) with approximately 1,500 students in total. Those who have encountered disrupted education number approximately 100 students. Whilst these numbers present a clear picture, many of the students will fall across multiple eligibility criteria, so it is important that the data analysis recognises this intersectionality and that the next, more intensive and specialist phase of the offer can be developed as quickly as possible.

Understanding the journey that UP students experience is critical to the development of the programme of support. An UP student will often begin their university experience long before they arrive at university, with 'younger years engagement' both on campus and in primary schools from the university's WP team. This support continues through secondary education, through to enrolment and beyond. The Careers and Employability team collaborate with the WP team to create a bespoke programme of induction and orientation for first-generation students and other students who can have a very different experience from their peers – mature students, those with a disability, and those who reside in the travel-to-work area rather than living in student accommodation (commuter students). In helping these students to connect with one another, with university support services, and with the campus, inclusion and belonging are embedded into the student journey and are never just an afterthought or an intervention added in later down the line.

This ecosystem approach is a hugely important part of the UP journey. Even before students have been targeted, their aspirations have been raised, they have been introduced to role models, helped to grow their network, inducted into the concept of the peer-to-peer Career Studio and have been encouraged to engage with the university's support offer. By the time students receive their first invitation to join the UP programme, they are already equipped with the mindset of embracing opportunities for success. They know the campus, they know the teams who can help them, and they can begin to work with us to explore opportunities and work to address any barriers to success. Of course, every student experience is unique, and not everyone will follow this designated route to success, which is why addressing the barriers which affect under-represented students is so important.

Barriers to student success are a complex combination of factors which differ for each student, dependent on their individual circumstances. Examples can include a lack of social capital, such as mentors and networks, and a lack of confidence and sense of belonging, leading to an increased sense of 'imposter syndrome'. Something which the university has identified as a consistent barrier is a lack of access to financial support, which can make it more difficult for UP students to take part in employability activities. In addition to this, UP students are more likely to have other 'identities' which they must balance alongside being a student, such as being a parent, carer or having to work long hours whilst studying, and some may face discrimination, in a range of forms, as they attempt to reach their goals. In the face of all these obstacles, the university seeks to work with students to recognise and address the difficulties they face, but also to demonstrate that their difference may also be their strength and the very thing that makes them the best candidate for a role.

So how does UP work? It's complex ... Firstly, data is used to inform the approach, looking at a range of information such as careers registration (which measures students' levels of career readiness and meaningful experience gained within the previous 12 months), graduate outcomes and sense of belonging, measured through surveys at various points of the student journey. This enables the identification of specific cohorts and areas of need – for example, a lack of digital skills amongst commuter students was addressed through the Digital Accelerator Programme, funded by the Office for Students, which saw a cohort of students from the local area undertake a 12-week paid internship with a local marketing agency along with a research project to investigate the skills gap in the Liverpool City Region. Through their internship, the students gained expertise in a specific digital skill and delivered peer-to-peer workshops to share their learning with more students.

Secondly, the university recognises the importance of the student voice in the work, and strives to co-create activities with the students it is trying to help. Team planning meetings are attended by the student career coaches and there is regular engagement with student societies such as the Mature Students Society, Disabled Society, 93 per cent Club (representing state-school-educated students) and the Afro-Caribbean Society. The Careers and Employability team coordinates a 'Commuter Hub' via our Virtual Learning Environment (Canvas) and a Microsoft Teams network for all UP-eligible students, enabling the provision of instant, personalised support.

UP is wide-ranging and flexible, with support in the form of asynchronous content and resources, which students can engage with at a time to suit them, regular targeted emails, personal interactions, prompts and reminders through the 'UP Network' on Microsoft Teams, bespoke events, ring-fenced opportunities, embedded modules, and cohort-specific experiential projects. UP permeates all activity with the Careers and Employability team, and has become the team's shorthand for accessibility, equality and inclusion.

To explain UP in more detail, it is useful to think of it in three levels:

Level One	A low intensity 'business as usual' offer open to all UP-eligible students with a communications focus. Key dates throughout the year are used to raise awareness and highlight role models across the institution (such as LGBTQ+ Pride Month, Black History Month and International Women's Day). UP is relaunched to new students each year and eligible students are encouraged to engage with resources and UP-labelled opportunities via Handshake. UP students are also offered the chance to apply for an Employability Support Award Bursary – offering them up to £400 to help with the costs of undertaking any employability-related activities, such as attending an interview or buying suitable work clothing, IT equipment, short courses or enterprise opportunities.
Level Two	Each year one or two key groups are identified as the focus for the coming academic year, supported by data on progression, student experience and outcomes, and aligned with APP targets. In 2022, the priority at this level was to enhance the employability of disabled students, capitalising on increased employer-awareness of the benefits of employing a diverse workforce which includes disabled graduates. Interventions here include targeted communications, workshops, internships and mentoring opportunities, and awareness-raising.
Level Three	At this level there are a range of high-intensity projects focusing on specific groups at Faculty, School/Department or even programme level. These projects have specific targets, again supported by data on career readiness and progression.

LEVEL THREE ACTIVITY

Examples of Level Three activity are:

Law UP Project – 2021

Although progress has been made to increase diversity within the legal sector workforce, evidence suggests there is still work to be done to enable aspiring lawyers from under-represented groups to break into the sector. The aim of this project was to support a small group of UP-eligible law students to better understand what is required to be successful in the profession by developing skills, a wider network and increased confidence. After identifying a small group of students, the project consisted of six engagements – little and often – over a six-week period with a range of interventions. This included guidance from a professional mentor, membership of a student society, alumni panel events and specialist careers planning. While the impact has yet to be evaluated in terms of graduate progression, there was an immediate impact in participants' confidence levels: 'I got the most out of talking to other students. The discussions around imposter syndrome and wellbeing definitely help with a positive mindset. I feel prepared for what I need to do in the near future.'

EDI in the Curriculum – Chemistry

In 2020, EDI was successfully embedded into the curriculum for the first time as a part of the UP programme. Working with the entire chemistry first year cohort (c.150 students), a digital storytelling task was designed specifically to address student expectations, experiences and understanding of diversity issues. Students were divided into small, mixed groups and assigned to a shared digital workspace in Microsoft Teams. Using the Royal Society of Chemistry's Inclusion and Diversity Strategy 2025, each group was set a question:

> Why is equality, diversity and inclusion important in chemical sciences? Support your answer with reference to how a key employer in the chemical sciences is committed to equality, diversity and inclusion in the workplace.

The students worked collaboratively to share personal experiences, listen to others and agree their approach to answering this question. A digital story – a short film with each group member contributing – was submitted to present the students' thoughts and this formed 10 per cent of the module assessment.

Enterprise in the Life Sciences Challenge 2021

An exclusive opportunity for Black, Asian and ethnic minority students from the School of Life Sciences, this three-week challenge offered a platform for students across all years of study and all programmes within the School of Life Sciences to connect with employers across the life sciences sector. They were introduced to key concepts of entrepreneurial activity and gained industry knowledge to develop an enterprising mindset. Over 40 students worked together in small groups on 'real world' challenges set by employers from sectors including pharmaceuticals, health technology, animal and ecology, and medical communication. All students received an accredited award and the chance to present to the employers who set their challenge. They were then invited to their employer's premises for an insight day to meet other members of the organisation and further widen their industry knowledge and networks.

EVALUATION AND MEASUREMENT OF IMPACT

Each of the interventions with students recognises the importance of evaluation and measuring impact. The projects are reviewed and evaluated on an annual basis, whilst recognising that some outcomes may require a longer timescale to measure impact, e.g. graduate outcomes. The team tries to avoid over-surveying students with lengthy questionnaires and instead focuses on key questions which measure confidence levels and subsequent intended actions.

Of course, measuring the long-term success and outcomes of the activities is more difficult and, in many ways, a waiting game. The vision for the future is clear, however; that EDI will be embedded into every aspect of work within the Careers and Employability team:

- supporting UP students' transition into university;
- increasing the visibility of diversity on campus so that students are no longer 'unseen and unheard';
- helping UP students to develop their skills, networks and aspirations whilst they are studying at the university and working to remove any barriers that may hinder them;
- continuing to provide training and awareness-raising amongst the Careers and Employability team, employers, and the university community as a whole, to help everyone to recognise the benefits of a diverse workforce and diverse leadership;
- supporting UP students' transition into the workplace, or further study, ensuring that they can advocate themselves, recognise their own strengths and align their values to their chosen career;
- continuing to work with UP alumni, highlighting their successes and working with them as role models who will inspire each future cohort.

CONCLUSION

We know that helping our students overcome all the challenges they face as they plan their future represents an almost impossible challenge. But that does not stop us from trying. The distance we have travelled in developing the UP programme since 2019, plus the early indications of the impact we have had, provide the encouragement we need. We have set out an exciting vision for the future: we are developing new expertise, connecting with new partners, and understanding our students better every day. As we move into a new world of graduate recruitment in a post-Covid future, we are determined to ensure that no student is left behind.

REFERENCE

Frobisher, A. (2020), *BAME students apply for 45% more jobs than their white counterparts*. Debut. Available at: https://debut.careers/bame-students-apply-for-45-more-jobs-than-their-white-counterparts/ (accessed: 12 January 2023).

REFLECTION

From an International Business and Economics student

'Devotion, determination, and destination'. These three powerful words present a guideline to success.

Much like hard work and recognition, they go hand-in-hand, except the latter is deceiving, at least for some.

A few months ago, I was under the impression that we all began from the same starting line, advancing objectively as time progressed. Although I was aware of issues regarding unequal opportunities, my naïveté and wishful thinking led to the view that it was not commonplace because, after all, we are in 2022.

It was during my placement (with an organisation that focuses on empowering and rewarding successful women) that I learned the importance of collective support, to be more precise, women supporting women. Support comes in all forms, through respect, strong networks, mentoring or a listening ear and of course, a just acknowledgement of any efforts and victories. Too often, we see fantastic women overlooked because of an unconscious bias that remains unregulated and unrelenting, despite women's diligence. Yes, for some, hard work inspires recognition or vice versa, but for others, especially women, they only achieve one part of the equation, hard work.

My intention of bringing this issue forward is perhaps a little selfish. Like my fellow women graduates, I want to strive hard, be conscientious, have support and receive credit where it is due, helping pave the pathway to success. We cannot do that at the same pace as our male counterparts, if there are barriers on the road before we even have a chance to get to our destination, regardless of whether we have the devotion or determination. This is unfortunately not something new. Yes, it is going to be hard to resolve but the real question is, are we, as society, using the development of personal and employability skills able to solve it?

23. Social mobility and London's left-behind graduates

Emily Dixon

IS LONDON A SOCIAL MOBILITY HOT SPOT?

London is frequently cited as a 'social mobility hot spot' and a success story for graduate employability (Social Mobility and Child Poverty Commission, 2016; Swinney and Williams, 2016). In the 2021 Sutton Trust research brief (Britton et al., 2021), the top 12 universities in the country ranked in order of social mobility at the access stage were all in London.

In conversations about social mobility and employability, London can be viewed as irrelevant to or outside the discussion, such as in the 2016 Social Mobility Index, which expressed concern about London pulling ahead of the rest of the country (Social Mobility and Child Poverty Commission, 2016). Viewing London as the standard that other areas aspire towards could imply there is no progress to be made in London. This chapter aims to expose some gaps in London's employability landscape where graduates fall behind, and to explore how these gaps can be identified in the data and tackled in real life.

The Graduate Outcomes Survey (GOS) invites graduates to indicate whether they view their employment 15 months after graduation as skilled, meaningful and 'on-track' – meaning useful to their future plans (HESA, 2021). London graduates are more likely to view their work positively than the UK average, but nuances can be obscured when we view the data this way. If the average London graduate is happy in skilled employment, it does not hold true that every Londoner can access these opportunities equally, and the intersectionalities of disadvantage mean that 'left behind' graduates are more likely to be BAME, have disabilities or be from lower socio-economic groups. In this chapter, the employability gaps that persist in London's higher education (HE) landscape are identified and case studies used to illustrate how higher education institutions (HEIs) are tackling them.

To make this argument, specific focus will be given to 'left behind' students in health care from London's MillionPlus (a representative body for many UK universities formed post 1992) and post-1992 institutions and graduates in creative subjects from under-represented demographic groups.

Looking at Graduate Outcomes data in the 2021 Higher Education Statistics Authority (HESA) report, London graduates in most subjects had scores that were equal to, or slightly better than, national averages for likelihood of being in skilled and meaningful work. However, three areas in which London's graduates scored consistently worse than other areas were medicine, other health-care subjects and veterinary science. These gaps are only a few percentage points, but they mark these disciplines out as different. While London graduates in general were three percentage points more likely to view their work as 'on-track' than nationally (73 per cent vs 70 per cent), graduates in these three areas were three to four percentage points less likely to say this.

Employability gaps also varied across HEI types. While London's pre-1992 and Russell Group providers produced graduates who were more likely to be in skilled work than their peers nationally (73 per cent in London, compared with 67 per cent nationally for Russell Group, and 71 per cent London compared with 65 per cent nationally for pre-1992) the opposite happened for post-1992 and MillionPlus institutions, which can be referred to as modern universities. Across all disciplines, London's modern university graduates were less likely to be in skilled work. Gaps were widest for health care, with London six percentage points behind the UK.

These statistics raise the question of what 'on-track' or 'meaningful' means to graduates, and it is hard to answer with certainty. Meaningful solutions must conceptualise clearly what pathways their own graduates find meaningful and 'on track'.

In London's creative industries, the challenge is different. While London's creative graduates enjoy better employability statistics than nationally, this success is unequal across demographic groups (Allen et al., 2013; Brook et al., 2020). It is dangerous to assume that because London's creative graduates are generally successful, every graduate is in the same position. Carey et al. (2021) tell us that BAME graduates and graduates from poorer backgrounds are less likely to find creative employment and progress to senior roles. If minoritised graduates are shut out of opportunities in London's vibrant and successful creative industries, interventions must be put in place to level the playing field.

London HEIs are isolating different aspects of these problems to tackle. Targeted interventions for demographic groups, skills gaps or industries exist in many HEIs, and will be relevant to regions which share common challenges. The following sections will consider some of these interventions.

Health Care

Widening participation in health-care disciplines is a challenge, and in 2022 specifically, training needs to fill specific labour shortages. Health Education England (2014) noted that 'the diversity profile of the current workforce in England is not representative of the general population that it seeks to serve, nor is the diversity profile of those employed by the NHS representative across the key staff groups'. These issues are particularly acute in London, which has been hardest hit by Covid-19 pandemic labour shortages (Iacobucci, 2022), and where the UK's most diverse population grows more heterogeneous all the time (Atherton and Mazhari, 2018). The London Mayor has announced a strategic focus on 'good work', meaning jobs paying a living wage in strategic industries for pandemic recovery, including health care (London Assembly, 2022).

At the University of East London (UEL), two pre-entry courses create pathways through health-care degrees into good jobs – 'Get Into Nursing' (GIN) and 'New Beginnings'. These provide a bridge between adult Londoners (who may be underemployed or re-entering employment) and good work. Because many health-care roles require specific qualifications, this can be a barrier for adults who do not hold undergraduate or foundation degrees. HE is also not always as easy to complete for mature learners; challenges include, but are not limited to, caring responsibilities, financial worries, working while studying and commuting to study (Hubble and Bolton, 2020). Students with longer commutes are less likely to complete courses than students who live nearby (Liz Thomas Associates, 2019; Shah, 2019), and general mature students' challenges can cause particular emotional challenges in nursing (Christensen and Craft, 2021). Interventions linking mature learners with health-care jobs, then, need to be flexible enough to avoid the many pitfalls keeping mature learners out of degree study and encourage course completion and employability in the context of mature student numbers in nursing trending downwards over the 2010s (MillionPlus, 2018). Pre-entry courses (foundation years or shorter courses) can improve academic skills as well as confidence, going some way to tackling access gaps (Sanders and Daly, 2012). This can improve employability for adults who would otherwise not have been qualified for these jobs and simultaneously contribute to the NHS's diversity targets.

'New Beginnings' provides access into UEL's Public Health BSc, alongside other degrees. More than 200 students from widening participation backgrounds enter HE study from New Beginnings annually, according to UEL's Lecturer in Pre-Entry Programmes. In their HE courses, New Beginnings students have higher completion, progression and success rates than their peers and the degree-awarding gap for BAME students is reduced by over 10 per cent compared to students on the same courses. This flexible pre-entry programme has demonstrable employability benefits several years later.

In 2021, GIN began to bring New Beginnings' successes to health care specifically. While New Beginnings provides entry to many programmes, GIN is tailored to the Nursing Associate Level 5 qualification. Thirteen applicants have completed the course and progressed to the Nursing Associate programme as of January 2022, and three more deliveries of the programme are planned to build on its early successes. Pre-course eligibility checks ensure students can pass the course, enter the Nursing Associate programme and work in nursing. Though a GIN applicant is more than two years from work, this pipeline is designed with employability in mind, with academic and professional course content delivered by Nursing lecturers. This focused approach aims to minimise non-continuation and maximise learners entering health-care jobs locally after qualifying.

In addition to these students' statistical employment prospects, we must remember qualitative evidence of changes to individuals' confidence and aspirations. This is harder to measure but important for helping underemployed or unemployed adults work in health care. Accordingly, this discussion is rounded out with a quotation from a 2021 GIN student: 'I have loved turning up each week, knowing that I am working towards having an actual career that I chose and don't just do as a job because I have a family to feed.'

Creative Industries

London's creative industries face challenges that differ from other London industries and the national creative landscape. Overall employability is high; Siepel et al. (2020) identify London as the centre of British creative microclusters, with significantly more clusters than Manchester, the second most creative city. London contains excellent graduate opportunities in these industries across a broad sweep of creative areas from West End theatres to video game studios, but it cannot be assumed that the playing field for accessing these opportunities is level. In the government's much-discussed Levelling Up White Paper, the issue of cultural inequality between London and the rest of the country is discussed with reference to theatre, video game studios and other creative industries (Department for Levelling Up, Housing and Communities, 2022).

Students from under-represented groups (including working class, BAME, disabled and neurodivergent graduates) face persistent barriers entering London's creative industries. In some cases, student numbers at creative specialist institutions in these groups are so low that it is barely possible to determine the size of the gaps. One illustrative example can be found in the Access and Participation Plan (APP) from the Royal Academy of Dramatic Art

(RADA), where analysis of continuation and progression for disabled students is affected by having data for fewer than 60 individuals (RADA, 2019).

The numbers being so obscure makes targeted interventions difficult to plan and evaluate, and points to issues further down the access pipeline, in schools and the pre-application stage, which need different forms of attention. While understanding employability problems at HE level is hard for these reasons, there is still a need to find ways to work on these issues.

Creative employability interventions are challenging even when the data to evaluate what is needed does exist. Creative industries, in London as elsewhere, are disparate and specialised and this can lead to difficulty engaging in co-creation, as well as not fitting traditional graduate recruitment strategies (MillionPlus, 2015). Measuring progression gaps is particularly difficult because of the preponderance of freelance and short-term work, making 'good employment' very different to other industries and therefore harder to analyse.

GuildHE, whose membership contains close to 20 specialist arts institutions, recently examined the invisible issues faced by BAME students in specialist postgraduate research (GuildHE, 2022). While the report focuses on BAME students, it notes the importance of intersectionality and the additional barriers faced by students with multiple under-represented identities. Regarding employability, students spoke about the difficulty of building important relationships with industry professionals in order to transition into work; 'connecting ethnic minority [students] to networks which understand the specific experiences of ethnic minorities in the labour market is deemed crucial'. In London, while the opportunities exist, students who lack social networks and cultural capital are less able to benefit from the capital's thriving creative industries (Brook et al., 2020).

Parkinson et al. (2015) found that the proportion of BAME employees in creative and cultural industries was only 7 per cent on average. The report also notes that disabled individuals are under-represented, and employers rarely understand their support needs. With employers and HEIs both unsure how to support minoritised graduates into equitable employment, and the problem's scale obscured by averaged-out statistics, equality in creative employment becomes an even thornier issue.

London's creative specialist institutions' Access and Participation Plans (APPs) reveal a range of approaches to understanding and addressing these issues. A few examples illustrate the breadth of approaches. The Conservatoire for Dance and Drama's (CDD) graduate destinations project is evaluating skills provision, cultural capital and attitudes to employment across the student body to understand how barriers to good creative employment affect different demographic groups (CDD, 2019). Taking a different approach, a pilot project from the Royal Central School of Speech and Drama will use qualitative and quantitative data to look at barriers for BAME learners entering creative academia (Royal Central School of Speech and Drama, 2019). Rose Bruford College (RBC) is looking at opportunities to build on existing music industry research to explore how employers can adapt to fit the needs of neurodivergent creatives (RBC, 2019). These programmes are at early development stages and cannot offer answers yet, but they illustrate that London's creative specialists recognise the unequal playing field that several demographic groups face.

This handful of examples illustrates how London's creative specialist institutions acknowledge the complex problems of equitable employability in creative industries. Tackling these issues takes different forms for different demographic groups and requires a granular approach, with deaf graduates in a different situation from autistic graduates, and Black graduates in a different situation from Asian graduates. There cannot be a single path to ensuring that employment for every role in every creative pathway is equally accessible, as London Higher has discussed previously in the context of examining whether combining Black, Asian and Minority Ethnic students into a single demographic term is even useful (Atherton and Mazhari, 2021). Nevertheless, the problems being multifaceted and deeply rooted does not mean they should not be solved. Through careful attention to hidden gaps in London's creative employability landscape, interventions can be planned to increase equitable employability for London's creative graduates.

CONCLUSION AND RECOMMENDATIONS

Based on this discussion of the challenges affecting Londoners in health care and creative industries, we find within the capital's employability numbers a set of challenges for students in disadvantaged and under-represented groups. These issues are not only hard to tackle, they are hard to get into view clearly because of small datasets, overlapping challenges and averaged-out statistics.

To get a clearer sense of how we can keep London's disadvantaged graduates from being left behind, two recommendations are made:

- Firstly, more research is needed on the problems faced by students in specific demographic categories. Where student numbers are low enough to make quantitative analysis difficult, qualitative research in the form of interview and focus groups can help the sector build understanding of how to provide support.
- Secondly, the sharing of data between institutions and researchers will be essential to improve awareness across industries and provider types of the issues that are more likely to affect particular demographic groups of students. Through rigorous, granular research that acknowledges the differences in ability to find good employment that two individuals in the

same city can face, we can build solutions that are as complex and multi-faceted as the problems.

REFERENCES

Allen, K., Quinn, J., Hollingworth, S. and Rose, A. (2013), 'Becoming employable students and "ideal" creative workers: exclusion and inequality in higher education work placements', *British Journal of Sociology of Education*, 34(3), 431–452.

Atherton, G. and Mazhari, T. (2018). *Preparing for Hyper-diversity: London's Student Population in 2030.* London: AccessHE.

Atherton, G. and Mazhari, T. (2021), *Higher Education Awarding Gaps and Ethnicity in London: Going Beyond BAME.* London: AccessHE.

Britton, J., Drayton, E. and van der Erve, L. (2021), *Universities and Social Mobility: Summary Report.* London: Sutton Trust.

Brook, O., O'Brien, D. and Taylor, M. (2020), *Culture Is Bad for You*, Manchester: Manchester University Press.

Carey, H., O'Brien, D. and Gable, O. (2021), *Social Mobility in the Creative Economy: Rebuilding and Levelling Up?* London: Creative Industries Policy and Evidence Centre.

CDD (2019), *Access and Participation Plan 2020–21 to 2024–25.* London: Office for Students.

Christensen, M. and Craft, J. (2021), '"Gaining a new sense of me": mature students' experiences of undergraduate nursing education', *Nurse Education Today*, 96, 104617.

Department for Levelling Up, Housing and Communities (2022), *Levelling Up the United Kingdom* (CP 604). London: HMSO.

GuildHE (2022), *Understanding the Lived Experience of Ethnic Minority Students in Postgraduate Research.* London: Institute for Community Studies.

Health Education England (2014), *Widening Participation – It Matters! Our Strategy and Initial Action Plan.* NHS Health Education England.

HESA (2021), *Graduate Outcomes Respondents Full Person Equivalent (FPE) (Version 1).* (Not publicly accessible.)

Hubble, S. and Bolton, P. (2020), *Mature Higher Education Students in England.* House of Commons Library Briefing Paper number 8809.

Iacobucci, G. (2022), 'Military drafted in to tackle staffing crisis in London hospitals', *BMJ*, 376, o47. doi:10.1136/bmj.o47.

Liz Thomas Associates (2019), *Qualitative Perceptions of Students about Commuting and Studying in London.* London: London Higher.

London Assembly (2022), 'Mayor offers free skills training to unemployed and low-income Londoners'. [Press release].

MillionPlus (2015), *Creative Futures: Ten Steps to Support the Creative Economy.* London: MillionPlus. Available at: https://dera.ioe.ac.uk/24771/1/Creative_Futures_-_Ten_steps_to_support_the_creative_economy.pdf (accessed: 13 January 2023).

MillionPlus (2018), *Forgotten Learners: Building a System that Works for Mature Students.* London: MillionPlus. Available at: https://dera.ioe.ac.uk/32235/1/Forgotten_learners_building_a_system_that_works_for_mature_students.pdf (accessed: 13 January 2023).

Parkinson, A., Buttrick, J. and Wallis, A. (2015), *Equality and Diversity within the Arts and Cultural Sector in England: Evidence and Literature Review Final Report.* Manchester: Consilium Research and Consultancy and Arts Council England.

RADA (2019), *Access and Participation Plan 2020–2025.* London: Office for Students.

RBC (2019), *Access and Participation Plan 2020/21 to 2024/25.* London: Office for Students.

Royal Central School of Speech and Drama (2019), *Access and Participation Plan 2020–21 to 2024–25.* London: Office for Students.

Russell Group (n.d.), *Russell Group*. Available at: https://russellgroup.ac.uk/about/ (accessed: 13 January 2023).

Sanders, L. and Daly, A. (2012), 'Building a successful foundation? The role of foundation year courses in preparing students for their degree', *Widening Participation and Lifelong Learning*, Special Issue Winter 2012–13, 42–56.

Shah, P. (2019), *Results of a Pilot Project on Factors Affecting Continuation.* London: London Higher.

Siepel, J., Camerani, R., Masucci, M., Velez Ospina, J., Casadei, P. and Bloom, M. (2020), *Creative Industries Radar: Mapping the UK's Creative Clusters and Microclusters*. Creative Industries Policy and Evidence Centre and The University of Sussex.

Social Mobility and Child Poverty Commission (2016), *The Social Mobility Index*.

Swinney, P. and Williams, M. (2016), *The Great British Brain Drain: Where Graduates Move and Why*. London: Centre for Cities.

REFLECTION

From a languages student

My passions and my talents always lay with languages. I knew it was what I needed to do at university, but languages alone do not make for a lot of options outside of translation and interpreting, which were not for me. However, I was able to expand my experiences and skill set through my activities outside of the classroom. Some of my most impactful experiences at university were my time spent in Student Staff Partnerships, as a Student Representative and Peer Mentor, as well as the broad range of volunteering opportunities available on campus. I was also lucky enough to study abroad three times and join a UQ volunteering group to India as an English teacher. At the time, I was doing this to be fun and social, and for the element of adventure. However, I also gained skills in event management, team leadership, research, teaching, technology, as well as multiple soft skills as a result.

This was particularly important to me, as I was unsure of what I wanted to do as a career and was successful in applying to multiple different fields using this skill set. Ultimately, I have worked as a researcher, school teacher, kindergarten teacher, tour guide, conversationalist, hotel staff, and a volunteer team leader across three countries. I was able to do these jobs with confidence and convince employers of my suitability for these roles through the methods taught to me through the employability workshops offered by my university.

As a person who is autistic and has anxiety, it has been so important to have programs where I can practice and be guided in a safe environment, as well as receive clear direction on how to develop my employability (such as through the Employability Award). I now work part-time as a researcher in a field outside of my degree while also studying further, which I never would have dreamed of without all of the opportunities available to me during university.

PART VIII

International students

24. Using the net promoter score to understand international alumni satisfaction
Shane Dillon

INTRODUCTION

This chapter explores the relationship between international student graduate employment and recommendations made by international alumni of UK universities to future international students. It reports on critical outputs from research conducted by Cturtle in 2019, as part of their International Student Employment Outcomes and Satisfaction (ISEOS) project, which was sponsored by government and international higher education industry stakeholders in Australia, the UK and the USA.

INTERNATIONAL STUDENTS AND THEIR ASPIRATIONS

Higher education is a globalised industry and one of the UK's top service exports. It was estimated to be worth £35 billion to the economy in 2020 (Department of Education, 2021).

Underpinning international higher education's importance to the UK is research, which demonstrates that international students primarily choose to invest in international education to improve their employability and employment prospects after graduation (Austrade, 2019; Cturtle, 2019; Higher Education Policy Institute (HEPI), 2021; Nilsson and Ripmeester, 2016; Universities UK, 2020). Thus, it makes sense that marketing material from universities to attract international students focuses on the improved employment outcomes attainable through investment in international education (Blackmore et al., 2015, Divan et al., 2019).

As Tran and Bui (2021: 1) state, 'International graduate employability has become an issue of growing concern for not only international graduates and their families but also host institutions and countries over the past decade.'

For international students, and their families, employability and employment outcomes are closely related to their professional aspirations and expectations of return on investment (ROI) in overseas study.

Recent surveys and studies provide strong evidence about the growing emphasis on employment prospects and career goals in shaping international students' decisions (QS, 2018, 2019; Tran et al., 2022). However, evidence on employment outcomes among international students is limited as students overwhelmingly return home, with conservative estimates suggesting that 90 per cent of international students do so after graduation or post-study work (Tran and Bui, 2021).

However, employability directly after graduation is a concern, as over 70 per cent of international students intend to stay in the UK after graduating to find work (HEPI, 2021) since post-study visa changes have been implemented in the UK that were not available in previous years. Despite this, the opinions and experiences of international students' careers services at their institutions indicate challenges in addressing student need in this area. For instance, the Universities UK 2019 report, *International Graduate Outcomes*, notes that only 2 per cent of recent international graduates from UK universities found their employment through their institution's careers advisory service (Universities UK, 2019).

Further, the UPP Foundation recently found that 56 per cent of UK institutions have no specialist support staff to cater for international employability (Shutt, 2022) and the Group of Eight in Australia (the top-ranked research-intensive universities in Australia) stated in 2022 that 'Australia's jobs-based pitch to international students is "clumsy"' and the 'focus should be on high-end jobs after students graduate – not low-end jobs while they study' (Ross, 2022).

It is in this environment, and using a net promoter score satisfaction framework with regard to international student expectations regarding postgraduate employment, that the ISEOS research project explored how employment outcomes affected international alumni becoming promoters of, neutral about, or detractors of their university to future international students.

ISEOS RESEARCH

The International Student Employment Outcomes and Satisfaction (ISEOS) research project was conducted in 2019 by the EdTech company Cturtle and sponsored by international education industry stakeholders in Australia, the USA, and the UK (Cturtle, 2019).

The research used a net promoter score (NPS) framework to identify the key variables that affect international alumni recommending their university and/

or country of education to future international students. Over 80 independent variables were identified and explored, fitting into three broad categories:

(1) experiences with the university while a student and as an alumnus;
(2) experiences living in the country of education;
(3) employment outcomes while a student and as an alumnus.

METHODOLOGY

The research used a net promoter score model which is a customer loyalty and satisfaction measurement taken from asking customers, in this case international alumni, how likely they are to recommend their university and host country of education to future international students, on a scale of zero to ten. A range of independent variables, including categories related to employment outcomes, costs, safety, university and living experiences, were then analysed to identify the relative importance of variables or variable sets on the likelihood of international alumni recommending their university and/or host country of education to future international students. Additionally, a range of statistical analysis was used in the report to rank countries and universities based on these independent variable sets and the net promoter scores.

The research goal was to provide unique insights into the relationship between international student satisfaction with employment outcomes and future student recruitment.

The survey collected data from 14,694 unique international alumni, collecting 16,830 university reviews from international alumni from China, Hong Kong SAR, India, Indonesia, Malaysia, Singapore, Thailand and Vietnam, of whom 4,673 had graduated from UK universities.

ISEOS KEY FINDINGS

The findings highlight the importance of employability in shaping perceptions among international alumni. Among reasons cited by international students for choosing to study in the UK, the top two related directly to employment prospects: improving career opportunities (83 per cent) and pursuing a specific career (43 per cent). Seven of the top eight factors affecting an international student's likelihood of recommending their country of education to future international students were also employment related. This is even more critical in some international student cohorts, for example Indian students, where the top six factors to recommend the country of education were employment related.

Regardless of degree level, international students tend to go back to work in their home countries and this places great importance on the development and rollout of appropriate career support services for this returnee majority. A report from the UK Home Office in 2017 stated that 97 per cent of international students leave the UK after studies (Home Office, 2017) and similar reports from Australia and the USA show that at least 90 per cent of international graduates leave after graduation and/or post-study work rights expire (Cturtle, 2019).

International students had a global satisfaction rate with their perceived ROI of 68 per cent, with international alumni of UK universities scoring the lowest with an average of 65 per cent. International alumni of US (73 per cent) and Canadian (74 per cent) universities reported the highest satisfaction with ROI. Around 71 per cent of international alumni get a job within three months of graduation, with 79 per cent finding their first job back in their home country.

Alumni who studied at international campuses in Asia tended to earn higher incomes than alumni studying at campuses in the country of education, indicating the effect of local networks in employment outcomes. Alumni who graduated more than seven years ago feel the most positive and satisfied with their education and they can be the best promoters of both universities and country of education to future international students. Around 44 per cent of international alumni felt satisfied with career support from their university and 35 per cent of international alumni were satisfied with their alumni support in their home country.

The research found that undergraduate students appreciated career-orientation programmes being delivered during their studies, whereas postgraduate students appreciate those programmes after their graduation across all host countries of education.

INTERNATIONAL GRADUATE – FIRST JOB AFTER GRADUATION

There is variability in location of the first job, with 9 per cent of international graduates of US universities finding their first job in their host country of education compared with Australia with 4 per cent, and the UK with 2 per cent.

Students' access to information on migration, employment opportunities and work rights prior to study was limited, with under half of students having access to reliable sources of information prior to study.

Recent graduates, those within three years of graduation, earned on average US$1,770 per month in their first job. Income disparity was highly dependent on the location of first employment, with postgraduate students also tending to have a higher income than undergraduate students, with the income gap narrowing over time.

FACTORS AFFECTING INTERNATIONAL ALUMNI RECOMMENDING COUNTRY OF EDUCATION

International alumni are a powerful source of information for future students and the net promoter score (NPS) for international alumni recommending their host country of education was +19 (40 per cent promoters and 21 per cent detractors). The NPS is calculated by subtracting the percentage of detractors from the percentage of promoters with a higher score indicating a higher overall positive NPS.

The NPS for all countries of education was worse among Indian graduates with a score of −9 (41 per cent detractors, 27 per cent neutral, 32 per cent promoters).

The UK had the lowest NPS (a score of +10) among all major study destinations in relation to alumni's recommendation of their country of education as a study destination to future students (27 per cent actively detract, 37 per cent neutral, 37 per cent promoters). Indian students were the largest detractors of the UK, with 50 per cent actively discouraging future international students from studying in the UK (see Figure 24.1).

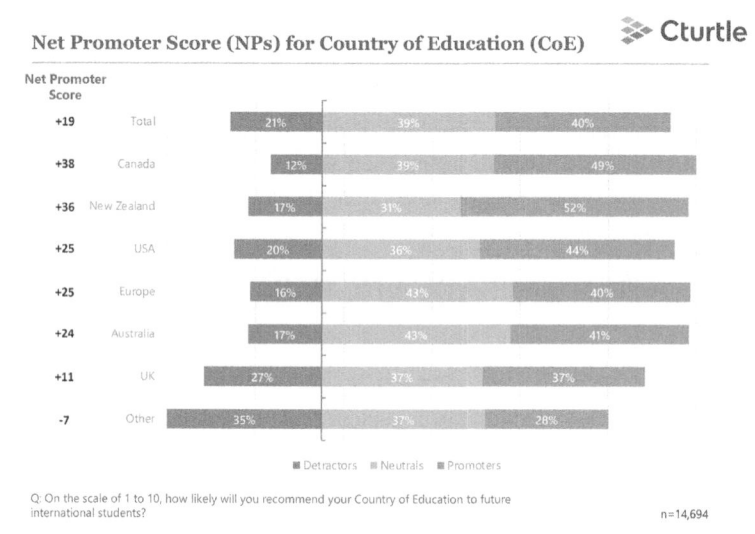

Net Promoter Score (NPs) for Country of Education (CoE)

Net Promoter Score	Country	Detractors	Neutrals	Promoters
+19	Total	21%	39%	40%
+38	Canada	12%	39%	49%
+36	New Zealand	17%	31%	52%
+25	USA	20%	36%	44%
+25	Europe	16%	43%	40%
+24	Australia	17%	43%	41%
+11	UK	27%	37%	37%
−7	Other	35%	37%	28%

Q: On the scale of 1 to 10, how likely will you recommend your Country of Education to future international students? n=14,694

Source: Cturtle (2019), *International Student Employment Outcomes and Satisfaction.* Available at: https://cturtle.co/2019/12/23/iseos-global-report/ (accessed: 23 January 2023).

Figure 24.1   NPS for country of education

For the UK, six of the seven top factors affecting international alumni recommending the country of education were employment-related, while the 'overall sense of feeling welcomed in the country' was the most important factor in recommending the country of education among North Asian and South-East Asian students. The six top factors affecting international alumni's recommendations of the UK to future students were employment related, with the number one factor being 'job opportunities available after graduation related to their field of study'.

For undergraduates, the 'overall sense of feeling welcome' and the 'overall satisfaction with working in country of education' were the two main drivers, while for postgraduates, general perceptions of job opportunities and other job/working-related factors play the key role in recommending or not recommending the country of education (see Figure 24.2).

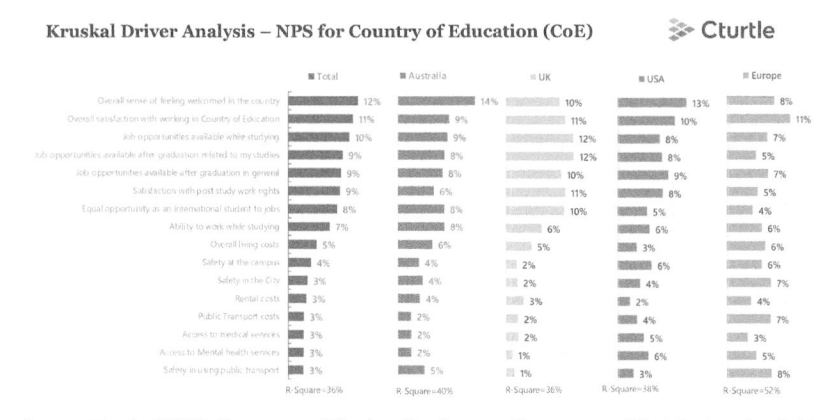

Source: Cturtle (2019), *International Student Employment Outcomes and Satisfaction.* Available at: https://cturtle.co/2019/12/23/iseos-global-report/ (accessed: 23 January 2023).

Figure 24.2   Kruskal driver analysis – NPS for country of education

FACTORS AFFECTING INTERNATIONAL ALUMNI RECOMMENDING UNIVERSITY

Across all countries of education, the average NPS for universities was +18 (21 per cent detractors, 40 per cent neutral, 39 per cent promoters) (see Figure 24.3). The most important factors driving international alumni's promotion of their universities (see Figure 24.4) were the

- overall satisfaction with working in the country of education;
- job opportunities available while studying;

- job opportunities available after graduation 'related to my studies'. Forty-four per cent of international alumni felt satisfied with career support from their university, with the UK having the lowest satisfaction from international alumni, with satisfaction from university career support services being at 40 per cent, career support after graduation at 33 per cent, university's network for job opportunities at 36 per cent, access to mentor programmes at 32 per cent, access to career help at 38 per cent, and support from alumni team in home country at 31 per cent;
- seventy-seven per cent of all international students are satisfied with the relevance of their education to their careers and 81 per cent are satisfied that their education had a positive impact on their career.

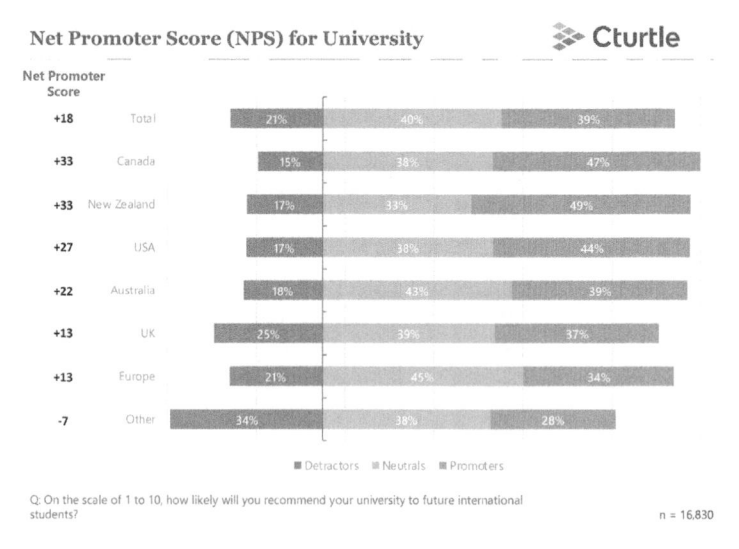

Net Promoter Score (NPS) for University — Cturtle

Net Promoter Score		Detractors	Neutrals	Promoters
+18	Total	21%	40%	39%
+33	Canada	15%	38%	47%
+33	New Zealand	17%	33%	49%
+27	USA	17%	38%	44%
+22	Australia	18%	43%	39%
+13	UK	25%	39%	37%
+13	Europe	21%	45%	34%
-7	Other	34%	38%	28%

Q: On the scale of 1 to 10, how likely will you recommend your university to future international students? n = 16,830

Source: Cturtle (2019), *International Student Employment Outcomes and Satisfaction.* Available at: https://cturtle.co/2019/12/23/iseos-global-report/ (accessed: 23 January 2023).

Figure 24.3   NPS for university

CONCLUSION

The research outputs show the importance of international student employment outcomes to the UK higher education system as a form of promotion for the UK as an education destination and for individual universities. Further, it shows UK universities have work to do in supporting international student employment outcomes, in particular for the majority of students who do return home after graduation. Supporting employment outcomes could be one of the

Kruskal Driver Analysis – NPS for University

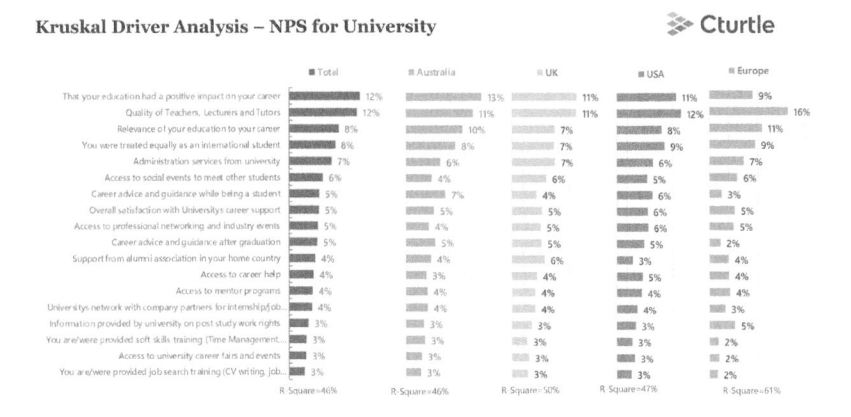

	Total	Australia	UK	USA	Europe
That your education had a positive impact on your career	12%	13%	11%	11%	9%
Quality of Teachers, Lecturers and Tutors	12%	11%	11%	12%	16%
Relevance of your education to your career	8%	10%	7%	8%	11%
You were treated equally as an international student	8%	8%	7%	9%	9%
Administration services from university	7%	6%	7%	6%	7%
Access to social events to meet other students	6%	4%	6%	5%	6%
Career advice and guidance while being a student	5%	7%	4%	6%	3%
Overall satisfaction with University's career support	5%	5%	5%	6%	5%
Access to professional networking and industry events	5%	4%	5%	6%	5%
Career advice and guidance after graduation	5%	5%	5%	5%	2%
Support from alumni association in your home country	4%	4%	6%	3%	4%
Access to career help	4%	3%	4%	5%	4%
Access to mentor programs	4%	4%	4%	4%	4%
University's network with company partners for internship/job...	4%	4%	4%	4%	3%
Information provided by university on post study work rights	3%	3%	3%	3%	5%
You are/were provided soft skills training (Time Management...	3%	3%	3%	3%	2%
Access to university career fairs and events	3%	3%	3%	3%	2%
You are/were provided job search training (CV writing, job...	3%	3%	3%	3%	2%
	R Square=46%	R Square=46%	R Square=50%	R Square=47%	R Square=61%

Source: Cturtle (2019), *International Student Employment Outcomes and Satisfaction.* Available at: https://cturtle.co/2019/12/23/iseos-global-report/ (accessed: 23 January 2023).

Figure 24.4   Kruskal driver analysis – NPS for university

most effective ways to recruit future international students via the creation of a global alumni footprint of brand ambassadors and promoters. For this reason, UK universities need to develop employment support for international students as a flagship pillar of their learning experience to remain globally competitive.

Globally, Covid-19 has changed the landscape of international education. The concerns posed by this pandemic on the future of universities and the international education sector are closely linked to the economics of many top study destinations as countries navigate through and after this health crisis.

The post-study work visa is currently the standard model employed by major destination nations worldwide to entice international students as a marketing tool and a reward for investing in overseas education. The question will be how many opportunities related to the subject of study are available in the destination countries, as well as how companies in those countries are informed about the advantages of recruiting graduates from other countries.

To draw in students, post-Covid employment results and return on investment will be crucial, and the emphasis should be on high-end jobs after students graduate rather than low-end jobs while they are students.

To effectively communicate to consumers the value and return on investment that international education offers, the sector must embrace statistics on international graduate employment results.

For most graduates who return home, it will become increasingly crucial for universities to offer career support by giving them data-driven insights into their domestic labour markets and advice on how to connect with graduate prospects there. Careers services need to consider strategies more adapted to the volatile, uncertain, complicated, and ambiguous environment that graduates will enter in the next decade.

REFERENCES

Austrade (2019), *Australian International Education 2025*. Available at: https://www.austrade.gov.au/Australian/Education/Services/australian-international-education-2025 (accessed: 16 January 2023).

Blackmore, J., Gribble, C. and Rahimi, M. (2015), 'International education, the formation of capital and graduate employment: Chinese accounting graduates' experiences of the Australian labour market', *Critical Studies in Education*, 58(1), 69–88.

Cturtle (2019), *International Student Employment Outcomes and Satisfaction*. Available at: https://cturtle.co/2019/12/23/iseos-global-report/ (accessed: 16 January 2023).

Department of Education (2021), *International Education Strategy: 2021 update: Supporting recovery, driving growth*. Policy paper. Available at: https://www.gov.uk/government/publications/international-education-strategy-2021-update/international-education-strategy-2021-update-supporting-recovery-driving-growth (accessed: 16 January 2023).

Divan, A., Knight, E., Bennett, D. and Bell, K. (2019), 'Marketing graduate employability: understanding the tensions between institutional practice and external messaging', *Journal of Higher Education Policy and Management*, 41(5), 485–499.

HEPI (2021), *Paying More for Less? Careers and Employability Support for International Students at UK Universities*. HEPI Report 143. Oxford: HEPI.

Home Office (2017), *Second Report on Statistics Being Collected under the Exit Checks Programme*. London: HMSO.

Nilsson, P. A. and Ripmeester, N. (2016), 'International student expectations: career opportunities and employability', *Journal of International Students*, 6(2), 614–631.

QS (2018), *International Student Surveys 2018*. London: QS.

QS (2019), *International Student Surveys 2019*. London: QS.

Ross, J. (2022), 'Australia's jobs-based pitch to international students "clumsy"', *Times Higher Education*, 22 June. Available at: https://www.timeshighereducation.com/news/australias-jobs-based-pitch-international-students-clumsy (accessed: 16 January 2023).

Shutt, E. (2022), *International Student Futures: Developing a World Class Experience from Application to Onward Career*. London: UPP Foundation Student Futures Commission.

Tran, L. T. and Bui, H. (2021), 'International graduate returnees' accumulation of capitals and (re)positioning in the home labour market in Vietnam: the explorer, the advancer or the adventurer?', *Journal of Education and Work*, 34(4), 544–557. doi: 10.1080/13639080.2021.1943334.

Tran, L. T., Phan, H. L. T., Tan, G. and Rahimi, M. (2022), '"I changed my strategy and looked for jobs on Gumtree": the ecological circumstances and international graduates' agency and strategies to navigate the Australian labour market', *Compare: A Journal of Comparative and International Education*, 52(5), 822–840. https://doi.org/10.1080/03057925.2020.

Universities UK (2019), *International Graduate Outcomes*. London: Universities UK.

Universities UK (2020), *Supporting International Graduate Employability: Making Good on the Promise*. London: Universities UK.

REFLECTION

From a director of a property consulting firm in Vietnam

I am the country director of a global property consulting firm in Vietnam and each year we employ between 10 and 20 university graduates to join our company. Our firm offers a wide arrangement of property related services from investment, valuation to leasing and project management to both domestic and international clients so it is imperative for our employees to have both local knowledge and a global perspective, as well as the ability to communicate at a professional level in English. Returning international students are a source for graduate talent that we try to tap into.

From my perspective as an employer, I want access to the best returning talent and that means being able to recruit from a wide network of universities and a wide range of graduates in terms of their level of education and also their areas of study.

My advice to universities would be to join larger employer networks as an individual university approach does not offer value to the international student or to me as an employer as you need the scale of both talent and opportunities that only networks can provide.

25. Meeting the employability expectations of international students in transition to higher education in the UK

Victoria Wilson-Crane and Linda Cowan

INTRODUCTION

As a provider of higher education (HE) to non-UK students, and as part of a global company working with universities in Australia, New Zealand, UK and the US, Kaplan International Pathways is well positioned and attuned to the interests and needs of these students, as well as the cultural and economic value that they bring to the learning experience. International students are a significant part of the HE scene – 538,615 international students were studying in the UK in the academic year 2019/20, of which 395,630 were from beyond the European Union (EU) (Universities UK International, 2021). It was reported that in 2018/19, international students brought £25.9 billion to the UK (London Economics, 2021).

Nilsson and Ripmeester (2016) discuss how international experiences enrich the academic work and life in general for university communities but question the degree to which those experiences improve employability. A large body of literature suggests that graduates entering many employment sectors beyond their degree studies are generally expected to have a range of job-related and human transferable skills. Weise (2021: 61) says 'the good jobs of the future will require ... a broader set of skills and competencies than the jobs of the past'. In all but the most vocational of subjects, knowledge of a particular discipline is of little significance. The types of skills that employers are looking for are changing in response to an evolving global world of work. A study by McKinsey in 2018 revealed that for most jobs, over one-third of the skills deemed necessary in 2016 would have changed or may no longer be required by 2020, an interesting observation even prior to the global Covid-19 pandemic, with the unforeseen acceleration in demand for digital skills and productive remote collaboration that this brought. Minocha et al. (2018) say 'more needs to be done to ensure graduates have the right *kind* and *level* of skills to succeed in a globally competitive market'.

Some time ago, reflecting on anecdotes about employers' perceptions of graduate work-readiness, Yorke (2004/2006) noted that graduates' perceptions of the services offered by universities to prepare students for future employment were not well researched. More recently, Cao and Henderson (2021) mentioned that there was limited literature to document how students manage their employability during the period of receiving overseas education. In 2021 Universities UK reported that International Student Barometer feedback indicates poorer work experience opportunities for international versus UK/EU students and the availability of information on those opportunities for countries overseas could be improved. Added to this is the potential for student disappointment with the lack of customised careers offerings, raised by Fakunle (2021), in the article on the intersection of internationalisation, employability and the international student experience. In their research with international students, disappointment was expressed that most careers fairs and presentations were thought to be designed with home students in mind.

EXPECTATIONS OF INTERNATIONAL STUDENTS

Kaplan International Pathways recruits 7,000 international students each year from over 100 different countries and regions to participate in higher education in the UK. The majority of those students study at colleges in which the company operates, in or close to the campuses of universities in England and Scotland. Courses prepare students for success at undergraduate and postgraduate study in the UK, and beyond. These students are looking for more from their pathway provider than simply a route to their degree programme. They are also wanting a programme that helps them make informed career decisions and build their skills for their future working life.

There is little in the academic literature or policy papers to guide organisations such as ours when looking for good practice in preparing students for their future jobs, so we undertook research alongside the Higher Education Policy Institute (HEPI) to find out more about the employability support expectations of international students. The report concluded:

- *Careers support is a big consideration when choosing where to study*: international students surveyed said the careers support (82 per cent) and employability skills (92 per cent) they thought they would receive at UK universities were 'important' or 'very important' when choosing their university.
- *Students on courses with embedded employability skills are more satisfied*: three-quarters (75 per cent) of students who say employability skills are

embedded in their course are happy with their course and university, compared to just 43 per cent for those who say employability skills are not part of their course.
- *Expectations of careers support after graduation vary*: students are split on whether their university careers service should provide tailored support about careers in their home country – 42 per cent of students say it should, another 42 per cent say they do not expect this.
- *International students struggle to find access to work experience opportunities in the UK*: four in ten (39 per cent) international students have done no work experience during their time at university (HEPI and Kaplan International Pathways, 2021).

Zhao and Cox (2022) note that much of the literature on the experience of students studying beyond their home countries is centred on 'managing the transition to a new learning environment and culture' whilst far less well documented are the benefits that studying overseas may bring to the student. It is expected that one perceived benefit is the increase in opportunities for fulfilling and lucrative employment upon completion of the degree and thus return on investment for the student, after graduation.

DEVELOPING EMPLOYABILITY SKILLS

Since 2019, we at Kaplan have taken several overt, deliberate steps to embed employability skills into our courses in response to student demand and to add value and improve employability outcomes. The benefits of this are twofold: firstly, to equip students with employability skills, and secondly, to ensure students are more familiar with the wealth of opportunities their degree will afford, once they progress. There are now a number of different elements to the Kaplan Pathways offering:

- Some are *led by college staff*, for example Applied Learning Weeks where students are off the normal timetable and participate in cross-curricular themed activities for the week, to apply the knowledge from their modules, participate in low- or no-stakes assessments and work with students from different disciplines.
- Some are *self-directed*, for example Kindness Curriculum self-access packages on the virtual learning environment where students can earn digital badges. This non-assessed feature of our wider learning experience focuses upon 12 attributes, such as collaboration, positivity and trust. This is in response to the prediction of a rapidly growing need for the development of social and emotional skills (Bughin et al., 2018) and to encourage self-regulation and self-management.

- Some are *required*, for example completion of a KapPACK e-Portfolio, evidencing skills developed and, crucially, reflections on learning and its contribution to future study and career plans.
- Some are *embedded into students' programmes*, for example internships across all programmes and authentic assessments.
- Some are undertaken by students as '*extracurricular*', for example joining relevant professional networking organisations, either discipline-specific (e.g. Institute of Biomedical Science), or more generic (e.g. Institute of Enterprise and Entrepreneurs or Association for Project Management), and participating in asynchronous and synchronous learning.

CAREER FOCUS

These offerings are drawn together into an Employability Framework, a reference tool to help Kaplan Pathways colleges plan the offering to students. It is expected that not every student will use each learning opportunity, but rather the framework serves as a menu that students may choose from. Learning is either self-directed, partly facilitated or fully led by staff.

Opportunities are displayed to students using the Career Focus logo to help students make the connection between the different activities and so that pre-undergraduate students, in particular, can recognise the value of these in terms of preparation for their future career, given that this is some years away. Students are sometimes slow to make the connections between what they are learning and the relevance and utility of this for their future careers, particularly in the case of human, transferable skills such as resilience, creativity and collaboration. Our approach of regular learning opportunities and multiple interventions from a range of activity types, drawn together under the theme of Career Focus, is helping students recognise the links and appreciate the importance of this learning.

Participation by students has been positive to date:

– attendance at Applied Learning Weeks is high, close to that for regular taught classes;
– around one-quarter of students each year take advantage of the chance to join a professional network;
– nearly 1,500 students in 2021–22 registered to earn Kindness Curriculum badges.

Students gave feedback on Career Focus in our 2021–22 Student Experience Survey and 97.33 per cent of students agreed that 'My programme helped me to develop knowledge and skills which will be useful for my future career', with 65.26 per cent choosing the highest rating.

Whilst comments are anonymous, this sample is indicative:

> [The programme] really helped for my future career.

> During this time, my skills have greatly improved, and I have a basic understanding of my major. I have made a lot of effort to improve my professional skills, which is a good experience.

> My project helped me to develop skills and knowledge for my future career.

> The course has helped me to a great extent in opening up my ideas and changing some of my ways of thinking, which will be of great help to my future study and life.

WHAT PARTICULAR EMPLOYABILITY NEEDS DO INTERNATIONAL STUDENTS HAVE?

International students are not a homogeneous group; however, in our experience, our students do frequently ask for:

- Useful contextual information on how to apply for jobs in their home countries and build the networks they have often lost from having chosen to study overseas. There are different expectations of quantity, quality and level of detail on CVs, application forms, etc. Higher education providers (HEPs) could usefully prepare students by explaining what employers typically expect in their home or target countries or regions.
- Intelligence on the current and predicted labour market needs of the home or target employment destinations.
- Assistance to integrate (back) into the labour markets in home countries.
- Information on how to apply for jobs in the UK. In addition to missed opportunities for individual students, employers and the UK economy may be unable to benefit from having international graduates working for them, if students are not successful in applications to employment via the graduate route.
- Cultural expectations of employment in different locations. Whilst it may not be possible to give all the information, HEPs might better equip students to be able to thrive in uncertainty and be aware of expectations so that graduates can be their authentic selves at work.
- Opportunities to learn languages or improve English if this is a second language, and perhaps to learn some discipline-specific language to ensure barriers to gaining employment are minimised and, in turn, potential future engagement in the workplace is maximised.
- Diversified offerings for students from different countries and regions, and entering emerging sectors, to help meet skills demands. Scott and Willison

(2021) mentioned this, explaining that '"catch-all" programmes may not be as effective as more bespoke provision'.

To meet these needs takes dedicated resources and involves training and development of existing staff or the appointing of specialist staff by HEPs. Standage (2018) observed that providers are investing more into employability and careers services. The Association of Graduate Careers Advisory Services (AGCAS) reported 82 per cent of respondents had confirmed a greater demand for services in 2020 compared to previous years and therefore resourcing the demand was said to be the number one challenge for careers service leaders (AGCAS, 2021). Fakunle (2020) recommended that universities could review the extent to which students are 'able to access opportunities to realise their aspirations, such as leadership opportunities'.

WHAT CAN INTERNATIONAL STUDENTS 'BRING'?

International students bring economic benefits to institutions and regions: tuition fee income, non-tuition fee income and other knock-on benefits via friends and families of the students (London Economics, 2021). As well as financial contributions, international students bring a wide range of experiences and skills that enrich the learning of other international and domestic students. Diverse learning environments are thought to be effective, allowing students to gain fresh perspectives (HEPI and Kaplan International Pathways, 2021). Done well, this significantly enhances the learning experiences of all students. Clarke (2018: 1933) tells us that 'universities have an important role to play in assisting students to build human capital. Degree relevant skills, knowledge, and competencies can be taught through well-designed curricula and evaluated through scaffolded assessment tasks.'

For example, discussions in taught sessions on cultural approaches can be richer if university staff draw from international students and encourage them to share, affording opportunities for all to compare and contrast. This can lead to greater understanding and empathy of approaches to solving business challenges in different contexts.

The International Education Strategy 2021 update indicates India, Indonesia, Saudi Arabia, Vietnam and Nigeria as immediate priorities for engagement (Department for Education, 2021). There is an opportunity for the government and higher education to work together to generate this intelligence and it would be logical to begin with a focus upon these countries.

CONCLUSION

Diversity of the student cohort was discussed by Standley (2015), reminding us that the perceptions of students of their experiences are of great importance to HEPs and this can have an influence on future recruitment. They go on to say that institutions have responded, to the benefit of in-person and remote students, from improvements in student support services.

The competition for students is fierce; positive testimonials from students about their experiences will help HEPs to attract well-qualified students with the potential for success. The all-important word-of-mouth recommendation can be achieved if institutions continue to develop and tailor their offering to meet the specific employability skills needs of international students.

HEPs could build or make use of established networks of former students, now the employees and perhaps even the employers, working in other countries and regions. These may be the source of the required intelligence which may only be available, at the appropriate depth, by those rooted in the countries of interest. This could be the basis of symbiotic relationships; for talented graduates, the possibility of work experience, internships or job offers, and for the employer, the reciprocal benefits of a pipeline of well-qualified graduates.

HEPs would benefit from reliable data on the employment outcomes for international students. As discussed by Graham (2022), institutions will gain much from having strong evidence of the achievements of students beyond their degree outcomes.

There is great potential, right now, for HEPs in the UK to meet, and even exceed, the career support expectations of international students. This focus on future career benefits could be – and our expectation is that this *will* be – an important differentiator as we continue to see greater choice for students on where, when and how they study.

REFERENCES

AGCAS (2021), *The resourcing of HE careers services during a pandemic and beyond.* Sheffield: AGCAS.

Bughin, J., Hazan, E., Lund, S., Dahlström, P., Wiesinger, A. and Subramaniam, A. (2018), *Skill shift: Automation and the future of the workforce.* Discussion paper. Washington DC: McKinsey Global Institute.

Cao, X. and Henderson, E. (2021), 'The interweaving of diaries and lives: diary-keeping behaviour in a diary-interview study of international students' employability management', *Qualitative Research*, 21(6), 829–845.

Clarke, M. (2018), 'Rethinking graduate employability: the role of capital, individual attributes and context', *Studies in Higher Education*, 43(11), 1923–1937.

Department for Education (2021), *International Education Strategy, 2021 update: Supporting recovery, driving growth.* Policy paper. Available at: https://www.gov.uk/government/publications/international-education-strategy-2021-update/

international-education-strategy-2021-update-supporting-recovery-driving-growth (accessed: 16 January 2023).

Fakunle, O. (2020), 'Developing a framework for international students' rationales for studying abroad, beyond economic factors', *Policy Futures in Education*, 19(6), 671–690.

Fakunle, O. (2021), 'International students' perspective on developing employability during study abroad', *Higher Education Quarterly*, 75(4), 575–590.

Graham, A. (2022), 'Now, more than ever, we need to expand our knowledge of international student outcomes', *HEPI*, 15 March. Available at: https://www.hepi.ac.uk/2022/03/15/now-more-than-ever-we-need-to-expand-our-knowledge-of-international-student-outcomes/ (accessed: 16 January 2023).

HEPI and Kaplan International Pathways (2021), *Paying more for less? Careers and employability support for international students at UK universities.* HEPI Report 143. Oxford: HEPI.

London Economics (2021), *The costs and benefits of international higher education students to the UK economy: Summary Report for the Higher Education Policy Institute and Universities UK International.* London: London Economics.

Minocha, S., Hristov, D. and Leah-Harland, S. (2018), 'Developing a future-ready global workforce: a case study from a leading UK university', *International Journal of Management Education*, 16(2), 245–255.

Nilsson, P. and Ripmeester, N. (2016), 'View of international student expectations: career opportunities and employability', *Journal of International Students*, 6(2), 614–631.

Scott, F. and Willison, D. (2021), 'Students' reflections on an employability skills provision', *Journal of Further and Higher Education*, 45(8), 1118–1133.

Standage, H. (2018), *How should universities teach employability?* Prospects Luminate. Available at: https://luminate.prospects.ac.uk/how-should-universities-teach-employability (accessed: 16 January 2023).

Standley, H. (2015), 'International mobility placements enable students and staff in higher education to enhance transversal and employability-related skills: Graphical Abstract Figure', *FEMS Microbiology Letters*, 362(19), fnv157.

Universities UK (2021), *International student recruitment data*. Available at: https://www.universitiesuk.ac.uk/universities-uk-international/explore-uuki/international-student-recruitment/international-student-recruitment-data (accessed: 16 January 2023).

Universities UK International (2021), *2021 International Facts & Figures*. Available at: https://www.universitiesuk.ac.uk/sites/default/files/field/downloads/2021-12/International%20Facts%20and%20Figures%202021_0.pdf (accessed: 24 January 2023).

Weise, M. (2021), *Long Life Learning: Preparing for Jobs That Don't Even Exist Yet.* New Jersey: Wiley.

Yorke, M. (2004/2006), *Employability in Higher Education: What It Is – What It Is Not.* York: The Higher Education Academy/ESECT.

Zhao, X. and Cox, A. (2022), 'Chinese students' study in the UK and employability: the views of Chinese employers, students and alumni, and UK teachers', *Journal of Education and Work*, 35(4), 422–440.

REFLECTION

From a senior manager in financial services

There has been a lot written in the press about young people in the UK having poor written English. My experience is that young people are really struggling with communication skills.

It seems that a lot of young people are using 'text speak' to talk to friends all day long, with lots of abbreviations and emojis. It is important to understand that this is not appropriate in business. It is not that this way of communicating is wrong, but young people do need to understand what is appropriate in different circumstances.

I do think it would be useful if universities were doing more to get students to be ready to communicate in business English. Academic writing is not always the right way to be communicating in the workplace, and neither is 'text speak'. Some focus on 'business English' and broader business communication skills would be very useful.

26. How partnerships can make a difference to securing jobs for international students

Jacklyn Tubb and Caroline Fox

INTRODUCTION

For all the discussion of the UK government's reforms to higher and further education, arguably their whole purpose can be boiled down to one top ministerial priority: achieving more jobs for students. This is equally true of the more established and modern universities, irrespective of whether the student comes from a disadvantaged background. The Department for Education and the Treasury are in lockstep in this pursuit of value for money. The University of Greenwich believes that it is already rising to the challenge.

It is undoubtedly true that when home tuition fees are being frozen, more international students coming to our institutions (Universities and Colleges Admissions Service (UCAS), 2022) help to keep balance sheets healthy. But the University of Greenwich has always felt that welcoming students from all over the world makes it a better place. In addition to them having a great learning experience, we want to support the international students into jobs, work placements or internships of the type which will put them on the road to a meaningful career. Of course, more students will increasingly be in employment from the start as a growing proportion opt for degree apprenticeship programmes.

Just like most universities, Greenwich prides itself in having a strong employment and careers service with an excellent team of employer partnership managers. But the scale of the employability challenge means that it considers partnership with other providers vital, even if the Office for Students' latest consultation proposals on quality assurance and partnerships may lead to a greater regulatory burden (Office for Students, 2022).

TEAMING UP WITH AN INDEPENDENT PROVIDER FOR EMPLOYER ENGAGEMENT

One of Greenwich's partners is Twin Group, an independent provider specialising in international education, skills training, work experience and employability. Because independent providers deliver apprenticeships and other skills programmes, employer engagement is their modus operandi and, overall, they work with approximately 350,000 employers a year.

In 2019, the university outsourced to Twin Group a pilot initiative to assist students on its MSc Engineering Management Industrial Practice and MSc Pharmaceutical Science Industrial Practice programmes in finding quality work placements in specialist areas over a two-year period. The MSc Industrial Practice programme gives international students an additional year in industry within the UK; together with the additional Graduate Route visa, this attracts more international students to the possibility of an extended stay in the UK.

> I was involved in a few opportunities, and this was down to a lot of people from Twin Group and the university placement officers. I received very good support and was very positive and calm throughout the whole process based on the support provided. (MSc Engineering Management with Industrial Practice student who completed a placement at Roadfill Ltd, an SME engineering company specialising in using recycled plastic waste to build, maintain and repair road networks)

Participants in the pilot are primarily international students from South Asia with varying levels of experience, academic ability and communication skills. With a goal to support more than 1,000 students in four years, the results are already extremely positive. Of the academically eligible students in the first cohort, 90 per cent achieved placements in industry despite the pandemic and 60 per cent of these students were then given roles in their placement company or received better offers.

Because of this success, the University of Greenwich has been able to increase the number of MSc Industrial Practice programmes, adding another seven programmes to its suite, with enrolment now higher, and at the same time the university can be more selective about the students which it accepts on to the programmes. This in turn means that more of the students in the second cohort of the pilot are academically eligible for placements, and they are more likely to apply, knowing that a high-quality placement is probably waiting for them after finishing their taught modules. The growing reputation of our industry placement programme with employers also pushes Greenwich's students to the front of the line, including with employers who would not necessarily consider hiring students. In a nutshell, this is the return on investment that the university has gained from using partnerships to develop its programmes.

HOW THE PARTNERSHIP WORKS FOR THE STUDENTS

The mandate for Greenwich's partner provider was to prepare students for the UK job market with the professionalism, behaviours, strategies and soft skills to find roles not only for their placement year but also for the jobs they would seek upon graduation and throughout their careers. In other words, instead of handing them a catch, we were teaching them how to fish. We felt that this would give the students an advantage over other newly graduated students with non-industry-specific employment services.

> Many students start their programme with a clear idea of where they want to end up in their careers, but they don't know where to begin. We are able to help them work backwards from their long-term goals in order to identify the steps they need to get there. (Student Engagement Manager, Twin Group)

All students have a one-to-one meeting with the partner provider at the start of their programme, where they discuss their expectations for their placement, and what kinds of roles will help them to gain the experience they need to achieve their longer-term ambitions. Many students are entering the programme from other industries, or straight from undergraduate study, so the one-to-one meeting is also an opportunity for them to identify the transferable skills they have gained through their previous experience.

They then receive individualised feedback to tailor their CV so that it is appropriate for a UK employer and emphasises the relevant skills for the placement they want. By working with us to understand their industry and careers in a UK context, students are able to work towards individual, attainable placement goals based on their level of experience. This aspect of the programme is particularly appreciated by our employer partners.

Over the pilot period, we have been able to improve this one-to-one process because Twin is so close to the employers offering the placements and therefore we know how the students can make their CVs more attractive to these employers. We also talk to the students about their expectations in the placement and then the CV can be customised to emphasise the skills and experience; for example, the three competences desired most by the employer, which will secure the placement they want. This 'constant innovation' aspect of the programme and the standard of CVs are particularly appreciated by our employer partners, and as the pilot has gone on, students are achieving better placements.

> The international students are doing productive work and it is a good opportunity for us to assess the students in the roles. These students become candidates for our graduate programme, the vital first step in their career. It is also good for the stu-

dents; they know what they are getting into – I have confidence that they understand the working culture of Kilnbridge and what is expected of them. This very positively reflects retention rates, so that our investment in the students will lead to a long-term relationship when they progress to the graduate scheme. (Head of Engineering, Kilnbridge Construction and member of the Civil Engineering Industrial Advisory Board at the University of Greenwich)

Kilnbridge Construction have also rated positively the onboarding process and support from Greenwich and Twin, calling the former 'painless', resulting in the securing of more suitable candidates.

Preparing students well for a placement can bring them the additional benefit of a placement salary, bearing in mind that some placements do not offer salaries at all. But this is a two-way street as the students are informed that their chances of securing a paid placement are significantly increased if they attend and are fully engaged in all the preparation sessions. By embracing this form of accountability, the benefit of being paid will be further enhanced; because their next job is unlikely to be at a lower salary than their placement offer, the students will enter their chosen industry on a stronger footing.

WHAT A STRONG PARTNERSHIP BRINGS

The placement is such a good option to gain practical knowledge. It's the beginning of a career. (A student who secured a placement at Bristol Laboratories Ltd in Luton as a Regulatory Affairs Trainee; she has gone on to become a Regulatory Affairs Officer at Kent-Athlone Pharma Group where she is responsible for submission of variations, change of ownership, notification of marketing status of products to respective regulatory authorities and other regulatory activities)

The value of the industry placement partnership can be clearly seen in a number of ways. Firstly, the independent provider works together with the university faculty to determine the services that would best suit the course type and industry placements students are seeking. This should involve working directly with the programme leaders to understand the role requirements and with the university placement team throughout the process to ensure consistent communication with students and to collaborate on identifying any additional areas for support, based on student and employer feedback. The independent provider will also work with the university to monitor students' well-being, development and visa compliance, once they have started their placement.

The university receives ongoing advice on what placements can be achieved according to current employment conditions and the student's academic status. It also receives regular updates on market trends. The external advice can help make a course even more attractive to both students and employers.

The partnership has led to the creation of targeted careers fairs where employers are given the opportunity to speak to specific groups of students who will be relevant to their needs. Similarly, students are guided to meet the employers that are suitable for their experience, and they can present to the employers the projects undertaken over the summer. We can even encourage an employer to adjust an advertised role to make it appropriate for a student who we feel has the potential to succeed. Moreover, half of the employers who participate in the careers fairs, including some global brands, are now offering placements as well as permanent positions.

Having partners has created a new community for the university. The independent provider can act as a conduit for the employer's interests in forging closer co-operation between the university and business in addition to increasing the number of connections made through, for example, networking opportunities. The employers can also be linked up to support faculty advisory boards and other initiatives such as the University of Greenwich's GreHacks (a two-day event where student teams complete challenges set by businesses) with support from the Office for Students (University of Greenwich, 2022).

A partner provider with international expertise can be particularly supportive in working with international student candidates. International students are operating in an unfamiliar market and many employers are not familiar with the nuances of the work permission situation for these students. International students may require extra support when interacting with employers or guidance on how to explain their work permission. Furthermore, they are less likely to be hired by British employers, who prioritise home students who do not have complicated work eligibilities.

By taking advantage of the services of an external provider who is experienced in working with both international students and UK employers, Greenwich is able to prepare international cohorts to have the same opportunities as home students by working with them on employability and interview skills that are customised to their situation and their industry.

In addition to individual support, the placement partner delivers a series of employability workshops, which are designed for each programme and cohort. These are continually updated to include real-time market updates and feedback from employers, and as we have learnt more from students about how job searching differs in their home countries, we have been able to integrate specific and timely advice to ensure that students know what to expect. We are able to make sure that students have all the information and tools to find roles that are suitable for them and also fit the requirements of their course.

The provider partnership offers extra capacity to engage with students individually at every stage of the placement process. This means that we can see students' progress in terms of professional writing, spoken English and technical knowledge in real time and we can give students ongoing feedback to boost their confidence. Because the work is undertaken by a small team, they interact regularly with the same students, and the team is able to adapt to the needs of specific cohorts. For example, we saw that our last cohort were struggling to implement self-evaluation skills, particularly when reflecting on their interview performance. We developed a resource to guide them through this process, which has enabled the interview practice that they do with us to become more focused.

JOBS SECURED WITH GLOBAL BRAND EMPLOYERS

> Twin Group advocated for me with employers, finding roles especially for me, checking my CV multiple times and explaining my visa status to employers. (A Pharmaceutical Science graduate who also progressed into fixed employment on completing her award during 2021 with multinational brand, Target Healthcare)

Placements on the pilot initiative have been found in global brands such as AstraZeneca, Thermo Fisher Scientific and Bristol Laboratories, as well as in many small and medium-sized enterprises.

A total of 555 student journeys were completed during 2021, having secured quality industry-based placements, and the combined student satisfaction rating on completing a programme during this period was 4.9 out of 5. Despite opportunity shortages reported due to the pandemic, 60 per cent of students went on to secure independent employment with their placement organisation. It is also very encouraging that most of the employers are willing to offer further placements and so the university will build on this initiative.

Furthermore, the employers report that students' confidence improves over time. By the end of the placement and before starting a graduate scheme, the students have demonstrated huge leaps forward in terms of self-confidence.

FURTHER PROGRAMME VALUE BEING ADDED POST-PANDEMIC

Our employer placement partners, especially those who have become members of the university's advisory boards, are helping to make improvements to the placement programme.

> By feeding back industry requirements to the forum, we are able to share information and our input helps curriculum to become more relevant to industry. That improves the capabilities of the candidates who come on placement and also who graduate, making them more ready for the work environment. (Head of Engineering, Kilnbridge Construction)

Another benefit of the programme is that it can help employers tackle gender imbalance within certain sectors. This year, for example, three out of four students who will be offered graduate roles by Kilnbridge Construction are women who it has recruited from the University of Greenwich.

With the partnership involving programme leaders, careers services and specialist providers working together in the same direction, a clear understanding of the expectations of the university and its students helps the programme evolve and it continues to adapt to the needs of the students and employers who are offering the placement opportunities. Ultimately the reputation of Greenwich benefits as the students secure better jobs than they would without specialist help. We are also seeing opportunities improve for students with different levels of ability and confidence.

Due to the Home Office UK Visas and Immigration's Graduate Route visa pathway, two global companies, who previously relied on European students before Brexit, are now offering placements with a view to hiring graduating international students. Seventy-five per cent of partnered employers are saying that they will offer more placements; of these, 20 per cent are taking multiple students as part of their recruitment cycles, expanding organisational capacity, and offering more career opportunities.

Challenges remain in an uncertain economy, and it is important to maintain a focus on the level of English communication, as this can directly impact career progression after a placement. That said, international students tend to go the extra mile. They are flexible and have shown resilience and eagerness to learn and do what is required to develop in their careers.

Overall, our view is that while the government's reforms present significant challenges for the higher education sector, they are not at all insurmountable. With the objective of securing more job outcomes for their students, universities should not be afraid to explore partnership arrangements with other providers because the opportunity to scale up employer engagement is immense.

BIBLIOGRAPHY

Office for Students (2022), *Student outcomes and teaching excellence*. Retrieved from https://www.officeforstudents.org.uk/publications/student-outcomes-and-teaching-excellence-consultations/ (accessed: 17 January 2022).

Tubb, J. (2022), 'How partnerships can make a difference to securing jobs for students', *Employability Blog – HEPI*, 27 May. Available at: https://www.hepi.ac.uk/2022/05/27/employability-blog-series-how-partnerships-can-make-a-difference-to-securing-jobs-for-students/ (accessed: 17 January 2023).

UCAS (2022), *The UK continues to be a top destination for study, with applications set to rise by almost 50% within five years*. UCAS News, 26 May. Available at: https://www.ucas.com/corporate/news-and-key-documents/news/uk-continues-be-top-destination-study-applications-set-rise-almost-50-within-five-years (accessed: 17 January 2023).

University of Greenwich (2022), *#GreHacks*. Generator. Available at: https://www.gre.ac.uk/business/generator/get-started/bootcamps/grehacks (accessed: 17 January 2023).

REFLECTION

From a Media Studies graduate

I did a placement when I was at university in the summer holidays between my second and third year. It was not paid, and that was really difficult for me because I really needed to be using the summer to earn some money. However, I got a part-time job in my third year instead. I think that did impede on my studies a bit, but I still completed my degree.

In my placement I was doing a proper job in the organisation. Someone had left, and I did their job in the gap between the new permanent person being appointed. It seemed a bit unfair that this was not paid, given that it was a 'proper' job, but I was really pleased to get the work experience and so I accepted it. I did then get a job in the same company when I graduated, so that made it feel worthwhile.

A placement was a really good way of me making new contacts, and it was through those contacts that I got my current job. It was never advertised, I was just contacted to see if I was interested. Building up effective networks seems essential to getting a good job.

PART IX

Insights from around the world

27. How England's policy and regulatory levers have shifted accountability for graduate employment

Lizzy Woodfield

INTRODUCTION

In England, universities are being held ever more accountable for their graduates' employment outcomes. This chapter examines how this came to be the case, looking at the related policy and regulatory developments of the past decade or so, bookended by the two independent reviews of higher education finance – the Browne Review in 2010 and the Augar Review, which reported in 2019.

Three distinct turning points in policy and regulation are identified. First is the link made between graduate outcomes and value for money in a reformed student finance regime. Second is the related provision of information to prospective students about employment outcomes. Third is the recent move into directly regulating universities in relation to their graduates' employment outcomes.

These turning points incorporate substantial policy and regulatory agendas – such as student finance reform, the introduction of the Teaching Excellence Framework, and the establishment of England's higher education regulator, the Office for Students (OfS), as well as a myriad of facilitating developments in data.

This chapter looks at how English universities are responding to these policy and regulatory levers, and argues that they have led to a significant shift in how universities prioritise, embed and resource the employability agenda – and that this is likely to intensify further in future, as well as become more challenging, in light of multiple competing pressures on a shrinking unit of resource.

Finally, this chapter considers universities' civic and place-based roles, particularly in relation to encouraging graduate retention, and working with employers to stimulate employment prospects and career pathways in their local areas, responding to the UK government's latest policy preoccupation: levelling up.

TURNING POINT ONE: THE LINK MADE BETWEEN GRADUATE OUTCOMES AND VALUE FOR MONEY IN A REFORMED STUDENT FINANCE REGIME

Lord Browne's 2010 independent review of higher education funding and student finance laid much of the groundwork for the Coalition Government's 2011 White Paper, 'Students at the Heart of the System'.

Though the White Paper (a government policy document which set out proposals for future legislation) made significant interventions on employability, including by commissioning the influential Wilson Review (2012) on business–university collaboration, it is largely remembered for confirming the government's intention to make sweeping student finance reforms – the introduction of £9,000 a year tuition fees and a reformed graduate contribution system, alongside the liberalisation of student number controls.

The reforms were intended to tip the balance of who bore the financial cost of higher education more towards its direct beneficiaries, graduates themselves, who, as noted in the White Paper, earn more on average than non-graduates:

> There is of course far more to higher education than financial benefit. It can transform people's lives for the better as their intellectual horizons are broadened. Nevertheless, graduates do, on average, earn more than non-graduates and their higher education is one reason for this. So it is fairer to finance the system by expecting graduates to pay, if and when they are in better paid jobs. (Department for Business, Innovation and Skills, 2011: 17)

A subsequent 'value for money' narrative has emerged over the years, which was more recently expressed in the government's response to the latest independent review of post-18 education and funding, which was led by Sir Philip Augar:

> We want to ensure that HE delivers better outcomes and value for students, employers and the taxpayers who underwrite the HE system. We want to realise positive employment outcomes for students, enabling them to move into the high-skilled employment that our economy needs – ultimately equipping them with the skills and knowledge they will need later in life. We are clear that the government should seek to ensure taxpayer money is well-spent, on high-quality courses aligned with opportunities for graduates. (Department for Education, 2022: 12)

Graduates' prospects and, as we will see later on, their salaries, have become universities' business. This has led to significant investment by universities in employability, including large-scale curriculum work, a greater focus on work experience and work-based learning, and bespoke programmes to support graduates. New executive-level roles within university management teams have emerged, focused specifically on developing students' employability and supporting graduates to achieve good employment outcomes. Alumni teams, too, are strengthening their offer in supporting recent graduates' career development.

TURNING POINT TWO: THE PROVISION OF INFORMATION TO PROSPECTIVE STUDENTS ABOUT EMPLOYMENT OUTCOMES AND A POLICY PREOCCUPATION WITH GRADUATE SALARIES

How would prospective students, pondering where to make their significant financial investment, inform their decisions? Perhaps most significant in shaping what was to follow was the 2011 White Paper's emphasis on the provision of information about employment prospects, which made the following commitment: 'We will radically improve and expand the information available to prospective students, making available much more information about ... graduate employment prospects' (Department for Business, Innovation and Skills, 2011).

Key Information Set (KIS)

The 2011 White Paper set out plans to establish the KIS, which would incorporate employment data, alongside information about student satisfaction and costs. The KIS contained data on the destinations of students six months after completing their course; the proportion of students employed in a full-time 'graduate' job six months after completing their course; the average salary for the course in question six months after graduating; the salary for that subject across all institutions six months after graduating; and the salary for that subject across all institutions 40 months after graduating.

Employment outcomes data makes up a significant component of the KIS's more recent successor, 'Discover Uni', a website described by the OfS (the higher education regulator, which we will learn about later) as the 'official, authoritative source of information and guidance on higher education in the UK' (OfS, 2021a). It incorporates information on the employment outcomes and earnings from the Graduate Outcomes Survey (GOS) and the longitudinal education outcomes (LEO) data set, as well as graduates' perceptions of their work after graduating.

Longitudinal Education Outcomes and the Teaching Excellence Framework

In 2015, what was to become the Teaching Excellence Framework (TEF), was promised in the Conservative Party's election manifesto. It would 'require more data to be openly available to potential students so that they can make decisions informed by the career paths of past graduates' (Conservative Party, 2015: 35).

In the same year, the Small Business and Enterprise Act 2015 enabled government to link higher education and tax and benefits data together, and the provision of longitudinal education outcomes (LEO) data was made possible.

The LEO data allows the tracking of individuals through their school, college and university education, and into the labour market. It presents employment and earnings outcomes for leavers of higher education at one, three, five and ten-year intervals after graduation, and the data is broken down to a subject and provider level. Some fear an overemphasis on salaries serves to devalue certain degrees and careers – for example in the creative arts or in low-paid, but crucial, public services – and point to limitations, like its significant time lag making it less helpful in informing prospective students' decisions.

The 2016 White Paper, 'Higher Education: Success as a knowledge economy', revealed more detail on the aims of the TEF and how it would be implemented. The TEF would 'for the first time bring sector-wide rigour to the assessment of teaching excellence', and was originally intended to 'generate reputational as well as financial incentives', with providers awarded TEF 'ratings', and with a provider's performance in the TEF tied to its eligibility to increase its tuition fee cap in line with inflation (Department for Business, Innovation and Skills, 2016: 44–51). In setting out its plans for the TEF, government made clear its expectation that excellent teaching should lead to excellent outcomes for students:

> The Government believes that excellent teaching can occur in many different forms, in a wide variety of institutions, and it is not the intention of the TEF to constrain or prescribe the form that excellence must take. What we expect though, is that excellent teaching, whatever its form, delivers excellent outcomes. There is of course more to university than financial gain, but the idea that excellent teaching occurs in a vacuum, independent of its impact on students' future life chances, is not one we can or should accept. (Department for Business, Innovation and Skills, 2016: 43)

Measures relating to employment outcomes, therefore, featured strongly across both the 'core' and 'supplementary' metrics in the first full TEF exercise, drawing on data from the Destination of Leavers Survey from Higher Education (DLHE) and LEO data sets.

The prominence of employment outcomes in the TEF was controversial, with Dame Shirley Pearce's 2019 independent review of the TEF hearing strong views that it was too focused on employment and did not capture the wider social and cultural benefits of higher education. The review went on to recommend that graduate outcome metrics should be broader and control for region of employment. The review also questioned the extent to which the TEF had met one of its key purposes: to inform students' choices. It concluded that the primary purpose of TEF should instead be the identification of excellence and educational enhancement (Pearce, 2019).

The TEF, although never realising its intended direct financial incentive in relation to tuition fees (which have been frozen for several consecutive years), and not featuring strongly as a consideration for prospective students, has arguably been enough of a policy lever to bring universities' responsibilities for their graduates' employment outcomes strongly into focus. In its latest evolution the TEF forms a key component of the OfS's more direct and granular approach to regulating student outcomes, as we will learn later.

Crucially, the availability of comparable graduate outcomes data means that employment measures feature in university league tables – a further incentive, if it was needed, which drives university resources and focus to this important area, though arguably leaves scope for some degree of 'gaming' of the system (Blackwell and Edmondson, 2016). Perhaps inevitably, resources and focus on supporting graduates appear often at their most intensive in the period between graduation and the Graduate Outcomes Survey census.

The government's drive to improve the transparency of information available to prospective students about past graduates' employment status does not appear to have slowed. In 2022 the then Higher and Further Education Minister asked higher education providers to incorporate data on the percentage of students who have gone into either professional employment or further advanced study on all university and course advertisements (Donelan, 2022).

TURNING POINT THREE: DIRECT REGULATION OF STUDENT AND GRADUATE OUTCOMES

The 2016 White Paper set out plans to establish a new market regulator, the Office for Students (OfS). This body was established in 2018, following the Higher Education and Research Act of 2017. Two of the OfS's four primary regulatory objectives relate to progression *from* higher education (OfS, 2022a).

As well as funding projects aimed at identifying and sharing good practice, like the 'Graduate Re-tune' project which sees Birmingham City University and Aston University work in partnership with Jobcentre Plus to tackle graduate unemployment and underemployment, the OfS (2020) has significant regulatory levers at its disposal to achieve their objectives.

The underpinning regulatory mechanism is Quality and Standards Condition B3, which sets out that providers 'must deliver successful outcomes for all of its students, which are recognised and valued by employers and/or enable further study' (OfS, 2022a).

For the first time universities have become subject to 'numerical thresholds', in other words, minimum acceptable standards, for students' progression to managerial and professional employment or higher-level study, with performance scrutinised at a distinctly granular level. This is enabled by a plethora of split indicators, illuminating performance, for instance, at subject level, level of study, and for different student characteristics, to identify 'pockets of provision' that fall below the numerical thresholds. Failure to meet numerical thresholds does not represent an automatic breach of Condition B3 but could be a starting point for an assessment into whether a provider is compliant. Performance in relation to Condition B3 also reads across to the TEF, which features a progression measure as part of its assessment of student outcomes.

Ultimately, the OfS has powers to take intrusive regulatory action against non-compliant providers if they judge this is in the student's and taxpayer's interest, including applying monetary penalties and varying or revoking degree-awarding powers (OfS, 2022b).

Meanwhile, the possible reintroduction of student number controls in some form has been mooted by government, with the suggestion that such limits on student numbers could lead the higher education sector to 'prioritise provision with the best outcomes and to restrict the supply of provision which offers poorer outcomes' and which creates 'significant expense to the taxpayer' (Department for Education, 2022: 34).

Another key regulatory mechanism, the Access and Participation Plan, has, in recent years, had a stronger focus on progression. Institutions must analyse their performance across the whole student life cycle, and where there are significant gaps in outcomes (including at employment) for different student groups, they must agree ambitious targets with the regulator to narrow them. Ministerial guidance to the OfS in 2021 set out the need for further emphasis on progression, particularly for less-advantaged students:

> There has been a strong focus on ensuring more people can get into higher education, but not always as much focus in ensuring that the courses they are admitted to are genuinely high quality, with support for students to ... develop the skills and knowledge that will lead to graduate employment or further study. (Donelan and Zahawi, 2021)

A BALANCING ACT, ALL THE WHILE DOING MORE WITH LESS

How might universities respond to this deeper, more granular, and data-driven regulatory scrutiny of graduate outcomes? It is likely that providers will seek to improve their ability to analyse their own data in real time; take a more strategic and universal approach to developing employability for the whole student body; embed employability further and more consistently into the curriculum; develop more work experience opportunities for students – a tried and tested method of improving graduate outcomes; seek more employer input into the design, delivery and assessment of courses; and take a more critical look at graduate outcomes when it comes to reviewing existing programmes or introducing new ones. All these responses are desirable, but resource intensive, so we can expect to see employability activities competing more fiercely for a bigger share of a university's shrinking unit of resource.

Some may fear that a stronger line of accountability on delivering good graduate outcomes will lead to universities seeking to change the pool of potential students from which they recruit, focusing on those students more likely to achieve 'better' graduate outcomes by virtue of their backgrounds and prior attainment, which could hamper efforts to widen participation in higher education. This could be interpreted as an unintended consequence, though government's desire that university should not be seen as the only 'route to success' (Department for Education, 2021: 40), should not be overlooked here.

Given that it is widely accepted that considerable geographic disparities affect graduates, with ex-industrial areas and coastal towns having 'lower paid graduates and fewer graduates in highly skilled jobs' (OfS, 2021b), universities in these areas face a tension in balancing their dual responsibilities: encouraging mobility and supporting their graduates into well-remunerated jobs, and in pursuing their civic roles which encourage local graduate retention and, crucially, utilisation, for local economic development.

The government's levelling up White Paper discusses in detail the labour mobility of young graduates, pointing out that if graduates are less likely to move to more productive areas (as is the case for graduates from lower socio-economic status backgrounds), they could be working 'below their productive potential'. The White Paper concludes that 'skill-based sorting of people has amplified agglomeration in steaming-ahead places, while further depleting human capital in left-behind areas' (Department for Levelling Up, Housing and Communities, 2022: 94).

Increasingly, universities are working with partners to stimulate employment prospects and develop clear career pathways in their local areas. For instance, funding has been made available to encourage place-based collaborations, as in the case of Department for Education-backed Institutes of Technology. These are partnerships between employers, further education colleges and universities, brought together to meet the academic and technical skills needs of future jobs in regionally important sectors such as engineering and advanced manufacturing, for example, the Greater Birmingham and Solihull Institute of Technology.

The policy and regulatory changes discussed in this chapter have pushed graduate employability much more into focus, and there is much to welcome about this. Developing employable graduates – with the required mix of technical, academic and 'soft' skills, along with valuable work experience – is resource intensive, but it is worth the investment.

Yet, in a sector that is increasingly financially stretched – and in which we expect tuition fee income to be frozen for the foreseeable future – universities will find their employability responsibilities more challenging to achieve. This, in turn, may hamper the sector's ability to deliver the skills needed to meet the wider policy challenges the country faces.

REFERENCES

Augar, P. (2019), *Independent Panel Report to the Review of Post-18 Education and Funding*. London: HMSO. Available at: https://www.gov.uk/government/publications/post-18-review-of-education-and-funding-independent-panel-report (accessed: 17 January 2023).

Blackwell, R. and Edmondson, M. (2016), 'Why employment outcomes are important and how they should be measured in future', in P. Blackmore, R. Blackwell, and M. Edmondson (eds), *Tackling Wicked Issues: Prestige and Employment Outcomes in the Teaching Excellence Framework*, Oxford: Higher Education Policy Institute, pp. 55–56.

Browne, J. (2010), *Securing a Sustainable Future for Higher Education: An Independent Review of Higher Education Funding & Student Finance*. Available at: https://www.gov.uk/government/publications/the-browne-report-higher-education-funding-and-student-finance (accessed: 17 January 2023).

Conservative Party (2015), *The Conservative Party Manifesto 2015*. Available at: https://ucrel.lancs.ac.uk/wmatrix/ukmanifestos2015/localpdf/Conservatives.pdf (accessed: 17 January 2023).

Department for Business, Innovation and Skills (2011), *Students at the Heart of the System*. London: HMSO. Available at: https://assets.publishing.service.gov.uk/government/uploads/system/uploads/attachment_data/file/31384/11-944-higher-education-students-at-heart-of-system.pdf (accessed: 17 January 2023).

Department for Business, Innovation and Skills (2016), *Success as a Knowledge Economy: Teaching Excellence, Social Mobility and Student Choice*. London: HMSO. Available at: https://assets.publishing.service.gov.uk/government/uploads/system/uploads/attachment_data/file/523396/bis-16-265-success-as-a-knowledge-economy.pdf (accessed: 17 January 2023).

Department for Education (2021), *Skills for Jobs: Lifelong Learning for Opportunity and Growth*. London: HMSO. Available at: https://assets.publishing.service.gov.uk/

government/uploads/system/uploads/attachment_data/file/957856/Skills_for_jobs _lifelong_learning_for_opportunity_and_growth__web_version_.pdf (accessed: 17 January 2023).

Department for Education (2022), *Higher Education Policy Statement and Reform*. Available at: https://www.gov.uk/government/consultations/higher-education -policy-statement-and-reform (accessed: 17 January 2023).

Department for Levelling Up, Housing and Communities (2022), *Levelling Up the United Kingdom*. London: HMSO. Available at: https://www.gov.uk/government/ publications/levelling-up-the-united-kingdom (accessed: 17 January 2023).

Donelan, M. (2022), *Universities Minister Puts Quality at the Heart of Higher Education*. Available at: https://www.gov.uk/government/speeches/universities -minister-puts-quality-at-the-heart-of-higher-education (accessed: 17 January 2023).

Donelan, M. and Zahawi, N. (2021), *The Future of Access and Participation*. Available at: https://www.officeforstudents.org.uk/media/1ceabbe1-2d49-41db -9795-068f37c23631/dfe-new-dfap.pdf (accessed: 17 January 2023).

Higher Education and Research Act 2017. London: HMSO. Available at: https://www .legislation.gov.uk/ukpga/2017/29/contents (accessed: 17 January 2023).

OfS (2020), *Improving Outcomes for Local Graduates*. Available at: https://www .officeforstudents.org.uk/advice-and-guidance/skills-and-employment/improving -outcomes-for-local-graduates/ (accessed: 17 January 2023).

OfS (2021a), *Discover Uni and Unistats*. Available at: https://www.officeforstudents .org.uk/advice-and-guidance/student-information-and-data/discover-uni-and -unistats/ (accessed: 17 January 2023).

OfS (2021b), *Place Matters: Inequality, Employment and the Role of Higher Education*. Available at: https://www.officeforstudents.org.uk/publications/place-matters -inequality-employment-and-the-role-of-higher-education/ (accessed: 17 January 2023).

OfS (2022a), *Securing Student Success: Regulatory Framework for Higher Education in England*. Available at: https://www.officeforstudents.org.uk/publications/ securing-student-success-regulatory-framework-for-higher-education-in-england/ (accessed: 17 January 2023).

OfS (2022b), *A New Approach to Regulating Student Outcomes*. Available at: https://www.officeforstudents.org.uk/publications/student-outcomes-and-teaching -excellence-consultations/student-outcomes/ (accessed: 17 January 2023).

Pearce, S. (2019), *Independent Review of the Teaching Excellence and Student Outcomes Framework (TEF)*. Available at: https://www.gov.uk/government/groups/ teaching-excellence-framework-independent-review (accessed: 17 January 2023).

Wilson, T. (2012), *A Review of Business–University Collaboration: The Wilson Review*. Available at: https://assets.publishing.service.gov.uk/government/uploads/system/ uploads/attachment_data/file/32383/12-610-wilson-review-business-university -collaboration.pdf (accessed: 17 January 2023).

REFLECTION

From a lecturer who has moved into a management role

When I was a lecturer I had no idea that the university had so many regulations that it had to adhere to. I only became aware of that once I took on a management role in the university.

Now, I understand the pressure on the university to achieve good graduate outcomes for the students. Then, I just did my best for my students and hoped that they would take what I was offering and do well. If students did not engage I did not really worry about it. Now, I do everything I can to make students engage.

University students are adults, and so I do think that they have to take responsibility for their own destinies and careers. However, I also know that we are measured by what they achieve, and therefore it is very difficult to leave them to choose whether to engage or not.

28. Approaches to developing graduate employability in Australia

Judie Kay and Sonia Ferns

NATIONAL CONTEXT

Consistent with global higher education priorities, there is increased focus and ongoing debate around employability and graduate employment outcomes in Australia. The lack of a shared understanding of employability and confusion with graduate employment outcomes adds complexity (Campbell et al., 2022). Recent reports highlight the transformation occurring in the Australian workforce triggered by the rapid growth of the gig economy, the expectation that Australians will have 17 changes of employers across five careers in their lifetime, and the changing skill sets needed to succeed (Foundation for Young Australians (FYA), 2017; Australian Industry Group (AiG), 2021).

Peak Australian industry groups have long called for better-prepared graduates able to move seamlessly into the workplace to benefit the Australian economy. These peak bodies are now signalling that skill shortages post Covid-19 are urgent and constraining economic growth (AiG, 2021). 'Australia ranks 6th for attainment of tertiary education, but the ranking declines to 10th for the business relevance of tertiary education and 12th for the supply of business-relevant skills' (Bean and Dawkins, 2022: 17). Universities have responded with a steady increase in curricular and co-curricular employability and career development strategies and substantial expansion of work integrated learning (WIL) nationally (Ferns et al., 2014; Rowe and Zegwaard, 2017). National WIL and career associations in Australia, including the Australian Collaborative Education Network (ACEN) and the National Association of Graduate Career Advisory Services (NAGCAS) have expanded their role to support the development of higher education staff.

In 2014 the Australian government implemented the New Colombo Plan (NCP), which aimed to enhance Australian undergraduate students' knowledge of the Indo-Pacific region through providing financial support for Australian students to undertake internships in the region. A core aim of the NCP is to ensure Australian students have 'skills and work-based experiences to contribute to our domestic and regional economy' (Department of Foreign Affairs and Trade, 2021). Recent Australian government programmes and reports set out priorities for higher education with specific focus on producing job-ready graduates (Australian Government, 2021; Bean and Dawkins, 2022). A major initiative, the Jobs Ready Graduates Package, includes the National Priorities and Industry Linkage Fund (NPILF), providing AUD900 million over four years to support the development of job-ready graduates through expanded university–industry engagement (Department of Education, Skills and Employment, 2021). The aim of the package, implemented as a pilot in 2021, is threefold: to increase WIL experiences and innovation, increase the number of, and employment outcomes for, STEM students, and strengthen university partnerships with industry (Australian Government, 2021). The NPILF reinforces the expectation for expanded industry engagement by universities through metrics that link evidence of impact to university funding allocation. The intent is to drive and reward innovation and action to enhance graduate employability. Industry in Australia is seeking greater collaboration with universities with an aim to 'accelerate Australia's skills agenda in a post-pandemic world' (Bean and Dawkins, 2022: 7). Other government proposals include a unified national credentials platform, a micro-credential marketplace, and encouraging greater involvement of industry in course and credential development.

WIL is recognised as a key enabler of graduate employability and graduate employment outcomes nationally. In 2017 Universities Australia conducted a national WIL survey. Findings revealed that 37.4 per cent of university students enrolled in 2017 had a WIL experience (Universities Australia, 2019) indicating higher participation than many other countries. The key role that WIL plays in preparing students for the workforce in Australia was recognised in the formulation of the National WIL Strategy (ACEN, 2015). Peak Australian industry groups, Universities Australia and ACEN collaborated in the development of the strategy, which articulates eight approaches to expand and enhance the quality of WIL across Australia. The National WIL Strategy continues to influence government policy and developments in WIL across Australia.

The Graduate Outcomes Survey (GOS) is administered annually to graduates from Australian universities. The GOS collects information pertaining to graduates' satisfaction with their degree and employment and further study outcomes. The GOS is currently the only national metric in Australia that measures graduate employment outcomes, but it has limitations as it measures only short-term employment outcomes, given the data is collected four to six months after graduation. Nevertheless, the positive impact of WIL on graduate employment and students' perceptions of their preparedness for employment in Australia was recently affirmed through analysis of items on WIL in the

GOS (ACEN, 2021). In 2020 ACEN negotiated additional items focused on WIL for inclusion in the survey. The data enables benchmarking across Australian institutions and provides evidence to inform areas for improvement. Analysis of the GOS WIL items confirms that 'Embedding WIL into the curriculum appears to be far more effective for preparedness for work and employment outcomes than employability-related interventions under extra- or co-curricular arrangements' (ACEN, 2021: 22).

EQUITY AND EMPLOYABILITY

Despite endeavours to encourage inclusivity for marginalised groups in Australian higher education (Patrick et al., 2009), systemic change to improve access and equity remains elusive (Heffernan, 2021). Ensuring equitable student access to WIL presents even greater challenges that 'hinder efforts and perpetuate student exclusion' (Mackaway and Chalkley, 2022: 227). Socio-economic, culture, gender, academic, regional, and remote, disability, and personal and family commitments singularly and collectively impact on students' access to WIL, and by default, employability development. A range of targeted interventions to support marginalised student groups have been introduced in Australia. These include financial assistance (e.g. scholarships and bursaries), targeted career workshops and resources, allocating mentors, and specifically designed teaching programmes to cater to diverse cohorts (Jackson et al., 2017). Funds are allocated to universities via the Higher Education Participation and Partnerships Program (HEPPP) to improve access, retention and completion rates of diverse cohorts. Reforms to higher education outlined in the Job-Ready Graduates Package (2020) aim to address national priorities through initiatives that improve access and equity for all stakeholders. The transition to more flexible WIL models has provided greater opportunity for accommodating unique needs of students (Kay et al., 2019). A nationally funded research project developed institutional principles and guidelines for inclusive WIL (Winchester-Seeto et al., 2015). The principles highlight the importance of flexibility, support for stakeholders, inclusive curriculum design and teaching practices, collaborative partnerships, and adequate resourcing.

The Review of Higher Education Access for Aboriginal and Torres Strait Islander People in 2012 proposed recommendations for achieving parity for Indigenous students; cultural change and policy development to enhance successful engagement of Indigenous students in universities; effective Commonwealth Government programmes to improve outcomes for Indigenous students; and 'the recognition and equivalence of Indigenous knowledge in the higher education sector' (Australian Government, 2012: 2). While universities were proactive in responding to the review with clear and transparent strategies for encouraging participation of Indigenous students and nurturing a sense of belonging, Indigenous students are less likely to enrol and succeed at university than their non-Indigenous counterparts and are less likely to build employability capabilities through WIL experiences (Universities Australia, 2019).

International students comprise 30.9 per cent of the student population in Australian universities (Universities Australia, 2020: 44) and frequently cite the opportunity to enhance global employability and secure a graduate position through WIL as the driver for selecting Australia as their study destination (Bennett and Ferns, 2017). While the participation rates in WIL for international students are comparable with domestic students in Australia (38.2 per cent and 37.1 per cent respectively: Universities Australia, 2019), persistent challenges for international students include competition for placements, language barriers, lack of familiarity with Australian workplace cultures, and discriminatory behaviours (Mackaway and Chalkley, 2022). Australia values the diversity of international students and their contributions to economic prosperity (Australian Government, 2021). The Australian strategy for International Education 2021–2030 endeavours to optimise the benefits that cross-cultural influences and global alumni networks of international students afford. The strategy is positioned as a 'Roadmap to recovery' after the Covid-19 pandemic and an effort to reinvigorate international education. The document outlines a series of actions premised on four themes: diversification, meeting Australia's skills needs, students as central, and growth and global competitiveness.

UNIVERSITIES' ROLE

The multidimensional, complex nature of employability requires coordination across Australian university agendas, including external partnerships, teaching quality, staff expertise and willingness, innovation in curriculum and assessment design, actively engaged students, and a flexible and responsive policy environment. Approaches that promote and strengthen student employability differ from traditional educational approaches, thereby requiring a cultural shift to reconceptualise the student experience, establish sustainable and inclusive partnerships, and recognise, build and reward staff capability (Ferns and Lilly, 2015). Inspiring and visionary leadership in Australian institutions is imperative to driving change, building relationships, distributing leadership, and establishing a cohesive culture that encourages risk-taking and innovation (Ferns and Kay, 2021). Despite the expansion of WIL practice in Australian universities, and the abundant research advocating improved leadership, high-level institutional governance that supports and resources initiatives for fostering student employability is crucial, but needs strengthening in Australia (Patrick et al., 2014). Strategic, insightful, and courageous leaders who allocate resources accordingly to achieve optimal impact is a priority for driving the WIL/employability agenda in the Australian context (Ferns and Kay, 2021). Although many Australian universities have developed WIL strategies and policies, few have a university-wide employability strategy that drives a coordinated approach.

Student awareness of the importance of building employability from early in their studies and broadening their often-narrow career focus presents a challenge in Australian universities (Russell and Kay, 2019). Universities are adopting a range of strategies, based on career development frameworks such as Dacre Pool and Sewell (2007), to raise students' consciousness around enhancing employability skills across their programme through curricular and co-curricular strategies. Garnering students' attention, however, is complex. Students are inundated with university communication and many students, for example, from international, Indigenous, or low socio-economic backgrounds, focus on more pressing survival issues and often delay building employability until late in their final year.

Embedding employability skills across the curriculum ensures that all students are exposed to the concepts and maximises engagement. Embedding career development learning (CDL) in programme design is increasingly prevalent, though not without its challenges (Bridgstock et al., 2019). A lack of clarity of what CDL entails and finding space in an already crowded curriculum are some of these challenges. Australian universities utilise a range of strategies to establish students' career awareness, develop career management skills, and enrich employability skills to enable informed career choices. A whole-of-programme approach that scaffolds employability-focused activities, including WIL and CDL, is considered the most effective (Russell and Kay, 2019).

Australian universities have used a range of co-curricular strategies to gain student attention around developing employability skills including Employability Awards, mentoring programmes, university incubators, leadership programmes and more recently the use of a range of micro-credentials based on 21st century skills co-designed with industry. Key messages to students include taking responsibility early and being proactive in developing employability skills. Developing students' understanding of the dynamic work context encourages them to adapt careers over their working life (Russell and Kay, 2019). An increasing trend in Australia is the use of third-party providers to implement programmes around employability skills or industry experiences in partnership with universities. Some students, often international students, seek out these experiences and approach third-party providers independently to participate in these experiences. State governments in Australia have been active in supporting the development of employability skills through partnering with third-party providers. This growing use of third-party providers indicates demand for employability-focused programmes and the lack of universities' resources to implement them.

INNOVATION OF WIL IN AUSTRALIA

Australia has seen a growing need to diversify WIL offerings beyond that of the traditional placement model. Increasing student numbers, limited resources in university and industry settings, and enhanced digital technologies are drivers for WIL innovation. With a large percentage of Australian businesses being small to medium-sized enterprises (97.4 per cent), short-term, project-based WIL is a preferred option to long-term placements (Kay et al., 2022). Kay et al. (2019) undertook a nationally funded project to identify distinctive features of innovative WIL models and explore the associated enablers and challenges. Characteristics fundamental to innovative WIL are robust stakeholder partnerships, specified design elements, and WIL experiences that are co-designed with students and industry partners. Co-design is becoming more common across the higher education landscape in Australia, with recognition of the benefits for all stakeholders through working collaboratively and sharing expertise (Kay et al., 2019). Furthermore, co-designing innovative WIL models ensures experiences reflect contemporary industry practices (FYA, 2017) and establishes 'a shared responsibility in the work-readiness of graduates' (Ferns et al., 2019: 107). With increasing workplace disruption, a strong demand for entrepreneurial skills in the Australian workplace, and start-ups becoming a popular graduate destination, the development of enterprise capabilities is a growing priority (Smith et al., 2022).

STAFF ROLES

Both professional and academic staff in Australian universities play critical roles in implementing employability agendas. The sector is recognised for attracting committed and passionate staff working across a broad range of employability-focused roles (Healy et al., 2021). Ensuring that staff have both capability and capacity, are supported through professional development, are recognised, and have long-term employment tenure is key. Ensuring continuity and longer-term planning to enhance student employability is often made complex by the short-term or project-linked nature of staff employment contracts. Analysis of job advertisements between 2013 and 2019 showed only 40 per cent of roles were continuing, making it challenging to achieve a longer-term integrated employability strategy (Healy et al., 2021).

Building the capacity of staff involved in WIL has been high priority in the Australian context and considered essential for designing and enacting WIL programmes that optimise employability outcomes for students (Patrick et al.,

2014; ACEN, 2015). The capabilities required of university staff to design and enact WIL curriculum are transforming as WIL approaches diversify and expand (Kay et al., 2019). Delivering quality WIL programmes where external partnerships are integral to successful execution, and flexible and creative approaches to curriculum and assessment essential, requires staff with relevant expertise and support where the focus is on real-world learning and empowering the learner (Zegwaard et al., 2022). However, strategies to build staff capability in universities are patchy, with many staff relying on institutional communities of practice and in some instances activities initiated by groupings of universities such as the Australian Technology Network. ACEN has taken an active role in the provision of professional development in response to increasing demand due to expansion of WIL. The Covid-19 pandemic was the catalyst for rapid transition to innovative WIL approaches, thereby escalating the demand for staff development (Kay et al., 2020). Participating in WACE events and the Global WIL Modules has enabled global collaboration with many Australian WIL practitioners (Ferns et al., 2022). Career Development staff are well supported through a suite of professional development programmes delivered by the NAGCAS and the Career Development Association of Australia (CDAA).

CONCLUSION

Although often misunderstood, employability continues to be a strategic focus of Australian universities, as in many countries. This importance, however, has not necessarily been matched with the required resources. The introduction of government performance-based funding is now sharpening that focus. Strong university leadership and a cohesive strategy are required to build employability activities into curricula to ensure impact and reach to all student cohorts, particularly Indigenous and international students. WIL continues to be a key driver that enhances student employability skills and employment outcomes. The strong record of WIL in Australia needs to continue and be supported. In addition, enhancing and expanding partnerships with industry and community is critical, with strategies to ensure stronger engagement. Staff play a critical role in the employability agenda and building their capability is key to ensuring great employability outcomes for students/graduates.

REFERENCES

ACEN (2015), *National Strategy on Work-integrated Learning in University Education*. Available at: http://cdn1.acen.edu.au/wp-content/uploads/2015/03/National-WIL-Strategy-in-university-education-032015.pdf (accessed: 17 January 2023).

ACEN (2021), *Summary Report for Graduate Outcomes Survey Items*. Available at: https://drive.google.com/file/d/18trRxxgbvY7Ee17rjRZNGSUfB4OiWwUr/view (accessed: 17 January 2023).

AiG (2021), *Skills Urgency: Transforming Australia's Workplaces: April 2021*. Available at: https://cdn.aigroup.com.au/Reports/2021/CET_skills_urgency_report_apr2021.pdf (accessed: 17 January 2023).

Australian Government (2012), *Review of Higher Education Access and Outcomes for Aboriginal and Torres Strait Islander People: Final Report*. Available at: https://opus.lib.uts.edu.au/bitstream/10453/31122/1/2013003561OK.pdf (accessed: 23 January 2023).

Australian Government (2021), *Australian Strategy for International Education 2021–2030*. Available at: https://www.education.gov.au/australian-strategy-international-education-2021-2030 (accessed: 23 January 2023).

Bean, M. and Dawkins, P. (2022), *Review of University–Iindustry Collaboration in Teaching and Learning*. Available at: https://www.education.gov.au/higher-education-reviews-and-consultations/resources/universityindustry-collaboration-teaching-and-learning-review (accessed: 17 January 2023).

Bennett, D. and Ferns, S. (2017), 'Functional and cognitive aspects of employability: implications for international students', in G. Barton and K. Hartwig (eds), *Professional Learning in the Work Place for International Students: Exploring Theory and Practice*, Cham: Springer, pp. 203–222.

Bridgstock, R., Grant-Iramu, G. and McAlpine, A. (2019), 'Integrating career development learning into the curriculum: collaboration with the careers service for employability', *Journal of Teaching and Learning for Graduate Employability*, 10(1), 56–72.

Campbell, M., Cooper B., Smith, J. and Rueckert, C. (2022), 'The framing of employability policy and the design of work-integrated learning curriculum', in S. J. Ferns, A. D. Rowe and K. E. Zegwaard (eds), *Advances in Research Theory and Practice in Work-Integrated Learning: Enhancing Employability for a Sustainable Future*, Abingdon: Routledge, pp. 17–27.

Dacre Pool, L, and Sewell, P. (2007), 'The key to employability: developing a practical model of graduate employability', *Education + Training*, 49(4), 277–289.

Department of Education, Skills and Employment (2021), *NPILF Pilot (2022–24) Guidance Document*. Available at: https://www.dese.gov.au/job-ready/resources/npilf-guidance-document (accessed: 17 January 2023).

Department of Foreign Affairs and Trade (2021), *New Colombo Plan: Connect to Australia's Future – Study in the Region*. Available at: https://www.dfat.gov.au/people-to-people/new-colombo-plan (accessed: 17 January 2023).

Ferns, S. and Kay, J. (2021), 'Needed now: exceptional leaders for Work-integrated learning', *Campus Morning Mail*, 8 August. Available at: https://bit.ly/3IqJ3Ib (accessed: 17 January 2023).

Ferns, S. and Lilly, L. (2015), 'Driving institutional engagement in WIL: enhancing graduate employability', *Journal of Teaching and Learning for Graduate Employability*, 6(1), 116–133. Available at: https://ojs.deakin.edu.au/index.php/jtlge/article/view/577/572 (accessed: 17 January 2023).

Ferns, S., Campbell, M. and Zegwaard, K. (2014), 'Work integrated learning', in S. Ferns (ed.), *HERDSA Guide: Work Integrated Learning in the Curriculum*, Milperra, NSW: Higher Education and Development Society of Australasia, pp. 1–6.

Ferns, S., Dawson V. and Howitt, C. (2019), 'A collaborative framework for enhancing graduate employability', *International Journal of Work-Integrated Learning*, 20(2), 99–111.

Ferns, S., Kay, J., Hoskyn, K., Zegwaard, K. E., Johansson, K., and McRae, N. (2022), 'Introducing the global work-integrated learning modules: Global connectivity for practitioners', *Refereed Proceedings of the 4th WACE International Research Symposium on Cooperative and Work-Integrated Education, 2022, Kanazawa Institute of Technology, Japan*. Kanazawa, Ishikawa Prefecture, Japan, 31 August to 2 September. Available at: https://waceinc.org/resources/Documents/IRS%20Conference%202022/WACE%20IRS%20Proceedings%202022.pdf (accessed: 23 January 2023).

FYA (2017), *The New Work Smarts: Thriving in the New Work Order*. Available at: https://www.fya.org.au/app/uploads/2021/09/FYA_TheNewWorkSmarts_July2017.pdf (accessed: 17 January 2023).

Healy, M., Brown, J. L. and Ho, C. (2021), 'Graduate employability as a professional proto-jurisdiction in higher education', *Higher Education*, 83, 1125–1142. https://doi.org/10.1007/s10734-021-00733-4.

Heffernan, T. (2021), 'Forty years of social justice research in Australasia: examining equity in inequitable settings', *Higher Education Research & Development*, 41(1), 48–61. Available at: https://www.tandfonline.com/doi/full/10.1080/07294360.2021.2011152 (accessed: 17 January 2023).

Jackson, D., Ferns, S., Rowbottom, D. and McLaren, D. (2017), 'Improving the WIL experience through a third-party advisory service', *International Journal of Training Research*, 15(2), 160–178. http://dx.doi.org/10.1080/14480220.2016.1259005.

Kay, J., Ferns, S., Russell, L., Smith, J. and Winchester-Seeto, T. (2019), 'The emerging future: innovative models of work-integrated learning', *International Journal of Work-Integrated Learning*, Special Issue, 20(4), 401–413. Available at: https://www.ijwil.org/files/IJWIL_20_4_401_413.pdf (accessed: 17 January 2023).

Kay, J., Ferns, S., Russell, L., Smith, J. and Younger, A. (2022), 'Innovation in work-integrated learning', in S. J. Ferns, A. D. Rowe and K. E. Zegwaard (eds), *Advances in Research Theory and Practice in Work-Integrated Learning: Enhancing Employability for a Sustainable Future*, Abingdon: Routledge, pp. 133–144.

Kay, J., McRae, N., & Russell, L. (2020), 'Two institutional responses to work-integrated learning in a time of COVID-19: Canada and Australia', *International Journal of Work-Integrated Learning*, Special Issue, 21(5), 491–503. Available at: https://www.ijwil.org/files/IJWIL_21_5_491_503.pdf (accessed: 23 January 2023).

Mackaway, J. and Chalkley, T. (2022). Student access and equity in work-integrated learning: A work in progress. In S. J. Ferns, A. D. Rowe and K. E. Zegwaard (eds), *Advances in Research Theory and Practice in Work-Integrated Learning: Enhancing Employability for a Sustainable Future*, Abingdon: Routledge, pp. 227–238.

Patrick, C. J., Peach, D., Pocknee, C., Webb, F., Fletcher, M. and Pretto, G. (2009), *The WIL (Work Integrated Learning) Report: A National Scoping Study*. Office for Learning and Teaching. Available at: https://eprints.qut.edu.au/216185/1/WIL-Report-grants-project-jan09.pdf (accessed: 17 January 2023).

Patrick, C.-j., Fallon, W., Campbell, M., Devenish, I., Kay, J., Lawson, J., Russell, L. and Tayebjee, F. (2014), *Leading WIL: A Distributed Leadership Approach to Enhance Work Integrated Learning*. Sydney: Australian Government Office for Learning and Teaching. Available at: https://ltr.edu.au/resources/LE11_2084_Patrick_Report_2014.pdf (accessed: 23 January 2023).

Rowe, A. D. and Zegwaard, K. E. (2017), 'Developing graduate employability skills and attributes: curriculum enhancement through work-integrated learning', *Asia-Pacific Journal of Cooperative Education*, Special issue, 18(2), 87–99.

Russell, L. and Kay, J. (2019), 'Building student employability from day one', in J. Higgs, W. Letts and G. Crisp (eds), *Education for Employability (Volume 2): Learning for Future Possibilities*, Rotterdam: Brill, pp. 133–142.

Smith. J., Russell, L., Bliemel, M., Donnet, T., Elkington, R. and Larkin, I. (2022), 'Developing university learners' enterprise capabilities through entrepreneurial work-integrated learning', in S. J. Ferns, A. D. Rowe, and K. E. Zegwaard (eds), *Advances in Research Theory and Practice in Work-Integrated Learning: Enhancing Employability for a Sustainable Future*, Abingdon: Routledge, pp. 145–156.

Universities Australia (2019), *Work Integrated Learning in Universities: Final Report*. Deakin ACT: Universities Australia. Available at: https://bit.ly/3Lk3f0d (accessed: 17 January 2023).

Universities Australia (2020), *2020 Higher Education Facts and Figures*. Canberra ACT: Universities Australia. Available at: https://www.universitiesaustralia.edu.au/wp-content/uploads/2020/11/200917-HE-Facts-and-Figures-2020.pdf (accessed: 17 January 2023).

Winchester-Seeto, T., Mackaway, J., Peach, D., Moore, K., Ferns, S. and Campbell, M. (2015), *Principles, Guidelines and Strategies for Inclusive WIL*. Available at: http://acen.edu.au/access-participation-progression/wp-content/uploads/2015/11/FINAL-Principles-Guidelines_and_Strategies-Inclusive-WIL-as-at-6_11_15.pdf (accessed: 17 January 2023).

Zegwaard, K., Ferns, S. and Rowe, A. (2022), 'Contemporary insights into the practice of work-integrated learning in Australia: Editorial', in S. J. Ferns, A. D. Rowe and K. E. Zegwaard (eds), *Advances in Research Theory and Practice in Work-Integrated Learning: Enhancing Employability for a Sustainable Future*, Abingdon: Routledge, pp. 1–14.

REFLECTION

From an international student

In 2016, the attractive part-time work rights and post-study open work visa strongly influenced my decision to choose New Zealand as a study destination over Australia, the US and the UK.

Participating in volunteer clubs and societies were accessible ways to gaining experience while studying. The ability to work part-time in a non-study related job, e.g., hospitality, supported living expenses; however, having done this for a year and a half, caused concern about the lack of relevant career experience to secure work in my discipline of study. Reality proved challenging to secure a study-related part-time job, despite having work experience. A couple of barriers to these roles were employer hesitation/unawareness of international student work rights, residency/citizenship eligibility to apply, and some part-time jobs requiring more than 20 hours a week, which were hours over the international student quota. Internships were not offered as a part of the degree, further limiting opportunities to gain degree-related work experience.

At the end of the second year, leveraging connections with university staff, I secured my next part-time job on campus supporting other international students. The university, as an employer, was also more accustomed to international student work rights and hiring processes. The influence of networking and connections strongly shaped my employment opportunities hereafter. I no longer considered the industry or discipline; securing any skilled job soon after graduation was the focus. While the post-study work visa allowed me to work in any sector, it only seemed an advantage if you had a foot in already. And as mentioned earlier, there are many obstacles to getting that foot in on a part-time basis. And so, my employability profile and career steps after graduation relied on developing relationships on campus to secure professional opportunities.

29. Enabling employability in New Zealand

Brett Berquist

INTRODUCTION

New Zealand's small and homogeneous university sector has always had an eye on employability as it delivered the knowledge and expertise required for an economy that for decades has called for diversity, but to a large extent remained primary industry-focused (Harrington, 2007). Yet it is only in recent years that the country's eight universities have sharpened their focus on graduate employability. Given the sector's strong regulatory oversight and recent government concern about the country's skills needs, an examination of the approach to employability in the New Zealand (NZ) context offers a valuable perspective.

NEW ZEALAND'S HE LANDSCAPE AND EMPLOYABILITY

The tertiary system in New Zealand is composed of three major kinds of institutions: (a) the eight public universities enrolling 177,655 students in 2020 (Education Counts, 2022); (b) Te Pukenga, the new national entity that has recently combined the country's 16 institutes of technology and polytechnics (ITP); and (c) private training establishments (PTEs), some of which also receive government funding.

The Education and Training Act 2020 guides all education activity, but the universities self-regulate programme development and monitoring through the Committee on University Academic Programmes (CUAP) within the peak body Universities New Zealand (UNZ). ITPs and PTEs are overseen by the New Zealand Qualifications Authority (NZQA).

Like other countries, New Zealand has seen growing access to tertiary education, rising from 54 per cent in 2001 to 64 per cent in 2020 (Ministry of Education, 2021). Attainment of a bachelor's degree or higher has more than doubled to 35 per cent in the same time frame (Ministry of Education,

2021). However, continued underachievement by Māori and Pacific students, at roughly half the national average (Ministry of Education, 2021) has seen a sector and government focus on support. This has intensified in recent years with the government allocating targeted funds and requiring institutions to support these students to succeed.

Currently (2018 census data and 2020 enrolments), Māori are 7.5 per cent of the population and 11 per cent of domestic tertiary enrolments. Pacific peoples represent 5.4 per cent of the population and 16 per cent of domestic tertiary enrolments (Education Counts, 2022; Stats NZ, 2020a).

Importance of Migration

From its colonial history, migration has continued to play an important role in the country's formation with net migration peaking in 2017 at just over 72,000 new immigrants (Stats NZ, 2018). International connections are embedded in NZ life, with over 27 per cent of the population born overseas at the last census (Stats NZ, 2020a). Record numbers of New Zealand's extensive diaspora returned home during the global Covid-19 pandemic (Stats NZ, 2020b), empowering the Prime Minister's slogan, 'Team of Five Million', in health compliance campaigns. Prior to the pandemic, NZ was very successful in attracting international students with one of the OECD's highest ratios of international students to tertiary education population (OECD, 2017). Among the eight universities, 17 per cent of enrolments were international in 2020, and approximately half of doctoral enrolments, reflecting the government's policy to subsidise PhD students regardless of nationality (Berquist, 2017).

International Student Work Rights

As a trading nation, New Zealand has maintained progressive policy settings to grow its economy and enrich its workforce. New Zealand currently has the most progressive policy settings for international students (Berquist et al., 2019). Relatively closed borders for 2020 and 2021 gave the Labour government an opportunity to reset migration in the NZ economy, including work rights for international students (Ministry of Business, Innovation and Employment, 2022).

The Big OE (Overseas Experience)

New Zealand university graduates are among the most mobile in the world, with one in three heading overseas within seven years of graduation and one in three international graduates remaining in NZ long term (Park, 2014, 2017). A series of studies reviewing available government data set out to analyse postgraduation mobility patterns of domestic and international graduates (Berquist and Moore, 2019). These meta-studies looked at the tertiary sector holistically. More recently, in the consultation process for potential revisions to work rights, Universities New Zealand has analysed during and post-study work behaviours for domestic and international students in the university sector only. This is an important distinction for NZ because 44 per cent of international tertiary enrolments in 2019 were in the sub-university sector (Universities New Zealand, 2021).

In some respects, the 'Big OE' tradition perhaps hampered the inclusion of experiential learning related to employability within the university curriculum. For previous generations of Kiwis, both education abroad and hands-on work experience were achieved through a stint abroad, rather than during university. Working during study was undertaken for budgetary need and work training was considered the domain of more applied studies in the ITP and PTE sector, rather than university. The levels of students working during study has remained relatively stable over the past decade with domestic students working at over double the rate (81 per cent) of international students (37 per cent) (Universities New Zealand, 2021).

In response to the current generation's demand, this trend has reversed, with NZ universities now engaging with more-inclusive learning abroad opportunities (Berquist and Moore, 2019) as well as the rise of work-integrated learning (WIL) (Hay and Fleming, 2021).

Working Collaboratively

An increased focus on employability and employment outcomes has been observed globally. A national definition of employability has empowered the rise of WIL in the UK (O'Leary, 2018) whereas Australia adopted a national WIL strategy in 2015 (Blackman, 2018). New Zealand encourages the focus but stops short of a national definition or mandate. Across these countries and many others, a shared metric is effective employment of graduates several months after completion, usually measured through graduate surveys (Rowe and Zegwaard, 2017). In addition to their own institutional surveys, all New Zealand universities participated in a ten-year longitudinal study of the 2011 graduating cohort for deeper information on career and social outcomes (Tustin et al., 2016).

The university career centres co-manage a shared job board 'nzunitalent', white-labelled for each university and delivered through the Abintegro platform. University Careers and Employability New Zealand (UCENZ) facilitates the universities' interface with professional associations, government, a national careers fair calendar, etc. Half the universities are firmly engaged with work-integrated learning (WIL) and Waikato recently made WIL mandatory for all programmes, effective from 2018 (Quigley, 2020). The NZ government has expanded the code of pastoral care for international students to now apply to all students (NZQA, 2021), leading to universities reviewing their governance and support systems for the full range of external workplace and community learning experiences (Fleming and Hay, 2021; Hay and Fleming, 2021). In a similar vein, this may eventually lead to all universities adopting a unified programme management system (Murray, 2022).

INTEGRATING EMPLOYABILITY INTO THE LEARNING EXPERIENCE AT THE UNIVERSITY OF CANTERBURY

NZ universities are required to state expected outcomes from qualifications and use core graduate attributes or profiles as a means to inform programme design and evaluation (Sampson et al., 2018). Strategic planning may include revision to graduate profiles with an expectation that this will influence curriculum design.

As already noted in other chapters in this volume, employability skills and employment outcomes are related but separate constructs (Jackson, 2016; Rowe and Zegwaard, 2017). Employment is a definite outcome that can be observed and often reported through graduate surveys, whereas employability communicates a broader set of skills that an institution believes may help the student succeed in a fulfilling career, for example, self-leadership (Zenatti-Daniels et al., 2018). Employability connects with engagement, student success, and equity, as we will illustrate through a particular NZ institution, the University of Canterbury.

Founded in 1873, Canterbury revised its graduate attributes in 2014 to include four categories: bicultural competence and confidence; community engagement; globally aware; and *employable, innovative and enterprising*. Foundational documents note that innovative and enterprising could be considered subsets of employability. Observing the link with employment, academics are encouraged to examine the types of employment graduates obtain, as evidenced through the Graduate Destination Survey and discussions with employers (University of Canterbury, 2016). Drawing on research from Australia and NZ, Canterbury outlines the 'core transferable skills that all UC undergraduates should obtain by graduation' (University of Canterbury, 2016): working effectively and professionally with diverse communities; communication; analytical, critical thinking and problem solving in diverse contexts; digital literacy; innovation, enterprising and creativity.

Guidelines for staff suggest that syllabi list relevant employability skills that may result from the course. Faculties are encouraged to offer a 'range of pedagogical-informed WIL opportunities'. They are also encouraged to consider modifying assessment activities to align with industry practices. Finally, academic staff should incorporate time for students to reflect on their learning, with a particular focus on transferable skills (University of Canterbury, 2016).

Priority Learners at the University of Canterbury

In 1840, Te Tiriti o Waitangi was signed, establishing the bicultural nature of New Zealand and giving specific rights to Māori as Tangata Whenua (Palmer, 2008, cited in Russell et al., 2021). This responsibility for universities was further reinforced in the Education Act of 1991 (Education Amendment Act 1991). Education strategy in New Zealand instructs providers to focus specifically on access and success for Māori and Pacific learners (Ministry of Education, 2020), and captures performance through mandatory reporting mechanisms.

Consequently, NZ universities share common diversity priorities. For the University of Canterbury, priority learners include Māori, Pacific, Rainbow/LGBTQIA+, people with long-term disabilities (physical and mental health-related), and first in Whānau students. As noted above, higher education attainment gaps exist for Māori and Pacific groups.

Kia Angitu – The University of Canterbury Student Success Ecosystem

In order to increase the effectiveness of various support initiatives, Canterbury has established the Kia Angitu initiative, a comprehensive ecosystem for student success. Kia Angitu aims for a 'comprehensive, strategic, and coordinated vision to lengthen and support the runway to tertiary education' (University of Canterbury, 2020).

First-year advising services have been physically relocated to an open area with easy access within the central library. Analytics for Course Engagement is working with revisions to the student information system and learning management system to identify and track early indicators of student engagement with their courses. Takere is a new residential first-year transition programme focused on Māori and Pacific students, and provides subsidised housing. Peer-assisted learning support has been developed to provide a different perspective of support for targeted learners. The project also aims to further embed career education into the curriculum, particularly in first-year courses.

Ako ā-mahi (WIL) at the University of Canterbury

Since the development of the 2014 graduate attributes, Canterbury's focus on WIL has increased. The NZ pastoral care code was expanded from international to all students in 2021 and increases the institutional duty of care

(NZQA, 2021). The onus on risk management has placed renewed importance on adequate management and support for students undertaking external learning activities and/or placements through their association with the university. Following a health and safety audit on field work, WIL, and study abroad (PwC, 2020), an external review was undertaken in 2021 to represent the user experience navigating placements through UC, from the student, partner, and staff perspectives (Purple Shirt, 2022). The report recognises the learning and personal development potential benefits of well-designed and well-executed experiential learning related to community engagement and/or the world of work. These benefits have been widely covered in the experiential learning literature and are reflected in various examples throughout this book. The report also identified the resource strain and risks that insufficiently resourced or guided experiential learning can create.

WIL is closely connected to community engagement, another graduate attribute at Canterbury. Canterbury has a long tradition of community engagement, with notable moments of intensity, such as the creation of the Student Volunteer Army in response to the earthquakes of 2010 and 2011. A degree programme in Youth and Community Leadership was developed through the Faculty of Education as a result of this outpouring of student involvement in community. The naming of internship courses, developed in the Faculty of Arts but open to all students, reflects this strong connection – Professional and Community Engagement (PACE). In the spirit of Kia Angitu and the university's focus on student success and priority learner groups, a proposal is in development to establish a hub for Ako ā-mahi (WIL) in order to address some of the recommendations that have surfaced through external reviews. As with Kia Angitu, the student success ecosystem, the Ako ā-mahi project is led by the Deputy Vice-Chancellor Academic, reflecting how much the impetus is driven by learning outcomes and graduate attributes. Through this process, Canterbury intends to develop strong support systems for WIL and the opportunity to further embed its benefits and opportunities within the curriculum.

Virtual Engagement

The difficult conditions of the global pandemic have engendered creative thinking on how to support students' engagement with companies and communities virtually. Even before the global crisis, a number of internship organisations were developing 'virtual internships' in response to the coming Fourth Industrial Revolution (Berquist, 2018) and universities such as Aston University in the UK have partnered with Virtual Internships to increase their capacity. Canterbury established micro-internships online for international students in business, providing a high level of mentoring and support for students unable to enter the country (University of Canterbury, 2021). The University of Auckland piloted three-week virtual micro-internships, in partnership with a local employers' organisation and leveraging Practera's platform (University of Auckland, 2020). This was then scaled to 1,500 micro-internships with NZ employers for international students both on- and offshore in 2021.

Technological and pedagogical developments empower increased access to work-related learning. With this increased access comes the need for strong support mechanisms to support students in these experiences.

CONCLUSION

The small size and homogeneous nature of New Zealand's university sector, operating within a strong regulatory environment, amplifies the impact of strategic policy settings. This in turn offers the opportunity to combine several threads of university strategy – diversity, access and inclusion, student success, and employability – in innovative ways that might be more challenging to achieve in larger higher education systems. The recent upscaling of technological and pedagogical innovations in delivery, empowered by the global pandemic, increase the opportunity to enhance our focus on these areas in a comprehensive approach.

REFERENCES

Berquist, B. (2017), *New Zealand's international PhD strategy: a holistic analysis 2005–2015*. University of Auckland. Available at: https://tinyurl.com/ya9fjn92 (accessed: 18 January 2023).

Berquist, B. (2018), 'Development of the international internship industry', in B. Berquist, K. Moore, and J. Milano (eds), *International Internships: Mission, Methods & Models: A Collection of Papers from the Global Internship Conference*, Boston, MA: Academic Internship Council, pp. 14–40.

Berquist, B. and Moore, A. (2019), 'Internationalization and employment: the case of the Kiwi overseas experience (OE)', in R. Coelen and C. Gribble (eds), *Internationalisation and Employability in Higher Education*, Abingdon: Routledge, pp. 129–137.

Berquist, B., Hall, R., Morris-Lange, S., Shields, H., Stern, V. and Tran, L. T. (2019), *Global perspectives on international student employability*. International Education Association of Australia (IEAA). Available at: https://www.ieaa.org.au/research/global-perspectives-on-international-student-employability (accessed: 18 January 2023).

Blackman, A. (2018), 'Creating and managing a quality academic WIL program for business students', in B. Berquist, K. Moore and J. Milano (eds), *International Internships: Mission, Methods & Models: A Collection of Papers from the Global Internship Conference*, Boston, MA: Academic Internship Council, pp. 124–140.

Education and Training Act 2020, Public Act 2020 No, 38. Available at: https://www.legislation.govt.nz/act/public/2020/0038/latest/LMS170676.html (accessed: 18 January 2023).

Education Counts (2022), *Tertiary Participation*. Available at: https://www.educationcounts.govt.nz/statistics/tertiary-participation (accessed: 16 April 2022).

Fleming, J. and Hay, K. (2021), 'Strategies for managing risk in work-integrated learning: a New Zealand perspective', *International Journal of Work-Integrated Learning*, 22(4), 553–564.

Harrington, A., (2007). The Contribution of the Primary Sector to New Zealand's Economic Growth. Working paper. Te Tai Ōhanga The Treasury. Available at: https://www.treasury.govt.nz/publications/wp/contribution-primary-sector-new-zealands-economic-growth-pp-05-04-html (accessed: 15 April 2022).

Hay, K. and Fleming, J. (2021), 'Keeping students safe: understanding the risks for students undertaking work-integrated learning', *International Journal of Work-Integrated Learning*, 22(4), 539–552.

Jackson, D. (2016), 'Re-conceptualising graduate employability: the importance of pre-professional identity', *Higher Education Research & Development*, 35(5), 925–939.

Ministry of Business, Innovation and Employment (2022), *Immigration settings for international students. Education sector peak body consultation 2–18 February 2022*. Wellington: Ministry of Business, Innovation and Employment. Unpublished.

Ministry of Education (2020), *The Statement of National Education and Learning Priorities (NELP) and the Tertiary Education Strategy (TES)*. Available at: https://assets.education.govt.nz/public/Documents/NELP-TES-documents/FULL-NELP-2020.pdf (accessed: 18 January 2023).

Ministry of Education (2021), *Tertiary Participation: Participation in Tertiary Education in New Zealand*. Available at: https://www.educationcounts.govt.nz/statistics/tertiary-participation (accessed: 24 January 2023).

Ministry of Education (2022). Educational attainment in the adult population. Available at: https://www.educationcounts.govt.nz/__data/assets/pdf_file/0009/208827/Educational-attainment-in-the-adult-population-2022-Indicatorb.pdf (accessed 23 January 2023).

Murray, C. (2022), *Ako ā-mahi | Work-Integrated Learning Business Case*. Christchurch: University of Canterbury. Unpublished report.

NZQA (2021), *The Education (Pastoral Care of Tertiary and International Learners) Code of Practice 2021*. Available at: https://www.nzqa.govt.nz/assets/Providers-and-partners/Code-of-Practice/Tertiary-and-International-Learners-Code-2021/NZQA_Pastoral-Care-Code-of-Practice_English.pdf (accessed: 16 April 2022).

OECD (2017), *Education at a Glance 2017: OECD Indicators*, Paris: OECD Publishing. http://dx.doi.org/10.1787/eag-2017-en.

O'Leary, S. (2018), 'Internships and graduate employability', in B. Berquist, K. Moore and J. Milano (eds), *International Internships: Mission, Methods & Models: A Collection of Papers from the Global Internship Conference*. Boston, MA: Academic Internship Council, pp. 108–123.

Palmer, M. (2008), *The Treaty of Waitangi in New Zealand's Law and Constitution*, Wellington: Victoria University Press.

Park, Z. (2014), *What young graduates do when they leave study: New data on the destination of young graduates*. Wellington: New Zealand Ministry of Education.

Park, Z. (2017), *Moving places – Destinations and earnings of international graduates*. Wellington: New Zealand Ministry of Education.

Purple Shirt (2022), *Ako ā-mahi Work-Integrated Learning Research Report*. Christchurch: University of Canterbury. Unpublished report.

PwC (2020), *University of Canterbury Health and Safety: Field Activities, Work-Integrated Programmes and Study Abroad*. Christchurch: University of Canterbury. Unpublished manuscript.

Quigley, N. (2020), *VC's perspective: Integrating learning and work: benefits, challenges*. Available at: https://www.universitiesnz.ac.nz/latest-news-and-publications/vcs-perspective-integrating-learning-work-benefits-challenges (accessed: 16 April 2022).

Rowe, A. and Zegwaard, K. (2017), 'Developing graduate employability skills and attributes: curriculum enhancement through work-integrated learning', *Asia-Pacific Journal of Cooperative Education*, Special Issue, 18(2), 87–99.

Russell, D., Tamanui-Hurunui, R., Vahl, M., Tamati-Elliffe, J. and Welsh, R. (2021), *Equity Review 2020/2021*. Christchurch: University of Canterbury.

Sampson, K., Moltchanova, E., Robertson, I., Bridgman, C., Suszko, A. and Russell, D. (2018), 'A roadmap for the evaluation of attributes in university graduates', New Zealand Journal of Educational Studies, 53(1), 119–134.

Stats NZ (2018), *Migration drives high population growth*. Available at: https://www.stats.govt.nz/news/migration-drives-high-population-growth (accessed: 16 April 2022).

Stats NZ (2020a), *2018 Census data allows users to dive deep into New Zealand's diversity*. [Press release, 21 April 2020].

Stats NZ (2020b), *NZ citizens migrating home in record numbers*. Available at: https://www.stats.govt.nz/news/nz-citizens-migrating-home-in-record-numbers (accessed: 16 April 2022).

Tustin, K., Gollop, M., Theodore, R., Taumoepeau, M., Taylor, N., Hunter, J., Chapple, S., Chee, K.-S. and Poulton, R. (2016), *Graduate Longitudinal Study New Zealand: First follow-up descriptive report*. Wellington: Universities New Zealand. Available at: https://www.glsnz.org.nz/files/1468361988403.pdf (accessed: 16 April 2022).

Universities New Zealand (2021), *Working while studying*. Available at: https://cdm20045.contentdm.oclc.org/digital/collection/p20045coll17/id/1165/rec/2 (accessed: 16 April 2022).

University of Auckland (2020), *Stranded international students provide global solutions for Auckland businesses*. Available at: https://www.auckland.ac.nz/en/news/2020/07/08/stranded-international-students-provide-global-solutions-for-auc.html (accessed: 16 April 2022).

University of Canterbury (2016), *Framework for the Graduate Attribute: Employable, Innovative and Enterprising*. Christchurch: University of Canterbury. Unpublished manuscript.

University of Canterbury (2020), *Graduate Destinations 2020*. Available at: https://www.canterbury.ac.nz/careers/academic-and-professional-staff/graduate-destinations/DVCR1030_Graduate_Destination_Survey_WEB.pdf (accessed: 18 January 2023).

University of Canterbury (2021), *International students to share knowledge with Canterbury businesses*. Available at: https://www.canterbury.ac.nz/news/2021/international-students-to-share-knowledge-with-canterbury-businesses.html (accessed: 16 April 2022).

Zenatti-Daniels, E., Napiersky, U. and Griffiths, I. (2018), 'From the inside out', in B. Berquist, K. Moore and J. Milano (eds), *International Internships: Mission, Methods & Models: A Collection of Papers from the Global Internship Conference*. Boston, MA: Academic Internship Council, pp. 267–280.

REFLECTION

From a New Zealand graduate

Whether it be the New Zealand culture, or the social bubble I grew up in, having some international experience was and is never a question of 'if' but 'when'. Another certainty that I have, and share with many of my friends, is that I know that I will eventually settle in New Zealand and progress most of my career here.

Although my overseas experiences have not been for longer than nine months, they have been valuable nonetheless.

I had my first overseas experience straight after high school. It was a spontaneous decision, and one which I had absolutely little expectation for. It took me out of my comfort zone, and it was challenging and eye-opening. I learned so much from the experience, and it really shaped me as a person at such a crucial time in my life.

Beyond the specialised skills and learnings that are available with programmes or work experiences overseas, my main motive for looking beyond our borders is for personal growth – living in a different culture without the comforts of home, meeting new people and networking, reflection, pursuing passions and so on.

I see workplaces accommodating and even encouraging overseas experiences nowadays. They know that an overseas experience is a significant learning opportunity and that most Kiwis will return someday.

30. Lessons from Germany

Patrick Glauner

INTRODUCTION

Universities of Applied Sciences are tertiary education institutions that specialise in a particular applied science or applied art, such as engineering, technology or business. They were first founded in Germany in the late 1960s and early 1970s and were initially referred to as *Fachhochschulen*, or *FH* for short.

The focus of Universities of Applied Sciences has been teaching professional skills and bridging the gap between academia and real-world demands by employers. Furthermore, they traditionally have a more diverse student body than research universities as there are broader entrance qualifications beyond A levels. In the following years, Universities of Applied Sciences were adopted in a number of countries, including Austria and Switzerland.

Prior to the Bologna Process (a transnational reform of higher education in the 1990s which was aimed at the creation of the European Higher Education Area, which standardises courses and degrees across Europe and promotes the international mobility of students), graduates of (research) universities received a *Diplom* after about five years of study. A *Diplom* is equivalent to a master's degree. Graduates of Universities of Applied Sciences, however, received a *Diplom (FH)* after about four years of study. A *Diplom (FH)* is roughly equivalent to a bachelor's degree. Due to the Bologna process in the early 2000s, (research) universities and Universities of Applied Sciences now award legally equivalent academic bachelor's and master's degrees. A bachelor's degree in Germany typically takes three to three-and-a-half years, while a master's degree takes one-and-a-half to two years. In recent years, most German Universities of Applied Sciences were renamed as *Hochschulen*, *Hochschulen für angewandte Wissenschaften* or *Technische Hochschulen*. Education is not centrally organised in Germany. All 16 German states have their own higher education laws. That is why these terms and regulations may slightly vary within Germany.

This chapter shows how Universities of Applied Sciences in Germany address the challenge of employability, how they work with industry, and how they build an understanding of what employers want and develop those skills during the degree. Recent developments, such as a stronger focus on research and new PhD programmes, are also discussed.

Universities and Employability in the 21st Century

Universities are facing major challenges as a result of the rapidly advancing digital transformation of teaching. These include, in particular, competition from massive open online courses (MOOCs), which focus on providing students with practical skills that allow them to solve real-world problems. By contrast, most German research universities teach purely academic skills. However, most research university graduates will not stay in academia upon graduation and do not necessarily possess the skills sought by industry.

An introduction to MOOCs is given in Ng and Widom (2014). This transformation is further being accelerated by the demographic change in developed countries and could result in a dwindling number of potential students in the near future. These courses enable learners to study high-quality content from renowned professors, remotely, at their own speed and at little or no cost (Bylieva et al., 2020). Furthermore, renowned universities have started to offer courses and entire degree programmes via MOOC platforms. Some MOOC platforms offer career coaching, too. Companies have also launched collaborative programmes with MOOC platforms to train their employees. However, if universities address those challenges swiftly, ambitiously and sustainably, they can even emerge stronger from this situation by providing better, more modern and more hands-on courses to their students and thus increase their employability.

DEGGENDORF INSTITUTE OF TECHNOLOGY: CASE STUDY

Deggendorf Institute of Technology is located in Eastern Bavaria, on the Danube. It has a diverse student body of different educational and cultural backgrounds and has been ranked 29th worldwide of the most innovative universities in the 2021 World's Universities with Real Impact (WURI) ranking. Founded in 1994, the multi-award-winning university has become the most successful University of Applied Sciences in Bavaria, which is confirmed by the WURI ranking as well as national rankings. This is due to the vision which has always been at the forefront of the development strategy: they have continuously developed attractive fields of study supplemented by a range of further education courses, generated intensive research, knowledge and technology transfer to the modern economy, followed economic and social trends, and developed a vast regional and international network.

The total student population is currently more than 8,000, including 30 per cent international students from all over the globe. The degree programmes at undergraduate and postgraduate levels, both full-time and part-time, cover engineering, digitalisation, health care, and business, taught in either English or German. Additionally, they offer three English-language undergraduate exchange programmes in the fields of engineering, computer science, and business for international students. All courses meet international quality standards. Three teaching campuses accommodate all students: in addition to the main campus in Deggendorf, there is the European Campus Rottal-Inn in Pfarrkirchen, which specialises in international bachelor's and master's degrees in health care and engineering, which are taught exclusively in English, and the newest addition, Campus Cham, offers degrees in engineering in both languages. Due to ongoing globalisation, graduates need to be fluent in English, both from a technical and business perspective. The English-language programmes increase employability of the students in that regard.

The university has a strong social and economic cohesion with the town of Deggendorf and the beautiful surrounding Bavarian Forest national park. The development of the university has evolved the town into a vibrant, international and multicultural hub of young academics intermingled with traditional Bavarian culture. There are 13 unique technology and health-care campuses dotted around neighbouring districts in the Bavarian Forest region. In these technology campuses, staff and students work closely together with local and international companies to create specific pioneering solutions for immediate implementation; for example, the students complete internships, research projects or thesis projects in the research campuses. The close collaboration with industrial partners thus increases their employability. The companies, in return, are supported by the university in research, development and consulting work and therefore the companies innovate to create new perspectives for young, qualified people.

DEGREE PROGRAMMES AT UNIVERSITIES OF APPLIED SCIENCES

Degree programmes at German (research) universities are known to be very theoretical. By contrast, degree programmes at Universities of Applied Sciences are fit for purpose because they bind together theoretical foundations and practical applications. Professors also typically include in their lectures the lessons they learned in their (past) practical experience or their ongoing consulting projects. Some professors also invite practitioners from industry for guest lectures or carry out coursework projects together with industrial partners.

There are also extended opportunities for students to apply their skills to the real world and gain more experience: first, almost all degree programmes at Universities of Applied Sciences include a mandatory internship semester, which is typically at the end of the second year or the beginning of the third year. Second, students are encouraged to complete their thesis project together with an industrial partner. That opportunity provides students not only with additional real-world experience, but often leads directly to a job offer by the industrial partner upon graduation.

At Deggendorf Institute of Technology, for example, an English language undergraduate programme in artificial intelligence (AI) is offered. Its structure is depicted in Figure 30.1, which also confirms the balance between theory at the beginning of the programme and applications later on.

The fascinating world of AI involves programming computer-controlled machines to independently make decisions and perform tasks usually conducted by humans. AI students acquire the expert knowledge required to build AI systems initially in foundation topics such as mathematics, programming, algorithms and data structures, operating systems, networks and databases. Later on in the course, they study complex AI such as machine learning, computer vision, natural language processing, Big Data, Deep Learning, autonomous robotics and computational logic (Glauner, 2021).

They customise their degree through individually selected elective courses that allow them to focus on particular subjects, depending on their interest areas in AI and its applications. They benefit from the mandatory internship semester, in which they have the opportunity to apply their newly acquired skills to challenges in a work environment. The department closely collaborates with industrial partners to provide them with a possible environment to complete their thesis project in the last semester, providing them with the perfect preparation to launch their career in AI upon graduation. The students increase their employability in multiple ways when doing their thesis project in industry: on the one hand, they are exposed to real-world problems and acquire additional skills that they will need in industry upon graduation. Second, they get to know their potential future employer during the time frame of their thesis project, which takes some four to six months. Most of the students benefit from that setting and get an offer from the industrial partner upon graduation.

PROFESSORS IN GERMANY

Most professors in Germany work at public universities, as private universities play only a minor role in the German university system. Professors at public universities are usually civil servants. Therefore, their employment is particularly safe because it could only be terminated for major misconduct. In addition, professors have a far-reaching freedom in their academic affairs

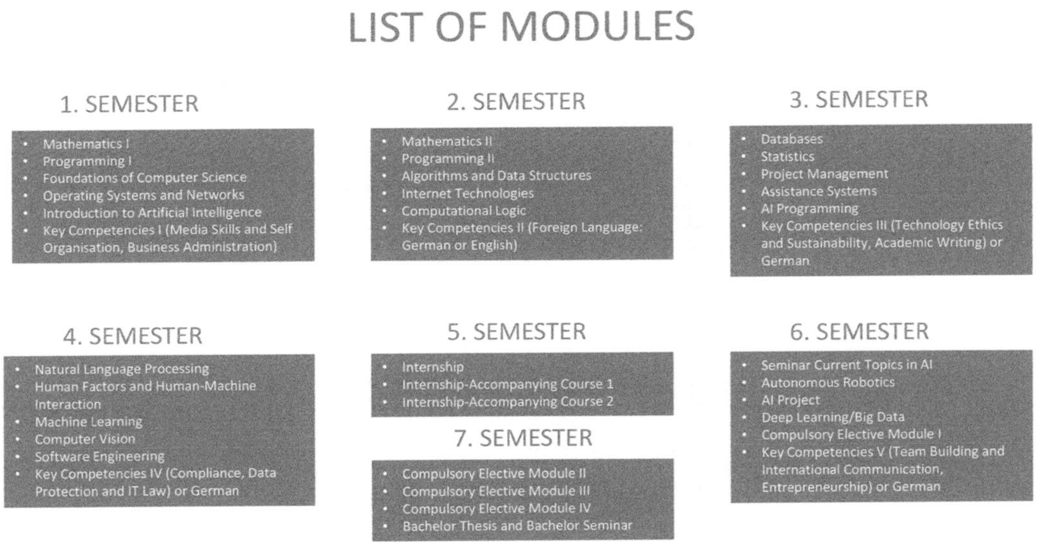

LIST OF MODULES

1. SEMESTER
- Mathematics I
- Programming I
- Foundations of Computer Science
- Operating Systems and Networks
- Introduction to Artificial Intelligence
- Key Competencies I (Media Skills and Self Organisation, Business Administration)

2. SEMESTER
- Mathematics II
- Programming II
- Algorithms and Data Structures
- Internet Technologies
- Computational Logic
- Key Competencies II (Foreign Language: German or English)

3. SEMESTER
- Databases
- Statistics
- Project Management
- Assistance Systems
- AI Programming
- Key Competencies III (Technology Ethics and Sustainability, Academic Writing) or German

4. SEMESTER
- Natural Language Processing
- Human Factors and Human-Machine Interaction
- Machine Learning
- Computer Vision
- Software Engineering
- Key Competencies IV (Compliance, Data Protection and IT Law) or German

5. SEMESTER
- Internship
- Internship-Accompanying Course 1
- Internship-Accompanying Course 2

6. SEMESTER
- Seminar Current Topics in AI
- Autonomous Robotics
- AI Project
- Deep Learning/Big Data
- Compulsory Elective Module I
- Key Competencies V (Team Building and International Communication, Entrepreneurship) or German

7. SEMESTER
- Compulsory Elective Module II
- Compulsory Elective Module III
- Compulsory Elective Module IV
- Bachelor Thesis and Bachelor Seminar

Figure 30.1   Artificial intelligence undergraduate programme at Deggendorf Institute of Technology

because the constitution of Germany, the Basic Law for the Federal Republic of Germany, grants them the right to academic freedom. As a consequence, professors do not really have a boss and are free to choose the topics they teach or conduct research in. Even the university president is considered the *primus inter pares*, the first among equals, and not the supervisor of professors.

Career development in German universities is very different compared to the English-speaking world. In Germany, there are only a very limited number of positions between the levels of postdoc and (full) professor. Tenure-track positions do not exist in most universities. As a consequence, career development is challenging as most researchers do not make any progress beyond the level of postdoc. They may thus never gain experience as a faculty member and ultimately be forced to leave academia once they run out of limited duration funding. By contrast, talented researchers may get promoted to the level of (full) professor very early in their career, i.e. soon after completion of their PhD.

Universities of Applied Sciences have a very unique demand profile for professors: first, applicants must have at least three years' full-time experience of working in industry. In exceptional circumstances, work in applied research institutions (which are not universities) may count too. Second, they must have at least five years' full-time experience of working in total, which may partially include working experience at a university. Finally, applicants must possess a PhD. Therefore, most professors at Universities of Applied Sciences switch from industry to academia some years after completion of their PhD. The actual length of past experience of working in industry of professors varies substantially and may range from three to more than 20 years.

Furthermore, professors at Universities of Applied Sciences are allowed to work one day per week outside the university. Some professors may keep working part-time for their previous employer. However, others run their own consulting businesses because of the increased flexibility. Keeping a foot in industry helps professors to stay up to date, retain a network and incorporate their experience in curriculum development. Both options help their Universities of Applied Sciences to increase employability of students by connecting them to potential employers. Furthermore, that situation helps Universities of Applied Sciences to retain talent, as the professors may earn a substantial additional income through their side jobs. Some universities have, therefore, also started to hire part-time professors who work more than one day per week in industry.

ABOUT THE AUTHOR

I have been interested in computer science and mathematics since I was a teenager. I finished my A levels in 2008 and initially aimed for a career in industry.

That is why I wanted to learn how to bind together theoretical work and practical work. Subsequently, I chose to study computer science at Karlsruhe University of Applied Sciences. Their computer science department was one of the leading ones in terms of employability at that time in Germany. During my first job at the European Organisation for Nuclear Research (CERN), I become more interested in research, though. Later, I received an MSc in Machine Learning from Imperial College London and a PhD in Computer Science from the University of Luxembourg.

Looking back, I am glad I had completed my undergraduate degree at a University of Applied Sciences as my professors had real-world experience and taught me how to produce concrete outcomes by applying theoretical foundations. I subsequently worked in industry as an executive in high-tech R&D and in the consulting business. In 2020, I joined Deggendorf Institute of Technology as a professor of artificial intelligence.

CONCLUSIONS

In recent years, Universities of Applied Sciences have undergone a number of changes. Historically, their professors have focused on teaching and technology transfer through side jobs. Nowadays, most Universities of Applied Sciences have also started to put an emphasis on active research and publications. Some state governments have even started to establish PhD programmes at selected Universities of Applied Sciences. The motivation for those changes is to attract more third-party research funding and to increase performance in research-related rankings. In order to achieve those goals, more professors without a classic industry background have been hired.

Some universities have also started to introduce a limited number of tenure-track assistant professorships that support career development and attract younger talent, with a stronger focus on research. It remains to be seen whether those changes will allow Universities of Applied Sciences to keep a competitive edge, though. They could, however, also become indistinguishable from research universities and subsequently lose relevance. This would ultimately decrease the employability of graduates, as they might not possess the real-world skills sought by employers anymore. Therefore, Universities of Applied Sciences must retain their close links to industry and keep in mind the real-world demands of industry in their curriculum development and when hiring new professors.

REFERENCES

Bylieva, D., Bekirogullari, Z., Lobatyuk, V. and Nam, T. (2020), 'Analysis of the consequences of the transition to online learning on the example of MOOC philosophy during the COVID-19 pandemic', *Humanities & Social Sciences Reviews*, 8(4), 1083–1093.

Glauner, P. (2021), 'Staying ahead in the MOOC-era by teaching innovative AI courses', in K. M. Kinnaird, P. Steinbach and O. Guhr (eds), *Proceedings of the 2nd Teaching in Machine Learning and Artificial Intelligence Workshop, Proceedings of Machine Learning Research*, 170, 5–9.

Ng, A. and Widom, J. (2014), *Origins of the modern MOOC (xMOOC)*. Technical report. Stanford University. Available at: http://ai.stanford.edu/~ang/papers/mooc14-OriginsOfModernMOOC.pdf (accessed: 18 January 2023).

REFLECTION

From a student working in a large American video game company

I originally only knew I wanted to work with computers, but there are a lot of options if that is your only condition. I chose to study computer science at a University of Applied Sciences instead of a research university, because I was not only interested in the theory, I wanted to create things as well.

Looking back, it definitely was the right choice for me. I did also study at a research university for one semester, to get my master's degree, and it was miserable. I switched back over to a University of Applied Sciences and finished my degree without a hitch.

I think that applying the things I learned together with my fellow students prepared me far better for my work life than any professor ever could on their own. In fact, I once sat in an interview for a student job in a software company where they asked me if I ever worked with a computer. A bit flabbergasted I asked why they would even ask that, and they explained that they get a lot of research university student applications from people that could not tell a computer mouse from a real mouse.

Always trying to make new stuff and trying to push the limit of a computer also put me into the position where I am now. After I published a few prototypes on my webpage, I was hired by a video game company to work on their game engine and push the limits on what computers can simulate in real time graphics. I could not have found a better job if I tried and I am grateful for everyone on my way who made it possible.

31. European University initiative in enabling student success

Renáta Tomášková, Ida Andersson-Norrie, Bice Della Piana, Anna Chudy, Melpo Iacovidou and Colombine Madelaine

INTRODUCTION

NEOLAiA which means 'Youth' in Greek, is a close-knit alliance of nine young universities based in the European regions: Bielefeld University in Germany, the University of Salerno in Italy, the University of Jaén in Spain, the University of Ostrava in the Czech Republic, the University of Örebro in Sweden, Stefan cel Mare University in Romania, the University of Tours in France, Siauliai State University of Applied Sciences in Lithuania, and the University of Nicosia in Cyprus (NEOLAiA, n.d.).

The establishment of the alliance was inspired by the European University Initiative arising from the 2017 Gothenburg Summit of EU leaders. In its December 2017 Conclusions, the European Council called on Member States, the Council and the Commission to take forward 'strategic partnerships across the EU between higher education institutions and encouraging the emergence by 2024 of some twenty "European Universities"', consisting in bottom-up networks of universities across the EU which will enable students to obtain a degree by combining studies in several EU countries and contribute to the international competitiveness of European universities (European Commission, n.d.a). Today it is one of the flagship initiatives of building a cohesive European Higher Education Area.

The aim of this initiative is to bring together a new generation of creative Europeans able to cooperate across cultures, languages, borders, and disciplines to address global challenges and skills shortages faced in Europe. Representing the diversity of Europe, NEOLAiA universities are at the same time unified by shared strategic goals. They are anchored in the regions most of their students come from, often first-generation students and with a migration background within the family. Unlocking the potential of our students is essential for raising the potential of the regions and the key to this achievement is seen in the synergy of the expertise and experience of all the partners in the alliance.

HOW CAN COLLABORATION WITHIN THE ALLIANCE BOOST THE EMPLOYABILITY OF THE GRADUATES?

There are two main points that answer this question:

First, universities in the alliance work together in all areas of university activities and are interconnected on multiple levels, through a wide variety of agendas. NEOLAiA represents a pool of researchers, teachers, and expert staff in research, teaching and learning, social engagement and internationalisation, as well as student services, and offers opportunities to learn from each other, share practices, search jointly for solutions, and test them in diverse environments. In that vein the management of students' academic and professional career skills is also open to sharing and learning from partners in the alliance, which enables partner universities to revise and improve their employability support activities.

Second, the students admitted to the member universities also become NEOLAiA students, and it is the principal goal of the alliance to make sure they can benefit from all the opportunities that the whole of NEOLAiA offers. Having access to career support activities at nine European universities, providing a wide range of job-ready knowledge and skills tailored for diverse European regions, is an invaluable asset for the professional careers NEOLAiA students may choose to seek both in the local and the wider European labour market.

Workshops on job-seeking skills on virtual platforms open to students across the alliance and on-site job-hunting training equip the participants with cross-cultural awareness. Students have a chance to explore the similarities and differences in personal branding, CVs and motivation letters, job-hunting techniques, and job interview styles, including the dress code, across European regions.

The students' career path, and their journey towards professions which would provide them with long-term job performance, job security, and also personal satisfaction, starts well before they enrol at university and is not completed with their graduation. To help students acquire knowledge and skills for high-level careers, or for the several careers they may eventually pursue, and to develop their job search competences, requires a comprehensive approach involving relevant study opportunities, work experience, entrepreneurial training, personal development and career counselling, and finally up-to-date information on the job market. Prospective students, and students at all levels, from bachelors to PhDs, as well as alumni, are all included and supported to make the best of the student journey and navigate successfully through professional life.

This chapter aims to offer an insight into the strategies and activities addressing this complex endeavour in the NEOLAiA alliance.

WIDENING PARTICIPATION IN HIGHER EDUCATION

The first step in getting students employed is to get them into university and into a suitable programme. Universities invite high school students, as well as mature prospective students, to open days, which is not only an opportunity to present their offer but also to hear directly from students on their plans, desires and needs. During Covid-19, open days were moved successfully online, and the virtual format has stayed afterwards as an alternative to the on-site events inviting visitors to the campuses again.

The University of Jaén, for instance, organises 'Encuentros UJA' (UJA Meetings) as a university fair at which it is mainly the current students who welcome their visiting peers at stands around the campus and introduce them to the Jaén University environment. Prospective students get acquainted with the university offer, including entrepreneurship training and internships, or financial aid. Open days and fairs, however, may not be enough to widen recruitment and to address groups that for reasons such as socio-economic background, disabilities and family situation are more remote from higher education than others.

An important area of collaboration in the alliance is the sharing and application of best practices in fostering diversity and inclusion (D&I) in the NEOLAiA campuses and regions, in alignment with the EU's D&I goals. One example of best practice that can be shared, adopted, and developed is Örebro University's broadened recruitment. In 2001, it was included in the Swedish Higher Education Act that all Swedish higher education institutions shall actively promote widened recruitment to higher education. As a step towards this, Örebro University, together with the municipality of Örebro, started the 'Linje 14' project in 2003 to motivate high school students towards higher education. The project is named after bus route #14, which runs between one of Örebro's suburbs, Vivalla, which has low socio-economic status and a high proportion of immigrant population, and the university. Within Linje 14 there are several activities in which high school students get to meet student ambassadors from the university in different settings. Activities include workshops, homework support and visits to the campus. The partnership has expanded to involve six high schools and three leisure centres. In 2018, a research group initiated a study of the long-term effects of Linje 14. One of the focus areas of the report targeted students who did not have a parent with an academic background. The result showed that the tendency to study at a university had increased by over 50 per cent at one school in Vivalla.

Linje 14 shows how a single university working together with regional stakeholders, such as the municipality and local schools, really can make a difference. The practice is especially relevant for NEOLAiA universities due to their regional collaboration, which is central to the alliance. Also, it is an idea that can be adjusted to suit the local context of the NEOLAiA partners.

Identifying one's own strengths and weaknesses, and finding a best fit among the numerous degree programmes on offer, is a challenge for teenagers today. There is a growing demand for counselling services and the number of students who decide to quit their degree programme and start a different one during or after the first year is relatively high. How to provide them with meaningful help is one of the areas for sharing of best practices in NEOLAiA. Many of the partner universities offer guidance for prospective students both through counselling services and online tools. The network of NEOLAiA staff committed to this agenda investigates the similarities and differences in practices due to culture, regional setting, and societal infrastructure and can discuss, review, or adopt them as needed.

NEOLAIA STUDENT EXPERIENCE FOR PROFESSIONAL CAREERS

The universities in NEOLAiA strive to join forces and resources to provide widening cohorts of students with knowledge, skills, and experiences that would help them develop careers which they would like to see themselves in and which would also be beneficial to the regions and society at large. The crucial ingredients to this are the way this ambitious vision in research-based study opportunities responds to global trends, work experience gained during studies, entrepreneurial training, personal development support, and continuous career counselling, including information on the current job market.

STUDY OPPORTUNITIES

To make sure the diverse community of students is motivated to find university studies that match students' interests and talents the alliance develops two lines of opportunities: firstly the NEOLAiA universities increase the accessibility of their courses and degree programmes through a variety of mobility formats and by opening virtual courses to students across NEOLAiA; and secondly, the task force of experts develop new research-based courses as joint ventures of NEOLAiA partners.

Currently there are seven courses in blended formats – designed to run online during the term and concluded by a short-term placement at the end of the term – equipping students with the knowledge and skills required to tackle current global challenges such as health research, artificial intelligence and social robotics, digital resources and tools in social research and research in humanities, cultural awareness and intelligence, entrepreneurial competence, self-directed learning skills, and emotional awareness. Not only the content and goals, but also the realisation of the courses, is an intercultural endeavour, as all the courses are led by teams of academics and attended by students from several of the NEOLAiA universities. The courses represent the foundations of the NEOLAiA Focus Academy, which is set to grow into a rich resource of specialised courses furnishing students with the micro-credentials sought after in the job market.

One of the most important assets of the alliance is the international environment it naturally offers – a cultural playground for students to learn languages, build cultural awareness, and practise intercultural competences. Multilingualism and cultural awareness and expression are recognised key competencies for lifelong learning, which is central to long-term employability, according to the European Commission (European Commission, n.d.b).

Whereas English is spread across the alliance as the dominant medium of instruction in international groups, students also have a chance to learn any of the nine languages of the participating countries, either on the spot through study abroad stays or through the Language and Culture Exchange (LACE) programme. In the LACE programme, the students themselves become advocates of their cultures and tutors of their first languages, teaching their peers in person or online. A long-term experience with focused cultural awareness training was brought to the alliance by the University of Salerno, where cross-cultural competences and cross-cultural management had been embedded in the curriculum as well as in extra-curricular entrepreneurial and knowledge transfer courses since 2013. NEOLAiA is drawing upon Salerno's know-how to design cultural awareness activities for all students going out on a placement for training before they leave, and as mid-term and after-placement reflections to make sure they get the most from their stay abroad for their future work in multicultural teams either in their home countries or on the international job market.

WORK EXPERIENCE

The importance of gaining early work experience during studies is widely acknowledged on the European and global scale. It is also requested by students themselves and recommended by alumni to their younger peers at the university. NEOLAiA universities strive to improve and broaden the offer of internships, and include them in the curriculum, even in degree programmes that did not traditionally employ them. The experience and data universities share clearly show that internships help regional companies recruit quality employees and bring job security to students; for example, 50 per cent of the students placed under the Industry Liaison Programme of the University of Nicosia have been offered permanent work contracts at the host organisations.

Besides opening up the placement bank platforms and internship counselling services at individual partner universities to all students in the alliance, NEOLAiA has also designed two new international internship formats: first, 'We-start-you-up' shadowing placements in new and innovative companies, boosting students' entrepreneurial competences and encouraging them to consider their own business plans, coordinated by Stefan cel Mare University in Suceava (Romania); and second, traineeships for regional leadership, coordinated by Ostrava University (Czech Republic), exploring leadership practices in institutions and organisations that contribute to regional development, such as municipal and regional authorities, innovation centres, non-profit organisations, and the NEOLAiA universities themselves. The added value of NEOLAiA internships is in the guarantee provided by the universities of selecting suitable companies and institutions in their regions, and in the international work experience from diverse European regions that students will gain.

ENTREPRENEURIAL TRAINING

While all member universities had well-developed internship support before joining forces in the alliance, the choice of programmes in entrepreneurship and knowledge and technology transfer support had been relatively uneven. Some universities have had long-term experience, with entrepreneurial schooling integrated into the curriculum and a number of university spin-off companies (e.g. the University of Salerno with 44 spin-offs supported by the UNISA Incubator). Other universities have shared their experience from regular extra-curricular training in entrepreneurship and knowledge transfer competences (e.g. summer schools in entrepreneurship at the University in Suceava; the University of Tours and their PEPITE Centre-Val de Loire programme; the University of Nicosia's participation in the Beyond Pre-Accelerator programme of Junior Achievement Cyprus; BizOU start-up workshops at Ostrava University; or the University of Salerno and their Student Entrepreneurship Hub).

Many universities have recently launched new strategies and activities to boost entrepreneurial skills and knowledge and technology transfer ambitions in students as well as academics (e.g. Master Plan for Knowledge Transfer, Employability and Entrepreneurship at the University of Jaén; a PhD course 'Utilisation of Research' at Örebro University; and Start Cup Campania at the University of Salerno). The aim of NEOLAiA collaboration in this field is to pool resources and build new capacities together. We are thus launching a joint international training and mentorship programme and an international Summer Academy to introduce NEOLAiA students to the European arena of contexts and practices in entrepreneurship education and enterprise.

CONNECTING STUDENTS WITH JOB OPPORTUNITIES

The knowledge and competences we try to help our students acquire and improve only become employability skills when they are required and appreciated by employers and open the doors to students' desired professional careers. NEOLAiA universities thus make sure they are connected to the job market, providing students with up-to-date information on demand and facilitating their search for jobs. All universities run online platforms with job offers, preferably platforms which enable both employers and students to present their profiles and find matches, such as the Job Teaser platform for the students of the University of Ostrava. The key task for NEOLAiA is to open these platforms to international students from partner universities and make the job offers accessible across the alliance. Authentic experiences of meeting reality in person are provided by career festivals and fairs inviting companies, institutions, and non-profit organisations to the campus. Local as well as international students can talk with employers, listen to presentations, take an active part in job dating, and apply for jobs on the spot.

NEOLAIA ALUMNI STAY ON BOARD

University alumni's professional careers are living proof of the employability of university graduates, and universities cherish their reports on the positions they achieve as well as their feedback on the knowledge, skills and training that they see as valuable parts of higher education. NEOLAiA universities keep in touch with their alumni, not only to survey their views of university studies, but also to introduce the alumni to the current students to provide advice, challenge and insight and help them take the first important steps after university with confidence and enthusiasm (as, for example, in the Örebro University Mentor Match programme).

Alumni entrepreneurs are involved in entrepreneurial training that is designed as a joint venture of the NEOLAiA alliance: they are connected with current students wishing to start their entrepreneurial journey by finding internships in alumni's start-ups or fully fledged companies, or to be invited for shadowing stays and mentorship. Both students and alumni can be in touch with all the universities in the alliance, building further on their cultural awareness, language, and intercultural communication skills.

Alumni are not just giving, though, they are also supported: they can choose re-skilling or upskilling courses in the lifelong learning offer, and join the Focus Academy courses to get new micro-credentials to meet the job market's fast-changing needs. Integrating younger students with returning students, who have work experience between their degree and the new programme, contributes to the diversity of student groups in which junior students can then benefit from the experience of their mature colleagues. Alumni can also benefit from career counselling, job search platforms, and career festivals and fairs, which remain open to all graduates during their professional life. Engaging alumni in all these activities is a way for them to gain new skills and build their transnational networks, something that will hopefully be reflected in their long-term employability, or job security.

CONCLUSIONS

Contemporary society is developing and changing fast and the needs and demands of the labour market are dynamically evolving alongside this. By pooling the resources across the alliance and joining forces to expand the study, training, and coaching opportunities NEOLAiA students are offered, we hope to help students as well as alumni to navigate successfully through their studies and professional careers. We also want students to feel welcome across a range of European regions, embrace life-long learning, and land jobs which will be beneficial to society as well as bring them happiness and satisfaction. Guiding students on their career paths together, the NEOLAiA alliance aims to boost their employability in the European as well as in global job markets.

REFERENCES

European Commission (n.d.a), *About the European Universities initiative*. Available at: https://education.ec.europa.eu/sr/node/1525 (accessed: 18 January 2023).

European Commission (n.d.b), *Council Recommendation on Key Competences for Lifelong Learning*. Available at: https://education.ec.europa.eu/focus-topics/improving-quality-equity/key-competences-lifelong-learning (accessed: 18 January 2023).

NEOLAiA (n.d.), *A high quality European Universities proposal recognised by the European Commission*. Available at: https://neolaiacampus.eu/ (accessed: 18 January 2023).

REFLECTION

From a French graduate

I always wanted to spend some of my undergraduate degree studying in another country. I thought that would be an exciting experience, and I also thought it would help me get a job in a multinational company, which I knew I wanted.

I spent one term studying in England. At first I struggled with the language. I thought that I was quite fluent in English, but it was very different learning in a different language to my native language. There was a lot of technical terminology which I found difficult to translate. I also struggled to settle in, I was the only exchange student on my course and everyone else had already studied together for two years, and therefore it was difficult to enter into a friendship group.

However, I did it and I succeeded. I have now got a job in a multinational company. At my interview I spoke a lot about the experiences I had in England, and how that had developed me. I am sure that made a difference and helped me get my job.

PART X

Institutional response

32. Widening the reach of employability skills development

James Forde

INTRODUCTION

In September 2020, the University of Huddersfield launched a brand-new initiative: the Global Professional Award (GPA). The GPA is a three-year programme that focuses on the following key themes: Employability and Enterprise; Wellbeing; and Global and Social Awareness. Most full-time undergraduates studying a first degree are automatically enrolled onto this centrally delivered programme, thereby bucking popular trends within higher education institutions (HEIs) for voluntary employability-based programmes or for embedding employability skill-building within existing academic curricula. Students attend workshops each term with dedicated GPA trainers, and they have access to a range of self-directed learning materials to supplement their learning. To progress each year, students must pass a range of assessment items and develop a portfolio of experiential learning opportunities. If a student meets all the requirements of the Award, they also receive a Level 5 Award in Leadership and Management from the Chartered Management Institute (CMI).

The GPA has been devised to meet a number of aims at the University of Huddersfield, in line with its 2025 Strategy. This includes a desire to see a significant increase in the number of Huddersfield graduates gaining highly skilled employment. While the UK HE sector as a whole experienced a drop in this area in 2018–19, the impact on Huddersfield was particularly pronounced, with 65 per cent of its graduates obtaining highly skilled employment in this year (down from 72 per cent in 2017–18). Secondly, the university has a significant proportion of first-in-family (FiF) undergraduates — 56 per cent of full-time undergraduates at the university in 2020–21 did not have a parent who had attended an HEI as a part of their own education. As has been documented extensively, FiF learners can face significant barriers to achieving both academic success and successful graduate outcomes, particularly compared with peers who have university-educated family members (Stebleton and Soria, 2012). A key strategic aim of the university is to provide targeted support for these students both during and after university. Finally, a significant proportion of Huddersfield undergraduates might be considered non-traditional students, and these learners can also be susceptible to a range of challenges to building the skills and knowledge necessary for academic and career success (Wong and Chiu, 2019).

This chapter outlines in more detail what the GPA programme is, and how it aims to meet the needs of its undergraduate cohorts. The purpose of this chapter is to provide a case study that can contribute to growing scholarship on the approaches HEIs can take to enhance students' chances for future success by addressing directly the barriers certain cohorts face as graduates. The chapter summarises some key learnings so far from the programme that may be of interest to other HEIs that are reconsidering their approach to employability skill-building.

CLOSING THE SKILLS-DEVELOPMENT GAP

In the initial design of the programme, the GPA team looked to a number of approaches adopted widely by HEIs to develop skills and capabilities for their graduates, with a particular focus on the mechanisms used to support non-traditional students. Students from these backgrounds can face significant barriers when competing for highly skilled employment opportunities, particularly in comparison with their more socially privileged peers, who tend to be able to better demonstrate to employers that they have the necessary soft skills to accompany the technical knowledge acquired through their degrees (Bathmaker et al., 2013). A key aim for the GPA, therefore, is for the award to be as inclusive as possible, with students from all backgrounds acquiring the key employability skills that are increasingly desired by employers.

GPA workshops, self-directed materials and assignments are designed with all undergraduates in mind, and workshops are framed in a way to inform students of how such skills are desirable across industries and disciplines. Crucially, self-reflection of these skills and knowledge is a central component of all workshops and assignments. This adheres to the growing evidence that students need to view reflective practice as a continuous process, rather than a one-off event or a skill to be developed at the end of their university experience (Reid et al., 2021). The GPA programme, therefore, provides students with the time and space to reflect on the importance of the skills developed, how they can improve further, and how they can apply these skills in their desired career paths.

Developing key employability skills can be significantly enhanced by the undertaking of experiential learning opportunities at university (such as placements or internships) or by exploring other extra-curricular activities such as volunteering. Non-traditional learners, such as those that are prominent within Huddersfield's undergraduate cohort, tend to be less inclined or able to participate in these activities, despite these opportunities enhancing students' employability and social skills, and as a result becoming increasingly sought-after additions to graduate CVs by employers (Hinchliffe and Jolly, 2011). Students from middle-class backgrounds are more likely to engage with these opportunities, as their less-privileged peers are either unable financially to participate in unpaid opportunities, or may focus more attention on obtaining academic success (Bathmaker et al., 2013).

To ensure Huddersfield students from all backgrounds are provided with the best chance for success as graduates, a strategic priority of the GPA is to provide students with as many opportunities as possible to engage with extra-curricular activities (ECAs) throughout their time at university, and by motivating students to undertake these. This motivation is provided by the inclusion of GPA electives as part of the robust requirements to pass each year of the programme, with students needing to undertake a minimum of 15 hours of ECAs each year. Studies have indicated that non-traditional students can be less inclined to participate in traditional (i.e. university-based) ECAs, but that these students may in fact be developing skills within alternative ECAs, such as religious or family-based activities (Stuart et al., 2011).

GPA students, therefore, are largely able to choose how they make up these hours, as long as the opportunities undertaken meet the learning outcome to provide personal or professional development. This flexibility allows students to view extra-curricular skills development through a wider lens than university-based offerings that may not speak to their interests or beliefs. Central to the electives component of the programme is the written reflection students provide about the opportunities undertaken. By asking students to consider what skills they gained from the opportunity, how they applied pre-existing knowledge in the role, and how they will further develop these skills and knowledge in the future, the electives portfolio helps to build students' social and cultural capital in a very tangible sense, and it demonstrates to learners the value of continued engagement with these opportunities throughout their studies and as early-career graduates.

THE HUDDERSFIELD WAY

In addition to the GPA's focus on skills development and experiential learning opportunities, a number of approaches that deviated from more widespread HEI programmes were necessary to meet the needs of Huddersfield's undergraduate cohorts and to aim to have an immediate impact on these students. One such approach is the weaving of interlinking themes that may traditionally be delivered through separate learning platforms. The first theme—Employability and Enterprise—is a central focus, building the capabilities of students and enhancing their prospects for future career success. But in the programme design, students and other stakeholders made it clear that it was necessary to think broader than this in terms of the support students need during their time at university and as graduates.

Therefore, a second theme of Wellbeing focuses on introducing students to key concepts and strategies for supporting their own wellbeing, and that of their peers, both at university and in the workforce. By doing so, the programme aims to help students to support themselves during difficult periods of their studies and to equip them with the knowledge and tools to have sustainable and fulfilling career paths. It is important to note that this work in no way aims to replace the in-depth and crucial work of wellbeing professionals at the university. Rather, content is developed in consultation with these experts to determine suitable introductory concepts and pathways.

The third theme to be woven into the GPA is Global and Social Awareness, something that is a crucial addition to help the university to meet its strategic aims, particularly in the support of its diverse learning communities. This theme also helps students to enhance their status as well-rounded graduates who have an understanding of issues beyond the knowledge delivered as part of their degrees. Through workshops, self-directed resources and targeted experiential learning opportunities, the GPA addresses topics such as the UN's Global Goals, equality, diversity and inclusion, intercultural effectiveness, and workplace rights and ethics. A main focus of these learning resources is skills development, but by framing this development within subjects such as these, the GPA enriches students' awareness of key societal, political and economic issues, as well as their intercultural understanding. By doing so, the programme aims to enhance students' employability (Jones, 2013), as well as possibly broadening students' horizons in terms of what opportunities they may like to explore in the future.

In addition to interweaving these key themes into the programme, staff members and students responsible for the initial design of the GPA expressed a clear desire for students to receive a tangible output on completion of the programme, ideally one that would be desirable for employers. As a result, the programme has been designed in consultation with the Chartered Management Institute (CMI), an internationally recognised body with over 75 years of experience delivering management and leadership training. By completing the GPA, students receive a CMI Level 5 Award in Leadership and Management, as well as access to CMI's vast library of management training resources. By introducing students to the CMI throughout the programme, and by equipping them with a leadership qualification at the end, the programme aims to build confidence among students that leadership and management positions can be attainable regardless of learners' social or economic backgrounds. Through its partnership with CMI, the GPA demonstrates to learners that the development of leadership skills can be a unique selling point in the job market for graduates of all disciplines, regardless of whether a management position is a desired end point for them.

The final approach to the design and delivery of the GPA, that may differ from other HEI offerings, is the fact that the award is a three-year programme in which eligible students are automatically enrolled. By delivering the programme over three years, the GPA aims to provide a scaffolded and sustainable approach to students' learning, with a cyclical approach to the themes introduced and often revisited the following year. The delivery over three years, as opposed to a semester-long programme or one-off workshops at various times in the year, allows students the time and space to reflect regularly on the skills and experiences obtained within the programme and in their academic courses.

By automatically enrolling students, the programme aims to engage as many students as possible to benefit from the GPA. Voluntary programmes can be a resource-efficient method of giving opportunities to students to build their capacity as skilled employees, but such programmes can struggle with low participation among non-traditional students, with more socially privileged peers more inclined to utilise university opportunities to enhance their employability (Bathmaker et al., 2013). Embedding employability skills and knowledge-building within academic curricula can have demonstrable impacts for learners, but such an approach can be resource heavy and time intensive to work institution wide. Through the GPA, the University of Huddersfield outlines the development of employability and wellbeing skills as a learning outcome and expectation of all its students, rather than relying on students to volunteer their time. In doing so, the GPA is inclusive of as many students as possible by immediately including all students within its enrolment. This approach does not, of course, mean that every student in fact engages with the programme. But it has allowed for a wide reach to date, with over half of all enrolled undergraduates having attended at least one workshop, and with over 10,000 workshop attendees in total over an 18-month period.

Full engagement with the programme is also encouraging, with approximately one in four students having met the complete requirements of the year one module in 2020–21. A university-wide approach also enables workshops to be scheduled with students across different schools and disciplines, enabling interaction and knowledge exchange between learners from different backgrounds. Student feedback has been positive about this aspect of the programme in particular, because it has pushed students out of their comfort zones and introduced them to different ways of thinking about the topics introduced within the workshops.

CONCLUSION

Inevitably, the approach adopted by the University of Huddersfield has presented a number of challenges in terms of the management and delivery of the GPA programme. Although the time required to complete the programme translates to approximately one hour per week during term time, some students and academic staff have raised concerns about additional demands on students' time and workloads. Related to this, but a separate challenge in its own right, is requiring students to engage with experiential learning opportunities or extra-curricular activities in every year of the programme. In addition to the demand on students' time that this brings, this also requires students to be aware of what activities are available both within and external to the university setting, and it requires confidence-building within some students that these opportunities are attainable. A final challenge is motivating students over three years to engage fully and complete the programme—a particular challenge in the final year of their degrees when academic demands are often at their peak.

But these challenges are not insurmountable, and HEIs interested in adopting a similar approach to the GPA may be interested in the following solutions. To begin with, targeted communication to students from the very start of their degrees is imperative so that they understand the minimal time requirements of the programme. GPA trainers, alongside GPA student ambassadors, attend university induction days on a course-by-course basis to deliver this information first hand to students, and this has proved to be effective.

Further to this, assignment deadlines are now placed early in the academic year with no penalties for late submissions, and all workshops are recorded for students who are absent. This allows flexibility around students' academic commitments and is something that has been received particularly favourably in end of year evaluations. As an institutional strategic priority, Students' Unions, professional services and academic colleagues should work together to encourage students to engage with extra-curricular activities. The GPA team works closely with these important stakeholders to identify opportunities available to students, and these are promoted regularly throughout each term and in workshops, including via a dedicated webpage to direct and inform students of such activities. Course leaders are regularly consulted to understand what experiential opportunities students already undertake as part of their degrees that would align with the aims of the GPA.

The aim should not be to add additional work or hurdles for students, particularly those who are already meeting the requirements of the award. Therefore, GPA trainers are invited to present to cohorts of students to explain to them how the experiential learning undertaken in their degree can contribute to the award through the reflection piece of the GPA electives. Although progress has been made in this area, encouraging take-up of ECAs, particularly for students less inclined to do so, continues to present a challenge and will be a priority area of focus for the foreseeable future.

Finally, to encourage motivation throughout the three years, resources in the team have been allocated to ensure motivational communications are sent each year to students engaging with the programme. Equally important, targeted interventions are made each term with students who have not engaged sufficiently. Provision within the structure of the team is also available for students to book one-to-one virtual appointments with GPA trainers for further support. Whether these measures will translate to sustained engagement and completion remains to be seen and will be reported on in future publications.

The Global Professional Award is a young programme with a number of unanswered questions. As with similar programmes across HEIs, these may be summarised as: how many students will actually engage and complete the programme over three years? What impact will this have on students' immediate futures, particularly in the workplace? And is this approach the one that students as graduates will reflect on as having met their needs? It is therefore imperative that programmes such as these constantly, and honestly, evaluate and reflect on the work undertaken. Working in partnership with students, alumni, university staff, students' unions and employers is a fundamental aspect of the programme's aims to be relevant and impactful and to evolve with students' needs and the ever-shifting socio-political landscape for HEIs.

REFERENCES

Bathmaker, A. M., Ingram, N. and Waller, R. (2013), 'Higher education, social class and the mobilisation of capitals: recognising and playing the game', *British Journal of Sociology of Education*, 34(5–6), 723–743.

Hinchliffe, G. W. and Jolly, A. (2011), 'Graduate identity and employability', *British Educational Research Journal*, 37(4), 563–584.

Jones, E. (2013), 'Internationalization and employability: the role of intercultural experiences in the development of transferable skills', *Public Money & Management*, 33(2), 95–104.

Reid, A., Richards, A. and Willox, D. (2021), 'Connecting experiences to employability through a meaning-making approach to learning', *Journal of Teaching and Learning for Graduate Employability*, 12(2), 99–113.

Stebleton, M. J. and Soria, K. M. (2012), 'Breaking down barriers: academic obstacles of first-generation students at research universities', *Learning Assistance Review*, 17(2), 7–19.

Stuart, M., Lido, C., Morgan, J., Solomon, L. and May, S. (2011), 'The impact of engagement with extracurricular activities on the student experience and graduate outcomes for widening participation populations', *Active Learning in Higher Education*, 12(3), 203–215.

Wong, B. and Chiu, Y. L. T. (2019), '"Swallow your pride and fear": the educational strategies of high-achieving non-traditional university students', *British Journal of Sociology of Education*, 40(7), 868–882

REFLECTION

From a Speech and Language Therapist

I qualified as a Speech and Language Therapist (SLT) in September 2020 in the midst of the pandemic, with a longstanding aspiration to work for the National Health Service (NHS), ideally in a hospital setting. My university provided me with everything I needed to embark on this journey of finding my first job as a newly qualified SLT. From helping me develop the skills and knowledge I needed to enter this field, to arranging a series of lectures delivered by recruiters, alumni students, and experienced professors on the NHS application and interview process. In fact, we had a whole week dedicated to 'careers'.

However, the thorough preparation did not translate to fast results. The NHS had reduced scope to prioritise recruitment in 2020, particularly recruitment of newly qualified healthcare professionals like myself, who needed additional training, support, and guidance from NHS staff for the first few months of employment. These NHS staff were unlikely to have the time or energy to provide this level of training, amidst fighting in the frontline against Covid-19. This seemed to contribute to a reduced supply of jobs being advertised. Meanwhile the demand for jobs was arguably rising, with most SLT graduates across multiple universities in the UK qualifying at the same time, with fewer opportunities to take a gap year or work abroad, due to travel restrictions. The low supply and high demand cycle created by the pandemic meant that it took significant patience and perseverance to find employment as an SLT in a London hospital.

33. An integrated institutional approach to employability

Dino Willox, Anna Richards and Madelaine-Marie Judd

INTRODUCTION

Globalisation and massification of higher education, coupled with digital and technological automation, means that graduates entering the workforce must be able to articulate their value to employers. The technical knowledge that their degree has provided is no longer sufficient to guarantee employment; graduates must be able to stand out from the crowd to demonstrate their employability (Donald et al., 2018; Healy, 2015; Knight and Yorke, 2003; McKinsey, 2017; PricewaterhouseCoopers, 2017; Sander, 2017). Similarly, while graduates must be demonstrably more than just their degree, universities must be more than just knowledge transmitters; they must prepare graduates for uncertain futures to the satisfaction of students, employers, government, and themselves (Jackson and Bridgstock, 2019; Kinash et al., 2016; Small et al., 2018). Whilst it is uncontested that a degree is no longer sufficient for graduates to secure employment, it is contestable that universities are the sole purveyors of such a guarantee.

In the Australian context, the Federal Government, industry, and policymakers are placing greater emphasis on universities to guarantee employment outcomes for graduates (Tomlinson, 2012). A raft of recent legislative changes in Australia continue to alter the very nature of universities, with the "distinctive purpose" of universities now legally requiring "engagement with industry and the local community to enable graduates to thrive in the workforce" (Higher Education Support Amendment Job-Ready Graduates Supporting Regional and Remote Students Act (Cth) 2020 (part 2, item 3)). Two of the most recent legislative changes include performance-based funding (PBF) which requires universities to "achieve the best possible graduate outcomes" (Australian Government, Department of Education, 2022), and the "Job-Ready Graduates Package" (Australian Government, Department of Education, 2020), which promises an increase in funding from A$18 billion in 2020 to A$20 billion by 2024. What these legislative instruments have in common is that they both explicitly tie to graduate employment outcomes and signal from the Federal Government the role of universities in producing employable graduates to positively impact economic development (Cranmer, 2006; Small et al., 2018).

Employability, however, is more than employment and while there is a relationship between the two, it is not causal. There is a difference between the existence of a job (economics), being able to secure a job (recruitment), and being able to do that job well (employability). The legislative instruments that universities now find themselves beholden to slip effortlessly between employability and employment – carelessly equating one with the other – and the responsibility for both is placed firmly with universities, albeit in partnership with industry. Governments, it seems, have abrogated any responsibility for the economic landscape within which education and industry coexist, and positioned employment as a critical success factor not only of graduates, but also of universities themselves. Placing responsibility for graduate employment solely in the hands of educators appears to enact the logical fallacy *post hoc ergo proctor hoc*: developing student employability will result in employed graduates.

Nonetheless, to be effective in this landscape universities must steer a careful path between the short-termism of government funding based on employment, and the necessarily developmental and educational approach to employability. This chapter describes how one university in Australia has navigated this path, outlining the iterative enactment of an employability framework from initial inception, implementation, and refinement, to the current reimagining that draws on transition pedagogy to ensure continued currency and impact in the employability articulation and value transfer space.

A WHOLE-OF-INSTITUTION APPROACH TO EMPLOYABILITY DEVELOPMENT

The University of Queensland (UQ) is a research-intensive institution with six faculties housing over 30 schools, eight research institutes, more than 6,500 staff, and over 53,000 students. Staff responsible for enhancing student employability are based across schools, faculties and central units. The co-authors of this chapter are based within a central unit, Student Enrichment and Employability Development (SEED), which is responsible for coordinating and managing a range of experiential learning experiences and related educational workshops through which students reflect upon and realise their employability development across curricular, co-curricular and extra-curricular experiences.

Given the complexity of the university, a strategic approach to student employability needed to be discipline-agnostic and able to be enacted in discipline-specific and context-relevant ways. The resulting institution-wide framework approach was developed under the proviso that it must be both simple enough to be easily recognisable by multiple stakeholders, yet sophisticated enough to be applied across a complex landscape.

The grounding of this approach lay in a clear definition of what employability should be. Shaped by the uncertainty of future needs and expectations, it was clear that the focus must be on developing agility and resilience in students to help them deal with uncertain futures (Black et al., 2016; Foundation for Young Australians, 2016; McKinsey, 2017; PricewaterhouseCoopers, 2015). Critical to achieve this are the capability and capacity to reflect on, and learn, from lifelong and life-wide experiences.

The definition was founded on two leading approaches to employability: the "Understanding; Skills; Efficacy beliefs; Metacognition" or USEM model (Knight and Yorke, 2002) and the CareerEDGE model (Dacre Pool and Sewell, 2007). Both emphasise the importance of self-efficacy and require the individual to reflect upon their experiences to unlock the value through a process of meaning-making (Boud et al., 1993; Jarvis, 2006; Kolb, 1984; Park, 2010).

By foregrounding the self-reflective learning experience as the critical component, the framework emphasised that it is not simply the activity or experience that matters, but what is learnt from it. The aim is to facilitate learning from experiences through assigning significance to the experience and interpreting it in ways that support expansion or transformation of existing perspectives and capabilities (Merriam and Clark, 1993).

The framework relied on the reflective process (situation, effect, action, learning (SEAL)) developed in partnership with students and the broader employability community of academic and professional staff. Both the framework (Figure 33.1) and the SEAL self-reflection method draw on the principles of experiential and transformative learning theory (Kolb, 1984; Mezirow, 2000). Together, they enable students to translate their learnings from curricular, co-curricular, and extra-curricular experiences into employability development.

Once the theoretical foundation, framework, and self-reflection methodology were established, an embedded collaborative model was co-created in partnership with faculties. Collaborative agreements with each faculty enabled implementation of the framework, taking into consideration relevant industry needs, existing operational strengths, and student cohort expectations, resulting in the design and delivery of tailored services that were fit for purpose.

This model enhanced the relevance of programmes and experiences that were designed and delivered with, by, and for both students and industry, ultimately leading to greater reach and uptake. Discipline-specific and context-relevant initiatives became fundamental to the success of both the

| Awareness | Experience | Learning | Transfer |

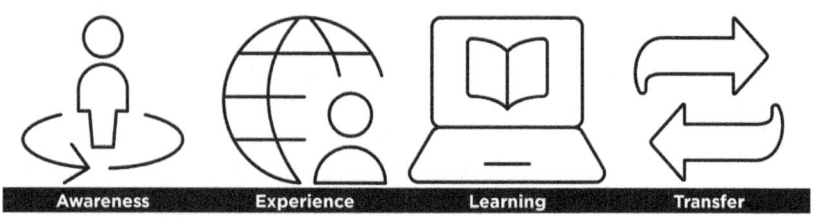

Source: Authors' own.

Figure 33.1   The UQ Employability Framework

model and the overarching framework of the institution, improving the student experience and employability development through a combination of conceptual consistency and cohort relevance. This holistic strategic approach was recognised as best practice across the Asia Pacific through a sector-wide Embedding Employability Exchange Initiative, led by Advance HE, Higher Ed Services, and Online Peer Solutions.

Over three years, UQ invested almost A$19 million in this collaborative model, including over A$12 million in direct funding to students. This resulted in over 7,000 students accessing more than 9,000 enrichment experiences, and 40,000 students undertaking almost 65,000 work-integrated learning (WIL) experiences. This facilitated a strategic shift in organisational mindset, elevating awareness of the importance and impact of self-reflection as a critical component of employability development, and resulted in recognition as an international leader in student employability across the sector and beyond.

The next phase of development coincided with the advent of further changes in government policy. The 2020 Job-Ready Graduates Package of higher education reforms placed greater focus on measurable outcomes (employment) and directly linked funding to universities through the National Priorities and Industry Linkage Fund (NPILF). The NPILF allocates block grants to universities to help engage industry to produce job-ready graduates, with a focus on increasing access to innovative WIL opportunities, on science, technology, engineering, mathematics (STEM)-skilled graduates and their employment outcomes, and on partnerships with industry. Having established the fundamental importance of experiential learning, consideration was given to ensuring that graduates were able to articulate their value to industry and transfer their self-reflective practice into the workforce.

Recognising that success in this economic ecosystem was beyond the control of any single entity, the approach was to focus on the part that education plays. The transfer stage of the employability framework was foregrounded through a shared language of value creation and transfer and the application of transition pedagogy.

THE NEXT FRONTIER FOR EMPLOYABILITY: APPLYING TRANSITION PEDAGOGY AND A THIRD-GENERATION APPROACH

In order to centre employability as "everyone's business", an integrated and holistic approach is vital (Coates, 2005; Kift et al., 2010; Krause et al., 2005). One such approach for tackling institution-wide transformation is the third-generation approach, as defined by Kift (2009: 1): "This optimal approach will only occur when first generation co-curricular and second-generation curricular approaches are brought together in a comprehensive, integrated, and coordinated strategy that delivers a seamless FYE [first year experience] across an entire institution."

Transition pedagogy can serve as a powerful mechanism to achieve broader cultural transformation within an institution. According to Kift et al. (2010: 11), transition pedagogy can be defined as an "intentional first year curriculum design that carefully scaffolds, mediates and supports first year learning for contemporary heterogeneous cohorts". The strategies that underpin transition pedagogy include:

1. curriculum that engages students in learning;
2. proactive and timely access to learning and life support;
3. intentionally fostering a sense of belonging;
4. sustainable academic–professional partnerships (Kift et al., 2010).

The Employability Framework was developed cognisant of these strategies and pedagogy. Table 33.1 provides a high-level overview of how the Employability Framework aligns with the strategies that underpin the third-generation approach to transition pedagogy.

The focus of transition pedagogy in the employability context relates to preparing students throughout their studies to successfully transition *out* of university and contribute positively to our local and global communities through their engagement with society.

Applying transition pedagogy to the journey from student to the workforce focuses on providing students with timely and relevant employability and career development information and support throughout their studies, creating opportunities for students to engage in experiential learning activities, and empowering them to become self-reflective practitioners.

Table 33.1 Alignment of the Employability Framework to the third-generation approach to transition pedagogy strategies

Strategy	Alignment of the Framework to the strategies	Enactment
Curriculum that engages students in learning	The Employability Framework has a specific focus on learning and self-reflection	Embedding the SEAL self-reflection process in experiential learning activities in curriculum, and in extra-curricular activities
Proactive and timely access to learning and life support	Students can engage in the Framework throughout their student journey and activities, workshops and offerings are scaffolded to the Framework depending upon the learning outcomes	Providing career development support at all stages of a student's employability journey, through a range of accessible supports and resources
Intentionally fostering a sense of belonging	All offerings that align to the Framework seek to foster a sense of belonging to the university community, local or global community, or professional community	Supporting students in the development of their professional identities
Sustainable academic–professional partnerships		Connecting academic staff to industry partners and supporting collaborative delivery of both curriculum and extra-curricular activities

As outlined in Table 33.1, transition pedagogy for employability is demonstrated in the following ways across the institution:

1. Curriculum that engages students in learning:
   The SEAL self-reflection process is embedded in experiential learning activities in curriculum, such as WIL placements, in extra-curricular activities such as research projects and global experiences, and the degree-long UQ Employability Award requires students to reflect on all submitted experiences. Workshops to support students to use the SEAL process and unpack their experiences are also provided.

   The learning from this reflective practice supports the development of a student's professional identity and enables students to understand and articulate their unique value. It also reinforces the importance of self-reflection as a career management tool.

2. Proactive and timely access to learning and life support:
   Career development support is available at all stages of a student's employability journey – recognising that students come to study with different life experiences (e.g., varied exposure to work environments when they enter study) and a linear career development pathway is not appropriate for all.

The UQ My Career Adviser online tool allows students to access "just in time" and relevant support, regardless of their stage of study.
3. Intentionally fostering a sense of belonging:
Through connection to industry partners, professional communities and the provision of industry-based experiences, students start to construct their professional identities from early in their degree. Building this identity and forging professional networks fosters in the students a sense of how they will contribute to the wider community through work and consolidate their place outside the university.
4. Sustainable academic–professional partnerships:
Building staff capacity is critical to supporting students' employability development. Connecting academic staff to industry partners and supporting collaborative delivery of both curriculum and extra-curricular activities familiarises students with industry and professional expectations, contextualises academic learning, and makes content relevant and relatable.

This approach to employability development accepts that experiential learning (both inside and beyond the curriculum) forms the basis of significant employability development. Further, that self-reflective practice allows students to identify their capabilities, and both understand and articulate the value that they offer to the workforce.

This recognition of personal value, in conjunction with a defined sense of professional identity, enables students to articulate their value and potential more confidently in recruitment situations, as well as understand how and where they can put their capabilities to use in specific work environments.

CONCLUSION

Graduate outcomes have retained, and gained, prominence as a central issue within higher education. In the Australian context, legislative changes, and correlative changes to funding streams, have highlighted the need for academic and professional staff members within institutions to work in partnership for the betterment of student and graduate employability. As the literature has suggested, strategic, whole-of-institution programmes and approaches are required to successfully and meaningfully provide adequate support for heterogeneous students (Coates, 2005; Kift et al., 2010; Krause et al., 2005).

This chapter shows how a whole-of-institution approach to employability development, based on a discipline-agnostic framework, can be made discipline-specific and industry-relevant through a collaborative delivery model. Further, this can be enhanced to meet the continuing changes to expectations from governments and funding bodies through the application of transition pedagogy, empowering students to articulate their employability and value as they transition from university to the workforce.

REFERENCES

Australian Government, Department of Education (2020), *Job-Ready Graduates Package*. Available at: https://www.education.gov.au/job-ready (accessed: 23 January 2023).

Australian Government, Department of Education (2022), *Performance-Based Funding for the Commonwealth Grant Scheme*. Available at: https://www.dese.gov.au/higher-education-funding/performancebased-funding-commonwealth-grant-scheme#:~:text=Performance-Based%20Funding%20for%20the%20Commonwealth%20Grant%20Scheme%20As,places%20at%202017%20levels%20for%202018%20and%202019 (accessed: 19 January 2023).

Black, L., Furnell, S. and Tye, G. (2016), *Future of Work Whitepaper 2016*. Brisbane: RedEye. Available at: https://www.voced.edu.au/content/ngv%3A73895 (accessed: 19 January 2023).

Boud, David, Cohen, R. and Walker, D. (eds) (1993), *Using Experience for Learning*. Buckingham: Society for Research into Higher Education and Open University Press.

Coates, H. (2005), "The value of student engagement for higher education quality assurance", *Quality in Higher Education*, 11(1), 25–36. https://doi.org/10.1080/13538320500074915.

Cranmer, S. (2006), "Enhancing graduate employability: best intentions and mixed outcomes", *Studies in Higher Education*, 31(2), 169–184. https://doi.org/10.1080/03075070600572041.

Dacre Pool, L. and Sewell, P. (2007), "The key to employability: developing a practical model of graduate employability", *Education & Training*, 49(4), 277–289. https://doi.org/10.1108/00400910710754435.

Donald, W. E., Ashleigh, M. J. and Baruch, Y. (2018), "Students' perceptions of education and employability: facilitating career transition from higher education into the labour market", *Career Development International*, 23(5), 513–540. https://doi.org/10.1108/CDI-09-2017-0171.

Foundation for Young Australians (2016), *The New Basics: Big data reveals the skills young people need for the New World Order*. Sydney: AlphaBeta. Available at: https://www.fya.org.au/app/uploads/2021/09/The-New-Basics_2016.pdf (accessed: 19 January 2023).

Healy, J. (2015), "Graduating into a weak job market: why so many grads can't find work", *The Conversation*, 28 July. Available at: https://theconversation.com/graduating-into-a-weak-job-market-why-so-many-grads-cant-find-work-45222 (accessed: 19 January 2023).

Higher Education Support Amendment (Job-Ready Graduates Supporting Regional and Remote Students) Act (Cth). 2020.

Jackson, D. and Bridgstock, R. (2019), "Universities don't control the labour market: we shouldn't fund them like they do", *The Conversation*, 8 October. Available at: https://theconversation.com/universities-dont-control-the-labour-market-we-shouldnt-fund-them-like-they-do-124780 (accessed: 19 January 2023).

Jarvis, P. (2006), *Towards a Comprehensive Theory of Human Learning*. Abingdon: Routledge.

Kift, S. (2009), *Articulating a Transition Pedagogy to Scaffold and to Enhance the First Year Student Learning Experience in Australian Higher Education*. Final report for ALTC Senior Fellowship Program.

Kift, S., Nelson K. and Clarke, J. (2010), "A third generation approach to FYE: a case study of policy and practice for the higher education sector", *International Journal of the First Year in Higher Education*, 1(1), 1–20. https://doi.org/10.5204/intjfyhe.v1i1.13.

Kinash, S., Crane, L. H. and Judd, M.-M. (2016), *Good Practice Report: Nurturing Graduate Employability in Higher Education*. Sydney: Australian Government Office for Learning and Teaching.

Knight, P. T. and Yorke, M. (2002), "Employability through the curriculum", *Tertiary Education and Management*, 8(4), 261–276. https://doi.org/10.1080/13583883.2002.9967084.

Knight, P. T. and Yorke, M. (2003), "Employability and good learning in higher education", *Teaching in Higher Education*, 8(1), 3–16. https://doi.org/10.1080/1356251032000052294.

Kolb, D. A. (1984), *Experiential Learning: Experience as the Source of Learning and Development (Vol. 1)*. Englewood Cliffs, NJ: Prentice-Hall.

Krause, K.-L., Hartley, R., James, R. and McInnis, C. (2005), *The First Year Experience in Australian Universities: Findings from a Decade of National Studies*. Canberra, ACT: DEST. Available at: https://www.voced.edu.au/content/ngv%3A11049 (accessed: 19 January 2023).

McKinsey (2017), "Getting ready for the future of work", *McKinsey Quarterly*, 12 September. Available at: https://www.mckinsey.com/business-functions/people-and-organizational-performance/our-insights/getting-ready-for-the-future-of-work (accessed: 19 January 2023).

Merriam, S. B. and Clark, C. (1993), "Learning from life experience: what makes it significant?", *International Journal of Lifelong Education*, 12(2), 129–138. https://doi.org/10.1080/0260137930120205.

Mezirow, J. (2000), *Learning as Transformation: Critical Perspectives on a Theory in Progress*. San Francisco, CA: Jossey-Bass.

Park, C. L. (2010), "Making sense of the meaning literature: an integrative review of meaning making and effects on adjustment to stressful life events", *Psychological Bulletin*, 136(2), 257–301.

PricewaterhouseCoopers (2015), "A smart move: future-proofing Australia's workforce by growing skills in science, technology, engineering and maths (STEM)". Available at: https://www.pwc.com.au/publications/a-smart-move.html (accessed: 19 January 2023).

PricewaterhouseCoopers (2017), "Workforce of the future: the competing forces shaping 2030". Available at: https://www.pwc.com.au/pdf/workforce-of-the-future-the-competing-forces-shaping-2030.pdf (accessed: 19 January 2023).

Sander, E. (2017), "Lack of workers with 'soft skills' demands a shift in teaching", *The Conversation*, 28 February. Available at: https://theconversation.com/lack-of-workers-with-soft-skills-demands-a-shift-in-teaching-73433 (accessed: 19 January 2023).

Small, L., Shacklock, K. and Marchant, T. (2018), "Employability: a contemporary review for higher education stakeholders", *Journal of Vocational Education & Training*, 70(1), 148–166.

Tomlinson, M. (2012), "Graduate employability: a review of conceptual and empirical themes", *Higher Education Policy*, 25(4), 407–431. https://doi.org/10.1057/hep.2011.26.

REFLECTION

From a PhD student

I have a bachelor degree in Mathematics and Biology and a master in Experimental Biology, currently I am completing my PhD in Molecular Biology. I have also been teaching mathematics at a high school for several months, preparing myself to leave the academia. It has become clear over the last few years that the direction I choose will probably not have much to do with where I see myself in the future.

I don't think a PhD in molecular biology will ever be useful to me outside the lab but the research group I have been a part of is worth mentioning regardless of whether or not I continue in this direction. It is a lab dedicated to cutting-edge research. Thanks to the international team, I have been in an English-speaking work environment, which I value immensely and now build on it at an international school. I appreciate the personal and professional qualities of my supervisor, who has been in many ways a role model for me. I have learnt from the team many soft skills applicable across disciplines: the ability to organise work, process information, handle resources, plan and manage one's own projects, or collaborate in a team.

There is a lot science has taught me even for my personal life and relationships. I'd also like to mention the university counseling center: I greatly appreciate self-development activities I participated in and without career counselling I would have had a hard time navigating the confusion when I realised after six years of university study that I was doing something I did not want to do in my life. It was only thanks to my career counselor that I was able to figure out who I am and where I want to go next so that my career makes more sense.

34. A strategic institutional approach to employability

Susan Smith and Emily Huns

POLICY CONTEXT

'We aim to ensure that every student, whatever their background, has a fulfilling experience of higher education that enriches their lives and careers' (Office for Students, 2022).

The UK's Office for Students has firmly articulated that employability and value for money lie at the heart of the contemporary UK higher education experience (Office for Students, 2022). Its regulatory agenda seeks to: set minimum thresholds for progression to employment; narrow gaps in graduate outcomes through monitoring of institutional Access and Participation Plans; and embed employability outcomes into institutional Teaching Excellence Framework (TEF) assessments.

Another influence on university behaviour is university league tables, which have a significant impact on student recruitment (Bradley et al., 2021). All domestic (and some international) league tables adopt algorithms that draw on graduate outcomes data (Christie, 2017) whilst longitudinal employment outcomes (LEO) are also influential (Britton et al., 2020).

Accelerated by the Office for Student's latest strategy (Office for Students, 2022), policy and league tables are shaping employability definitions and the actions of universities to achieve various metrics. Each university has sought its own approach to adapting to this landscape with impacts felt through teaching, learning and assessment practice, extra-curricular student support, business/university relationships and resource allocation.

This chapter offers an example from the University of Sussex – a mid-sized, research-intensive university situated in the south-east of England – of taking a strategic institutional approach to employability, exploring challenges and opportunities.

INSTITUTIONAL CONTEXT

The components of graduate employability are generally agreed in the higher education literature to comprise the following: (applying) disciplinary knowledge, transferable generic skills, emotional regulation, career management skills, self-management and self-efficacy (Römgens et al., 2020). Meanwhile, the 'vehicles' for building student employability capitals (Caballero et al., 2020) are diverse. Each institution's culture, student demographic, setting, community, discipline mix and strengths provide a unique set of opportunities with which to construct these vehicles. So, a university with an arts focus located in a wealthy urban area might establish a street market where students sell their own designs; whilst a law school in an area facing social and economic disadvantage might run student-led pro bono legal services for their community (Alexander and Boothby, 2018). Through these two very different routes, students learn to apply their discipline knowledge whilst further developing soft skills, networks and 'real-world' experience. Collectively, these employability assets provide a launchpad into the job market.

APPROACH

Alongside much of the sector, the University of Sussex has examined its unique set of strengths and has built an employability strategy and provision that reflect that context. The university – known for its modernist architecture on the edge of a rural national park – was founded in 1961, one of the 'plateglass universities', with an emphasis on cross-disciplinary research and teaching. Through the activity of its faculty and Students' Union, Sussex has maintained a tradition of disruptive and experimental interventions and innovations, a tradition which sits comfortably within the modern-day culture of the neighbouring City of Brighton, with its international population and reputation for creativity, digital innovation, open- and eco-mindedness.

Now a multi-faculty university with $c.2,500$ staff and $c.18,500$ students from over 100 countries, the Sussex Strategic Framework 'reimagines the pioneering spirit of the original purpose of our university but does so for new times and a new generation'. In 2020, inspired by this framework – and following a period of co-creation with students, employers, and staff – the senior leadership team launched an institution-wide employability strategy to outline how employability-building at the university could be developed in a uniquely Sussex way. The Sussex World Readiness and Employability Strategy emphasises civic and political engagement, entrepreneurialism and world readiness. The vision is for all Sussex students to graduate 'confident, knowledgeable and skilled, with clear career choices and real opportunities, ready to be citizens of the world – connected, civically and politically engaged, entrepreneurial and creative'. The strategy has five objectives; the 'interconnect' between these five objectives is key to the strategy's impact.

OBJECTIVE 1: EMBEDDING INTO CURRICULA

Embedding employability and entrepreneurship into the curriculum is a means of ensuring that all students, whatever their background, develop the skills, knowledge, and experience needed for a successful transition into the job market on graduation. An embedded approach is particularly important for students who cannot engage with extra-curricular provision due to the need to work to finance their studies, caring responsibilities and other constraints, which reflect the increasingly heterogeneous student base (Bradley et al., 2021). The rationale for embedding is well evidenced (Tibby and Norton, 2020), but the tensions between disciplinary curricula and employability persist, ranging from philosophical objections related to the purpose of higher education to practical hurdles such as timetabling, staff time and skill set.

The approach has been to empower academic schools to embed in ways that work for their discipline cluster, whilst providing tools and resources to guide and support the process. There are three guiding priorities. Students should be given opportunity through the curriculum to: apply their discipline knowledge to real-world contexts; enhance job market-relevant soft skills; and develop career management skills. Career management skills are defined here as the skill set to access and progress within the job market. This includes the skills to explore options, make career decisions, find vacancies, network, and successfully apply for jobs.

To support embedding work, the university's Careers and Entrepreneurship Team has developed an embedding toolkit, which shares principles, practical guidance and best practice examples (internal and sector-wide). Referring to this toolkit, each academic school develops an annual plan to define its priorities and outline actions for the year ahead. Schools are supported in this activity by a dedicated school careers consultant and an academic developer. Good practice is shared across and between academic departments via the toolkit.

The most difficult element to embed proves to be career management skills because these cannot easily be integrated with discipline learning. To date, students have developed these skills via extra-curricular activity provided by the Careers and Entrepreneurship Team. To address the challenge, a collection of learning materials is under design which teaching staff will draw into their modules from the embedding toolkit as appropriate.

The opportunity for infusing the curriculum with real-world experiences that reflect the Sussex context has proved significant. The local employer community participates with enthusiasm, providing faculty with live business challenges for students to address, applying their discipline knowledge and skills. Students work on briefs such as: how to reimagine Council-owned green spaces to enhance community well-being; how to design products from upcycled materials; and how to rethink local policy to reduce the carbon emissions of the visitor economy. Through these activities, students develop confidence in the value of their skills and knowledge to business and community; they become more aware of their career options, develop networks and write better job applications.

> I have gained skills in communication, research, professional writing, time management and so many more. I really liked our team meetings when we could talk about what we had done because it made me feel proud. I am ready to start working now. (Sussex student)

OBJECTIVE 2: COHERENT EXTRA-CURRICULAR SUPPORT

'It is clear that added value can be gained by facilitating students to engage in this process by multiple means and in a range of contexts' (Dalrymple et al., 2021: 40). The extra-curricular employability offer in universities must complement and enhance in-curricular embedding. Alongside a coherent core (and increasingly digital) provision for all students, at Sussex two flagship schemes have been developed: The Sussex Career Lab and the Sussex Entrepreneurship Programme. Again, these programmes embody Sussex context and strengths.

Sussex Career Lab

The Sussex Career Lab is a menu of 800 opportunities across 15 activities to build skills, experience, employer connections and confidence. Students select from a menu of activities stepped by year group. Student choice is important to the popularity of the programme, recognising and celebrating each student's unique starting points, skill set and direction. The programme is open to all, but places are prioritised for under-represented groups, helping to close graduate outcomes gaps. Recognising, in particular, the needs of these under-represented cohorts, activities include: connection to alumni role-models through a career mentoring scheme (Turner, 2014); paid virtual internships with businesses outside the UK; paid in-person internships to businesses (including start-ups) local to the university; paid opportunities to become a student consultant to business; digital skills accelerators; and an inclusive global leadership programme.

> If you're like me and feel as though university is just another step in a path that's clouded and blurry, Career Lab offers a vision of the future. My experience led me

to have the confidence to apply for a job that three months ago I would've thought would not be within my reach because I just didn't have enough experience. (Sussex student)

Sussex Entrepreneurship Programme

The Sussex Entrepreneurship Programme engages $c.$500 students annually. The programme honours the university's tradition of disruptive and experimental interventions. Prioritising social innovation, sustainability and accessibility for under-represented groups, it offers multiple entry points and support for students exploring their entrepreneurial capabilities – from point of curiosity to point of trading and beyond. Activities include inspirational events, hackathons, one-to-one coaching, an annual competition, grants, an accelerator and an incubator. A regular podcast streams interviews with inspiring student entrepreneurs from various backgrounds and at various stages of their journey. At Sussex, the programme is as much about student employability and personal development as it is about new business creation. Whilst a significant number of students register new businesses each year, all participants further develop their entrepreneurial mindset and the skills sought by graduate recruiters across the globe.

> I have a multi-disciplinary education and it's one of the very few times that I have felt actively enabled to go on a journey to not only explore the uniqueness of my academic background but also my life experience. Combined, I think that is a powerful way to support people and ideas. We all have a story to tell and a voice about how we want to make the world better but it's finding that place where your ideas will be listened to and then given a platform. The Sussex entrepreneurship programme was that place for me. The last year has been a life-changing experience and I'll take everything I've learned with me as I go forward. (Sussex student entrepreneur)

OBJECTIVE 3: CO-CREATION

To address the complex challenge of student engagement, particularly of under-represented groups, a team of 300 'student connectors' are hired by the university annually to co-create student support programmes and curriculum content. Connectors are selected from under-represented groups. Staff–student partnership activity has been linked to a variety of individual benefits including motivation and learning (Cook-Sather et al., 2014), sense of belonging (Cook-Sather et al., 2014; Curran and Millard, 2016), improved employability skills (Dickerson et al., 2016), engagement (Curran and Millard, 2016) and student outcomes and retention (Lubicz-Nawrocka and Bovill, 2021). Twenty-five of these connectors work with staff on employability provision.

Connectors were instrumental in design of the Sussex Career Lab and Sussex Entrepreneurship Programme. Some of the most successful engagement has been achieved through student-controlled events, where students set the agenda and run an activity independently, lightly enabled by staff as needed (through funding or other forms of resource). Outcomes of co-creation have been positive with examples including growth in students securing a placement (thanks to peer-to-peer support) and higher levels of academic attainment amongst connectors themselves.

OBJECTIVE 4: DATA-INFORMED DEVELOPMENT

Within an increasingly heterogeneous student body, a one-size-fits-all approach to employability is neither accessible nor equitable. Rather, a nuanced approach is required which balances core learning for everyone with the channelling of the highest-impact interventions (such as funded internships) to target groups to close gaps in outcomes. Identifying these high-impact interventions and target groups requires a complex cross-mapping of datasets, including graduate outcomes, career readiness, engagement and the student record. With datasets often held on different platforms and shaped for different purposes, drawing a clear picture from the data has required a significant development project at Sussex. The work has proved worthwhile, however, as findings have led to more informed decisions around resource allocation with reduced investment in some areas of provision and expansion of others. Further data-driven developments are underway; notably a system to personalise employability messaging to students and a self-service dashboard to improve reporting to staff.

OBJECTIVE 5: EXPANSION OF REAL-WORLD OPPORTUNITIES

One of the findings emerging from the Sussex data development project supports the long-established argument that work-based and work-related experience is one of the strongest predictors of future job market success (Helyer and Lee, 2014). Consequently, this is an area of focused expansion. In the curriculum, some course leaders are giving students the opportunity to work in groups on a live business challenge instead of writing a dissertation; and expansion of year-long in-programme placements is underway. Out of the curriculum, there has been investment in diversifying and scaling fully funded work-based opportunities under The Career Lab banner, prioritising access for under-represented groups. To ensure access for these groups, all opportunities are paid the National Living Wage. To help address the career management skills challenge, activities such as CV and LinkedIn profile-writing are integrated into wrap-around training.

Around half of work-based and work-related opportunities are provided by employers local to the university. Employers may go on to recruit their intern or student consultant on a more permanent basis. Many students seek to stay in Brighton or the south-east on graduation so this regional focus to employer engagement has proven effective in raising student access to local, highly skilled employment opportunities. Similarly, the Sussex Entrepreneurship Programme places fully funded interns with newly registered student start-ups. All of this activity supports the university in its knowledge exchange objectives, closes outcomes gaps for under-represented groups and helps to address geographic inequalities (Office for Students, 2021).

> Last summer our first Sussex intern joined us. She came with an open mind to learning and a willingness to get stuck in. But most importantly what impressed us was that she came willing to share her ideas and opinions which our team and clients really valued. She hit the ground running and we offered her a full-time job at the end of her six weeks. (Local employer)

CONCLUSION

At Sussex, a strategic institutional approach to employability is driving real change in opportunity for students, whilst helping to showcase the university's strengths and spirit. It is raising its regional impact, encouraging smarter use of resources and revealing the power of co-creation in engaging under-represented groups. Whilst the approach has surfaced weaknesses in areas such as business intelligence, and the complexity of embedding employability across diverse curricula, these challenges have often led to constructive dialogue and improved practice. There are signs across the university community that the institutional approach is taking root, and that employability is gradually becoming more integral to thinking, design and delivery.

REFERENCES

Alexander, J. and Boothby, C. (2018), 'Stakeholder perceptions of clinical legal education within an employability context reviewed article', *International Journal of Clinical Legal Education*, 25(3), 53–84.

Bradley, A., Quigley, M. and Bailey, K. (2021), 'How well are students engaging with the careers services at university?', *Studies in Higher Education*, 46(4), 663–676. doi:10.1080/03075079.2019.1647416.

Britton, J., Dearden, L., van der Erve, L. and Waltmann, B. (2020), *The Impact of Undergraduate Degrees on Lifetime Earnings*. Institute for Fiscal Studies. Available at: https://www.ifs.org.uk/publications/14729 (accessed: 23 January 2023).

Caballero, G., Álvarez-González, P. and López-Miguens, M. J. (2020), 'How to promote the employability capital of university students? Developing and validating scales', *Studies in Higher Education*, 45(12), 2634–2652. doi:10.1080/03075079.2020.1807494.

Christie, F. (2017), 'The reporting of university league table employability rankings: a critical review', *Journal of Education and Work*, 30(4), 403–418. doi:10.1080/13639080.2016.1224821.

Cook-Sather, A., Bovill, C. and Felten, P. (2014), *Engaging Students as Partners in Learning and Teaching: A Guide for Faculty*. San Francisco, CA: John Wiley & Sons.

Curran, R. and Millard, L. (2016), 'A partnership approach to developing student capacity to engage and staff capacity to be engaging: opportunities for academic developers', *International Journal for Academic Development*, 21(1), 67–78. doi:10.1080/1360144X.2015.1120212.

Dalrymple, R., Macrae, A., Pal, M. and Shipman, S. (2021), *Employability: A Review of the Literature 2016–2021*, York: AdvanceHE.

Dickerson, C., Jarvis, J. and Stockwell, L. (2016), 'Staff–student collaboration: student learning from working together to enhance educational practice in higher education', *Teaching in Higher Education*, 21(3), 249–265. doi:10.1080/13562517.2015.1136279.

Helyer, R. and Lee, D. (2014), 'The role of work experience in the future employability of higher education graduates', *Higher Education Quarterly*, 68(3), 348–372. doi:10.1111/hequ.12055.

Lubicz-Nawrocka, T. and Bovill, C. (2021), 'Do students experience transformation through co-creating curriculum in higher education?', *Teaching in Higher Education*. doi:10.1080/13562517.2021.1928060.

Office for Students (2021), *Place Matters: Inequality, Employment and the Role of Higher Education*. Available at: https://www.officeforstudents.org.uk/publications/place-matters-inequality-employment-and-the-role-of-higher-education/#local (accessed: 23 January 2023).

Office for Students (2022), *Office for Students Strategy*. Available at: https://www.officeforstudents.org.uk/about/our-strategy/ (accessed: 23 January 2023).

Römgens, I., Scoupe, R. and Beausaert, S. (2020), 'Unraveling the concept of employability, bringing together research on employability in higher education and the workplace', *Studies in Higher Education*, 45(12), 2588–2603. doi:10.1080/03075079.2019.1623770.

Tibby, M. and Norton, S. (2020), *Essential Frameworks for Enhancing Student Success: Embedding Employability*, York: Advance HE.

Turner, N. K. (2014), 'Development of self-belief for employability in higher education: ability, efficacy and control in context', *Teaching in Higher Education*, 19(6), 592–602. doi:10.1080/13562517.2014.901951.

REFLECTION

From a marketing graduate

Rewind to 2015/16. I am in the final year of my marketing degree and working as a Weekend Duty Manager for a soft play centre. Throughout my three years of study, there were placement opportunities for Level 4 and Level 5 students but it wasn't until my final year that a work-based option was introduced for Level 6 students.

This module allowed me to experience being an aspiring marketing professional. For one day per week, I implemented the skills and knowledge I was developing throughout my studies for the soft play centre I was also working at.

Then, as I was approaching the end of my degree, I managed to obtain full-time employment as a Marketing Assistant for one of Yorkshire's largest FE colleges. I worked there for two years and it enabled me to practice the skills I had learned, developed and gained throughout my studies.

Fast-forward to the summer of 2020, when the world was suffering and changing due to the pandemic. Like many others, I lost my job due to budget cuts. However, the pandemic became something of a blessing in disguise because it opened up the opportunity to grow my freelancing business. Through the success of SME clients, I was able to offer ten students from my former university placement opportunities in various roles.

I am now working as Digital Marketing Manager for a cyber security company whilst still committed to growing my freelance alongside this.

35. Student experience(s) and an integrated pastoral approach to employability

Matthew Vince and Thea Jones

INTRODUCTION

With the steady expansion of approaches to employability, there has been increasing concern about where employability provision fits within the auspices of higher education (HE) (Dalrymple et al., 2021). Debates have tended towards a focus on curricula, and a delineation between embedded (into the curriculum) and non-embedded approaches to employability (Dalrymple et al., 2021). Yet, emerging thinking suggests that such delineation is unhelpful, highlighting instead that engaging students 'by multiple means and in a range of contexts' seems to add significant value to employability provision (Dalrymple et al., 2021: 40). As a result, emphasis is instead placed on employability provision that enriches the student experience of HE throughout the entire student life cycle (Tibby and Norton, 2020).

Within such discussions, however, the concept of student experience tends to take a limited view (see, for example, the focus of case students from Norton and Dalrymple 2020). Typically, student experience is reduced to siloed experiences of career-related skills development and provision, associated learning through curricula teaching, or enrichment via engagement with employers (Hayes and Jandrić, 2018). Specifically, it is rare for these discussions to consider the individuality of student experiences (Hayes and Jandrić, 2018). As Hayes and Jandrić (2018) contend, a consequence of this is that student experience, and associated concepts and initiatives such as employability provision, are simply packaged and delivered to students, rather than developed *by them*. This is problematic, as students' experiences are effectively erased from, rather than enriched by, such initiatives (Allen et al., 2013) and exemplifies the tyrannies of employability within neoliberal HE policy (Noonan and Coral 2015; Patrick, 2013). Additionally, such a narrow view of employability offers little motivation for students to engage with initiatives, which is a considerable barrier to the success of employability provision (Clements and Kamau, 2018).

By extension of questioning its fit, who is responsible for its provision is also a contested subject. Again, the question of responsibility has tended to prioritise concerns of curricula and teaching; asking whether it is the role of academics and lecturers, or bespoke roles of careers advisors (Dalrymple et al., 2021). Such critiques also overlap with other key academic themes, particularly in terms of pedagogy, assessment, and academic integrity. As a result, whose responsibility it is to provide this 'integrated' approach to employability provision is still debatable.

Accordingly, this chapter offers an example of an integrated approach to employability by framing it as a pastoral responsibility of the university. A holistic approach to employability provision is taken to mean an integrated approach; reflecting approaches that use both discrete and embedded modes for engaging students with employability through their whole HE experience (Römgens et al., 2020). We can see this approach adopted elsewhere, such as in the Gatsby Benchmarks, which adopt such a holistic approach to employability provision at both school and further education (FE) level (Gatsby Foundation, 2018).

In doing so, we argue that this positioning of employability resists a narrow view, and instead fosters a richer view more in keeping with the holistic nature of pastoral student support. This understanding is one that aims to support each student's needs to pursue their future life goals by beginning from their own experience. As Patrick (2013) has proposed, education that prioritises the flourishing of students must also recognise the realities of their experience and socioeconomic contexts.

In this chapter, University Centre South Devon is used as an example of this approach. At University Centre South Devon the responsibility for employability provision sits alongside other forms of student support within the Student Support Hub, existing as a discrete area of activity, general support, and also being embedded within wider curricula. Within the context of student pastoral support, employability is reimagined as a particular lens through which to reflect upon, and better understand, one's life experiences (including those outside academic study) alongside other lenses: in terms of one's potential life goals and career aspirations. Then, to practise articulating these goals, aspirations, and experiences to consider who one wants to be, and to convey this to others – some of whom may be employers.

This pastoral vibe builds on the student-centred ethos at University Centre South Devon, which provides dynamic support across the whole of the student experience through a well-developed pastoral and tutorial system (University Centre South Devon, 2020). As a result, within this framework, employability will be experienced as a form of pastoral support concerned with supporting students' future goals and ambitions, in concert with academic study, disability, and well-being support.

BACKGROUND

University Centre South Devon is a particularly interesting case study given its close linkages with the further education (FE) sector as a partner to South Devon College – a valuable perspective for employability in HE (Dalrymple et al., 2021: 39). University Centre South Devon is a higher education institution that is part of South Devon College, a medium-sized further education college in Torbay, Devon. University Centre South Devon, through South Devon College, was granted Foundation Degree Awarding Powers in early 2019 and, until 2021, has held the Teaching Excellence Framework Gold award. In the 2020–2021 academic year, University Centre South Devon supported approximately 740 students on a range of foundation degrees, bachelor's degrees, higher and degree apprenticeships, and Higher National Certificates, across diverse curriculum areas, to meet local need.

Eighty per cent of University Centre South Devon's students come from the local Torbay and South Devon postcode, with just 1.2 per cent of students currently coming from a non-Devon or Cornwall postcode. Torbay is ranked within the top 20 per cent most-deprived local authorities in England and is the most deprived in the south-west on a range of income and employment deprivation measures (Torbay Council, 2015).

This context highlights the importance of University Centre South Devon's pastoral and tutorial system, which is conceptualised as holistic support for the entire student life cycle for each of its 740 students (University Centre South Devon, 2020: 9). Many of University Centre South Devon's students face barriers to their studies, with higher levels of socio-economic deprivation and a higher number of mature students (Office for Students, 2020). Informed by its close ties to FE, this system keeps a tutorial model, whereby HE students remain in tutor groups and are guided by their personal tutors, who are also leaders in their academic programmes. A tutorial curriculum accompanies this, with weekly sessions that cover themes linked to each of the pastoral areas in the Student Support Hub. The Hub, within which the Employability Coordinator sits, also supports students directly through one-to-one sessions and training workshops.

APPROACH

Building upon this commitment to support the entire student's life cycle, employability provision at University Centre South Devon is built on two key aspects of students' experiences. First, it recognises that achieving career-related goals is often one of several motivations to embark on this learning journey, and that this journey starts before students arrive and continues long after their studies conclude (Watson and Turpie, 2020). Due to a high level of mature learners in the Centre, this is not just finding employment in the broadest sense, but in many cases the students supported want to progress, or change, their career towards 'higher level' or 'more skilled' employment, alongside students who simply want to achieve the qualification itself. The approach also acknowledges that the lives of students outside these academic ambitions bring unique challenges and needs, which have become even more apparent in the context of Covid-19 (Hughes and Walton, 2021). So, framed in terms of this pastoral and tutorial system, employability is understood as a form of support, in this case supporting students through this learning journey towards potential future goals and ambitions. This journey has a start point and an end point, between which their academic journey is recognised as a stepping stone.

From this pastoral ethos, employability activity at University Centre South Devon adopts a bottom-up approach. This begins with the diverse needs of students – their own unique experiences, identities, and backgrounds, and the opportunities and barriers these bring. Critical reflection on who the student is then leads to discussions about who they want to be, where they want to get to, and how to get there, building from their own positionality (Sánchez, 2010). This includes the skills and knowledge development from their academic studies as one aspect of this, alongside idealistic goals and practical considerations. Importantly, this discussion does not have to end up grounded in a route to a certain career, but rather a simple hope that the student has a better sense of where they want to go after their studies.

These foci extend to traditional employability-style workshops and one-to-one support provision. CV and cover letter writing sessions become framed as moments to take stock of one's experiences to date – not limited to work-related experience – and draw out what general skills, behaviours, and competencies those experiences represent to the student. Job searches can take the form of opportunities for self-reflection on who one wants to be, and how certain forms of employment may reflect on these ideas of the self. Doing so often means that a need for support for other aspects of a student's experience may be identified, and so students can be easily referred to other members of the Hub team, for well-being support, for example.

Thus, a consequence of this pastoral-orientated imagining of traditional employability activity is that the role is brought into close proximity with many other teams, meaning that employability forms part of the everyday fabric of the HE student experience, particularly in terms of support. Students are encouraged to visit the Hub for one-to-one disability support along with mapping out their studies and future career plans, working together to build in training needs analyses and to identify meaningful and accessible opportunities. Personal tutors and other pastoral teams also refer students to the Employability Coordinator as a result of their interactions, just as they would refer students who they are concerned about in other pastoral areas, such as academic attainment. Likewise, the Employability Coordinator, as a member of staff working under the umbrella of support, can find it easier to proactively target individuals who may need guidance but not always have the confidence, or awareness, to come forward and know what sort of guidance they are after. In this way, employability is integrated as a vital part of supporting a student's whole life cycle.

Moreover, this extends into curricula. Curriculum design is guided by the needs of the subject, the needs of the local market, and also the needs of students identified by the pastoral team. Alongside the use of labour market information data and consultation between local employers, teaching teams invite the Student Support Hub, including employability personnel, to shape programme design and delivery. As such, the relationship between academic, employer, and pastoral teams really shapes the programmes, guiding module content to bring together the experiences, knowledges, and selves that are needed by local employers, with the experiences, knowledges, and selves of our students. In doing so, student experiences are being framed with the specific needs of local employers in mind, and so are in turn being brought into conversation through the students' learning. Examples include a robust tutorial curriculum through which students engage with pastoral, academic and employability topics, which is essential to student engagement (de Main et al., 2022). Authentic assessments are also used across programmes to examine students in ways that reflect real local work contexts and allow them to demonstrate their own unique approaches to practice, as informed by the above conversations (Sotiriadou et al., 2020).

CONCLUSION

This chapter highlights that framing employability as a pastoral responsibility of the university opens up powerful opportunities for reimagining the nature of employability itself. In particular, employability frameworks and competencies such as University Centre South Devon's HE Employability Framework, adapted from AdvanceHE's framework, become tailored to the needs of individual students, as part of a wider network of support (Tibby and Norton, 2020). In doing so, this integrated approach blurs the lines between the academic, employment, and general skills that students develop during their student life cycle.

The pastoral approach is opposed to top-down approaches that focus on articulating abstract skills and competencies as siloes that students are made to fit into. We can see such criticisms in the language of employability, in its blindness to the individual experiences of students (Hayes and Jandrić, 2018: 127–143). Rather, and inspired by its pastoral context, employability provision begins from students' experiences and self-understanding and exploration considers how these wider skills and competencies make sense to them, conceptually and experientially. This then forms a dialectic to reflect on, understand, and articulate one's own goal-orientated journey. As Patrick (2013) has urged, this encourages students to engage in employability in a eudemonic sense that prioritises their agency as unique, goal-orientated actors. Hence, by attending to the employability of students as a form of support, it overcomes the tendency to depersonalise employability and prioritises delivery of the student experience.

Close proximity to other teams, both academic and professional, also increases opportunities for quality engagements with students in multifaceted and intersecting ways. Collaboration is encouraged within the Student Support Hub between support teams, with teaching teams at a curriculum level, and also with employers at the local level. In this way, an integrated approach to employability seems to overcome many of the barriers associated with binary embedded or non-embedded employability initiatives (Dalrymple et al., 2021: 34–37).

This approach requires significant support across HE institutions at all levels, and notably a robust tutorial system and a well-supported pastoral team. Given the linkages between University Centre South Devon and its close partnership with the FE institution South Devon College, it is important to acknowledge that this approach extends into this space – a relationship not available to all institutions. Here, HE has learnt considerably from the insights of FE, especially around the maintenance of the pastoral needs of students in the transition from one level of study to another.

REFERENCES

Allen, K., Quinn, J., Hollingworth, S. and Rose, A. (2013), 'Becoming employable students and "ideal" creative workers: exclusion and inequality in higher education work placements', *British Journal of Sociology of Education*, 34(3), 431–452.

Clements, A. and Kamau, C. (2018), 'Understanding students' motivation towards proactive career behaviours through goal-setting theory and the job demands–resources model', *Studies in Higher Education*, 43(12), 2279–2293.

Dalrymple, R., Macrae, A., Pal, M. and Shipman, S. (2021), *Employability: A Review of the Literature 2016–2021*, York: AdvanceHE.

de Main, L., Holmes, H. and Wakefield, L. (2022), 'Why won't they engage in extra-curricular opportunities?', *AdvanceHE*. Available at: https://www.advance-he.ac.uk/news-and-views/why-wont-they-engage-extra-curricular-opportunities (accessed: 19 January 2023).

Gatsby Foundation (2018), *Good Career Guidance*, London: The Gatsby Charitable Foundation.

Hayes, S. and Jandrić, P. (2018), 'Resisting the iron cage of "the student experience"', *Šolsko polje*, 29(1–2), 127–143.

Hughes, J. and Walton, D. (2021), 'Nurturing belonging in a diverse student group: transition and transitioning innovations in the University of Opportunity', *Widening Participation and Lifelong Learning*, 23(2), 31–38.

Noonan, J. and Coral, M. (2015), 'The tyranny of work: employability and the neoliberal assault on education', *Alternate Routes: A Journal of Critical Social Research*, 26, 51–73.

Norton, S. and Dalrymple, R. (eds) (2020), *Enhancing Graduate Employability: A Case Study Compendium*, York: AdvanceHE.

Office for Students (2020), *Access and Participation Data Dashboard*, London: Office for Students. Available at: https://www.officeforstudents.org.uk/data-and-analysis/access-and-participation-data-dashboard/ (accessed: 19 January 2023).

Patrick, F. (2013), 'Neoliberalism, the knowledge economy, and the learner: challenging the inevitability of the commodified self as an outcome of education', *International Scholarly Research Notices*, 2013, 1–8.

Römgens, I., Scoupe, R. and Beausaert, S. (2020), 'Unraveling the concept of employability, bringing together research on employability in higher education and the workplace', *Studies in Higher Education*, 45(12), 2588–2603.

Sánchez, L. (2010), 'Positionality', in B. Warf (ed.) *Encyclopedia of Geography*, Thousand Oaks: SAGE.

Sotiriadou, P., Logan, D., Daly, A. and Guest, R. (2020), 'The role of authentic assessment to preserve academic integrity and promote skill development and employability', *Studies in Higher Education*, 45(11), 2132–2148.

Tibby, M. and Norton, S. (2020), *Essential Frameworks for Enhancing Student Success: Embedding Employability*, York: AdvanceHE.

Torbay Council (2015), *Population Overview: An Overview of the Population on Torbay*, Torbay: Torbay Council.

University Centre South Devon (2020), *South Devon College: Access and Participation Plan*, Paignton: South Devon College.

Watson, E. and Turpie, T. (2020), 'Putting historians into work: a discipline-specific example of embedding employability at the centre of the student lifecycle in higher education', in S. Norton and R. Dalrymple (eds), *Enhancing Graduate Employability: A Case Study Compendium*, York: Advance HE, pp. 33–39.

REFLECTION

From an Education graduate

As an international student, I studied Education at Master's-level at a UK University. In China, overseas students with Master's degrees are competitive in the job market, especially for educational institutions, because it means good language level and personal ability. However, prior to my graduation, China's Ministry of Education issued a policy prohibiting educational institutions from providing after-school courses for students. As a result of this policy, many companies went bankrupt, and the job opportunities related to my major decreased sharply. Despite obtaining a good degree abroad, I couldn't find work, or an internship related to my major. I do not require my professional knowledge for my current internship position, as Human Resources Business Partner (HRBP) at an Internet company but I utilise the soft skills I got at university from group work and solving problems on my courses. Communication skill is the most important and fundamental skill for HRBP. In addition, there is the problem-solving skill. The work, however, is very unpredictable and troublesome and I do not want to make it my lifelong career.

Before graduation, I never thought I would do anything other than education, so I didn't make a detailed career plan. Regrettably, I did not contact the Career Service Department at university. I think it can help you get a clear view of employment status, provide related job opportunities and improve résumés. During my one-year postgraduate study abroad, I even did not know when, how and what kind of help I can get from the careers service. I think if you make more plans for your career development in advance, you may avoid some risks or provide yourself with more possibilities, which is very beneficial. In sum, I think we should actively cultivate soft skills at university as these are suitable for all jobs.

PART XI

A final reflection

36. Reflections on 20 years of research on employability and its effect on policy and practice

Helen Higson

INTRODUCTION

Recently, I was asked to write a blog for a well-known higher education policy organisation. In preparing for this I started looking back at the work on employability that I had been involved with over a 20-year period, and I began to reflect on the development of the research that I produced during this time. As a result, this chapter has ended up as a kind of retrospective, reviewing a research career and how this work has influenced strategy and delivery for my university and nationally. In doing so, it also charts the progress of the policy and practice environment on employability over these years.

In order to provide a framework for this reflection, it seems important to give an overview of the context in which I have been working. Aston University has been known for the transformational effect that it has on students since it became a university in 1966. The university grew from an institution (the Birmingham Municipal Technical College), set up in 1895 by the employers of Birmingham because they could not find enough employees with the appropriate skills.

The university's Charter, dated 22 April 1966, outlines its central purpose as being,

> to advance, disseminate and apply learning and knowledge by teaching and research, for the benefit of industry and commerce and of the community generally: and to enable students to obtain the advantage of a university education, and such teaching and research may include periods outside the University in industry or commerce or whatever the University considers proper for the best advancement of its objects.

This objective, to make its graduates the most employable global citizens, continues to this day.

The majority of degrees at Aston University have professional accreditation from the relevant sector accrediting body, and the curriculum is designed to ensure that students learn a set of relevant skills and competencies, integrated with their academic studies. The aspect that is most unique to Aston, however, is its year-long placement, which is assessed and integrated into the curriculum. Nearly 75 per cent of undergraduate students undertake a placement year annually, many studying for degrees with a compulsory placement year. The placement year and integrated work experience provide a lens through which I have examined the development of employability.

I have led initiatives across the university to encourage students to take a placement and to demonstrate to them, and to the wider policy community, the lasting impact which this integrated work experience has on their academic and employability achievements. Looking back on my research, I have become aware that it divides into four stages: basic practice, the employer angle, policy implications, and redefining employability. I reflect on these below.

BASIC PRACTICE

My exploration of placement activity began back in 2005 when I started observing how students engaged with placements and considered how to maximise the benefit they gained from this experience. It was building up to the time of the Leitch Review (2006), which shone more light on the value of UK universities in building the skills of the future, and set out what the government could do to ensure the skills gap was closed by 2020. The aim of the report was that the proposed activities would lead to higher productivity and employment, which would in turn generate 'significant economic and social benefits'.

This gave Aston University an opportunity to build on its strengths in placement education, but we had to make sure that placements were productive learning experiences. A number of my publications at the time explored ways to maximise the effectiveness of organising placements (Higson and Bullivant, 2006) and helping students to engage with their work experience (Higson and Parkes, 2006). These were often from a practitioner standpoint and did not explore the wider issues of research-informed policy. In retrospect, the comparative naivety of this early work demonstrates that the field of employability was relatively badly developed. Just assisting students to take up a placement opportunity was enough. The concept of employability we used at the time focussed on the students developing their skills, rather than anything more.

THE EMPLOYER ANGLE

By 2010 I was very interested in the part that employers had to play in developing graduate employability. This demonstrated an awareness that employability was not just about the student developing skills, but the skills being those that employers wanted and needed. It therefore seemed important to ensure that all partners in the tripartite collaboration to create an employable graduate were engaged to their maximum – students, universities and employers. This led to studies looking at the part that employers played in developing employable graduates (Hall et al., 2010; McEwen et al., 2010). This focus was further developed in an EU-funded project looking at the role of employers and business students across Europe (Azevedo et al., 2011). That study identified variability, and little evidence of systematic relationships between employers and universities. An opportunity in 2012 allowed me to extend this approach. I was asked to co-write the chapter on skills for the government's review of business–university partnerships (Higson, 2012). The report built on best practice that was currently being undertaken in the field of work-based learning and recommended that aspects be expanded, such as work shadowing for academics, placements for PhD students, opportunities for students to set up their own businesses, incentives for businesses to employ placement students, as well as strongly advocating the integrating of internships systematically into degrees. This piece of work led me to start working on research which would influence national policy.

POLICY – INSTITUTIONALLY AND NATIONALLY

In the years being reviewed, the concept of the university's role in producing employable graduates has become increasingly stronger. As the fee regime in terms of the size of fees and the sources of funding changed, the case for the link between investment in students' education and their subsequent contribution to the economy and society became strongly espoused (Browne Report, 2010). It was time to use our research on value added, attainment gaps, and the role of universities in society, amongst other current topics, to contribute to the debates. Our contributions included an important analysis showing that an integrated placement experience is the only significant variable in closing the degree attainment gap between different groups of graduates (Birdi et al., 2017). We challenged a large body of previous research which suggested that a placement year would automatically enhance a student's academic performance (Driffield et al., 2011; Jones et al., 2017). In this work we discovered that the more engaged and academically stronger students choose to undertake a placement, but that those students who are less engaged and less strong academically benefit most from undertaking one. In order to build our university practice on this work, we needed to find out how we could get that latter cohort of students to choose a placement year. This led to publications on how to influence student choice before they come to university (Higson and Andrews, 2013), and how to increase engagement amongst students (Andrews et al., 2012). As a result of these papers the university appointed a pre-arrival Careers Advisor and integrated placement preparation more comprehensively into the first and second year curriculums. Many other institutions started more formally and more comprehensively doing the same.

REDEFINING WHAT EMPLOYABILITY IS AND ITS IMPLICATIONS FOR PRACTICE

Everything changed in the year that our article on graduate employability, soft and hard skills was published (Andrews and Higson, 2008). To this day, this paper is cited a few times a week. So, what was so groundbreaking? Firstly, it was one of the papers which started the process of redefining employability as a more complex concept than had previously been considered. Earlier research on employability often concentrated on the development of a combination of skills, competences and mindset, which it was suggested would lead students to be employable, just as we had done in our earlier outputs (Hillage and Pollard, 1998). What we pointed out was that the pervading economic conditions had also to be taken into account. Secondly, our paper discussed 'soft' and 'hard' skills, putting forward the argument that discipline-based technical skills were not enough to make students employable. They also needed to develop skills such as teamworking, decision-making, negotiating, presenting, for example; these skills were often best learned in the workplace.

We followed this up six years later, with a review of what was happening across Europe in terms of graduate employability (Andrews and Higson, 2014). We noted that the concept of partnership with employers and the embedding of soft skills via work experience had progressed, but that there were variable levels of development in different countries. The tradition of integrated paid work experience was not so highly developed in Austria, for example, but the short unpaid internship was very widespread.

To bring this chapter up to the present, the latest part of this research journey has culminated in the editing of a special issue, devoted to the discussion of the latest concepts of employability and their implementation in policy and practice across the world. Our introductory paper to this publication bears witness to the now increasingly prevalent awareness of the many facets which need to make up the definition of employability (Omolabake and Higson, 2021). As we say in the abstract of this paper, we are making two new contributions to the study of graduate employability:

> First, drawing from existing literature, this introductory paper proposes three categorisations of employability as: outcomes approach, process approach and conceptual approaches. This moves beyond normative conceptualisation of employability from mostly the outcomes approach. The applicability of the categorisation is further

enumerated by the diversity of contributions to this special issue that highlights (a) the complexity in the field and (b) the interrelatedness of the categories. Second, the special issue puts together a rarely combined collection of global perspectives on conceptualisations of employability ... The papers, therefore, illustrate the need to widen our scope of understanding employability beyond current dominant perspectives. The broadening that is required in employability discourses is further needed in view of unprecedented disruption brought on higher education during the Covid 19 pandemic. This suggests the need to rethink our conceptualisations of employability amidst uncertainty and potential disruption to the future of work.

CONCLUSION

In conclusion then, it is clear that research into employability needs to continue to be produced with an open mind, and that the link into policy and practice has never been so important in this field. At Aston University we will continue to be at the forefront of this. For all of us, however, the Covid-19 pandemic has meant that we have needed to continue to be creative in how we envision the world of work, and how we develop students to thrive in it. Taking into account our previous research, we made the decision not to cancel the placement experience for students during the pandemic. That would have perhaps been the easiest action to take, but it would have deprived students of the development of that crucial work experience, just at the time when they were most in need of it. As a result we developed the portfolio placement, based on the concept of those at the end of their careers, using their skills, built up over many years in a range of different job roles. The weeks I had with students work-shadowing me as part of this scheme were rich in learning for both me and the students.

Looking forward, we will clearly need to revisit our concept of employability again, and how we prepare students to thrive in the new hybrid world of work. Expectations of both employees and employers have changed and how we prepare students for this change needs some developing. We need to take the three employability features that we identified in our special issue: outcomes approach, process approach and conceptual approaches (Omolabake and Higson, 2021). My next project will be looking at what post-pandemic graduate employment looks like, with its increased precarity and need for flexibility. How can we empower students to be able to navigate this environment, and how can we help them develop the resilience to thrive in workplaces where the need for soft and hard skills will not be enough? I see the next five years of employability research, and its implications for practice and policy, ahead.

REFERENCES

Andres, J. and Higson, H. (2008), 'Graduate employability, "soft skills" versus "hard" business knowledge: a European study', *Higher Education in Europe*, 33(4), 411–422.

Andrews, J. and Higson, H. E. (2014), 'Is Bologna working? Employer and graduate reflections on the quality, value and relevance of business and management education in four EU countries', *Higher Education Quarterly*, 68(3), 267–287.

Andrews, J., Higson, H. E., Green, J. P. and Jones, C. W. (2012), 'How to encourage student engagement in placement learning', *Society for Research into Higher Education Annual Research Conference*. Newport, 12–14 December.

Azevedo, A., Gomezelj Omerzel, D., Andrews, J., Higson, H. E., Caballero, A. and Frech, B. (2011), 'Satisfaction with knowledge and competencies: a multi-country study of employers and business graduates', *American Journal of Economics and Business Administration*, 4(1), 23–39.

Birdi, G. K., Moores, E. and Higson, H. E. (2017), 'The pervasive problem of the higher education BME performance gap: reflections on prior experience, policy and placements, *Frontiers in Psychology*, 8, article 1518.

Browne Report (2010), *Securing a Sustainable Future for Higher Education: An Independent Review of Higher Education Funding and Student Finance*. Available at: https://assets.publishing.service.gov.uk/government/uploads/system/uploads/attachment_data/file/422565/bis-10-1208-securing-sustainable-higher-education-browne-report.pdf (accessed: 20 January 2023).

Driffield, N. L., Foster, C. S. and Higson, H. E. (2011), 'Placements and degree performance: do placements lead to better marks, or do better students choose placements?', in D. Siva-Jothy (ed.), *ASET Annual Conference 2011*. Leeds, September 2011. Sheffield: ASET, pp. 4–27. Available at: https://research.aston.ac.uk/en/publications/placements-and-degree-performance-do-placements-lead-to-better-ma (accessed: 20 January 2023).

Hall, M., Higson, H. and Bullivant, N. (2010) 'The role of the undergraduate work placement in developing employment competences: results from a five year survey of employers', *Graduate Market Trends*. Available at: https://www.educationandemployers.org/wp-content/uploads/2014/06/graduate_market_trends_2010_-_hecsu.pdf (accessed: 23 January 2023).

Higson, H. E. (2012), contribution to *A Review of Business–University Collaboration*, chaired by Sir Tim Wilson, for the Department of Business Innovation and Skills.

Higson, H. E. and Andrews, J. (2013), 'How to enhance your degree: the value of placements and work based learning', in D. Siva-Jothy (ed.), *ASET Annual Conference 2013*. Greenwich, September 2013.

Higson, H. and Bullivant, N. (2006), 'Encouraging Aston Business School students to reflect on their employment experience', in N. Becket and P. Kemp (eds), *Enhancing Graduate Employability*, Newbury, Threshold Press, pp. 552–559.

Higson, H. and Parkes, E. (2006), 'Preparing Aston Business School students for placements', in N. Becket and P. Kemp (eds), *Enhancing Graduate Employability*, Newbury, Threshold Press, pp. 42–51.

Hillage, J. and Pollard, E. (1998), *Employability: Developing a Framework for Policy Analysis*, Research Report 85. Brighton: Institute of Employment Studies.

Jones, C.M., Green, J. P. and Higson, H. E. (2017), 'Do work placements improve final year academic performance or do high-calibre students choose to do work placements?', *Studies in Higher Education*, 42(6), 976–992. http://dx.doi.org/10.1080/03075079.2015.1073249.

Leitch, S. (2006), *Leitch Review of Skills. Prosperity for all in the global economy – world class skills*, London: HMSO.

McEwen, L. et al (including Higson, H.) (2010), 'Integrating employers in effective support for student work-based learning in placements: learning for assessment', *Learning and Teaching in Higher Education (LATHE)*, 4(2), 62–89.

Omolabake, F. and Higson, H. E. (2021), 'Interrogating theoretical and empirical approaches to employability in different global regions', *Higher Education Quarterly*, 75(4), 525–534. https://doi.org/10.1111/hequ.12345.

Index

3Es (employability, enterprise and entrepreneurship) 179–84
4i Careers Education 140–45
21st century skills 190

accessibility 154–5, 307
accountability for graduate employment *see* England, policy and regulation, and accountability for graduate employment
accounting students and profession
    professional skills module to develop student confidence 100–106
    see also employers' and students' perceptions of skills and knowledge needed by accounting graduates in Greece
agency 3
Agri-Food Tech and Sustainability Consortium 40
Ako ā-mahi (University of Canterbury) 288–9
alumni
    NEOLAiA (European University initiative) 310–11
    see also international alumni satisfaction, using net promoter score
alumni-engaged student projects 89–92
anxiety 128, 131
apathy 119
Apollo 191–2
artificial intelligence (AI) 298, 299
ARU Peterborough *see* creating a new university
ASEAN region 142
Asia, international students from *see* international students from Asia
Asia Careers Group 137, 140–41

Asia School of Business (ASB) 144
assessment
    authentic 109–14
    centres 18
    for learning, and creativity 60–61
    as motivator 121–2
    see also employer input to curriculum and assessment
Aston University 352–3
Australia
    developing graduate employability 273–9
    integrated institutional approach to employability 323–30
authentic assessment 109–14

BAME students/graduates 199, 200, 216, 221, 228–9
Big Challenge 159–65
Birmingham Skills for Entrepreneurship and Employability (BSEEN) programme 188–95
blended format courses 307–8
Bologna Process 295

capital 169, 170, 198, 211–12
    cultural 208, 228
    human 67, 68
    social 4, 9, 19
care-experienced and estranged students/graduates 199, 200
career coaching (My Generation Career Coaching programme, University of Southampton) 207, 208–12
career development, in German universities 300
career development learning (CDL) 277
Career Focus (Kaplan International Pathways) 247–8
career management skills 336
career outcomes, intended 120–21

Career Pathway Scheme (Derby Law School) 120–23
career readiness 200
Career Readiness Test 209, 211–12
Career Studio (University of Liverpool) 127–32
Career Zone (University of Exeter) 199–203
careers education, 4i 140–45
careers fairs 31, 256–7
careers guidance, benefits of 203
careers services 14–15, 30–31, 140
careers sessions and activities, attitudes towards 118, 119, 122–3
careers support
    expectations after graduation 246
    importance of 245
    for international students 139–40
Change Project (Leeds Trinity University, LTU) 171–4
Chartered Management Institute (CMI) 317
chemistry students 221
City Graduate Schemes 20
clinical legal education (CLE) 47–8, 50
co-creation 338–9
co-design 278
community, supporting local 152–3, 154, 155–6
community engagement 289
competencies 43
confidence 19–20, 161, 208, 212
    professional skills module to develop 100–106
connectedness 173
constructive alignment 119–20, 122–3
COVID-19 pandemic 28, 42, 47, 49, 50, 51, 53, 152, 356
Cradle 143–4
creating a new university 36
    context 36–8
    impact 42–4
    new curriculum 38–40
    objectives 38
    working with industry 40–42
creative industries and institutions, London graduates in 225, 227–9
creativity 56–7, 63–4, 143
    difficulties relating to 57–8
    nature and definitions of 58
    role of higher education in developing 59–63
Cturtle 234, 235
cultural awareness 308
cultural capital 208, 228
curriculum
    creating new 38–40
    design and development 118–23, 130, 347
    embedding employability in 101, 336–7
    social action in 153–4
    transition pedagogy 328
    see also employer input to curriculum and assessment; real-world opportunities in curriculum

datasets, use of 339
Deggendorf Institute of Technology 296–7, 298, 299
degree programmes, universities of applied sciences (Germany) 297–8, 299
Derby Business School
    Professional Development for Accounting and Finance Graduates (PDAFG) module 101–6
    see also real-world opportunities in curriculum
Derby Law School
    Career Pathway Scheme 120–23
    Student Legal Advice Centre 47, 48–9, 50, 51–2
disabled students/graduates 199, 200, 218
disadvantaged groups see widening participation (WP) students
diversity
    and creativity 61–2
    and international students 249

ecosystem model, authentic assessment 112–13
embedding employability in curriculum 79–80, 101, 336–7
employability

approaches to 68, 169–70, 325, 343, 355–6
employer view of 6–7
meaning and definitions of 2–4, 13–14, 24
models 182–3
student view of 5–6
university view of 7–9
employability, enterprise and entrepreneurship (3Es) 179–84
employability development opportunities (EDOs) 25
Employability Monsters project (University of Exeter) 199–203
employer input to curriculum and assessment 79
case studies (University of Liverpool) 82–6
considerations and challenges 81–2
framework for embedding employers 79–80
teaching, inclusion and industry connections 80–1
employer-led skills development 84–6
employers
involvement in creation of new university 38–43
responsibility for employability 17–19
skills and competencies required/valued by 43, 50–53, 244–5
views of employability 6–7
employers' and students' perceptions of skills and knowledge needed by accounting graduates in Greece 67–9
methodology 69
students' perceptions 71–3
understanding desirability of accountancy graduates to employers 69–71
employment and employability, difference between 324
employment outcomes *see* graduate outcomes
engagement with employability activities 118–23, 127–8, 130, 132, 160–61, 163

England, policy and regulation, and accountability for graduate employment 263–70
enterprise and entrepreneurship
3Es 179–84
life sciences students 221
NEOLAiA (European University initiative) 309–10
support, extra-curricular (BSEEN programme) 188–95
University of Huddersfield, Global Professional Award (GPA) 316–17
University of Sussex 338, 340
equity and employability, Australia 275–6
Ericsson 145
European University initiative (NEOLAiA) 304–11
experiential learning 48, 111, 289
extra-curricular activities (ECAs) 6, 316
extra-curricular enterprise and entrepreneurship support (BSEEN programme) 188–95
extra-curricular support 337–8

finance, as barrier to accessing opportunities 202
first-generation students 19, 207–12, 314–15
Future Talent and Skills Network 40

Germany, universities of applied sciences 295–301
Get into Nursing (GIN) (University of East London, UEL) 226, 227
global and social awareness 317
Global Professional Award (GPA) (University of Huddersfield) 314–20
Gradcore 14, 16, 20
graduate jobs, defining 14
graduate outcomes 7–8, 25, 100–101, 168–9, 180
Australia 274–5, 323–4
intended career outcomes 120–21
London graduates 224–5
New Zealand 287
and value for money 264–5

widening participation (WP) students 198–9, 208
see also international alumni satisfaction, using net promoter score
graduates, responsibility for employability 19–20
Greece *see* employers' and students' perceptions of skills and knowledge needed by accounting graduates in Greece

health-care subjects, London graduates 225, 226–7
higher education, value of 3
holistic approach to employability provision 344
human capital approach 67, 68

IBM 145
inclusion 80
India, graduate employment 137–8
Indian Institutes of Technology (IITs) 139–40
Indigenous students
    Australia 275–6
    New Zealand 285, 288
innovation
    4i Careers Education 141, 142–3
    Social Innovation Programme (SIP) 150–51, 152–3
institutional approaches to employability 17
    integrated 323–30
    strategic 334–40
integrated pastoral approach to employability 343–8
interdisciplinary development of employability skills 159–65
international alumni satisfaction, using net promoter score 234
    factors affecting alumni recommendations 238–40, 241
    first job after graduation 237
    International Student Employment Outcomes and Satisfaction (ISEOS) research project 235–6
    international students and aspirations 234–5
    ISEOS key findings 236–7
    methodology 236
international opportunities (4i Careers Education) 141, 142
international students
    Australia 276
    'benefits' of 249
    New Zealand 285–6, 289–90
    particular employability needs 248–9
    partnerships to secure jobs for 253–9
    post-study, staying-on or returning home 136–7, 237
    in transition to UK higher education, meeting employability expectations of 244–50
international students from Asia 136–9
    4i Careers Education 140–45
    careers support for 139–40
internships 5, 202–3, 289–90, 298, 308–9
    see also placements
INTI International College Subang 145
intrapreneurship (4i Careers Education) 141, 143–4
#iwill Campaign 150

'Job-Ready Graduates Package', Australia 323–4, 326

Kaplan International Pathways 244, 245, 246–8
key information set (KIS) (2011 White Paper, England) 265
Kia Angitu (University of Canterbury) 288
Kilnbridge Construction 256, 258–9
Knowledge Exchange Framework (KEF) 181

law clinic, developing employability skills through working in 47
    clinical legal education (CLE) 47–8
    skills required by employers 50–52
    Student Legal Advice Centre (Derby Law School) 48–9
leadership
    Australian universities 276–7

Global Professional Award (GPA) (University of Huddersfield) 317–18
league tables 180–81, 267, 334
learning
  assessment for, and creativity 60–61
  attitudes towards 119
  career development learning (CDL) 277
  experiential 48, 111, 289
  outcomes 119–21, 122–3
  participatory 170
  SEAL (situation, effect, action, learning) self-reflection method 325, 328
  see also work-based learning/work integrated learning (WIL)
Leeds Trinity University (LTU) 168, 169, 170–74
legal profession
  Career Pathway Scheme (Derby Law School) 120–23
  skills required by employers 50–53
  widening access to 220
levelling-up 37, 269
liberal arts education *see* student voice
life sciences students/sector 41, 84–6, 221
liminality 199–200
London Higher 229
London's left-behind graduates, and social mobility 224–30
longitudinal education outcomes (LEO) data 266

Malaysia
  graduate employment 137–8
  tech companies 144–5
Māori and Pacific students, New Zealand 285, 288
marketing students, and authentic assessment 111–12
massive open online courses (MOOCs) 296
mature students/graduates 199, 200, 218, 226, 346
migration, New Zealand 285
mission, universities 15–16

motivation of students to engage in employability activities 118, 119, 121–3
My Generation Career Coaching programme (University of Southampton) 207, 208–12

National Priorities and Industry Linkage Fund (NPILF) (Australia) 274, 326
NEOLAiA (European University initiative) 304–11
net promoter score *see* international alumni satisfaction, using net promoter score
New Beginnings (University of East London, UEL) 226–7
New Colombo Plan (NCP) (Australia) 273–4
new university, creating *see* creating a new university
New Zealand, enabling employability 284–90
non-traditional students 315–16

Office for Students (OfS) (England) 100, 168, 207, 267–8, 334
Örebro University 306–7

partnerships 269–70
  academic-professional 329
  co-creation 338–9
  to secure jobs for international students 253–9
pastoral approach to employability 343–8
peer-to-peer mentoring and careers support 127–32, 131–2, 203, 209
perceptions of skills and knowledge *see* employers' and students' perceptions of skills and knowledge needed by accounting graduates in Greece
performance-based funding (PBF), Australia 323–4
Peterborough *see* creating a new university
placements 150, 152, 170–72, 202, 254–9, 353, 354–5, 356
  see also internships

POLAR4; 215–16
policy and regulation, England *see* England, policy and regulation, and accountability for graduate employment
pre-professional identity (PPI) formation 100
process approach to employability 25, 26, 27
Professional Development for Accounting and Finance Graduates (PDAFG) module (Derby Business School) 101–6
professors, Germany 298, 300, 301
promotion, university staff 16
psychological contract 7, 16
psychological risk, and creativity 62

real-world employer projects 82–4
real-world experience and learning 19–20, 29–30, 48, 50–52, 336–7, 339–40
real-world opportunities in curriculum 89
    fostering alumni-engaged student projects 89–92
    social media 92–4
    Workplace Development Module (WDM) 94–7
recruitment for skills 17–18
regulation, England 267–8
resilience 143
responsibility for employability 13, 344
    case study (City Graduate Schemes) 20
    employers 17–19
    graduates 19–20
    understanding graduate employability 13–14
    universities 14–17
role models 208

SEAL (situation, effect, action, learning) self-reflection method 325, 328
sector interest groups (SIGs) 40
self-reflection 325, 328
shared mental models 62–3
skills
    21st century 190
    career management 336
    employability 121
    forecasting 18–19
    recruitment for 17–18
    required by employers 43, 50–53, 244–5
    soft and hard 43, 355
    see also creativity; employers' and students' perceptions of skills and knowledge needed by accounting graduates in Greece
skills development
    and authentic assessment 109–14
    Birmingham Skills for Entrepreneurship and Employability (BSEEN) programme 188–95
    employer-led 84–6
    Global Professional Award (GPA) (University of Huddersfield) 314–20
    interdisciplinary 159–65
    Kaplan International Pathways 246–8
    professional skills module to develop confidence 100–106
    using social action to support 149–56
    see also law clinic, developing employability skills through working in
small and medium-sized enterprises (SMEs) 20, 37
social action 149–56
social capital 4, 9, 19
Social Innovation Programme (SIP) 150–51, 152–3
social media 92–4
social mobility, and London's left-behind graduates 224–30
South Devon College 345
start-ups 143–4, 181
    Birmingham Skills for Entrepreneurship and Employability (BSEEN) programme 188–95
strategic institutional approach to employability 334–40
'student connectors' 338–9

student consultancy projects 150–52, 153, 154
student experience, and integrated pastoral approach to employability 343–8
student finance 264
Student Hubs 149, 150, 153–4, 155
Student Legal Advice Centre (Derby Law School) 47, 48–9, 50, 51–2
student voice 24–6
  conceptual framework and methodology 26–7
  perceptions of liberal arts degree in relation to employability 27–31
supportive environment, and creativity 62
Sussex Career Lab 337–8, 339–40
Sussex Entrepreneurship Programme 338, 340

Teaching Excellence Framework (TEF) 266–7
teams, and creativity 60, 61–3
tech companies 138–9, 144–5
technology
  and creativity 61
  skills 72, 109, 169, 189–90
third-generation approach 327–9
transferable competencies 43
transition pedagogy 327–9
Twin Group 254, 255–6, 258

under-represented students *see* widening participation (WP) students
universities
  mission 15–16
  purpose 24
  responsibility for employability 14–17
  role, Australia 276–8
  views of employability 7–9
  see also creating a new university
universities of applied sciences, Germany 295–301
University of Birmingham 188, 267
University Centre South Devon 344–8
University of Canterbury 287–90

University of East London (UEL), pathways to 'good' health-care jobs 226–7
University of Edinburgh 29
University of Exeter 199–203
University of Greenwich, partnerships to secure jobs for international students 253–9
University of Huddersfield, Global Professional Award (GPA) 314–20
University of Jaén 306
University of Liverpool Careers and Employability Service
  Career Studio 127–32
  Unlock Your Potential (UP) programme 215–22
  see also employer input to curriculum and assessment
University of Queensland (UQ) 324–6
University of Salerno 308
University of Southampton, My Generation Career Coaching programme 207, 208–12
University of Sussex 334–40
Unlock Your Potential (UP) programme (University of Liverpool) 215–22

'value for money' 264–5
Very Group 84
virtual internships 289–90

wellbeing 128, 131, 317
widening participation (WP) students
  Australia 275–6
  breaking barriers to employability for 198–203
  first-generation students 19, 207–12, 314–15
  graduates from poorer backgrounds 169
  involvement in extra-curricular activities 80
  NEOLAiA (European University initiative) 306–7
  social mobility, and London's left-behind graduates 224–30
  under-represented students 215–22

work-based learning/work integrated
    learning (WIL)
  4i Careers Education 141, 144–5
  Australia 273–9
  Change Project (Leeds Trinity
    University, LTU) 171–4
  New Zealand 286–90

work experience *see* real-world
    experience and learning
Workplace Development Module
    (WDM) (Derby Business School)
    94–7
'workplace readiness' 13

youth social action 150